Office Milestones

Englisch für Kaufleute für Büromanagement

von
Dr. Richard Hooton
Ulrich Boltz
Ruth Feiertag
Annely Humphreys
Jason Humphreys
Veronica Leary

Ernst Klett Verlag
Stuttgart · Leipzig

So arbeiten Sie mit Office Milestones

Einsteigen

Online-Code
zu ergänzenden Materialien im Internet

Warm up-Einstiegsfrage
führt direkt in das Thema

Word Bank
Schlüsselvokabular

Erweitern und Vertiefen der Fachinhalte

Office expert-Seiten
erweitern und vertiefen die Fachkenntnisse von Industriekaufleuten

Lernen, Üben, Anwenden

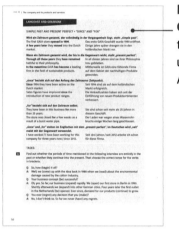

Language- and Grammar-Boxen
trainieren sprachliche und grammatikalische Aspekte

Audio-Aufgaben ⊙ A1.2
trainieren das Hörverständnis

Differenzierungsaufgaben
auf drei Stufen (○ A2 – ◐ B1 – ● B2) ermöglichen binnendifferenziertes Unterrichten

Communication-across-cultures-Boxen fördern die interkulturelle Kompetenz

Vorbereiten auf die Prüfung

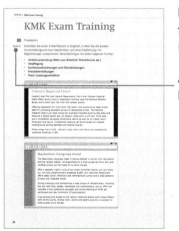

KMK Exam Training
für eine gezielte KMK-Prüfungsvorbereitung

Auszeichnung der **KMK-Stufe** (I, II, III)

Phrases
Satzbausteine für die mündliche und schriftliche Kommunikation

Anhang

Authentische Videos
auf zwei Niveaustufen
in der **Video Lounge**
schulen das Seh- und
Hörverständnis

Mock Exam mit einem
kompletten Prüfungssatz
für optimale Prüfungs-
vorbereitung

Role cards

Chronological word list

Alphabetical word list

Symbole

Differenzierung:
○ Niveau A2
◑ Niveau B1
● Niveau B2

 Partneraufgabe

 Gruppenaufgabe

KMK Aufgaben zur Vorbereitung auf die
Prüfung zum KMK-Fremdsprachenzertifikat

P, M, I, R Produktion, Mediation,
Interaktion, Rezeption

 Internetrecherche

◎ A1.2 Audioverweis

 3sg2tt Auf den Einstiegsseiten finden Sie Milestones-
Codes. Diese führen zu den Audios sowie zu
weiteren Materialien im Internet. Geben Sie
einfach den Code auf www.klett.de ein.

UNIT

1 | Introducing yourself   ⊕ 3sg2tt

TOPICS / SKILLS Introducing and talking about yourself • Talking about traineeship and profession
OFFICE EXPERT Job profiles • Streamlining office procedures

2 | Taking care of visitors   ⊕ p238rz

TOPICS / SKILLS Greeting visitors • Making conversation • Giving directions • Taking foreign visitors
to a restaurant
OFFICE EXPERT Corporate entertainment • Preparing a conference

3 | The company and its products and services   ⊕ 972j5i

TOPICS / SKILLS Describing a firm and its history • Describing products and services
OFFICE EXPERT Presenting your company online

4 | The Office   ⊕ w8pm9c

TOPICS / SKILLS Describing the office • Catering • Describing departments and responsibilities
OFFICE EXPERT Handling stressful situations • Office suite applications

5 | Telephoning   ⊕ ts73ac

TOPICS / SKILLS Appliances • Receiving and redirecting calls • Taking messages / Spelling •
Making telephone calls • Messages for the answering machine • Text messaging
OFFICE EXPERT Mobile madness

6 | Making arrangements   ⊕ b9f9qd

TOPICS / SKILLS Booking flights, hotel rooms and exhibition stands / Hiring cars • Making appointments •
Preparing a meeting • Taking the minutes
OFFICE EXPERT Handling schedules

7 | Presentations and meetings   ⊕ c232sk

TOPICS / SKILLS Preparing and delivering presentations • Describing graphs and diagrams • Meetings
OFFICE EXPERT The structure and design of presentations

8 | Forms of written communication   ⊕ 8dy3ft

TOPICS / SKILLS Layout and components of business correspondence • Writing e-mails, faxes and letters
OFFICE EXPERT Word processing

9 | Enquiries   ⊕ r73tp6

TOPICS / SKILLS Making enquiries in writing and by phone • Discounts
OFFICE EXPERT Negotiating in trade

10 | Offers   ⊕ 8u35iu

TOPICS / SKILLS Making offers in writing and by phone • Comparing options • Incoterms® 2010
OFFICE EXPERT Evaluating services • Office supplies fair

UNIT	

VIDEO LOUNGE	

01

Think about introductions. How do you introduce yourself in different situations?

Introducing yourself

In business people have to introduce themselves all the time. So it's a good idea to know what to say and what information to include. You may, for instance, need to explain your professional role or duties in the firm you work for. In a business situation introductions and greetings are often more formal than among friends and the people you know well.

1 Decide which of the following introductions and greetings are more formal and which are more informal or casual. Match the phrases with the photos above.

1
Hi Pauline, how's it going?

2
Good morning, Mr Stanton. I hope you had a pleasant flight.

3
Hello, I'm Martin Fielding from Global Exchange Ltd.

4
Hi, you guys. Fancy going out for a coffee?

WORD BANK

- apprentice
- to attend school
- to be a …
- to be interested in
- to be into
- to be on a programme
- to be training to become a …
- to do a traineeship as a …
- to qualify as a …
- to take part in
- to train / to be training as a …
- to train to be a …
- to work as a …
- to work at / with / for …
- clerk
- consultant
- I was born in / on …
- I'm / my name is …
- I'm from …
- management assistant
- specialist
- trainee
- traineeship / apprenticeship
- vocational school

A | Talking about yourself

The British company Enterprise Exchange organises placements for young trainees from other European countries for a minimum of one month at British companies. Mark Freshfield is talking to a group of trainees who have just arrived from Germany.

1 Take the roles of Mark Freshfield and the trainees and read the introductions.

Mark: Hi, I'm Mark Freshfield from Enterprise Exchange and I'm going to be acting as co-ordinator of your programme and generally looking after you while you're on your placements in the Brighton area. So if you have any questions or problems I'm the person to contact. I think it would be a good idea if we all introduced ourselves. Perhaps you could mention what job you're training for, what company you're working with and in what sector etc. I'll start the ball rolling: I'm Mark, 38 years old, my background is mainly in HR and I've been with Enterprise Exchange for about 4 years – oh, and I come from South London. Right, (turning to the girl on his right) what about you?

Emma: Hi, I'm Emma Petersen. I'm 18 years of age and come from Rostock on the Baltic coast. I'm training to be a freight forwarding and logistics services clerk with a logistics company in Rostock. My training will be finished next year. I'm a member of a canoeing club.

Mark: Sounds very adventurous! Thank you, Emma. Let's move on to this young man now.

Ben: Hi! My name's Ben Hartmann. I am doing an apprenticeship with an import-export company in Krefeld near Düsseldorf. I'm training to be a management assistant in wholesale and foreign trade. I'm in my final year. When I finish, I'd like to move into the IT field and plan to do some further training. I enjoy designing websites. Oh, and I'm 19 years old.

Mark: Thank you, Ben.

Cem: Hi! My name's Cem Batuk. I'm 20 and I come from Munich but I was born in Istanbul. My traineeship is in the field of event management and that's the area I want to work in. Munich is a good place to be as the city and Bavaria are very popular with tourists.

Mark: And not just the Oktoberfest! Have you got a hobby?

Cem: Yes, I like cooking Turkish food for my friends.

Mark: Thanks, Cem.

Lina: Hi, I'm Lina. I'm working for an advertising agency and training to become a management assistant in advertising. I'm in my final year and want to work in the advertising and media field. Social media are my hobby and I'm especially interested in online advertising. Eventually, I want to start my own company.

Mark: Great! That certainly is a growth area. How old are you, Lina?

Lina: I've just turned 19.

Adriana: Hi, I'm Adriana. I'm 20 years old, I was born in Belgrade and now live in Berlin. I'm training as a foreign language secretary with a big industrial company. My hobby's buying and selling vintage clothes online.

Mark: Gosh! That sounds enterprising. Thank you Adriana. Thank you all. Right. Monday and Tuesday you go to the company where you're doing your placement. Our shuttle bus will pick you up at 8.30 am and take you there. On Wednesday we're back here to meet the other four people on the programme who are arriving tomorrow. We've also arranged for you to visit the local Further Education College and meet a few of the students who are roughly at the same stage as you. On Saturday we've got a day of sightseeing in London lined up. Anyway, hope you all get off to a good start! See you Wednesday.

R **2** Say whether the following statements are true or false.

1. Mark Freshfield has a background in IT.
2. Lina is training to become an advertising assistant.
3. Adriana is 20 years of age.
4. Cem was born in Ankara.
5. Ben is doing a traineeship as a freight forwarding and logistics services clerk.
6. Emma is training with a logistics company.
7. Cem wants to work in the hotel and tourism business.
8. Adriana is working at a vintage clothes company.

3 Complete the following sentences using prepositions from the box.

at · in (3×) · on (2×) · near · from · for

I was born **1** Ditchling **2** 7 June 1996. Ditchling is a small village **3** Brighton **4** the south coast of England. My family originally comes **5** Zagreb **6** Croatia. I work **7** an advertising agency and am taking part **8** a training programme as an advertising assistant. I regularly work out **9** a local fitness centre.

R **4** Listen to the following introductions and answer the questions.

⊙ A1.1

Luca

1. Where does Luca come from?
2. What is he training as?
3. What is his hobby?

Lily

1. How long has she been living in Germany?
2. How old is she?
3. Where does she come from?

Tobias

1. Where does he come from?
2. What is he training to become?
3. What's his hobby?

P **5** Work in groups and make up similar introductions using the following
 information.

Training or working as: IT management assistant,
insurance clerk/insurance business management assistant, office
management assistant/office administration clerk, event management
assistant/event consultant, wholesale and export clerk/management
assistant in wholesale and export trade, bank clerk/bank business
management assistant, management assistant in advertising, freight
forwarding and logistics services clerk/management assistant in freight
forwarding, management assistant in retail business, publisher's
assistant, industrial clerk/industrial business management assistant
Firms: Osiris GmbH (IT), Feinmechanik AG, Intereuropa Logistik Schulz
GmbH, Publice-Werbung, Polis-Veranstaltungs-Management GmbH, Jäger
& Braun Weinhandel – Import-Export, PUNTAS AG, Schmitt – Dobermann
und Co. KG
Hobbies: hang-gliding, clubbing, designing websites, horse-riding,
reading, cooking, chilling out, playing tennis, socialising, volunteer work,
watching TV, billiards

6 Work in groups. Choose task a, b or c.

a. Use the examples on the previous pages and in the box below and introduce yourself briefly in writing.

b. Introduce yourself briefly in writing. You can use imaginary details if you want. Read your introduction out to the group.

c. Introduce yourself in writing. Include further details such as work experience, hobbies etc. You can use imaginary details if you want.

LANGUAGE AND GRAMMAR

INTRODUCING YOURSELF

Im Englischen werden Geburtszeitpunkt und Geburtsort mit „simple past" angegeben.

I **was** born in Rostock in 1997.	Ich **bin** 1997 in Rostock geboren.
My mother **was** born in Turkey.	Meine Mutter **ist** in der Türkei geboren.
Cem **was** born on 7 June 1995.	Cem **ist** am 7. Juli 1995 geboren.

Es wird in der Regel zuerst der Ort und danach der Zeitpunkt genannt.
Im Deutschen ist die Reihenfolge umgekehrt.

I was born **in Turkey in 1995**.	Ich bin **1995 in der Türkei** geboren.

Im Englischen steht zur Angabe des Berufs der unbestimmte Artikel.
Im Deutschen steht kein Artikel.

I'm doing a traineeship as **an** industrial clerk.	Ich mache eine Ausbildung als Industriekaufmann.
She's **a** tourism consultant.	Sie ist Kauffrau für Tourismus und Freizeit.
He's working as **an** IT practitioner.	Er arbeitet als Informatikkaufmann.

Im Englischen wird zwischen männlicher und weiblicher Berufsbezeichnung oft kein Unterschied gemacht.

He / She is a teacher.	Er ist Lehrer. / Sie ist Lehrerin.

Ausnahmen (z. B.):

a waiter	ein Kellner
a waitress	eine Kellnerin
an actor	ein Schauspieler
an actress	eine Schauspielerin

TASK:

7 Übersetzen Sie folgende Sätze ins Englische.

1. Sergio arbeitet als Industriekaufmann.
2. Emily ist in Glasgow geboren.
3. Birthe ist Veranstaltungskauffrau.
4. Alina ist Fremdsprachenkorrespondentin.
5. Cem ist in der Türkei geboren.

INTRODUCING AND GREETING PEOPLE

In English-speaking countries people often give only their first name when introducing themselves. "Hi, I'm Nicholas" or "Hello, I'm Sophia." In more formal situations and business contexts they may give their first name and surname – but **never** just their surname as is often the case in Germany. "Good morning, I'm Olivia Rowlinson". She may add "Please call me Olivia" or the other person may simply address her by her first name: "Good morning Olivia, I'm Finn Armstrong."

"How do you do" is a formal greeting which is not much used nowadays: "How do you do, I'm Liam Hopkins." The other person might reply: "How do you do, I'm Emily Grant. Pleased to meet you." "Good morning" or "Good evening" are also rather formal.
 "Hello" is both formal and informal. A common greeting is "Hello, how are you?" The other person says something like "Fine, thanks / not so bad / so-so" and immediately adds "How are you?" "Hi" is always informal. Friends usually say something like "Hi Emily, how are you doing?" or "Hi Paul, how's things?" Emily might reply "Fine, how's things with you?" Young people sometimes use the greeting "Hi you guys" to address a group – the group may be all male, or female or mixed.

TASK:

8 | Answer the following questions on the text.

1. Do people in English-speaking countries introduce themselves using their surname only?
2. What sort of a greeting is "How do you do?"
3. Is the greeting "Hi Joe, how's things?" formal or informal?
4. How do you reply to "Hi, I'm Pete"?
5. "Good morning, Mrs Armstrong?" – is this formal or informal?

B | Young people talk about their future professions

Mark has taken the trainees from Germany to visit a local Further Education College near Brighton Pier to meet some of the students there.

R **1** Listen to them introducing themselves in the cafeteria and then answer the
◉ A1.2 questions.

1. What course is Liam doing?
2. What is the examination called that he is preparing for?
3. Where does Aleksandar come from originally?
4. What is Paul's chosen profession?
5. What does Cem want to do when he finishes his course in Munich?
6. Where does Chloe come from and what does she have in common with Cem?
7. Where does Dragana come from and what is she specialising in?
8. Where did Giancarlo grow up?
9. Who is doing an engineering apprenticeship?
10. How does Mark suggest they spend the last half hour at the college?

2 Choose task a, b or c.
○ a. Match the German phrases with the English idioms in the box below.
◐ b. Match the German phrases with the English idioms and make complete sentences using the idioms.
●●● ● c. Work in pairs. Match the German phrases with the English idioms and make up dialogues using the idioms.

1.	den Anfang machen	a.	to jump at an offer
2.	einen erfolgreichen Start haben	b.	to line something up
3.	ein Angebot begeistert annehmen	c.	to be into something
4.	etwas planen/organisieren	d.	to fancy doing something
5.	Lust auf etwas haben	e.	to be dying to do something
6.	auf etwas stehen, etwas gerne machen	f.	to start the ball rolling
7.	darauf brennen, etwas zu tun	g.	to get off to a good start
8.	sich gut mit jemandem verstehen	h.	to get on well with someone

3 Match the German occupations listed below with their English paraphrases.

1.	Informatikkaufmann	a.	advertising assistant/management assistant in advertising
2.	Fremdsprachenkorrespondentin	b.	wholesale and export clerk/management assistant in wholesale and foreign trade
3.	Kauffrau für Versicherung und Finanzen	c.	management assistant for tourism and leisure
4.	Kaufmann im Groß- und Außenhandel	d.	automobile sales management assistant
5.	Kauffrau für Marketing-kommunikation	e.	secretary/PA with foreign languages/foreign language correspondent
6.	Kaufmann für Büromanagement	f.	management assistant for event management/event organiser
7.	Automobilkaufmann	g.	office management assistant
8.	Industriekauffrau	h.	IT practitioner/management assistant in informatics
9.	Veranstaltungskauffrau	i.	management assistant in freight forwarding and logistics/freight forwarding and logistics clerk
10.	Kaufmann für Spedition und Logistikdienstleistung	j.	insurance business management assistant/insurance clerk
11.	Kauffrau für Tourismus und Freizeit	k.	industrial clerk/industrial business management assistant

M   Übertragen Sie folgende Aussagen ins Englische:

1. Ich mache eine Weiterbildung als Fremdsprachen-korrespondentin.
2. Ich möchte als Kaufmann für Tourismus und Freizeit arbeiten.
3. Ich nehme an einem IT-Weiterbildungsprogramm teil.
4. Ich will eine Ausbildung als Veranstaltungskauffrau machen.
5. Ich bewerbe mich um einen Ausbildungsplatz als Kauffrau für Büromanagement.
6. Ich mache eine Ausbildung als Werbekaufmann.
7. Ich möchte mich um eine Stelle als Industriekauffrau bewerben.
8. Ich habe eine Ausbildung als Kauffrau für Marketingkommunikation gemacht.
9. Ich werde als Kaufmann im Groß- und Außenhandel ausgebildet.
10. Ich bin Versicherungskaufmann.

I   Work in groups of three. Act out the following conversation, inserting your own names and training courses.

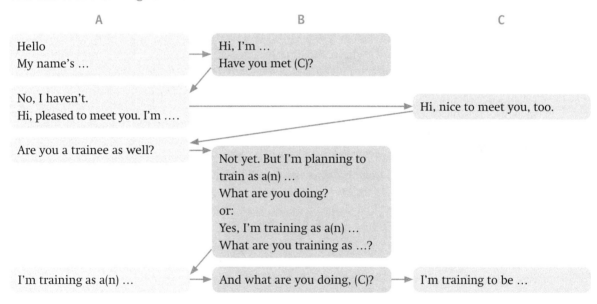

A	B	C
Hello My name's …	Hi, I'm … Have you met (C)?	
No, I haven't. Hi, pleased to meet you. I'm ….		Hi, nice to meet you, too.
Are you a trainee as well?	Not yet. But I'm planning to train as a(n) … What are you doing? or: Yes, I'm training as a(n) … What are you training as …?	
I'm training as a(n) …	And what are you doing, (C)?	I'm training to be …

I   Work in groups of three. Use the phrases from the conversation above and make similar dialogues.

R   Listen to the dialogue and say which of the following statements are true
◉ A1.3   for Ethan or Emily.

1. I'm training to be a freight forwarding and logistics assistant.
2. I'm training to be an advertising assistant.
3. There are good prospects of promotion.
4. I can use my English a lot.
5. I get on well with the people I work with.
6. I enjoy telephoning with customers in other countries.
7. I can work on my own.

I **8** Work in pairs. Introduce yourselves and say what you do. Ask each other
ㅅㅅ what you like or dislike in your job.

P **9** Search the internet for job ads regarding the following international job titles.
🌐 Note down the details of one job ad. Compare and discuss your findings with
the group.

junior advertising assistant · freight forwarding clerk · insurance clerk ·
IT practitioner · trainee events assistant · bilingual secretary/secretary
or PA with foreign languages · assistant tourism/tourism clerk

COMMUNICATION ACROSS CULTURES

VOCATIONAL TRAINING IN BRITAIN AND GERMANY

Vocational education is organised somewhat differently in the UK and Germany. There is no equivalent to the large number of protected job titles with a prescribed course of training in Germany. However, the system of apprenticeships combining on the job training with 1 or 2 days a week at the local Further Education or Community College is similar to the German "dual training system" and was partly inspired by it. The advantage of apprenticeships is that young people are employed, earn a small salary (which differs depending on the type of work) and the training is work-related and practice-oriented. The apprenticeship courses (on three levels) in subjects ranging from accounting and business administration, hospitality and catering to carpentry, bricklaying and plumbing lead to external NVQ examinations (National Vocational Qualifications). Alternatively students take full-time courses combining practice and theory in work-related subjects and sit either NVQ or BTEC (Business and Technology Education Council) exams. BTECs are also external and taken in over 100 countries throughout the world.

As a result of these differences it is often difficult to translate German job titles literally into English. It is necessary to paraphrase them in such a way that a foreign employer can get a realistic idea of the level and nature of the qualification. If you are applying for a job, it is essential to find out what a similar qualification would be called in English.

The statement "Ich mache eine Ausbildung zum Kaufmann für Spedition und Logistik bei der Müller-Logistik GmbH" could be paraphrased as follows: "I am on a three-year training programme with Müller-Logistik to qualify as a freight-forwarding and logistics management assistant. During the training programme I attend courses at a vocational college either two days a week or in blocks of several weeks at a time. I spend the rest of the time in the company working through the various departments. At the end of the traineeship I sit an examination before the local chamber of commerce."

TASK:

10 Answer the following questions on the text.

1. What is the difference between vocational education in Germany and in Britain?
2. What was the British system of apprenticeships inspired by?
3. What are the advantages of doing an apprenticeship?
4. What do students do who do not opt for an apprenticeship?
5. Supposing you are a "bank business management assistant". What might the nearest equivalent be in English-speaking countries?

M/P **11** Choose task a, b or c.

You work with a medium-sized company manufacturing components for the car industry. Mr Rajinder Mohit, a supplier from India, visits your company. He is interested in the German dual training system. Your boss, whose English is a bit rusty, asks you to introduce yourself to the visitor and give a few particulars about your training. He says:

○ a. „Sagen Sie Guten Morgen, stellen Sie sich Herrn Mohit mit Namen vor, sagen Sie wie alt Sie sind und dass Sie hier eine Ausbildung zum Industriekaufmann / zur Industriekauffrau machen."

◐ b. „Begrüßen Sie Herrn Mohit, stellen Sie sich vor und sagen Sie, dass Sie hier seit einem Jahr zum Kaufmann / zur Kauffrau für Büromanagement ausgebildet werden, dass Sie schon in mehreren Abteilungen gearbeitet haben und jetzt im Einkauf tätig sind. Sagen Sie auch, dass Sie dienstags und donnerstags in der Berufsschule zusätzlich auf die Abschlussprüfung vor der Industrie- und Handelskammer vorbereitet werden, die nach drei Jahren stattfindet."

● c. „Begrüßen Sie unseren Gast angemessen, stellen Sie sich mit ein paar Einzelheiten zu Ihrer Person vor, sagen Sie, dass Sie Kaufmann / Kauffrau im Groß- und Außenhandel werden wollen und erklären Sie kurz das deutsche Schulsystem und das System der dualen Ausbildung mit Unterricht in der Berufsschule und praktischer Ausbildung in den verschiedenen Abteilungen unserer Firma. Führen Sie auf, wo Sie schon gewesen sind: Vertrieb Ausland, Buchhaltung, Einkauf, Personalwesen. Sagen Sie ruhig, dass Sie wegen guter Noten in der Berufsschule Ihre 3-jährige Ausbildung um ein halbes Jahr verkürzen dürfen und im Juni ihre Abschlussprüfung vor der IHK machen werden."

Basic structure of the German education system

GRADE						
	1–4	5–6	7–10		11–12	13
Kindergarten (pre-school)	Grundschule (elementary school)	Orientation Stage	Hauptschule (secondary modern school)	Hauptschule students usually graduate after 9 years. Realschule students graduate after 10 years.	Berufsschule (vocational school – part-time)	
			Realschule (higher secondary school)		Berufsfachschule (vocational school – full-time)	
			Gymnasium (grammar school)		Fachoberschule (higher secondary vocational school)	
			Gesamtschule (comprehensive school) may combine elements of other 3 schools		University and college preparatory classes in Gymnasium and some Gesamtschulen	
	3–5	6–9	10–11	12–15	16	16–17	18

AGE				
Pre-school	Elementary School	Secondary School (First Phase)		Secondary School (Second Phase)

Office expert

C | Job profiles

1 Many different verbs are used to describe job tasks in an office. Match the following English verbs (1.–10.) to their German equivalents (a.–j.).

1.	to complete	a.	pflegen, verwalten
2.	to conduct	b.	Berechnungen durchführen
3.	*to deal with*	c.	(durch)führen, leiten
4.	to maintain	d.	aufgeben (Anzeige, Bestellung)
5.	to make computations	e.	*sich befassen mit*
6.	to process	f.	prüfen, aussondern, durchleuchten
7.	to place	g.	verarbeiten, bearbeiten
8.	to post	h.	weiterleiten
9.	to route	i.	vervollständigen, ausfüllen
10.	to screen	j.	(per Post) verschicken

2 Now use the verb phrases and words from the two boxes above and below to form collocations, i.e. popular word combinations.

Example: "to deal with customers"

> incoming mail · *customers* · candidates · tours · job adverts · for accounts · schedules · data · files · outgoing correspondence

M **3** The duties performed by office assistants may include a combination of tasks. First assign the jobs (A.–E.) to the appropriate job duties (1.–15.) on the next page. Some duties may apply to more than one job. Then translate the job duties into German. If necessary, use a dictionary for help.

Jobs:
A. Secretary with foreign languages
B. Personal assistant
C. Human resources assistant
D. Accounting assistant
E. Office administration clerk

Job duties:
1. Answer telephones, direct calls and take messages.
2. Prepare graphics, statistics and tables for presentations.
3. Answer enquiries (phone, e-mail, in person) concerning payments.
4. Organise application and contract documents.
5. Conduct plant tours for foreign visitors.
6. Process information, maintain/update filing and database systems.
7. Create and design texts with the computer.
8. Translate company advertising material.
9. Screen applicant profiles and job adverts.
10. Complete schedules, manage diaries and arrange appointments.
11. Deal with English language correspondence and documents.
12. Make computations for balancing and maintaining accounts.
13. Open, sort and route incoming mail and prepare outgoing mail.
14. Create and place job adverts according to requirements.
15. Post payments and refunds to appropriate account or cost centre.

4 Choose task a, b or c.

○ a. Decide which tasks are stand-alone tasks that you can do on your own. Which ones are interactive where you need to work with other people?

◐ b. Write sentences describing the skills required to do the different tasks/ jobs.

Example: A personal assistant needs to be friendly, helpful and organized because she/he has to answer the phone and take messages.

● c. Discussion: Which of the duties do you prefer and why?

5 Complete the description of key soft skills with the words from the box.

command · communicator · detail · discretion · individual · intercultural · meeting · member · multi-task · organisational · pressure · professional

A personal assistant needs to be a good **1** in speech and writing with an excellent **2** of English. The ability to prioritise work and to **3** – which means being able to work on several tasks at any given time – are equally important.
Accuracy and an eye for **4** , as well as good **5** skills are also required. Personal assistants are often assigned to a group, not just an **6** , and, therefore, need to be able to work independently and as a **7** of a team. The position of an executive secretary or office management assistant requires **8** because such persons often have to deal with confidential information. A friendly, **9** manner, being able to work under **10** and **11** deadlines are essential criteria for all types of assistants. **12** awareness is a key factor when working for a company that deals with foreign customers.

6 Rephrase the skills to make questions for a survey of personal assistants.
Then use the survey to interview other students and report back to the class.

Example:

Questions	Yes	Usually	Sometimes	Not really
Are you a good communicator, both in speech and writing?				
Do you have an excellent command of ...?				

D | Streamlining office procedures

1 Complete the following definitions with suitable words from the box.

> characters · combination · downloaded · located · pre-formatted · storage

Tools for saving time

Templates are **1** files that serve as a starting point for creating new documents. They can be **2** and are available for letters, business forms, etc. A keyboard shortcut is a key **3** that performs a certain command. Most shortcuts are **4** in a programme's menu. Auto text is a **5** location for text or graphics you want to use again. The selections have to be at least five **6** long and each is recorded as an auto text entry and assigned a unique name.

2 Match the recommendations (1.–4.) with the examples (a.–d.).

1. Automate processes
2. Replicate repetitive tasks
3. Reuse information
4. Use shortcuts

a. Create and print labels and envelopes for mass mailings.
b. Learn keyboard shortcuts, such as pressing SHIFT + F10, to display the shortcut menu for the selected item.
c. Save time by using professional templates or create your own templates for text elements you use frequently.
d. Think about how you can automate tasks you do regularly.

3 Discuss which streamlining techniques you are already familiar with and can recommend. Which ones would you like to try?

4 Choose task a, b or c.

a. Find the English translations for the following German words:

> Abkürzung · sich wiederholende Vorgänge · ausgewählt · Briefumschläge · Sendungen · gespeichert · Befehl

b. Use the information above and write a brief definition for the following terms: templates, keyboard shortcuts, autotext.

c. Write a brief definition for the following terms: templates, keyboard shortcuts, autotext. Now make sentences using these words.

KMK Exam Training

1 Interaktion

Stufe II Work with a partner. Using the following prompts, conduct a conversation in English about your training jobs.

Partner A   Partner B

Begrüßen Sie Partner B und stellen Sie sich mit Ihrem eigenen Namen vor.

Erwidern Sie die Begrüßung und stellen Sie sich ebenfalls vor.

Fragen Sie Partner B, was er/sie beruflich macht und warum er/sie diesen Beruf ausgewählt hat.

Beantworten Sie die Fragen und erkundigen Sie sich nach dem Beruf des Partners/der Partnerin.

Antworten Sie entsprechend und fragen Sie nach den beruflichen Aufgaben und Verantwortlichkeiten des Partners/der Partnerin.

Beantworten Sie die Fragen und stellen Sie selbst geeignete Fragen.

Beantworten Sie die Fragen und fragen Sie nach Aufgaben und Tätigkeiten im Beruf nach.

Nennen Sie mögliche Aufgaben und Tätigkeiten.

2 Rezeption: Hörverstehen

Stufe I
⊙ A3.17
Listen to the following conversation between Monika, an office assistant trainee, and one of her new colleagues in London. Decide if the statements below are true or false.

1. Monika spent a summer at a camp in Sweden when she was 15.
2. Monika speaks quite fluent English.
3. Monika doesn't like working with children.
4. Monika's new colleague likes taking pictures of her friends.

3
Stufe I
⊙ A3.17
Listen to the conversation again and list three reasons why Monika chose to work in an office.

Phrases: Introducing yourself and others

To introduce yourself	
I'm Peter. / My name is Henry Myers.	Ich heiße Peter. / Ich heiße Henry Myers.
Please call me Harry.	Nennen Sie mich doch Harry.
My surname is Hillary, my first name is Tom.	Mein Familienname ist Hillary, mein Vorname Tom.
How are you? (How are you doing?)	Wie geht es Ihnen / Dir? (informelle Begrüßung)
I'm from Berlin and I am 20 years old.	Ich stamme aus Berlin und bin 20 Jahre alt.
I'm British / Irish.	Ich bin Brite / Britin / Ire / Irin.
I **was** born in Cyprus on 7 August 1982.	Ich bin am 7. August 1982 in Zypern geboren.
Have you met Mr Martens?	Kennen Sie Herrn Martens?
May I introduce Dr Bolt? (formal)	Darf ich Ihnen Herrn Dr. Bolt vorstellen?
Pleased / Nice to meet you.	Ich freue mich, Sie kennen zu lernen.
And how are you?	Und (wie geht es) Ihnen?
Didn't we meet at the Boat Fair?	Haben wir uns nicht schon auf der Boot-Messe kennen gelernt?
I've heard a lot **about** you **from** Mr Winter.	Herr Winter hat mir schon viel von Ihnen erzählt.

To talk about your hobbies	
I am interested in computers.	Ich interessiere mich für Computer.
I love travelling more than anything else.	Ich reise schrecklich gern.
I like to go clubbing.	Ich gehe gern in die Disco.
I'm **into** body-building.	Ich interessiere mich für Bodybuilding.
I do a lot of diving.	Ich gehe oft tauchen.

To talk about your training or your work	
I'm a trainee export clerk.	Ich mache eine Ausbildung zum Exportkaufmann.
I'm training to become …	Ich mache eine Ausbildung zum / zur …
… an industrial clerk / industrial business management assistant	… Industriekaufmann / -frau
… an office administration clerk / office management assistant	Kaufmann / -frau für Büromanagement

To talk about your training or your work

a wholesale and export clerk / management assistant in wholesale and foreign trade	Kaufmann / -frau im Groß- und Außenhandel
a freight forwarding and logistics services clerk / management assistant in freight forwarding and logistics	Kaufmann / -frau für Spedition und Logistik-dienstleistung
a bank clerk / bank business management assistant	Bankkaufmann / -frau
a retail clerk / management assistant in retail business	Kaufmann / -frau im Einzelhandel
a management assistant for tourism and leisure	Kaufmann / -frau für Tourismus und Freizeit
a publisher's assistant	Verlags- / Medienkaufmann / -frau
an insurance clerk / insurance business management assistant	Kaufmann / -frau für Versicherungen und Finanzen
a management assistant in advertising	Kaufmann / -frau für Marketingkommunikation
a management assistant in event organisation	Veranstaltungskaufmann / -frau
an automobile sales management assistant	Automobilkaufmann / -frau
I'm taking part in an ITC programme.	Ich nehme an einem ITC-Ausbildungsprogramm teil.
I'm in the catering **industry**.	Ich bin in der Cateringbranche.
I work **at** SITCOM Ltd.	Ich arbeite bei SITCOM Ltd.
I **attend** vocational school.	Ich besuche die Berufsschule.
What are you doing job-wise, Nina?	Nina, was machst du beruflich?
What are you training to be, Timo?	Was machst du für eine Ausbildung, Timo?
What do you like **about** your job?	Was gefällt dir an deiner Arbeit?
What industry are you in?	In welcher Branche arbeitest du?

To say what you like or dislike about your training or your work

I like my job because I get on well with the people I work with.	Ich mag meine Arbeit, weil ich mich mit meinen Kollegen gut verstehe.
I can work **on** my own.	Ich kann selbstständig arbeiten.
There are good prospects **of** promotion.	Die Aufstiegschancen sind gut.
I have to key in data all day long.	Den ganzen Tag muss ich Daten eingeben.
I have to work a lot of overtime.	Ich muss viele Überstunden machen.
I have plenty of opportunities to use my English.	Ich habe viele Gelegenheiten mein Englisch anzuwenden.

02

Imagine yourselves in a situation where you have to welcome visitors to your company. What would you do and say?

Taking care of visitors

Greeting visitors to your company and making them feel at home may be an important part of your job. You should always be friendly and helpful as first impressions are often decisive. You may be asked to entertain a visitor until the person they want to see appears. The language in which you can both communicate will often be English, even when the visitor does not come from an English-speaking country. English has become a global lingua franca.

WORD BANK

- *to chat*
- *to choose*
- *directions*
- *dish*
- *to entertain*
- *flight*
- *floor plan*
- *to follow*
- *to go*
- *to greet*
- *hobbies*
- *hotel*
- *to invite*
- *layout*
- *map*
- *meal*
- *to meet*
- *menu*
- *premises*
- *to receive*
- *refreshments*
- *restaurant*
- *sports*
- *to turn*
- *visit*
- *visitor*
- *weather*
- *to welcome*

1 Match the phrases with the photos above.

1 Welcome to Cosmo-Moden GmbH.

2 Have you met Mrs Denzel? She's head of marketing.

3 Take the lift to the first floor. The conference room is the first door on the right.

4 Mr Keller will join us after the break.

A | Greeting visitors

Jens Krüger, who works in the export department at Cosmo-Mode GmbH in Berlin, has been asked to look after Jayden Flaherty and Emma Hetherington from TopGuys Fashions which is well-known for its range of creative designer fashions for twenty-somethings supplying high-end boutiques and major fashion chains throughout the UK. They are interested in exploring the possibility of a joint venture with the German company.

R **1** Listen to the dialogue and answer the following questions.

⊙ A1.4

1. Who is Jens Krüger?
2. Why does Emma Hetherington ask for mineral water?
3. What is Jayden's role in the British company?
4. Where have Emma, Jayden and Frau Denzel met before?
5. Is Emma married?
6. Why has Herr Baumann asked Jens to take part in the meeting?
7. What is Frau Denzel in charge of?
8. What is Emma ashamed about?

2 Match the expressions on the left with those on the right.

1.	twentysomethings	a.	basic
2.	major fashion chains	b.	I've asked him to accompany us
3.	in charge of marketing	c.	important companies with many retail outlets
4.	we've met already	d.	I can't remember when and where we met
5.	I've asked him to come along	e.	I'll inform him
6.	rudimentary	f.	people somewhere in their twenties
7.	I can't quite place you	g.	we know each other
8.	joint venture	h.	the garment industry
9.	I'll let him know	i.	he holds the leading position in the marketing department
10.	rag trade (slang)	j.	project that two companies work on together on

B | Making conversation

R **1** Listen to the recording and complete the following dialogue on a separate
◎ A1.5 sheet of paper.

Jens: Did you have a pleasant journey?
Emma: Yes, it was OK. No major **1** . The flight from Gatwick to
Cologne was a bit **2** – makes me anxious. We had an
appointment there yesterday.
Jens: How did you get to Berlin?
Jayden: We **3** the ICE. They're so fast and beautifully comfortable.
Even the catering is quite good.
Emma: It was 20 minutes late, **4** – everybody in the UK (including us)
are convinced that German trains are 100 % punctual – unlike
ours.
Jens: I'm afraid they're often late! Which part of London are you
based in?
Jayden: Shoreditch in the East End – it's traditionally the centre of the
rag trade. Nowadays **5** creative people from the arts, media
and fashion. London is probably now the fashion start-up
capital of the world.
Jens: What's the weather **6** at the moment?
Emma: It's **7** ! We've been having the most wonderful summer
weather. The grass **8** to turn brown. Have you ever been to
London?
Jens: No I'm **9** . Everyone says it's so expensive. And the weather's
not so reliable.
Jayden: The South East is the driest part of Britain!
Emma: … and for anyone young like you and in the fashion business
to boot it's an absolute must! There are very cheap flights if
you book **10** and cheap places to stay for students and young
people – go on the internet.
Jens: You've really convinced me – OK, let's go to the…

2 Complete the following conversation with words from the box.

afraid (2×) · smooth · prefer · into · journey

You: Did you have a pleasant **1** ?
Visitor: The flight was incredibly **2** – not a hint of turbulence!
You: Great. What was the weather like in London?
Visitor: I'm **3** it was absolutely ghastly. Pouring rain!
You: Are you **4** football?
Visitor: No, I'm **5** I'm not. Why do you ask?
You: I'm a Chelsea fan.
Visitor: Good for you. I **6** cricket myself.

SMALL TALK

Some cultures engage in small talk more readily than others. Anecdotal evidence suggests that German-speakers are not much into small talk. You may think it is a waste of time. Far from it! It enables people to establish a relationship and bond with each other while avoiding any topics that might cause conflict or offence. Most connections start with small talk. However, permissible topics differ from culture to culture. For instance, in China or the USA, but less so in Britain or Germany, it is possible to ask people how much they earn. In Middle Eastern countries you may be asked about your family.

Because in Britain the weather is so changeable due to the maritime climate, it is an inexhaustible and harmless topic of conversation.

You might have the following kinds of conversation at the newsagent's, the pub, convenience store or supermarket checkout.

Customer in pub:	Isn't this weather wonderful!
Barmaid:	I don't think it's going to last, though.
Customer:	Don't say that! Have you seen the weather forecast?
Barmaid:	Yes, the forecast says cold and rainy the day after tomorrow.
Customer:	Well, let's enjoy it while it lasts. Maybe they've got it wrong!

Newsagent:	Good morning. How are you today?
Customer:	OK, but isn't this weather dreadful!
Newsagent:	What's happened to the glorious summer they promised us?
Customer:	It's supposed to get better towards the weekend.

TASK:

Make up similar small talk dialogues about the weather using the following words:

The weather is
☺ wonderful / superb / glorious / lovely.
☹ awful / ghastly / dreadful / terrible.

4 Work in pairs. Make up small talk dialogues using the following prompts and the phrases at the end of the Unit.

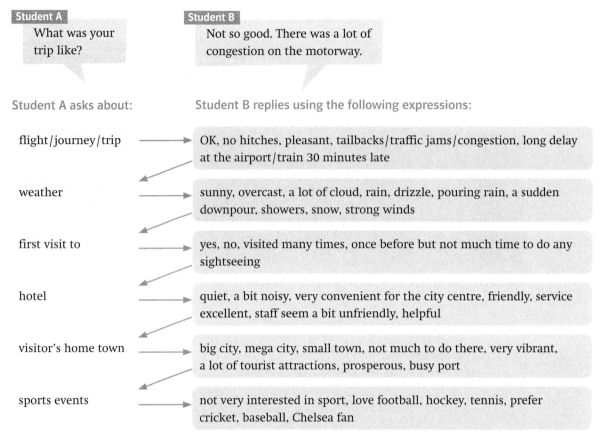

Student A
What was your trip like?

Student B
Not so good. There was a lot of congestion on the motorway.

Student A asks about: | Student B replies using the following expressions:

flight/journey/trip → OK, no hitches, pleasant, tailbacks/traffic jams/congestion, long delay at the airport/train 30 minutes late

weather → sunny, overcast, a lot of cloud, rain, drizzle, pouring rain, a sudden downpour, showers, snow, strong winds

first visit to → yes, no, visited many times, once before but not much time to do any sightseeing

hotel → quiet, a bit noisy, very convenient for the city centre, friendly, service excellent, staff seem a bit unfriendly, helpful

visitor's home town → big city, mega city, small town, not much to do there, very vibrant, a lot of tourist attractions, prosperous, busy port

sports events → not very interested in sport, love football, hockey, tennis, prefer cricket, baseball, Chelsea fan

C | Giving directions

P 1 A visitor has lost her way in the office building. She is standing at the reception desk. The receptionist directs her to Herr Baumann's office. Take the role of the receptionist. Use the floor plan and the phrases on the next page to give her directions.

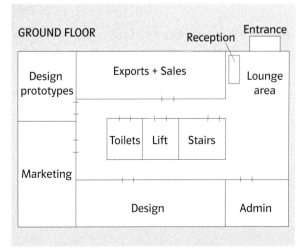

GROUND FLOOR

Reception — Entrance

| Design prototypes | Exports + Sales | Lounge area |

Toilets | Lift | Stairs

Marketing

Design | Admin

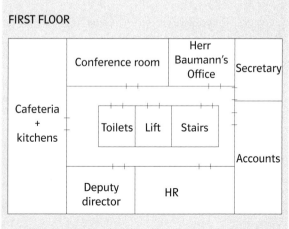

FIRST FLOOR

| Conference room | Herr Baumann's Office | Secretary |

Cafeteria + kitchens

Toilets | Lift | Stairs

Deputy director | HR

Accounts

Phrases: Giving directions (1)

Herr Baumann's office is on the left / on the right. · The women's / men's toilets are on the left / on the right. · Go up / down the stairs. · The entrance to the staircase is on the left / on the right. · Take the lift to the first floor. · Go down to the ground floor. · Go along the corridor. · Turn right / left into the corridor. · If you turn left / right you'll see the double glass doors of the cafeteria.

P **2** Emma and Jayden have somehow got separated. Emma rings Jayden on her mobile to find out where he is. He is in the cafeteria.
Emma: "I'm in the reception lounge. How do I get to the cafeteria?"
Take the role of Jayden and give her directions.

P **3** On leaving the building Jayden realises he has left his laptop in Herr Baumann's conference room. He has forgotten how to get there so he asks the receptionist: "How do I get to Herr Baumann's conference room?"
Take the role of the receptionist and give him directions.

P **4** As he comes out of the lift on the first floor another visitor says:
"Do you know by any chance where the Design Prototype room is?"
Jayden remembers where it is and directs the visitor to it. Take his role.

P **5** Jayden and Emma want to take advantage of their stay in Berlin to see some of the sights. They would like to walk from their hotel on the south side of Kronenstraße (a street that crosses Friedrichstraße) via Gendarmenmarkt to the Museumsinsel and then from the Museumsinsel to Brandenburger Tor. They ask Jens to tell them how to get there. Work in small groups. Taking the role of Jens, bring up a map of Berlin on your monitor and give directions.
Choose task a, b or c.
○ a. Write out a simple itinerary for them, using the expressions given below as appropriate.
◑ b. Write out a detailed itinerary for them, suggesting any alternative routes. Use the following expressions where appropriate.
● c. Write out a detailed itinerary for them, pointing out some of the sights or landmarks they may like to visit on their way.

Phrases: Giving directions (2)

Turn right / left when you leave your hotel. · Go along … street until the junction with … street. · Turn left / right at the junction. · Turn right / left into … street. · Take the first/second / third street on your right / left. · Cross over the main road. · After about 100 / 200 / 300 … metres you will see the museum buildings. · Go down this street until you see a church / cathedral / … . · Follow the bend in the road round to the right / left. · Then, go back to … street.

D | Taking the visitors on a tour of the premises

Herr Baumann, assisted by Jens, takes the visitors on a tour of the offices.

R **1**
⊙ A1.6
Listen to the dialogue and decide whether the following statements are true or false.

1. Everyone, without exception, works in an open-plan office.
2. Most people find working in an open-plan office more sociable.
3. The cafeteria also caters for vegetarians and vegans.
4. The food is always organic but not always free-range.
5. The main consideration is low price when buying in produce for the cafeteria.
6. Manufacturing is always outsourced.
7. Design and the creation of prototypes are done on the premises.
8. All the designers are directly employed by the company.
9. Neither side seems very happy about the outcome of the meeting.
10. They invite Herr Baumann to visit them in Shoreditch.

P **2**
Emma has agreed to write their joint report. Take Emma's role.
Choose task a, b or c.
○ a. Write a short report of their visit.
◑ b. Write a report covering the facts and impressions you had.
● c. Write a report outlining the facts, impressions of the company and how you feel about a possible joint venture or cooperation with them.

M **3**
KMK
Sie sind Jens Kröger. Verfassen Sie eine kurze Aktennotiz über die Betriebsbesichtigung und die Reaktionen der britischen Besucher.

P **4**
⊕
Emma and Jayden are returning to Cologne by ICE and plan to stop off at Düsseldorf to take a stroll along the famous "Kö", or Königsallee. They ask Jens to tell them how to get there from the main station.
He looks at a map of Düsseldorf on the internet and writes down a possible route for them. Take his role.

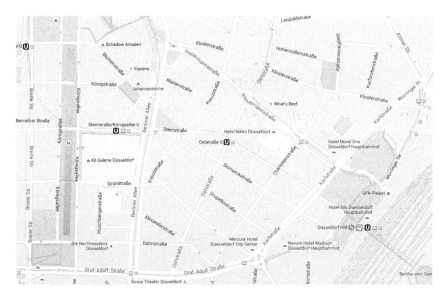

E | Taking foreign visitors to a restaurant

Jonas Färber from Färber Roboter GmbH and Noah Brady from Fenland Robotics Ltd have spent the day discussing whether their companies could market each other's healthcare robots at their office in Düsseldorf. After a lengthy discussion they decide to have dinner together. Noah is keen to go to a traditional German pub / restaurant with scrubbed tables although by his own admission, he is not a big meat eater.

R   **1**   Listen to them and write down what they order.
◎ A1.7

SPEISEKARTE

Vorspeisen
Avocado mit Vinaigrette
Leberknödelsuppe mit hausgemachten Leberknödeln
Blumenkohlcremesuppe
Honigmelone mit geräuchertem Schinken
Kraftbrühe mit Ei

***

Hauptgerichte
Himmel und Erde – Gebratene Blutwurst mit Apfelkartoffelpüree und Röstzwiebeln
Hirschgulasch mit Rotkohl und Kartoffelknödeln
Schweinefilet
Wiener Schnitzel mit Bratkartoffeln und Gurkensalat
Pfeffersteak mit Spargel und Petersilienkartoffeln.
Zanderfilet gebraten mit Spinat und Reis
Gratinierter Broccoli-Auflauf

***

Nachspeisen
Apfelstrudel mit Vanillesoße
Rote Grütze mit Sahne
Käseplatte

2   Study the descriptions below and decide which dishes they refer to.

> Kartoffelknödel · rote Grütze · Zander · Hirschgulasch · Blutwurst · Apfelstrudel

1. A freshwater fish – a member of the pike family.
2. Dumplings made of grated potato cooked in boiling water.
3. A kind of delicious apple pie.
4. A kind of red jelly containing red berries – not very sweet.
5. The English equivalent is "black pudding"- a kind of sausage made with pig's blood.
6. Goulash made of venison (meat of deer).

M **3**   Work in pairs. You are asked to accompany a foreign guest (your partner) to a restaurant. Refer to the menu on the previous page and the phrases at the end of the Unit.
Choose task a, b or c.

○   a.   Choose a starter, a main course and a dessert from the above menu and explain what they are to your imaginary foreign visitor.

◑   b.   Choose a starter, main course and dessert for your guest. Explain what they are. S/he doesn't like the main course and dessert you have chosen. Try and find something s/he does like. Can you recommend anything?

●   c.   Your foreign guest asks whether there is a vegetarian option on the menu. Is there a vegetarian starter and main course? Explain what they are. S/he isn't enthusiastic about the one vegetarian main course. Could s/he perhaps just have a vegetarian starter and a dessert? But which ones? Help your guest and suggest vegetarian options.

COMMUNICATION ACROSS CULTURES

DESCRIBING DISHES

There is often no direct translation for typical German dishes. You will have to describe them to your visitors from abroad. The following may help:

Which part of the meal is it?
It's a starter.
It's a main course.
It's a dessert.

What kind of food is it?
It's meat (pork, beef, lamb, veal).
It's chicken / turkey.
It's fish (cod, haddock, sardine).
It's game (rabbit, venison, wild boar).
It's a kind of pasta (noodles).
It's a vegetable (peas, beans, carrots, green / red / yellow peppers, cauliflower, cabbage, Brussels sprouts, asparagus).

How is it made?
It's made of mashed potatoes, ground / minced meat, chopped onions.
It's filled / stuffed with rice, vegetables, minced meat.
It's boiled, baked, stewed, grilled, fried, smoked.

What does it taste like?
It's hot / spicy.
It's sweet / sour.
It's tart.
It's savoury.
It tastes a bit like yoghurt, chicken, chocolate mousse, jelly.

4 Read the explanations below and decide what German dishes they refer to.

> Kohlrouladen · Semmelknödel · Eisbein · Speckpfannkuchen ·
> Königsberger Klopse

1. Pancake containing diced fried bacon.
2. Dumplings made of minced meat cooked in broth in a white sauce with capers.
3. Boiled pork hock served with sauerkraut and mashed potatoes.
4. They are made of mincemeat wrapped in a cabbage leaf in a sauce.
5. They go with the main course. They are dumplings made of bread and eggs.

P **5** Work in groups. Explain how to make two of the following dishes in English to the class. Get help where necessary from the internet.

> Gurkensalat · Semmelknödel · Sauerkraut · Wiener Schnitzel ·
> Frikadelle · Spätzle · Kartoffelsalat · Linsensuppe · gefüllte
> Paprikaschoten · Kartoffelsuppe · Grünkohl bürgerlich · vegetarische
> Maultaschen · veganer Schokoladenkuchen

R **6** A researcher from Omnipolis Research Services Ltd is doing a survey in an
⊙ A1.8 upmarket supermarket on changing consumer attitudes.
Listen to the dialogue and answer the questions.
Choose task a, b or c.

○ a. What items does the male shopper buy? What is important for him?
◑ b. How could you describe the young woman's approach to food? What kinds of things does she buy?
● c. Which of the above approaches is most like your own? Or is your approach entirely different from these three?

7 Match the English words with their German equivalents. Use a print or online dictionary if necessary.

1.	red pepper	a.	Vorspeise
2.	octopus	b.	Spargel
3.	free-range	c.	Seeteufel
4.	courgettes	d.	kurz anbraten
5.	asparagus	e.	Scholle
6.	salmon	f.	dünsten
7.	to stir-fry	g.	Hirsch/Reh
8.	monkfish	h.	rote Paprikaschote
9.	plaice	i.	Zucchini
10.	venison	j.	Freiland(-huhn)
11.	starter	k.	Lachs
12.	to steam	l.	Tintenfisch

COMMUNICATION ACROSS CULTURES

EATING OUT IN BRITAIN

Most pubs serve snacks and meals at lunchtime in a relatively informal atmosphere. You order and pay for your snack or meal and buy your drinks at the bar. The food is brought to your table. Otherwise, as a rule there's no table service and it is not usual to give a tip. Generally the food is inexpensive.

Some pubs, sometimes known as gastropubs, have more inventive and well-trained chefs who create more unusual and ambitious dishes. These pubs may also have both a bar area and a restaurant-style section.

In restaurants you may have to wait to be seated. A waiter/waitress will ask you how many you are and indicate a table. Of course you can state a preference such as "Could we sit over there by the window?" or "I'd like a corner table if that's possible."

The waiter/waitress who brings the menu may ask you whether you would like to order drinks straight away. After you have had time to study the menu the waiter/waitress will say: "Are you ready to order, madam/sir? If you've not yet decided, you could say: "We're not quite ready. We need a moment or two." If you have ordered but decide you would like something different, you can say: "Could I possibly change my mind?"

When the meal comes, the waiter/waitress will probably say: "Enjoy your meal" or often just "Enjoy!"

Complaining is very difficult. In Germany people tend to state the reason for their dissatisfaction clearly, even bluntly. In Britain you should avoid at all costs being confrontational, aggressive or loud. This will not have the desired result. Be friendly, understanding, humorous if possible.

TASK:

Answer the following questions on the text.

1. What is a "gastropub"?
2. How do you get drinks in a pub?
3. How do you find a table in a restaurant?
4. What do you say if you haven't decided what you want to order?
5. If you need to complain, what is important to avoid?

LANGUAGE AND GRAMMAR

WILL-FUTURE

Die „Will"-Zukunftsform (meistens in der abgekürzten Form I'll, we'll) drückt im Englischen spontane Entscheidungen aus und entspricht dem Präsens im Deutschen.

I'll give Herr Baumann a ring and let him know you're here.	Ich rufe Herrn Baumann an und sage ihm, dass Sie hier sind.
I'll have a white coffee.	Ich nehme einen Kaffee mit Milch.
I'll ring through and order tea.	Ich rufe an und bestelle Tee.

„Will" wird NICHT in Nebensätzen der Bedingung und der Zeit benutzt.

I'll fetch the newspapers if you **make** breakfast.	Ich hole die Zeitungen, wenn Du das Frühstück machst.
I'll tell him as soon as he **arrives**.	Ich werde es ihm sagen, sobald er ankommt.

TASKS:

9 Choose the correct forms of the verbs.

Paul: Hi Declan, I'm not sure when I'm moving. I (give / I'll give) you a ring in the next couple of days.

Declan: Hi Paul. If you (let / are going to let) me know in good time I (am / will be) able to help you with the move. I (ask / will ask) Emily if she can make it as well. I (tell / will tell) her to pass on the message to Noah. I (pick / will pick) up the Rent-a-Van if you (want / will want). David says he (stands / will stand) in for you at work if it (is / will be) necessary.

Olivia: I (do / will do) the typical female thing. I (do / will do) some tidying up and cook pasta with a creamy mushroom sauce when you (are / will be) finished.

Paul: Come on, Olivia. It (is not / will not be) a massive operation! It's only one room.

Olivia: We (make / will make) a party of it. I (invite / will invite) Joanna and her boyfriend. I (call / will call) them straight away.

10 Translate the following sentences.

1. Ich schicke die Sendung morgen früh ab.
2. Wir sagen Ihnen Bescheid, sobald wir die Artikel erhalten.
3. Ich ziehe den 10 %igen Rabatt vom Listenpreis ab.
4. Wir nehmen mit unserem Spediteur sofort Kontakt auf.
5. Ich werde ihn um einen Kostenvoranschlag bitten.

Office expert

F | Corporate entertainment

1 You work for an events management firm and have to choose an event for three groups of clients:

1. Anniversary celebration of a bank for 100 selected customers, their spouses and your staff
2. CEO of a major network corporation with his teenage sons and wife
3. Members of a forum for influential female company owners and executives

Choose task a, b or c.

○ a. Make a table comparing the special features, terms, food and prices of the three events below (A – C).

◑ b. Choose an event below (A – C) for each group. Give reasons for your choice.

● c. Choose one of the events below (A – C) and write an invitation to one of the groups mentioned in Exercise 1. Include these points:

- A friendly opening (e.g. You are cordially invited to attend …)
- Relevant details such as dates, transport, venue
- Some interesting highlights from the chosen event
- Deadline for sending your confirmation or RSVP (from French *répondez s'il vous plaît*)
- A suitable ending (e.g. We are looking forward to …)

A | FIFA World Cup

A hospitality package costs €1000 per person per match (minimum 4 customers or 4 matches) and includes:
- FIFA World Cup premium match ticket(s)
- High-end catering and unlimited bar service
- Special fan kit with football jersey and souvenirs
- On request accommodation and travel arrangements can be organized.

FIFA WORLD CUP
RUSSIA 2018

B | Danube River Cruise

Roll out the red carpet for your guest and treat them to an evening of dancing and dining on this exclusive river cruise.

Package includes a banquet of delicious finger food, salads and choice desserts with live music above deck and a disco below deck, all for just €40 per person (minimum of 200, maximum 275 guests).

Chelsea Flower Show

Mark your corporate calendar with this special event. Enjoy the best in British hospitality at the most famous flower show in the world. Experience this spectacular show together with delicious cuisine and fine wines. The entrance ticket – weekdays €250, weekends €280 – includes the show, a catalogue, morning coffee, a champagne reception with canapés and a four-course dinner with selected wines.

G | Preparing a conference

1 You brainstormed with your boss about all the things you need to do to prepare for a conference. Unfortunately, your notes from the meeting got mixed up.
Complete the "To do" list below with the right verbs from the box.
Then put the tasks into the correct order.

arrange · choose · draw up · make · prepare · send · send out · set

TO DO List

1. ... dates for conference
2. ... accommodation for participants
3. ... final arrangements
4. ... a suitable conference venue
5. ... the invitations
6. ... conference schedule
7. ... conference bags / folders
8. ... documentation with directions and details

2 Make up possible questions that correspond to the following answers.

1 A fully equipped conference room for up to 80 participants is available.

2 The hotel restaurant offers a wide variety of international cuisine and local Czech specialities.

3 Amenities include a bar, sauna, fitness centre and an underground car park.

4 It's only one hour's drive from the nearest airport.

5 It's located near the main railway station.

R **3** Listen to the following dialogue between a conference's organizer and
⊚ A3.18 assistant about choosing a suitable venue. Make notes of the questions asked.

KMK Exam Training

1 Produktion

Stufe II Schreiben Sie einen E-Mail-Bericht in Englisch, in dem Sie die beiden Veranstaltungsorte kurz beschreiben und eine Empfehlung mit Begründungen aussprechen. Berücksichtigen Sie dabei folgende Punkte:

- Verkehrsanbindung (Nähe zum Bahnhof / Abholdienste etc.)
- Verpflegung
- Konferenzeinrichtungen und Dienstleistungen
- Freizeiteinrichtungen
- Preis / Leistungsverhältnis

Ostrava Imperial Hotel

Located near the main square Masarykovo, the 4-star Ostrava Imperial Hotel offers luxury living in downtown Ostrava near the famous Stodolni Street and a short taxi ride from the railway station.

Offering hospitality for more than 100 years, this outstanding hotel prides itself on providing excellent service at reasonable prices. The Ostrava Imperial Hotel is an ideal choice for business travelers and tourists alike and features a stylish sports bar, an elegant restaurant, a 24-hour front desk and a completely equipped conference centre as well as an indoor swimming pool and sauna. Conference catering can be arranged on request. Underground parking facilities are located nearby.

Prices range from €120–160 per single room with discounts available for corporate bookings (+20).

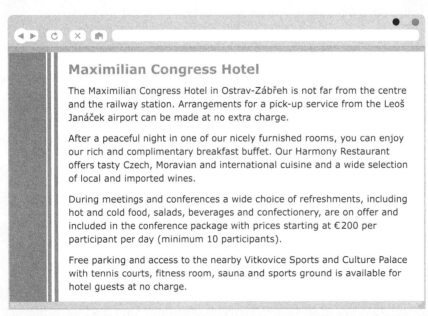

Maximilian Congress Hotel

The Maximilian Congress Hotel in Ostrav-Zábřeh is not far from the centre and the railway station. Arrangements for a pick-up service from the Leoš Janáček airport can be made at no extra charge.

After a peaceful night in one of our nicely furnished rooms, you can enjoy our rich and complimentary breakfast buffet. Our Harmony Restaurant offers tasty Czech, Moravian and international cuisine and a wide selection of local and imported wines.

During meetings and conferences a wide choice of refreshments, including hot and cold food, salads, beverages and confectionery, are on offer and included in the conference package with prices starting at €200 per participant per day (minimum 10 participants).

Free parking and access to the nearby Vitkovice Sports and Culture Palace with tennis courts, fitness room, sauna and sports ground is available for hotel guests at no charge.

2 Interaktion

Stufe II Use the role card below as a guide for exchanging information about hotels. Partner A uses the information provided about the Ostrava Imperial Hotel to answer Partner B's questions. Partner B then answers Partner A's questions about the Maximilian Congress hotel. Alternatively exchange information about local hotels you are familiar with.

> ## Role card A / B
>
> **Ask your partner questions about the following information:**
> - Location
> - Category and prices
> - Catering services
> - Hotel amenities
> - Nearby amenities
> - Corporate deals

3 Produktion

Stufe II Schreiben Sie eine Einladung in Englisch zu einer Konferenz für Techniker in Ostrava. Wählen Sie eines der beiden Hotels (Ostrava oder Maximilian) als Veranstaltungsort. Beachten Sie folgende Punkte in Ihrer Einladung:

- Zweck der Veranstaltung
- Relevante Details wie Ort, Datum, und Zeiten
- Mindestens zwei Details über den Veranstaltungsort
- Hinweise für die Anreise mit Zug oder Flugzeug oder mit dem PKW
- Sonstiges: Verpflegung, Freizeiteinrichtungen etc.
- Bitte um Rückmeldung

Phrases: Taking care of visitors

To welcome visitors	
Good afternoon. Can I help you? / What can I do for you?	Guten Tag. Was kann ich für Sie tun?
Please have a **seat**.	Bitte nehmen Sie Platz.
Can I offer you some refreshments?	Darf ich Ihnen etwas anbieten?
Coffee with milk and sugar, tea, herbal tea, fruit juice, sparkling / still mineral water, coke?	Kaffee mit Milch und Zucker, schwarzer Tee, Kräutertee, Fruchtsaft, Mineralwasser mit / ohne Kohlensäure, Cola?
Herr Färber **is expecting** you.	Herr Färber erwartet Sie.
I'm afraid, Frau Denzel is still in a meeting.	Frau Denzel ist leider noch in einer Besprechung.
She will be **with** you in a few minutes.	Sie wird in ein paar Minuten da sein.

To make conversation	
Where do you come from?	Wo kommen Sie her?
Did you have a pleasant flight?	Hatten Sie einen angenehmen Flug?
How was the **journey**?	Wie war die Fahrt / Reise?
The flight was rather bumpy.	Der Flug war ziemlich unruhig.
The trip was very pleasant. Thank you.	Danke. Die Fahrt war sehr angenehm.
Have you ever been to Oldenburg before?	Waren Sie schon einmal in Oldenburg?
Actually, I have been to Oldenburg twice, in 1999 and in 2002.	Ich war tatsächlich schon zweimal in Oldenburg, 1999 und 2002.
What was the weather **like** in Belfast?	Wie war das Wetter in Belfast?
The weather was fine. Not a cloud in the sky.	Das Wetter war schön. Kein Wölkchen am Himmel.

To give directions		
GB	**USA**	**Germany**
second floor	third floor	2. Etage / Stock
first floor	second floor	1. Etage / Stock
ground floor	first floor	Erdgeschoss
basement	basement	Untergeschoss / Keller

Take the lift to the third floor.	Fahren Sie mit dem Aufzug in den dritten Stock.
Herr Baumann's office is on the **right hand** side.	Das Büro von Herrn Baumann ist auf der rechten Seite.
At the junction **turn** right / left.	Gehen / Fahren Sie an der Kreuzung nach rechts / links.
Go straight ahead to …	Gehen / Fahren Sie gerade aus bis …
Go down this street till you come to the …	Gehen / Fahren Sie auf dieser Straße weiter bis Sie zu … kommen.
When you come to the roundabout, take the 3rd exit.	Am Kreisverkehr nehmen Sie die dritte Ausfahrt.
Follow the main road up the hill.	Fahren Sie die Hauptstraße weiter bergauf.
After 200 yards you will see the church to your left.	Nach (ca.) 200 m sehen Sie die Kirche auf der linken Seite.

To take visitors on a tour of your firm's premises

We would like to show you **round** the company's premises.	Wir möchten Ihnen unsere Firma auf einem Rundgang zeigen.
We have two open-plan offices.	Wir haben zwei Großraumbüros.
Production is outsourced.	Die Produktion ist ausgelagert.
We'll go through this door which leads to the canteen.	Wir gehen durch diese Tür, die zur Kantine führt.
The canteen looks very modern and airy.	Die Kantine wirkt sehr modern und luftig.
We leave this building and **cross** the car park.	Wir verlassen jetzt dieses Gebäude und gehen über den Parkplatz.
Our visit has certainly been very interesting.	Unser Besuch war wirklich sehr interessant.

To take visitors to a restaurant

This is a typical German restaurant.	Dies ist ein typisch deutsches Restaurant.
Let's have a look **at** the menu.	Lassen Sie uns einen Blick auf die Speisekarte werfen.
I think I'll just have a main course.	Ich nehme nur ein Hauptgericht.
I'll have the lamb cutlets with beans.	Ich nehme die Lammkoteletts mit Bohnen.
I prefer chicken **to** fish.	Ich esse lieber Geflügel als Fisch.
Is there a vegetarian / vegan option?	Gibt es ein vegetarisches / veganes Angebot?
What about ice cream as a dessert?	Wie wär's mit Eis als Nachtisch?
I'd **rather** have cheese. / I'll have cheese.	Ich hätte lieber Käse. / Ich nehme Käse.
It was delicious but I'm afraid I can't eat any more.	Es hat sehr gut geschmeckt, aber ich bin leider schon satt.

03

What national / international companies do you know? What do they produce and what services do they offer?

The company and its products and services

Companies generally project a particular brand image in their sales literature and media presence. Well-established companies may prize qualities such as reliability, experience, solidity and familiarity. Newly founded companies, on the other hand, will probably emphasise their dynamic and forward-looking approach. All companies point to their ability to innovate and adapt in order to survive in a competitive and changing market. This branding process is intended to speak both to customers and the companies' own employees, who will identify more readily with a positive brand.

1 Choose words from the box to describe an old established company and a recently founded company.

> flexible · reliable · experienced · adventurous · solid · dynamic · forward-looking · trustworthy · revolutionary · mature · quality-conscious · loyal

P **2** Work in groups. Use the internet and find five old-established companies and five recently founded companies. How are they described?

3 Which words best describe the company you are training at?

WORD BANK

- brand image
- business idea
- company brochure
- to establish
- family-owned firm
- to found
- forward-looking
- global player
- leading
- to manufacture
- manufacturing
- medium-sized
- old-established
- practical
- private limited company
- to provide
- provision of services
- public limited company
- range of products
- start-up
- state-of-the-art
- stock corporation
- sustainability
- traditional
- well-established
- workforce

A | Introducing a firm and giving a brief history

Tim Schneider comes across the English website of a German company while doing research for his coursework on "green business". When he clicks on 'about us', this is what he learns about the history of the firm:

GAIA – working towards a sustainable future

It all began in 1988 when my friend Pia – a very committed environmentalist – came up with the idea of creating and marketing ecological fashion. She had read several reports on the catastrophic environmental impact of the large-scale cultivation and processing of cotton. When she showed me statistics on the amount
5 of water needed to grow enough cotton to produce just one t-shirt, I was shocked: 2700 litres. 'But is there an environmentally-friendly alternative?' I asked. 'Oh, yes', she told me. 'There's hemp for instance. It can be grown anywhere and needs very little in the way of water or fertilisers. It's also very pest-resistant. And don't forget wool. Let's support sheep farmers and the local wool industry.'
10 So we worked hard to set up a business concept and, after securing an EU-funded loan to help with founding new businesses, we established contact with hemp growers, sheep farmers and spinning mills across Europe.
Finally, in 1990, we opened our first store in Berlin – in a former factory warehouse in the then up-and-coming
15 district of Prenzlauer Berg.
Today, we have 35 stores and boutiques throughout Germany and Europe. We have meanwhile established our own production facilities and employ more than 500 staff. During all these years we have remained faithful
20 to our corporate philosophy by offering locally-sourced and manufactured produce and goods – from fashion made from organically-grown linen, to honey and beeswax products from selected bee keepers. From 100 % plant-based cosmetics and essential oils, to
25 wonderfully soft pure wool knitwear and sturdy shoulder bags made from sustainably-grown hemp. The good health of our planet matters a lot, don't you agree? So let's work together towards a sustainable future.

Elise Glasbauer CEO
GAIA GmbH Berlin

R **1** Read the text about GAIA and answer the following questions.

1. When was the first store opened?
2. How many litres of water are needed to grow enough cotton for one t-shirt?
3. What plants used in the textile industry use much less water than cotton?
4. Who did Elise and Pia establish contacts with?
5. How many staff do GAIA employ?
6. What is special about their cosmetics?

2 Find the missing prepositions from the box with the help of the text on GAIA.

> across · in · on (2×) · throughout · to · from · of (2×) · towards

Back **1** 1988 Pia came up with the idea of creating eco-friendly fashion. She got the idea after reading reports **2** the negative environmental impact of the cotton industry. She showed her friend Elise shocking statistics **3** the enormous amount of water used by the cotton industry. After securing an EU-funded loan, they established contact with suppliers **4** Europe. Their first store to open in 1990 was in the Berlin district **5** Prenzlauer Berg. Today they have a large number of stores and boutiques **6** Germany and Europe. Through all these years they have remained faithful **7** their company's philosophy. Their bags are made **8** environmentally-friendly hemp. The good health **9** planet Earth matters a lot to them. They encourage their customers to work **10** a sustainable future.

R **3** Read the text on GAIA on the previous page again and find words or phrases that mean the same as the following expressions.

1. people employed by a firm
2. growing agricultural produce on an industrial scale
3. a business start-up
4. a large building for the storage of goods
5. good for the environment
6. it is not attractive to pests
7. produce from farmers in the region
8. a way of growing or manufacturing something that does not damage or destroy resources

4 Choose task a, b or c.
○ a. Give a short summary of the history of the company.
◑ b. Summarize the most important points regarding the company's history and explain what the motivation of its founders were.
● c. Give a brief account of the company's history, the motivation of its founders and comment on the importance of sustainability.

R **5**
⊙ A1.9   Mark Friedrichs has trained as an IT practitioner and would like to do a practical in an English-speaking country with an online services company. At a job fair he listens to a presentation by Philippa Jackson-Webb, founder and director of Zooks!, on setting up your own company. He hopes to talk to her about his plans.

Listen to Philippa describing her experience of setting up an online company and complete the following transcript on a separate sheet of paper.

"Zooks! was **1** in 2010. The business **2** behind our start-up was to provide an online market place for all those small manufacturers of high-quality **3** food and wines in the UK which are not big enough to **4** their own online service. Now we've **5** to three EU countries and are
5 preparing to move into two more in the summer. From the **6** we had a clear idea of what we wanted to do but we had no idea **7** how we could set about it. The government organisation www.start-ups… .co.uk and the local chamber of commerce gave us a lot of advice and put us in touch with experienced **8** who advise people like us in their free time
10 how to **9** their company and find **10** through the difficulties of getting start-up **11**. In the end we got one of the **12** loans the government provides for people who are struggling to get a **13** from a bank. We also got advice **14** how to do a feasibility study – it's obviously important to know how realistic your idea is. Of course, our first priority was to
15 have an attractive and efficient website but we had to **15** a lot of other problems as well – how to organise the logistics – putting in place a system for ensuring quick and **16** delivery of orders. Now, we also organise pop-ups, which are very popular. We rent an empty building or open-air **17** for a weekend or a few days and invite artists, designers,
20 musicians, the media and, of course, the companies that have signed **18** to our organisation and **19** it into a big event. Pop-ups are incredibly popular and are a very exciting development in **20**. They also help to establish us as a lifestyle company."

6   Match the English expressions with their German equivalents.

1.	to spread	a.	Finanzierung
2.	organic	b.	den Kontakt herstellen
3.	to set up	c.	sich ausdehnen
4.	from the outset	d.	unglaublich
5.	to set about	e.	bio(logisch)
6.	to put in touch with	f.	von Anfang an
7.	to give advice	g.	erfahren
8.	experienced	h.	Mitglied werden
9.	to find your way through	i.	gründen
10.	funding	j.	sich zurechtfinden
11.	feasibility study	k.	etwas verwandeln
12.	to ensure	l.	Machbarkeitsstudie
13.	to sign up to	m.	sicherstellen
14.	to turn something into	n.	an etwas herangehen
15.	incredibly	o.	beraten

R **7** Answer the following questions.

1. When was the company founded?
2. What was their business idea?
3. How did they get advice and funding?
4. What important problem does Philippa mention?
5. What are pop-ups and why does the company organise them?

M **8**
KMK
Mark Friedrichs fasst die Informationen, die Philippa über ihre Firma gegeben hat, auf Deutsch in einer Gesprächsnotiz für seine Personalabteilung zusammen. Übernehmen Sie seine Rolle.

GESPRÄCHSNOTIZ

Empfänger: _____

Verfasser: _____

Datum: _____

Betreff: _____

P **9** Choose task a, b or c.
- a. Briefly describe the firm you work for in writing.
- b. Briefly describe the firm you work for in writing. What is special about its products and / or services?
- c. Briefly describe the firm you work for in writing. Describe its products and / or services and say what kind of image it projects.

COMMUNICATION ACROSS CULTURES

JOINT STOCK COMPANIES (KAPITALGESELLSCHAFTEN) IN THE USA AND BRITAIN

The British Public Limited Company (abbreviated to PLC or plc after the company name) and the American Stock Corporation (abbreviated to Inc. or Corp.) are roughly comparable to the German Aktiengesellschaft. The British Private Limited Company (abbreviated to Ltd) and the American Closed Corporation are approximately equivalent to the German GmbH. British and American joint stock companies are managed by a Board of Directors under the leadership of a Chief Executive Officer (CEO) (chairman of the board or managing director), who may have the title of Chairman or President. The head of a Private Limited Company is generally called the Managing Director.

10 Search the internet for some national and international companies. Make notes on their products or services in English. Compare your notes with the group.

B | Describing products and services

Tim finds GAIA's history and business concept very interesting and decides to explore the website to get more information. He clicks on 'all products' and the following page comes up:

GAIA – working towards a sustainable future

about us | **all products** | shopping cart   contact us   FAQ   log into my account

Knitwear

Cosmetics

Honey and beeswax products

Women's fashion

Men's fashion

Fashion for kids

. All our products comply with the strictest EU environmental standards. We never
. use synthetic additives in our cosmetics. The hemp and linen we use for our textiles
. is grown organically in EU countries without any pesticides or herbicides.
. We support local businesses: The wool for our knitwear comes from German sheep
5 farms close to our production sites, the lavender oil we use in our cosmetics range
. comes from a lavender farm in Wiltshire, England, and our delicious honey and
. aromatic beeswax products are from carefully selected French and Scottish honey
. farms.
. For more information, click on any of the buttons above to take you to the product
10 group you are interested in.

1 Which buttons do you click on if you want to do the following?

1. find out about the firm
2. read frequently asked questions
3. get in touch
4. see what items you have bought
5. browse the range of pure wool articles
6. buy clothing for boys and girls
7. edit contact and payment details
8. buy moisturising hand cream

2 Replace the words in brackets with appropriate expressions from the box.

> artificial · weed killers · handpicked · insecticides · most rigorous · delectable

1. GAIA's products comply with the (strictest) **1** environmental EU standards.
2. They never use (synthetic) **2** additives in their cosmetics range.
3. Their (delicious) **3** honey and aromatic beeswax products are from (carefully selected) **4** honey farms.
4. The hemp and linen for their textiles is grown without any (pesticides) **5** or (herbicides) **6** .

M **3** Match the statements in German on the next page with the following statements in English.

A
Emily: I work for an international advertising agency. We specialise in online advertising.

B
Haluk: I work for a medium-sized company producing organic cosmetics.

C
Olivia: The company I work for is a leading manufacturer of fitness wearables.

D
Jonas: I work for a small family firm making quality reproduction furniture.

E
Kevin: The firm I work for is a catering start-up that provides fresh salads, soups and small vegetarian snacks for mobile sales outlets in the city.

F
Lina: My company is a wholesaler stocking a wide range of electronic devices.

G
Jörg: I work for a major manufacturer of foldable bicycles.

H
Elena: I work in the purchasing department at the head office of a major supermarket chain.

1. Meine Firma ist ein mittelständisches Unternehmen, das Biokosmetika herstellt.
2. Ich arbeite für einen großen Hersteller von Klapprädern.
3. Ich arbeite im Einkauf bei der Hauptverwaltung einer bekannten Supermarktkette.
4. Die Firma, bei der ich arbeite, ist ein Catering-Start-up, das frische Salate, Suppen und kleine vegetarische Gerichte an mobile Verkaufsstellen im Finanzzentrum London liefert.
5. Meine Firma ist ein führender Hersteller von tragbaren Fitnessgeräten.
6. Ich arbeite bei einem kleinen Familienunternehmen, das hochwertige Stilmöbel herstellt.
7. Ich arbeite bei einer internationalen Werbeagentur, die auf Online-Werbung spezialisiert ist.
8. Bei meiner Firma handelt es sich um eine Großhandlung mit einem breiten Sortiment von elektronischen Geräten.

P **4** Write similar descriptions of two firms and their products or services using a selection of the following words.

Types of firm	medium-sized company, import/export company, major manufacturer, start-up, old-established company, wholesaler, retailer, family firm, IT consultancy, publishing company, advertising agency, catering firm, public limited company, private limited company
Products/services	household appliances, central heating systems, IT services, organic foods, fabrics, cosmetics, advertising material, removal services, electrical goods, industrial design, legal services, furniture, lamps, camping equipment
Ways of describing firms and their products	modern, upmarket, high-quality, fresh, unique, reliable, well-designed, attractive, best-in-class, robust, user-friendly, low-maintenance, inexpensive, elegant, prompt (service), thorough, state-of-the-art, sophisticated, elaborate, bespoke, tailor-made, customized

Examples:
I work for a small manufacturer of well-designed, upmarket furniture.
We specialise in servicing company computer systems.

I **5** Work in small groups. Discuss what kind of online company you would like to found. If you wish, use the internet for inspiration. Note down your ideas and present them to the class.

Choose task a, b or c.
○ a. What would your business idea be? What would you call your company?
◑ b. What idea would your business be based on? How would you go about getting advice and funding. Think of a catchy name for your company.
● c. Give an account of your business idea, sources of advice and funding and mention some of the problems you might have to solve. Give your company an attractive-sounding name.

LANGUAGE AND GRAMMAR

SIMPLE PAST AND PRESENT PERFECT + "SINCE" AND "FOR"

Wird ein Zeitraum genannt, der vollständig in der Vergangenheit liegt, steht „simple past".

The first GAIA store **opened in 1990**.	Das erste GAIA-Geschäft wurde 1990 eröffnet.
A few years later they **moved** into the Dutch market.	Einige Jahre später drangen sie in den holländischen Markt vor.

Wenn ein Zeitraum genannt wird, der bis in die Gegenwart reicht, steht „present perfect".

Through all these years they **have remained** faithful to their philosophy.	In all diesen Jahren sind sie ihrer Philosophie treu geblieben.
In the meantime GAIA **has become** a leading firm in the field of sustainable products.	Mittlerweile ist GAIA eine führende Firma auf dem Gebiet der nachhaltigen Produkte geworden.

„since" bezieht sich auf den Anfang des Zeitraums (Zeitpunkt).

Since 1994 they have been active on the Dutch market.	Seit 1994 sind sie auf dem holländischen Markt erfolgreich.
Sales figures have improved **since** the introduction of new product ranges.	Die Verkaufszahlen haben sich seit der Einführung von neuen Produktsortimenten verbessert.

„for" bezieht sich auf den Zeitraum selbst.

They have been in this business **for** more than 25 years.	Sie sind schon seit mehr als 25 Jahren in diesem Geschäft.
The store was closed **for** a few weeks as a result of a burst water pipe.	Der Laden war wegen eines Wasserrohrbruchs einige Wochen lang geschlossen.

„since" und „for" stehen im Englischen mit dem „present perfect", im Deutschen wird „seit" meist mit der Gegenwart verwendet.

I have worked / I have been working for this company for three years now / since 2012.	Seit drei Jahren / seit 2012 arbeite ich schon für diese Firma.

TASKS:

6 **Find out whether the periods of time mentioned in the following interview are entirely in the past or whether they continue into the present. Then choose the correct tense for the verbs in brackets.**

Q: So, how (begin) it all?

A: Well, we (come) up with the idea back in 1988 when we (read) about the environmental damage caused by the cotton industry.

Q: Your business concept (be) successful?

A: Oh, yes. So far, our business (expand) rapidly. We (open) our first store in Berlin in 1990. Shortly afterwards we (expand) into other German cities. Four years later the first outlet in the Netherlands (be) opened. Ever since, demand for our products (continue) to grow.

Q: You ever (regret) any decision that you (make)?

A: No, I don't think so. So far we never (have) any regrets.

Office expert

C | Presenting your company online

1 Micron company, specialists for automotive solutions, has decided to present itself online. Before listening to a discussion between the website designer and a company representative match the English verbs (1.–12.) to their German equivalents (a.–l.).

1.	to access	a.	abschließen
2.	to appear	b.	aktualisieren
3.	to set up	c.	anbieten
4.	to enable	d.	aufnehmen
5.	to finalise	e.	betreffen, sich beziehen auf
6.	to include	f.	einfügen
7.	to insert	g.	einrichten
8.	to provide	h.	ermöglichen
9.	to refer to	i.	erscheinen
10.	to stand for	j.	stehen für, repräsentieren
11.	to suggest	k.	vorschlagen
12.	to update	l.	Zugriff haben

R **2**
◎ A3.19
Now listen to the discussion about the desired features and options and answer the questions below.

1. Name three elements the company wants to include on their website.
2. How many categories are suggested for the main menu of the homepage?
3. What does *PDF* stand for according to the text?
4. What happens if you click on a hyperlink?
5. What kinds of information are included under the category *Contact*?
6. What category can you click on if you want information about copyright?

R **3**
◎ A3.19
Listen again and decide if the following statements are TRUE or FALSE.

1. The company wants to be able to add newer information at a later date.
2. The homepage of a website is also called "home".
3. Clicking on a sub-category opens up a drop-down menu.
4. A drop-down menu includes different options or sub-categories.
5. Downloads and Support are to be included under General Services.
6. *Privacy Policy* and *Terms of Use* are types of legal information.

KMK Exam Training

1 Produktion

Sie arbeiten zurzeit im Verkauf und erwarten Besuch von einem schwedischen Neukunden, der sich ausschließlich für Ihre Spielwaren interessiert. Erläutern Sie ihm die Organisationsstruktur dieser Sparte auf Englisch.

Stufe I   Benennen Sie alle Zuständigkeitsbereiche und beschreiben Sie die hierarchischen Verhältnisse im Vertrieb.

Stufe II   Verdeutlichen Sie die hierarchischen Verhältnisse und die jeweiligen Verantwortungsbereiche anhand von Tätigkeitsbeispielen.

Stufe III   Verdeutlichen Sie die hierarchischen Verhältnisse sprachlich abwechslungsreich und beschreiben Sie die jeweiligen Verantwortungsbereiche anhand von Tätigkeitsbeispielen.

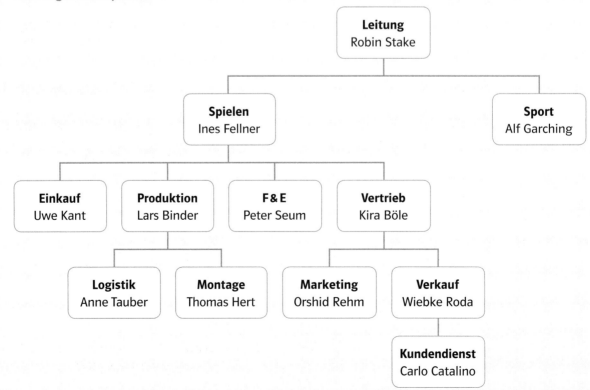

Phrases: The company and its products and services

To introduce your firm	
Our company was founded in 1972.	Unsere Firma wurde 1972 gegründet.
Our business idea was …	Unsere Geschäftsidee bestand darin …
In 1998 we were taken over by …	1998 wurden wir von … übernommen.
We are a leading manufacturer **of** …	Wir sind ein führender Hersteller von …
I work for an upmarket advertising agency.	Ich arbeite bei einer exklusiven Werbeagentur.
We are a **medium-sized** family firm.	Wir sind ein mittelständisches Familienunternehmen.
We are a wholesaler **specializing in** …	Wir sind ein Großhandelsunternehmen und sind spezialisiert auf …
My company is a major food retailer.	Meine Firma ist ein bedeutender Lebensmittel-einzelhändler.
We are a start-up company offering customized solutions.	Wir sind ein junges Unternehmen, das maß-geschneiderte Lösungen anbietet.
We are a chain of organic cosmetics suppliers.	Wir sind eine Kette von Anbietern biologischer Kosmetikprodukte.
The legal form of our company is a public limited company.	Juristisch gesehen ist unsere Firma eine (britische) Kapitalgesellschaft (vergleichbar einer deutschen Aktiengesellschaft).
FastTrack Inc. is a stock corporation.	FastTrack Inc. ist eine (US-) Kapitalgesellschaft.

To describe your firm's products / services	
We provide state-of-the-art solutions.	Wir bieten topmoderne Lösungen an.
Our high-quality products are well-known **all over** the world. They are unique.	Unsere erstklassigen Produkte sind weltbekannt. Sie sind einzigartig.
Our instruments are both reliable and durable.	Unsere Instrumente sind zuverlässig und haben eine lange Lebensdauer.
The software we offer is carefully adapted to suit your requirements.	Unsere Software wird Ihren Bedürfnissen sorgfältig angepasst.
We make a wide range of high-quality furniture.	Wir stellen ein breites Sortiment hochwertiger Möbel her.
The travel agency I work for **specialises in** high-end educational tours.	Das Reisebüro, bei dem ich arbeite, ist auf exklusive Bildungsreisen spezialisiert.

04

A | B | C | D

What does an office at your training company look like? What would you like your office to look like?

The Office

Offices may be spacious open-plan, purpose-built areas, perhaps taking up a whole floor of an office building, or small individual rooms to accommodate two to three people, or elegant premises at a prestigious address in a converted building. They may be back offices where employees have no contact with the public or front offices where members of the public are received. Many firms rent flexible office space furnished and fitted out with all the necessary electronic equipment from dedicated companies. Some create a business presence by renting a virtual office with a prestigious address and local telephone number with a (real) receptionist to deal with calls and mail.

WORD BANK

1 Match the following types of office with the photos above.

1. front office
2. back office
3. manager's office
4. open-plan office

2 Which type of office would you prefer to work in? Give reasons why. Discuss this in small groups.

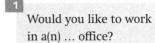
1 Would you like to work in a(n) … office?

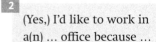
2 (Yes,) I'd like to work in a(n) … office because …

3 (No,) I'd prefer to work in a(n) … office because …

- *assistant*
- *back office*
- *business unit*
- *catering equipment*
- *colleague*
- *department*
- *electronic equipment*
- *front office*
- *furniture*
- *head*
- *to be in charge of*
- *internet access*
- *office supplies*
- *open-plan office*
- *organization chart*
- *to report to*
- *to be responsible for*
- *superior*

A | The office environment

1 Work in pairs. Make a list of all the stationery items shown in the picture. Use a dictionary if necessary.

R **2** Listen to Julia, Dragan, Vanessa und Sajid describing the office environment A1.11 in which they work and take notes. Work in pairs / small groups and compare your notes.

Vanessa   Julia

Dragan   Sajid

3 Choose task a, b or c.

○ a. Write a short summary of the kind of office these four young people work in.

◐ b. Give a detailed description of the kind of office the four young people work in and the office equipment available.

● c. Give an account of the offices the four young people work in and the equipment available. Explain each person's preferences.

M **4** Translate the following statements into German.

1. I work in a spacious open-plan office with air-conditioning. There is a wide range of office equipment.
2. We have a lot of visitors from client companies and potential new accounts. I work in a front office.
3. I work in the back office of a wholesaler. Our office looks out on to a public park. I like the privacy of a small office.
4. The photocopiers and printers are housed in a separate room.
5. I work free-lance from home. I am gradually building up a client base.

5 Choose task a, b or c.
○ a. What is your own office like? Give a brief description.
◑ b. Give a detailed description of your own office, its setting and the equipment available.
● c. Describe your own office and its setting. Discuss the pros and cons of the different types of office and your preferences.

6 Check out the latest products for the office including any innovative
⊕ features. Make notes and compare your findings with the class.

B | Catering in the office

M **1** Übertragen Sie die Aussagen von Julia, Dragan, Vanessa und Sajid ins Deutsche.
KMK

Julia

At my company we've got a small kitchenette attached to our office where we can make tea or coffee, and there's a fridge.
We also have a cafeteria where we generally have lunch as our lunch break is too short to go out. It is reasonably nutrition-conscious and serves light snacks, some of them vegetarian. My friend Luise is a vegetarian and I'm more or less permanently on a diet so we usually go for a fresh vegetable soup and a salad.

Vanessa

We have a kitchen with a tea and coffee machine, fridge and microwave. Our company doesn't have a canteen so we bring salads, sandwiches or convenience food that we can microwave. There's an upmarket supermarket nearby that has a good range of fresh soups and Thai or Chinese-style dishes. We have an hour lunch break so we sometimes go out and get a coffee to go.

Dragan

We've got a small kitchen with a coffee-machine, fridge and microwave. We usually bring our own sandwiches. We've got an hour for lunch so we sometimes go out when the weather's good. There's a mobile snack van nearby with good coffee and an interesting range of paninis and wraps. If we've got a deadline, which happens all the time, we just eat an apple or sandwich at our desks.

Sajid

On the days I'm in the office I usually just eat an apple or banana. There are coffee and tea making facilities. Occasionally, if the boss is in a good mood, we all go round to the pub, which also has sandwiches if anybody's desperate. When I'm working at home I don't have a set time for lunch. I just eat when I feel like it.

P **2** Describe the catering facilities at your company. Work in pairs to produce a brief description in writing that you can read out to the other students.

3 Choose task a, b or c.

○ a. Match the words on the left with the explanations on the right.

◐ b. Match the words with the explanations then choose five to make up your own sentences with.

● c. Match the words and explanations and include as many as possible in an imagined dialogue.

1.	it's more sociable	a.	equipment for making coffee
2.	free-lance	b.	pre-prepared food
3.	convenience food	c.	you have more contact with people
4.	snack van	d.	coffee to take away
5.	upmarket store	e.	fixed time
6.	to be desperate	f.	high-quality store
7.	nutrition-conscious	g.	you are your own boss
8.	coffee to go	h.	mobile snack bar
9.	a set time	i.	knowing what food is good and healthy
10.	coffee making facilities	j.	you can't wait a moment longer (here: to eat)

C | The company's organisation chart

1 Study the organisation chart below and complete the following text:

Antonia works for a family-owned company that sells lifts and escalators. The **1** is Markus Vogel who is also one of the three owners of the firm. His **2** is Lea Borawski, who has been working with the company for 15 years. Antonia Loretti reports to Vanessa Schultze who is a chartered accountant and head of the **3** Department. Mehmed Yildirim, an engineer, is in charge of **4**. The **5** manager is Frauke Vogel, Markus' wife. Lisa Steinke, Markus' sister in law, is the head of the **6** department, and Jonas Bergmann, who has just joined the firm and is training to become a management assistant, reports to her. The company is organised like this:

INFO: Large companies

The larger a company is the more complex its organisation tends to be. Large companies are headed by a chief executive officer (CEO) or a chairman of the board. They have many different business units and departments, such as a personnel, legal or marketing department. The scope of an individual employee's responsibilities will also be smaller and his or her duties more specialised in a large company than in a small one.

2 Refer to the text and the organisation chart on the previous page and find the equivalents of these German job titles.

Geschäftsführer · Einkaufsleiterin · Techniker · Buchhalterin · Leiter des Kundendienstes · Leiterin des Rechnungswesens · Sekretärin

3 Work in pairs. Partner A asks Partner B about his current department. Then change roles.

A Which department are you in?

B I work in the … department.

Partner A

Who is your boss?

What is he/she responsible for?

Who does he/she report to?

What's your general manager's name?

Who are your colleagues?

What are you responsible for?

Partner B

The head of our department is …

He/She is in charge of …

His/Her superior is …

Our general manager is called …

My colleagues are …

I process/I'm in charge of …

R **4** Listen to five trainees describing what they or their colleagues do in the
⊙ A1.12 departments they work in. Find out who works in what department.

	Lea	Marc	Marie	Zehra	Aslan
department	…	…	…	…	…

LANGUAGE AND GRAMMAR

INFINITIVE AND GERUND

Nach "too", "the first", "the last", "the only one" steht im Englischen der Infinitiv.

The company is too small **to compete with** multinationals.	Die Firma ist zu klein, um mit den Multis zu konkurrieren.
She was the first candidate **to be taken on**.	Sie war die erste Kandidatin, die eingestellt wurde.
He was the only one **to apply for** the post.	Er war der einzige, der sich für die Stelle bewarb.
This was the last problem **to be sorted out**.	Dies war das letzte Problem, das geklärt wurde.

In folgenden Fällen wird oft fälschlicherweise der Infinitiv benutzt. Es muss jedoch eine „Gerund"- Form benutzt werden.

We are looking forward to **doing** business with you.	Wir freuen uns darauf, mit Ihnen Geschäfte zu machen.
He is not used to **speaking** in public.	Er ist es nicht gewohnt in der Öffentlichkeit zu sprechen.
They objected to **paying** the top-up fees.	Sie waren dagegen die Zusatzgebühren zu bezahlen.
Sometimes there are problems **understanding** foreign business partners.	Manchmal gibt es Probleme ausländische Geschäftspartner zu verstehen.
We had great difficulties **convincing** him of the advantages of our new product.	Wir hatten große Schwierigkeiten ihn von den Vorteilen unseres neuen Produktes zu überzeugen.
It's no use **sending** these goods by ordinary mail.	Es hat keinen Zweck diese Waren mit der normalen Post zu verschicken.
I'd suggest **waiting** for the test results.	Ich schlage vor auf die Testergebnisse zu warten.

TASKS:

5 Translate the following sentences:

1. Unsere Firma war die erste, die dieses Produkt herausbrachte.
2. Wir hatten Schwierigkeiten damit das Treffen zu arrangieren.
3. Ich bin die Einzige, die sich um die Stelle beworben hat.
4. Man sagt, dass die Firma zu groß ist, um Bankrott zu machen.
5. Er hat als Letzter das Büro verlassen.
6. Ich freue mich darauf mit meinem Chef auf die Messe zu fahren.

6 Choose the correct form of the verbs in brackets:

1. He was the only candidate (to fail / failing) the exam.
2. We look forward to (meet / meeting) you in June.
3. They object to (work / working) till 8 pm every day.
4. I am having problems (to understand / understanding) his English.
5. We had some difficulties (to solve / solving) the problem.
6. This problem is too big (to be handle / handling) by our department alone.

ADDRESSING PEOPLE

In English-speaking countries hierarchical differences may seem less pronounced than in German companies. Certainly, they are not obvious from the way people address each other as first names are generally used. Immediate superiors are also usually addressed by their first name. Where there is a considerable difference in status the titles Mr / Mrs / Miss may be used when addressing a superior who may, however, use the employee's first name.

In Britain or the USA business contacts will call you by your first name and try to establish an informal atmosphere from the word go. When you are introducing yourself to English-speaking people, always give both your first name and your surname. If they call you by your first name, you should obviously do the same.

If the person you are speaking to is using English as a second / or foreign language, there may be some confusion about which rules apply. They may want greater formality, i. e. by sticking to titles (Mr / Mrs / Miss) and surnames.

In shops and restaurants customers may be addressed as sir / madam by the shop assistant / waiter, e. g.: "Are you ready to order, sir?" "Can I help you, madam?" You do NOT use these forms of address back!

TASK:

7   Answer the following questions.

1.   Why may hierarchical differences not be so obvious in English?
2.   How might your immediate superior address you?
3.   What are English-speaking associates trying to achieve by using your first name?
4.   What may happen when the person you are speaking to comes from a culture where more formality is expected?
5.   How would you translate the idiom "from the word go" (see above)?

Office expert

D | Handling stressful situations

1 Discuss stressful situations that you have to deal with in the office.

Step 1:   Brainstorm about possible stressful situations in the office and make a list of at least five situations. After completing the list, pass it on to another group.

Step 2:   Now brainstorm about possible solutions to the different situations on the list you received from another group (i.e. how to avoid or cope with stressful situations).

Step 3:   Have a classroom discussion about the most stressful situations and the best ways of dealing with them.

E | Office suite applications

1 Use the words below to describe different office applications.

1. Database: changes/any number of records/at one time / information/easily/retrieve
2. Spreadsheets: change/width of columns/calculate/display/values
3. Word processors:
   a.: create/edit/print/documents/texts
   b.: check spelling/mail merge/create and send/personalised letters
4. Presentation programmes: prepare/slide show/add/animation/ graphics
5. E-mail clients: store/manage/compose/receive/messages

2 Choose the correct word in brackets to complete the following sentences.

1. A(n) (record/item/folder) in a database is the collection of information about a certain person or product. (Datensatz)
2. If I want to get information from a database I have to (call/delete/ retrieve) it. (abrufen)
3. Excel is an example for (database/spreadsheet/mailing) software. (Tabellenkalkulation)
4. Another word for "values" is "(figures/words/money)". (Werte)
5. (Mail merge/multi-tasking/blogging) makes it easy for you to send a personal letter to a number of people at the same time. (Serienbrief)
6. Another word for "e-mail" is "electronic (post/message/memo)". (Nachricht)
7. To write a letter means to (compare/contain/compose) it. (erstellen)
8. You use an (edition/editor/addition) to change and improve, for example, graphics. (Editorprogramm)
9. I need a (remainder/remember/reminder) in order not to forget something. (Erinnerung)
10. Notes taken at a meeting are called (protocol/minutes/lists). (Protokoll)

KMK Exam Training

1 Produktion

Stufe II Verfassen Sie einen Bericht auf Englisch mit Bezug auf die Inhalte der folgenden Tabellenkalkulation. Berücksichtigen Sie folgende Punkte:

- Kurze Einführung zum Bericht
- Darlegung der Entwicklung der einzelnen Einnahmenpunkte über das Jahr
- Darlegung der Entwicklung der einzelnen Ausgabenpunkte über das Jahr
- Allgemeine Zusammenfassung der Jahresergebnisse
- Zwei begründete Empfehlungen für die Zukunft

	A	B	C	D	E
1		1st quarter	2nd quarter	3rd quarter	4th quarter
2	Sales	$890	$982	$1,200	$799
3	Fees	$420	$400	$432	$630
4	Dividends	$430	$760	$720	$870
5	Interest	$182	$60	$55	$66
6	Total revenue	$1,922	$2,202	$2,407	$2,365
7					
8	Payroll	$899	$904	$904	$904
9	Publicity	$390	$451	$350	$250
10	Administration	$232	$230	$256	$240
11	Operations	$550	$420	$399	$402
12	Total expenses	$2,071	$2,005	$1,909	$1,796
13					
14	Total	−$149	+$197	+$498	+$569

2 Rezeption: Hörverstehen

Stufe I Hören Sie folgenden Auszug einer Präsentation über eine Firma.
⊚ A3.20 Kopieren und ergänzen Sie dann das folgende Organigramm.

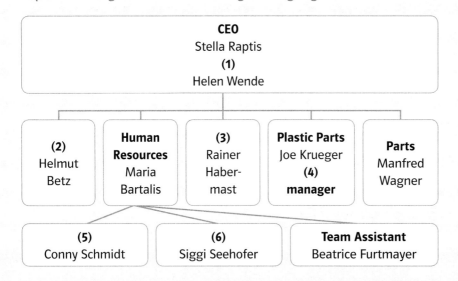

Phrases: The Office

To describe the office

I work in an open-plan office.	Ich arbeite in einem Großraumbüro.
She works in the back office / front office.	Sie arbeitet in einem Büro ohne Publikumsverkehr / mit Publikumsverkehr.
We all have tablets with internet access.	Wir haben alle ein Tablet mit Zugang zum Internet.
There is a photocopier and file shredders.	Wir haben einen Kopierer und Aktenvernichter.
The senior staff use the computer projectors for presentations.	Die leitenden Angestellten verwenden die Beamer für ihre Präsentationen.

To introduce the people in the office

He is the overall **boss**, the managing director.	Er ist der oberste Chef, der Geschäftsführer.
Mr Kent is the chief executive.	Herr Kent ist der Vorstandsvorsitzende.
She is **head** of department.	Sie ist die Abteilungsleiterin.
He **reports to** Frau Niemeyer.	Er untersteht Frau Niemeyer.
Frau Kramer is our **immediate** superior.	Frau Kramer ist unsere Vorgesetzte.
She is assistant / secretary **to** Mr Kent.	Sie ist Herrn Kents Assistentin / Sekretärin.
I'm **in charge of** exports.	Ich bin Exportsachbearbeiter / in.
I am responsible for sales to the EU.	Ich bin zuständig für den Verkauf in die EU-Länder.
He deals with / processes / handles complaints.	Er bearbeitet Mängelrügen.
He makes sure that instalments are paid **on** time.	Er kümmert sich um den pünktlichen Eingang der Ratenzahlungen.
Robert is one of the partners in this firm.	Robert ist einer der Partner in der Firma.
I hope to be **taken on** after I've finished my course.	Ich hoffe nach der Ausbildung übernommen zu werden.

To describe your company's organization chart

He is our **chief executive officer**.	Er ist der Chef unserer Firma.
The Marketing Department is part of Sales.	Die Marketing-Abteilung gehört zum Verkauf.
We are an international company and our **personnel** department is called "human resources".	Wir sind ein internationales Unternehmen und unsere Personalabteilung heißt „Human Resources".
The head of our legal department is a lawyer specializing in company law.	Der Leiter unserer Rechtsabteilung ist ein Fachanwalt für Gesellschaftsrecht.
Our company is divided **into** five business units.	Unsere Firma ist in fünf Geschäftsfelder unterteilt.

05

A

B

C

D

What are your thoughts on the subject of telephoning and text-messaging?

Telephoning

Telephoning customers and receiving incoming calls is an essential part of business life. Generally this involves the use of both landlines (fixed lines) and mobile phones. Mobile phones make it easy to make and maintain contact with business partners and help to complete transactions quickly and efficiently, especially when they or you are on the move. Many small businesses and start-ups cannot afford the expense of an office or secretarial back-up and rely almost entirely on the mobile or cell phone. Although text messages are not much used as formal communications in business it is, of course, useful to be able to text a business partner e.g. to check up on the time of a meeting. Now smartphones have combined the potential of the mobile phone with internet access and email, making it possible to check and respond promptly to both messages and emails when out of the office.

1 Describe the situations in the photos.

2 When do you prefer to text somebody instead of calling?

3 What are the major advantages of smartphones?

4 Are there any disadvantages of being available 24/7?

5 Are there situations where you would prefer to telephone rather than text or send an email?

WORD BANK

- *answering machine*
- *to catch*
- *clearly*
- *codes*
- *extension*
- *handset*
- *to hold*
- *landline*
- *mailbox*
- *mobile / cell phone*
- *number*
- *precisely*
- *to put through*
- *to read back*
- *to repeat*
- *slowly*
- *to spell*
- *symbols*
- *to take down*
- *telephone*
- *telephone alphabet*
- *text message*

A | Appliances and components

1 Match the German words below with their English equivalents.

1.	SMS	a.	landline/fixed line
2.	Freizeichen	b.	answering machine
3.	Hörer	c.	text (message)
4.	Handy	d.	headset/earphones
5.	Festnetz	e.	dialling tone
6.	Vorwahl	f.	extension
7.	Kopfhörer	g.	area code
8.	Anrufbeantworter	h.	engaged signal
9.	Besetztzeichen	i.	mobile (phone), cell (phone)
10.	Durchwahl	j.	receiver

NOTE

Mobile phone (often reduced to 'mobile' – e.g. He rang me on my mobile) is used more in Britain while cell or cell phone is used more in America.

B | Receiving and redirecting calls

1 Restore the correct order of the two jumbled dialogues between a receptionist and a caller. Then write them out.

Dialogue 1
- Oh, I'm sorry, her extension's engaged at the moment. Would you like to hold?
- Fenland Robotics Ltd. Good morning.
- Just a moment, Mr Weber. I'm putting you through to Amanda Browne.
- No thanks, I'll call back later.
- How can I help you?
- I'd like to speak to someone in marketing, please.
- Hello, this is Niko Weber from Brockhaus & Braun in Freiburg, Germany.

Dialogue 2
- Could you give me your name and room number, please?
- Hello. I want to make a complaint. I need to speak to the manager.
- Thank you. I'm putting you through to Customer Services.
- It's about the condition of our hotel room.
- Snowdonia Leisure Park. Good morning. What can I do for you?
- Jessica McGuire, room 312.
- May I ask what it is about?

2 Look at the following short telephone conversations. Note what expressions are used to deal with problems that arise.

Telephone conversation 1:

Moritz Meyer:	Good morning. Could I speak to Jessica McGuire, please?
Emily Davies:	I'm afraid there's no-one of that name here. This is a private address.
Moritz Meyer:	I'm terribly sorry. I must have got a wrong number.

Telephone conversation 2:

Emily Davies:	Good morning, Emily Davies speaking. Could you put me through to Niko Weber, please?
Julia Braun:	Good morning. I'll see if he's in his office. I'm afraid he's talking on the other line. Would you like to hold or shall we ring you back?
Emily Davies:	I'd prefer to hold – it's urgent.

Telephone conversation 3:

Alex White:	I'm trying to put you through to his extension but I'm afraid he's not answering.
Julia Braun:	What's the best time to catch him?
Alex White:	He's out a lot meeting customers. Why don't you try his mobile? Have you got the number?
Julia Braun:	No, I haven't. Could you give it to me?
Alex White:	Of course, it's 0 15 20 59 87 35 06
Julia Braun:	I didn't quite catch the last four digits. Could you repeat them more slowly, please?

Telephone conversation 4:

Miranda Crouch:	Good afternoon, Miranda Crouch from Fawkes & Fawkes Solicitors speaking. I've been trying to get Niko Weber on his extension but all I get is the engaged signal.
Julia Braun:	Sorry, could you speak more slowly please. I didn't quite get what you were saying. Could you give me your name again?
Miranda Crouch:	Sorry. My name is Miranda Crouch – that's C-R-O-U-C-H. Niko Weber's extension seems to be permanently engaged. Could you try it, please?
Julia Braun:	I'm very sorry about this. It seems to be engaged now as well. I'll look into it and get him to ring you back as soon as possible. Would you like to leave a message?
Miranda Crouch:	Please just ask him to ring me asap.
Julia Braun:	Certainly. Sorry, what was the company name? Could you spell it, please?
Miranda Crouch:	It's Fawkes & Fawkes Solicitors – that's F-A-W-K-E-S and then solicitors. He has the address and telephone numbers.

M **3** Now find equivalents for the following German telephone phrases:

1. Ich habe mich leider verwählt.
2. Möchten Sie warten oder sollen wir zurückrufen?
3. Hier gibt es keinen Jürgen Benders/niemanden, der so heißt.
4. Er spricht gerade auf der anderen Leitung.
5. Ich möchte lieber warten. Es ist dringend.
6. Das habe ich leider nicht mitbekommen/verstanden.
7. Möchten Sie ihm etwas ausrichten?
8. Wann kann ich ihn am besten erreichen?
9. Ich versuche Sie durchzustellen/zu verbinden.
10. Könnten Sie mir bitte seine Durchwahl/Handy-Nr. geben?
11. Könnten Sie das bitte langsamer wiederholen/buchstabieren?
12. Können Sie mich bitte mit Angela Harper verbinden?

R **4** Listen to the following telephone conversation between Tobias Heinze
⊚ A1.13 of Färber Roboter GmbH and Jessica Alderson, a receptionist at Fenland Robotics Ltd. Then decide whether the statements that follow are true or false.

1. Nicholas Able works for Buxton Engineering Ltd.
2. Tobias Heinze wishes to speak to Jessica Alderson.
3. Jessica knows for certain that Noah Brady is not in.
4. Tobias prefers to hold.
5. Tobias has got Noah's mobile phone number.
6. Tobias does not want to be put through to Alexandra Banwell.

R **5** Hören Sie sich den Dialog noch einmal an und achten Sie darauf, wie
KMK Folgendes auf Englisch formuliert wird.
⊚ A1.13

1. Was sagt Nicholas Able, als er den Hörer abhebt?
2. Was sagt Tobias Heinze, als er sich verwählt hat?
3. Wie entschuldigt er sich?
4. Was sagt Jessica Alderson, als sie Tobias Heinze durchzustellen versucht?
5. Wie drückt sich Jessica aus, als sie wissen will, ob Tobias warten möchte oder ob sie zurückrufen soll?

> **INFO: Telephoning in a foreign language**
>
> Telephoning, even in your own language, is different and potentially more difficult than speaking face to face, especially when you don't know the person on the other end. The non-verbal signals we rely on to read the other's reactions are missing. We can't see each other's facial expressions – smile, frown, raised eyebrows – or gestures. Obviously, there are other problems as well when you are telephoning in a foreign language. Will I know what to say if it's not the right number? What if the person I want to speak to isn't there? What if I don't understand what they are saying? Will I make a fool of myself? No wonder we often prefer to send an email where we can plan what we want to say and where there's no immediate comeback. So, when telephoning in English, it's all the more important to have the set expressions that are used at your fingertips.

6 Study the info-box on the previous page and choose task a, b or c.

○ a. Explain what makes telephoning in a foreign language difficult.

◐ b. Explain the differences between telephoning and face-to-face interaction.

● c. Explain the disadvantages of telephoning compared to face-to-face interaction and outline the main problems of telephoning in a foreign language.

R **7**

⊙ A1.14

Luise Wagner is in her second week of an internship at Gaia GmbH and is alone in the office as her colleagues are all at a conference. Suddenly the phone rings – for a moment she is tempted to ignore it.

Work with a partner. Listen to the telephone conversation. What phrases does Luise use to make sure she understands what Calum Buchanan is saying. How does Calum help Luise to understand him and feel good about her English. Discuss your findings with the class.

8 Complete the telephone phrases below using words from the box.

> cut · slowly · wrong · hold · repeat · louder · through · line · get · catch

Did you **1** that?

I'm sorry. I didn't quite **2** what you said.

I'm sorry, this is a bad **3** .

Could you speak a bit **4** , please?

Could you **5** that, please?

I must have got a **6** number.

Could you speak a bit more **7** , please?

I'm afraid we were **8** off.

Would you like to **9** or shall we ring you back?

Could you put me **10** to Anne Elliot?

I **9** Roleplay this telephone conversation with a partner. Refer to the phrases at the end of the Unit.

Firma: Hansen GmbH, Leipzig Company: Baltic Automotive, Riga, Latvia

Nehmen Sie den Anruf entgegen.

Nennen Sie Ihren Namen und den Namen der Firma.
Sie möchten Herrn Ackermann sprechen.

Sagen Sie, dass Sie den/die Anrufer/in schlecht verstehen und bitten Sie ihn/sie, etwas lauter zu sprechen.

Sprechen Sie etwas lauter und fragen Sie, ob Sie jetzt besser zu verstehen sind.

Es ist jetzt besser. Fragen Sie, worum es geht.

Es geht um einen Liefertermin.

Bitten Sie den/die Anrufer/in einen Moment zu warten.
Sie wollen ihn/sie mit Herrn Ackermann verbinden.

Bedanken Sie sich.

Sagen Sie, dass die Leitung leider momentan besetzt ist. Fragen Sie den/die Anrufer/in, ob er/sie warten möchte.

Sagen Sie, dass Sie lieber später zurückrufen möchten. Sie fragen nach der Durchwahl.

Die Durchwahl ist 3528. Herr Ackermann wird bis 17 Uhr im Büro sein.

Sie haben das nicht richtig verstanden und bitten um Wiederholung.

Wiederholen Sie die vorherige Information.

Bedanken Sie sich und verabschieden Sie sich.

Bedanken Sie sich für den Anruf und verabschieden Sie sich.

I **10** Work in pairs. Sit back to back. Use your notes from Exercise 5 and the phrases at the end of the Unit to act out a similar dialogue.

C | Taking messages

> **INFO: How to take a message**
>
> When you take messages, make sure that you note down all the relevant details. First take down the name of the caller – it will often be necessary to ask him / her to spell names and addresses. Be sure to get the postcode. Make sure you note down telephone numbers accurately. Mistakes lead to a lot of problems. Read back the number to the other person to check that you have got it right. Telephone numbers can be read differently in different countries. In England, the telephone number 370645 is simply read in the order it occurs: three seven oh six four five. Instead of "oh" the Americans generally say "zero". People often say "double" if there are two consecutive zeros or any other number (e.g. the country code: 0044 or 3998 etc).
>
> Always check the spelling of email addresses. The slightest mistake results in them being sent back. Note that @ is pronounced "at", (.) is read as "dot", / is pronounced "slash" and – is read as "hyphen" or "dash" (it doesn't matter which), _ is called "underscore".

1 There are different international telephone alphabets but people very often make up their own as they go along. Spell the following names using the international telephone alphabet below. Then listen and check.

> William Davy · Yvonne Waterhouse · Vincent McEwan · George Jameson · Jörg Müller-Jäger · Slobodan Vlasic · Ian McGuire · Siobhan O'Rourke · Gillian Gainsborough · Jimmy Joplin · Durim Januzai · Wendy Watson

2 Spell the following names making up your own English telephone alphabet.

> Wensleydale · Düsseldorf · Xaver Ziegler · Energize Ltd · Watford · Rhondda · Grinzing · Georgina Walton · Phillip Wade · Yolanda Smythe · Pierre-Yves Gide · Yitzak Johnson · Dragana Stefanovic

| **3** | Work in pairs: Sit back to back and spell your name and the name and address of your company using the international telephone alphabet. Then change roles and check the results. |

Symbol	Name	Example
'	apostrophe	O'Connor
@	at	info@
A/a	capital letters/small letters	USA/asap
-	hyphen/dash	t-online
Ö	o-umlaut/oe/o with 2 dots	Möller
:	colon	http:
/	slash/stroke	org/gla/
\	backslash	\docs.nt\
.	dot	.de
_	underscore/understroke	tourist_org.

Codes/numbers

+49	0(711)	664376-0
country code	**area code**	**office number**

34	04275	Leipzig
extension	**postcode/zip code**	**city**

| **4** | Work in groups. Group A uses the role card below and dictates the following telephone numbers, email addresses and websites. Group B uses the role card on page 259 and dictates the information given there. Then check your results. Ignore "…" when dictating. |

→ **ROLE CARD B:** page 259

Role card A

1. +44 (0) 12 73 72 85 75 …
2. (02 08) 865 38 89 …
3. (051) 26 91 11-12 …
4. +44 (0) 20 26 73 58 46 …
    +49 (0) 711 66 72 15 55 …
    001 941-921-55 55 …
5. buchanan@highlandwoollens… .co.uk
6. info@freshfield… .com
7. http://www.businessevents… .de/abo
8. mailto:noahbrady@fenland-robotics… .com

R **5** Choose task a, b or c.

○ a. First copy the form below. Then listen to the conversation and enter the
◎ A1.15   details in the form.

TELEPHONE MESSAGE

Message for: _____

Message taken by: _____ Date: *(today)* _____

Caller: _____

Subject: _____

_____

⬤ b. Following a telephone call Joachim Falcke has filled in the following
◎ A1.16   telephone message for his boss. Unfortunately there are some errors
         in his notes. Take his role, listen to the dialogue twice and correct the
         mistakes on a separate sheet of paper. See below what Joachim Falcke
         himself says in the conversation with the caller.

TELEFONNOTIZ

Nachricht für: *Alexander Boehmke* _____

aufgenommen von: *Joachim Falcke* _____ Datum: *(heutiges Datum)* _____

Anrufer: *Dylan Jones* _____

Betreff: *Miranda Stedman-Miller sollte Sie eigentlich in 3 Wochen auf der Light Engineering Fair in*

London treffen. Leider kann sie nicht kommen. Sie ist immer noch am Joint Venture interessiert und

möchte Sie stattdessen im September treffen, da sie dann in Dortmund ist.

Telephone call – Joachim Falcke:

Joachim Falcke:	Arndt GmbH, Falcke, Guten Tag.
Dylan Smyth:	…
Joachim Falcke:	Good morning, Mr Smith. I'm afraid he's in Scandinavia at the moment on a business trip. He's not due back until next week. Is there anybody else you would like to speak to?
Dylan Smyth:	…
Joachim Falcke:	Certainly. No problem.
Dylan Smyth:	…
Joachim Falcke:	OK, I'll let him know in good time.
Dylan Smyth:	…
Joachim Falcke:	Right. I'll pass on that information as well. Could you spell your boss' second name and the first part of the name of your company?
Dylan Smyth:	…
Joachim Falcke:	Thank you for ringing and I'll make sure Herr Boehmke gets the message. Goodbye.

● A1.16   **c.**   First listen to the dialogue. Then copy the following form and enter the details in the form.

TELEFONNOTIZ

Nachricht für: _____

aufgenommen von: _____ am: *(today)* _____

Anrufer: _____

Betreff: _____

_____

---

6   Work in pairs. Copy the English and German forms for taking messages. Partner A rings partner B and leaves a short message. Partner B takes down the message, either in German or English depending on the recipient. Use the role card on page 259.

→ **ROLE CARD A/B:** page 259

Example:

Partner A: "This is Dragan Petrovic speaking. I want to leave a message for your advertising manager, Ms Alexandra Scott. Please tell her that I've got the copy ready for your online ads. Could we arrange an appointment next week to finalise the texts? Please let me know asap".

Partner B takes down the message on the appropriate form:

TELEPHONE MESSAGE

Message for: *Ms Alexandra Schmidt* _____

Message taken by: *(you – your name)* _____ Date: *17 June 2015* _____

Caller: *Dragan Petrovic* _____

Subject: *Dragan Petrovic called to say that our online advertising copy is ready. He asked Ms Scott to ring him back asap to arrange a meeting to finalise the text.* _____

---

7   Use the phrases at the end of the Unit and choose task a, b or c.

○   **a.**   Make up a simple telephone message of the above type left by a customer who wishes to order a product.

◑   **b.**   Make up a message from a customer who is not satisfied with the goods you have delivered.

●   **c.**   Make up a message from a customer who wishes to complain about their hotel room. Give details.

D | Making telephone calls

TELEPHONING IN ENGLISH-SPEAKING COUNTRIES

You should use suitable polite phrases when telephoning in English-speaking countries. If you know the person you are ringing it is usual to ask how they are getting on etc. before you get down to business (e.g. "How are you doing? I haven't spoken to you for ages").

If you are about to mention a problem or difficulty you should begin with: "I'm afraid …". A request often begins with: "Could you possibly …?" ("Could you possibly repeat the address?") or "I would be grateful if you would / could …". When someone does you a service, however small, it is usual to say something like "Excellent!" or "Brilliant!" If someone thanks you for your help you can say: "You're welcome", or "Not at all". Do not just answer "yes" or "no". Say: "Yes, I think so"; "No, I'm afraid not". The problem for German speakers is that one-word answers (like "ja" and "nein"), which are NOT impolite in German, come across as rude, unfriendly, uninterested or impolite in English.

TASK:

1   Answer the following questions on text.

1. What phrase do you begin with if you are going to talk about a problem?
2. What do you say, for example, if the other person promises to send you some sales literature?
3. What does it sound like if you just answer "yes" or "no" in English?
4. If you know the person you are calling, how do you start the conversation?
5. How do you begin a request?

R   **2**   Listen to the conversation and note down the missing expressions on a
⊚ A1.17   separate sheet of paper.

AF: Good morning, Frame-it Ltd. Andrew Freeman speaking. How can I help you?

JA: Good morning. My name is Julia Alt. **1** from Germany. My boss saw your range of modern picture frames mentioned in a magazine article. He's **2** obtaining a catalogue and some **3** .

AF: Of course. As a matter of fact, we have just brought out a new print catalogue which I should be very happy to send you. We also have sales literature – in English, though, **4** . But we do also have a website af@frame-it… .com with illustrations and a lot of information.

JA: Thank you, I will **5** have a look at it.

AF: Could you give me your company name and address?

JA: Certainly. It's Hübbe GmbH.

AF: Could you **6** spell that?

JA: Yes, it's H for Henry, U for uncle 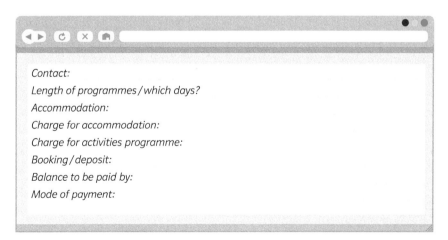, double B, E for egg. Then capital G, small m, small b, capital H – it is equivalent to Ltd. The street is Fürstenplatz 10 – F for Freddy, U for uncle with two dots, R for Richard, S for Sarah, T for Tommy, E for egg, N for nice, P for Peter, L for lovely, A for Andrew, T for Tommy and Z for Zebra, number 10. The city is Köln – K for Kevin, O for orange with two dots, L for lovely and N for nice, ⑧ goes before the place name, it's 50667.

AF: That was ⑨! I've noted everything ⑩. You'll receive the catalogue and sales literature in a couple of days.

JA: Thank you very much. Goodbye.

R **3**
⊙ A1.18
Lea Fischer works for a major German company. Her boss is very keen on corporate bonding and team building adventures. He likes the idea of Wales or Scotland, which would give the added benefit of being in an English-speaking environment. He asks Lea to search the internet and ring two or three companies for a quote. She finds an adventure company in the Brecon Beacons National Park in South Wales and decides to ring them.
Choose task a, b or c.

○ a. Read or listen to the following conversation. Then copy the form below and fill it in.

◐ b. Listen to the conversation. Then copy the form below and fill it in. Give details regarding accommodation and catering. Say what is included in the activities charge.

● c. Listen to the conversation. Then copy the form below and fill it in. Give details regarding accommodation, catering and insurance and list the activities available.

Contact:
Length of programmes / which days?
Accommodation:
Charge for accommodation:
Charge for activities programme:
Booking / deposit:
Balance to be paid by:
Mode of payment:

JW: Good morning. Argonauts Adventures Ltd, Jason Jackson speaking.

LF: Good morning. My name's Lea Fischer. I'm ringing from Germany. My boss is interested in bonding and team building events for our company.

JA: Great. We offer a wide range of outdoor team-building activities such as rock climbing, caving, canoeing, raft-building and rafting, kayaking, archery, abseiling, bush craft and mountain biking.

LF: That sounds like quite a range!

JA: It is! We can put a programme together to suit the interests and abilities of your group.

LF: How long do the events last?

JA: They generally last for five days, from Monday to Friday. We also have a wide range of weekend events. They go from Saturday to Sunday.

LF: I think my boss would be interested in a 5-day event. What about catering and accommodation?

JA: We provide accommodation in our log cabins – two to a room – and packed lunches. Breakfast and dinner are self-catering, but there is a restaurant on site. The accommodation is good value at £45 per person per night.

LF: What about the other charges?

JA: The activities programme costs about £600 per person for the week, depending on the activities you choose and the size of your group. It also includes insurance.

LF: Essential, I'm sure!

JA: Just a precaution. I'll send you our online brochure that gives you all the details and includes a booking form. Half the total cost is due when you make the booking and the balance is due four weeks before your programme starts.

LF: How can payment be made?

JA: By credit card or international bank transfer – the form gives our bank details. Is there anything else you'd like to know?

LF: I don't think so at the moment. Shall I give you our email address?

JA: Yes, please.

LF: It's lf@brueggemannco… .de.
I'll spell Brüggemann – it's B for Bertie, R for Richard, U for uncle, E for egg, double G for George, E for egg, M for mother, A for apple and double N for nice.

JA: Got that. Thank you very much, Lea. Do ring if there's anything you need to know.

LF: I will. Thank you. Goodbye.

| **4** Roleplay the telephone conversation with a partner.

Employee at Racer Motorradzubehör GmbH
(eigener Name)

British customer
John Stowe
Exclusive Biker Accessories Ltd

Melden Sie sich, wenn das Telefon klingelt. ⟶ Stellen Sie sich vor. Sie haben die neue Zubehörserie der deutschen Firma auf der Interbike-Austellung in Berlin gesehen und möchten eventuell einiges bestellen.

Erklären Sie, dass Sie Azubi sind. Sie sind allein im Büro. Fragen Sie, ob der Anrufer eine Nachricht hinterlassen möchte.

Sie haben Verständnis, sagen aber, dass Sie möchten, dass jemand so bald wie möglich anruft. Es ist dringend, da die großen Biker-treffen bald anfangen. Sie geben Ihre Telefonnummer in Leeds an: 01 13 27 03 24 53… .

Sie bitten den Anrufer, die Telefonnummer langsam zu wiederholen.
Den Namen haben Sie auch nicht mitbekommen. Bitten Sie den Anrufer, ihn zu buchstabieren.

Buchstabieren Sie den Namen und wiederholen Sie die Telefonnummer langsam und deutlich. Sie sind heute bis 18.00 Uhr britischer Zeit im Büro.

Sie bedanken sich. Es wird auf jeden Fall jemand im Laufe des Nachmittags anrufen.

Sie bedanken sich, sagen „nicht vergessen!" und verabschieden sich.

Sie danken dem Anrufer für seinen Anruf und verabschieden Sich ebenfalls.

5 Work in pairs. Search "Telephoning in English" on the internet for suggestions for role plays. Sit back to back and practise telephone dialogues with your partner. Refer to the phrases at the end of the Unit.

E | Leaving messages on an answering service, answering machine or voicemail

INFO: Leaving a message on an answering machine

- Wait for "the tone"! Pronounce your name clearly, give your company name and the place you are calling from.
- If you are calling from abroad, give the country.
- Dictate the telephone number slowly and clearly so that whoever hears the message can write it down (often people unthinkingly gabble telephone numbers!).
- Repeat important numbers and spell any names that might be difficult for the addressee.
- It may be a good idea to repeat your name and telephone number at the end (if there is time!).
- It goes without saying: Be friendly and polite!

P **1** The person you wish to contact is not answering his phones. Prepare a message to leave on his answering machine.

> Hello, Julian Smithson speaking · arrive Schipol · 3 pm · 15 June · staying Hotel Koninginnegracht Amsterdam · Look forward meet Mr Chan · discuss joint venture · Singapore · suggest working lunch · 16 June · 13.00 · contact on mobile +44 778 989 4347 · suggest place to meet · possibly restaurant · or this hotel · Best regards

---

INFO: Abbreviations used in text messages

The inclusion of predictive text apps in smartphone and tablet software has tended to reduce the need to use abbreviations in texting. Nevertheless some are still used and others like "ASAP" (as soon as possible), "FAQ" (frequently asked questions) and "FYI" (for your information) have become a

part of general usage. Others that are still in use are, for example, "u" (for you = CU / see you) and "2" (for to or too = 2nite / tonight). With the exception of "ASAP" they should generally not be used in business emails.

---

2 Choose task a, b, or c.
○ a. Match the German expressions with the English expressions.
◑ b. Match the German expressions with the English expressions and use them to form complete new sentences.
● c. Work in pairs. Match the German expressions with the English expressions and use some of them to form a dialogue.

a.	übertrieben	1.	to make a fool of yourself
b.	(hier) stören	2.	to make something up as you go along
c.	eine Bindung eingehen		
d.	sich lächerlich machen	3.	to catch
e.	sich etwas spontan einfallen lassen	4.	to be cut off
		5.	to look into something
f.	(hier) mitbekommen	6.	to bother
g.	einer Sache nachgehen	7.	at your finger tips
h.	getrennt werden	8.	over the top
i.	griffbereit	9.	to bond with

LANGUAGE AND GRAMMAR

TRICKY PREPOSITIONS (TYPICAL MISTAKES)

Verwendung von „by" oder until" für „bis"

Wenn etwas bis zu einem bestimmten Zeitpunkt geschehen soll wird „by" verwendet.

We need the shipment **by** Friday.   Wir brauchen die Sendung bis (spätestens) Freitag.

Falsch: We need the shipment ~~until~~ Friday.

Wenn etwas in einem begrenzten Zeitraum geschehen soll und danach abgeschlossen ist, wird „until" verwendet.

I need to employ additional staff **until** the   I brauche zusätzliches Personal (noch) bis
end of August.   Ende August (aber danach nicht mehr).

Falsch: I need to employ additional staff ~~by~~ the end of August.

Verwendung von „from ... to" für „von ... bis"

Der Beginn eines Zeitraums wird durch „from" gekennzeichnet, das Ende durch „to".

The London Fashion Fair will take place **from**   Die Londoner Fashion Fair (Modemesse) wird
30 June **to** 7 July.   vom 30. Juni bis zum 7. Juli stattfinden.

Falsch: The London Fashion Fair will take place from June ~~until~~ July.

Verwendung von „of", „from" und „by" für „von"

Vor dem Datum eines Briefs oder eines E-Mails steht „of" oder „dated".

We refer to your offer **of** (**dated**) 2 January.   Wir beziehen uns auf Ihr Angebot vom
                                                        2. Januar.

Falsch: We refer to your offer ~~from~~ 2 January.

Woher eine Mitteilung stammt wird durch „from" ausgedrückt.

We received a complaint **from** one of our   Wir haben eine Reklamation von einem
customers.   unserer Kunden erhalten.

Falsch: We received a complaint ~~of~~ one our customers.

Die Präposition „by" wird benutzt, um den Verfasser / Sprecher etc. zu benennen.

This is discussed in a report **by** an   Dies wird in einem Bericht einer unab-
independent research group.   hängigen Forschungsgruppe behandelt.

Falsch: This is discussed in a report ~~of~~ an independent research group.

TASK:

3   Choose the correct prepositions in the following short dialogues.

Dialogue 1
A: The meeting will last from 2 pm (until / to) about 5 pm.
B: But I need to get home (by / until) 7 pm at the latest.
A: You'll probably have to wait (until / by) 5.30 pm before you can go.

Dialogue 2
A: We enclose a description of the premises (by / of) an independent expert.
B: I have never heard (from / of) this firm.
A: Unfortunately we didn't hear (of / from) the company we wanted to use.
     Nevertheless, we will need to finalise the agreement (by / until) the beginning of next week.

Office expert

F | Mobile madness

With their often shrill ring tones and callers talking loudly, mobile phones, Blackberries and I-phones are everywhere: on buses, trains, on the street, at parties. What can you do to be a more polite mobile phone user?

1 Match the rules for mobile phone etiquette (1.–8.) to the texts (a.–h.).

1. Keep private conversations private
2. Lights out, phone off
3. Modulate your voice
4. Observe the proximity rule
5. KISS = Keep it short and simple
6. Don't talk and drive
7. Use common sense
8. Love the one you're with

a. Phoning while driving can cause accidents and is outlawed in many countries. Studies show that using a hands-free device doesn't solve the problem. Either wait or pull over to the side of the road.

b. Leave your phone off at funerals and job interviews or places such as libraries and places of worship where a quiet atmosphere is called for.

c. Keep your voice low, don't shout or argue if other people are nearby.

d. Keep your call brief if you're in a public place – arrange to call back later.

e. In public places such as restaurants or on buses avoid private conversations. Put the ringer on vibrate or silent mode and let the call roll over to voicemail. If the call is important, step outside or move off to the side to return it.

f. It's impolite to take a call in the middle of a conversation – after all if the caller were present they wouldn't just interrupt the conversation.

g. Move at least ten feet away from other people when talking on your mobile.

h. You should turn off your phone in the theatre, the cinema and at concerts – people are paying money to be entertained, not to listen to your ring tones.

2 Match the display indicators (1.–6.) with the correct description of the mobile phone functions (a.–f.).

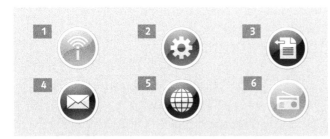

a. Appears when you receive a new message. It flashes when SIM card is full.
b. Camera function is activated.
c. Choose to customise your settings.
d. Indicates the strength of the signal.
e. Internet connection.
f. Scroll backward one page.

KMK Exam Training

1 Rezeption: Leseverstehen

Mobile Device Security

Smart phones now play an integral role in our daily lives. They are small, relatively inexpensive and multi-functional and have become almost indispensable for many people. Most feature GPS (Global Positioning System), multi-media capacity for taking photos and videos as well as recording sound, data processing and internet access.
Mobile devices, however, operate quite differently from how the internet works. Using a mobile device creates security challenges and puts a user's privacy at risk. This is why mobile device security is an important issue. It is important to understand that using a mobile device is inherently insecure. This means that the information you send from but also store on a mobile phone is vulnerable, i.e. can easily be accessed and stolen. In addition, such phones provide information about their location.

When people lose their purse or wallet, they report it to the police because of all the sensitive items it contains such as credit cards, driver's license, and insurance card and so on. When they lose their mobile phone they consider it a nuisance rather than a risk. They don't think of all the sensitive information it contains. This could include pictures and videos of family and friends as well as email and social networking applications and their passwords. In addition, banking applications with access to accounts as well as sensitive documents and private communication records are often stored on such mobile devices.
As a smartphone user you need to think of the risks and take precautionary measures to prevent someone stealing your valuable personal information. **259 words**

→ **VOCABULARY**
nuisance – Ärgernis

Stufe I Lesen Sie den obigen Text über Sicherheit im Zusammenhang mit Mobilgeräten und entscheiden Sie, ob folgende Aussagen richtig oder falsch sind.

1. Mobile Geräte werden immer teurer und für viele Leute immer wichtiger.
2. Mit einem Mobilgerät kann man die Standorte von Freunden und Familienmitgliedern feststellen.
3. Die Verwendung eines Smartphones stellt ein höheres Sicherheitsrisiko dar als die Verwendung eines PCs.
4. Auf Mobilgeräten gespeicherte Daten sind anfällig und können leicht gestohlen werden.

Stufe I Beantworten Sie folgende Fragen zum Text auf Deutsch.

1. Warum nehmen viele Leute den Diebstahl eines Smartphones nicht ernst genug?
2. Welche Arten von sensiblen Daten können auf einem Smartphone gespeichert werden?
3. Warum könnten solche Daten für potentielle Diebe interessant sein?

Phrases: Telephoning

To make friendly remarks at the beginning of a telephone conversation	
Oh, hello Julia. Nice to hear from you. How are things **over there**?	Hallo Julia. Schön von Dir zu hören. Wie geht's denn so?
Good morning Mrs Stanton. I hope you had a pleasant holiday.	Guten Morgen Mrs Stanton. Ich hoffe, Sie hatten einen angenehmen Urlaub.
Good afternoon Mr Llewellyn. **What's** the weather in Wales **like**?	Guten Tag Mr Llewellyn. Wie ist das Wetter in Wales?
Reactions	
Fine, thank you. And how are you?	Gut, vielen Dank. Und wie geht es Ihnen?
Thank you, it was really very relaxing.	Danke, es war wirklich sehr erholsam.
We've had an awful lot of rain recently, I'm afraid. What's it like in Germany?	Es hat in der letzten Zeit leider schrecklich viel geregnet. Wie ist das Wetter in Deutschland?

To ask the caller to speak more slowly / loudly, to spell sth., to repeat sth.	
Oh sorry. I didn't quite catch / get that. Could you repeat it more slowly, please?	Es tut mir Leid, das habe ich nicht verstanden. Könnten Sie es etwas langsamer wiederholen?
Could you possibly spell that? Is that the name of the town?	Könnten Sie das vielleicht buchstabieren? Ist das der Name der Stadt?
I'm afraid I didn't get the telephone number. Could you give me the number again, please?	Leider habe ich die Telefonnummer nicht mitbekommen. Würden Sie sie bitte wiederholen?
I'm afraid this is a bad line. Could you speak up a bit?	Die Leitung ist leider schlecht. Könnten Sie etwas lauter sprechen?

To ask for somebody	
Could I speak **to** Ms Hetherington, please?	Könnte ich bitte Ms Hetherington sprechen?
Could you put me **through** to Jason Jackson?	Könnten Sie mich mit Jason Jackson verbinden?
Could you give me his / her extension, please?	Könnten Sie mir bitte seine / ihre Durchwahl geben?
I'd like to speak to someone from the sales department.	Ich möchte gern jemanden im Verkauf sprechen.

To say that someone is not available	
I'm afraid Jason is not in the office at the moment. He …	Jason ist z. Zt. leider nicht in seinem Büro. Er …
… is in a meeting.	… ist in einer Besprechung.

To say that someone is not available

… has someone **with** him.	… hat Besuch.
… is **on** a business trip.	… ist auf Geschäftsreise.
… is out **at** lunch.	… ist zu Tisch.
… is no longer **with** the company.	… ist nicht mehr bei unserer Firma.

To offer to ring back or take a message

I'm afraid Jason is speaking **on** the other line. Would you prefer to hold or shall I ask him to ring back?	Jason spricht leider gerade auf der anderen Leitung. Möchten Sie warten, oder soll er Sie zurückrufen?
Can he call you back this afternoon?	Kann er Sie heute Nachmittag zurückrufen?
Can I give him a message?	Kann ich ihm etwas ausrichten?
Would you like to leave a message?	Möchten Sie eine Nachricht hinterlassen?

Reactions

Thank you. I'll ring back later.	Danke sehr. Ich rufe später zurück.
I'm afraid I won't be in the office this afternoon. I'll give you my mobile number.	Ich bin heute Nachmittag leider außer Haus. Ich gebe Ihnen meine Handy-Nummer.
Yes, please. Could you tell him that …?	Ja bitte. Könnten Sie ihm ausrichten, dass …?

To refer someone to someone else

I'm afraid I don't know the details.	Leider kenne ich mich damit nicht aus.
I'm afraid I am not familiar **with** this order.	Leider weiß ich über diesen Auftrag nicht Bescheid.
I'm afraid I am not in charge of this transaction.	Leider bearbeite ich diesen Vorgang nicht.
I'll put you through to Jayden Flaherty.	Ich stelle Sie zu Jayden Flaherty durch.
Shall I put you through **to** his secretary?	Soll ich Sie mit seiner Sekretärin verbinden?
Would you like to speak **to** somebody in the accounts department?	Möchten Sie mit jemandem aus der Abteilung Rechnungswesen sprechen?

Reactions

Yes, please. She may be able to help.	Ja bitte. Sie kann mir vielleicht helfen.
No thanks, I really need to speak **to** the export manager.	Nein danke. Ich muss unbedingt mit dem Exportleiter sprechen.

To ask for / about something

Would you please let me know if …?	Ich möchte gern wissen, ob …?
I'd like to ask **whether** it would be possible to …	Wäre es möglich, dass …
Could you possibly …?	Könnten Sie / Könntest Du …?

To ask for / about something

Do you think you could …?	Könnten Sie / Könntest Du vielleicht …?
You'd be doing us a great favour if you could …	Sie täten uns einen großen Gefallen, wenn Sie …
Please **make sure** that …	Bitte sorgen Sie dafür, dass …
I would really appreciate **it** if you could …	Ich wäre Ihnen sehr dankbar, wenn Sie …

Reactions

I see no reason why not.	Natürlich. Warum nicht.
Certainly. No problem.	Klar. Kein Problem.
I will certainly do my very best.	Ich werde bestimmt mein Bestes tun.
Definitely. I'll see to it myself.	Ganz bestimmt. Ich werde mich selbst darum kümmern.

To refuse something

I'm afraid we can't agree **to** your proposal.	Leider können wir uns mit Ihrem Vorschlag nicht einverstanden erklären.
We find this level of service quite unacceptable.	Für uns ist diese Art von Kundendienst absolut inakzeptabel.
This is unfortunately not what we had in mind.	Leider hatten wir uns das nicht so vorgestellt.

Reactions

That is a pity / most regrettable.	Das ist wirklich schade / überaus bedauerlich.
I can quite understand. We are trying hard to improve things.	Das kann ich verstehen. Wir bemühen uns nach Kräften um eine Verbesserung.
There must have been a misunderstanding.	Hier muss ein Missverständnis vorliegen.

To apologise

I'm terribly sorry but …	Es tut mir schrecklich Leid, aber …
I really must apologise for the inconvenience we've caused you.	Ich möchte mich für die Ihnen entstandenen Unannehmlichkeiten vielmals entschuldigen.
I'm sorry. Thank you for being so understanding.	Es tut mir Leid. Vielen Dank für Ihr Verständnis.
I can only repeat that I'm very sorry for …	Ich kann mich nur nochmals für … entschuldigen.

Reactions

It could happen to anyone.	Das hätte jedem passieren können.
It's a mistake that is very easily made.	So ein Fehler kommt oft vor.
Well, let's just hope it doesn't happen again.	Hoffen wir nur, dass es nicht noch einmal geschieht.
It has caused us a lot of embarrassment.	Es war für uns sehr peinlich.

To play for time	
Can I ring you back? I need to look **at** the file.	Kann ich Sie zurückrufen? Ich muss erst die Unterlagen einsehen.
I'll have to have a word with the line manager.	Ich muss das mit dem Bereichsleiter besprechen.
I'm afraid I can't give you a definitive answer **at** the moment.	Leider kann ich Ihnen z. Zt. keinen endgültigen Bescheid geben.

Reactions	
Certainly, but please give me your extension so that I can ring you direct if necessary.	Natürlich, geben Sie mir aber bitte Ihre Durchwahl, damit ich Sie nötigenfalls direkt anrufen kann.
I wish to settle the matter now. I should be grateful if you would put me through to the person responsible.	Ich möchte die Angelegenheit jetzt klären. Bitte stellen Sie mich zu dem entsprechenden Sachbearbeiter durch.
Fine. I leave the office **at** 4 pm your time.	Schön. Ich bin bis 16 Uhr Ihrer Zeit im Büro.

To insist that something is done by a certain date	
We need the goods **by** Wednesday **at** the very latest.	Wir benötigen die Ware bis spätestens Mittwoch.
We definitely need the documents **by** 3 May.	Wir brauchen die Unterlagen unbedingt bis zum 3. Mai.
Can we rely **on** that?	Können wir uns darauf verlassen?
Please make sure it arrives **no later than** the end of April.	Bitte sorgen Sie dafür, dass es spätestens Ende April eintrifft.
Monday 31 July is the final deadline.	Montag, der 31. Juli ist der letzte Termin.

To promise something	
We promise you that ...	Wir versprechen Ihnen, dass ...
You have my word. The documents will reach you **by** Monday.	Ich gebe Ihnen mein Wort. Die Dokumente treffen spätestens Montag bei Ihnen ein.
We will certainly **ensure** that ...	Wir werden bestimmt dafür sorgen, dass ...
The goods will definitely be dispatched tomorrow.	Die Ware wird mit Sicherheit morgen abgeschickt.

To end the conversation	
Goodbye Ms Hetherington. Thank you for calling.	Auf Wiederhören, Frau Hetherington. Vielen Dank für Ihren Anruf.
Thank you. Goodbye. Have a nice weekend.	Danke. Auf Wiederhören. Schönes Wochenende!

Reactions	
Goodbye Mr Llewellyn. You'll be hearing from us again soon.	Auf Wiederhören Mr Llewellyn. Sie werden bald wieder von uns hören.
Goodbye.	Auf Wiederhören.

New York Shanghai
London
Los Angeles **Dubai.**
Singapore

What sort of arrangements
may a personal assistant
(PA) have to make?

Making arrangements

An important part of the job of a secretary, administrative assistant or PA is
to make arrangements on behalf of management. This will include managing
the boss's calendar, making or rescheduling appointments, booking flights
or train tickets, making hotel reservations and hiring cars. It may also entail
booking tables at restaurants, recommending local places of interest to visit
and finding out about current entertainment. Many companies take part in
trade fairs and exhibitions and it will probably be the PA's task to book stand
space and help organise the company's participation, which may include
booking local interpreters. Finally, a secretary is responsible for welcoming
visitors, often from abroad. He / she may have to entertain them if the person
they are scheduled to see has been held up. They may also need help with
using public transport, calling taxis, finding their way around the city centre
etc. Obviously a good command of English is an absolute must.

WORD BANK

- accommodation
- application
- appointment
- arrangements
- arrival
- to book
- booking
- departure
- destination
- ensuite bathroom
- exhibition
- fair
- flight
- hotel
- to hire
- to organise
- PA (personal assistant)
- to record
- to (re)schedule
- reservation
- stand

M **1** Translate the above text into German.

2 Your boss is planning business trips to London and New York in the coming
month and has asked you to find out what musicals are on in both cities.

3 Check the internet and find out. Your boss has some Friday appointments in
Leeds and decides to stay over the weekend. He has heard that Harrogate is
attractive and asks you to find out more about it.

A | Flights and accommodation

Brandenburg Mechatronics AG is a German company based in Berlin specialising in engineering, robotics etc. Executives from the company's subsidiaries in several European countries are planning to take part in the International Mechatronics Exhibition in Shanghai where the company has a stand. The executives are scheduled to meet in Berlin for a conference before flying to Shanghai.

R **1**
⊙ A1.19

Elena Markovics, PA to Julius Braun, managing director responsible for sales to the Far East, has been asked to organise the conference from 5–7 May at the company's headquarters in Berlin. She decides to start by ringing Victoria Armstrong, her opposite number at Manchester Mechatronics UK. Listen to the dialogue and complete the following sentences.

1. The conference is to take place in `1` on `2` .
2. Erica Sanderson, our export sales manager, is `3` .
3. Elena Markovics will book `4` for her.
4. Victoria asks whether the hotel caters for `5` .
5. Lunch will be provided at `6` .
6. Victoria will book the flight from `7` to `8` .
7. Victoria will email the flight number and `9` .
8. Elena is organising `10` at the Shanghai Mechatronics Fair.

R **2**
⊙ A1.19
KMK

Als Auszubildende/r hören Sie das Gespräch mit und notieren sich die wichtigsten Punkte auf Deutsch:

1. Veranstaltungsort und -termin
2. Konferenzzeiten
3. Teilnehmer/innen
4. Details zur Flugbuchung
5. Details zur Buchung einer Unterkunft
6. Hinweise zu Essgewohnheiten
7. Vorbereitungen für Weiterreise zum nächsten Veranstaltungsort

P **3** Taking the role of Elena Markovics send an email to Victoria Armstrong confirming the reservation of a single room on 5, 6 and 7 May at the Hotel Strelitzer Hof, Glinkastr. 154, 10117 Berlin.

Confirm also that the hotel offers vegetarian cuisine. Ask for details of the flights to Berlin with flight number and times of arrival they have booked for their staff on 5 May.

To:	v.armstrong@mechatronicsmanchester….co.uk; ebba.almgren@mechatronicsmalmoe….se; eufrozyna.pomorski@mechatronicswarszawa….pl; simona.slavik@mechatronicsbratislava….sk
From:	e.markovics@brandenburgmechatronics….de

R **4**
A1.20

As she has not received a reply to her email sent to the Grand Yangtze River Hotel in Shanghai in which she booked rooms for the six executives taking part in the Mechatronics Fair, Elena decides to ring the hotel.

Listen to the telephone call and answer the following questions.

1. What rooms does Elena want to book?
2. What are the particular features of the rooms?
3. What are the nationalities of the executives?
4. What are the arrangements for breakfast at the hotel?
5. What catering arrangements does the hotel provide otherwise?
6. What catering arrangements are necessary for Erica Sanderson?
7. How will the executives get to the exhibition grounds?
8. Is it necessary to hire a car?
9. What information does Elena ask for re business facilities?

P **5** Elena has meanwhile booked the flights from Berlin to Shanghai.

Refer to the flight schedule below, take the role of Elena and send an email to the Grand Yangtze River Hotel (reception@grandyangtzeriverhotel . . . .cn) informing reception of the flight number and time of arrival of the Mechatronics executives from Berlin.

Flight	Departure Time	Arrival Time	Destination
XZE 175	Berlin: 8:45/8 May	14:45/9 May	Shanghai
XZE 178	Shanghai: 14:00/15 May	21:00	Berlin

P **6** In your role as Elena send an email to Victoria Armstrong (v.armstrong@ mechatronicsmanchester . . . .co.uk) and cc her opposite numbers in Sweden, Poland and Slovakia (cf email addresses above) giving them details of the flights and hotel accommodation in Shanghai. Ask them to email if they have any questions.

7 Work with a partner. Act out the following dialogue with the help of the prompts.

Ryan Linton

Marek Kotnik

Good morning/Fenland Robotics Ltd

Great Oriental Airlines

book flight/Singapore

date/one way/return?

return/outward journey 25 July/
return 30 July

one moment/look monitor/flight 8 am
25 July/London Heathrow/return Heathrow/
9 am 30 July

How many hours/flight?

flight duration about 13 hours

OK/price?

business/economy?

business

£ 897/return/book?/pay credit card?

book/pay Visa

name on card/long number/security
number/expiry date?

Ryan Linton/4731 5026 7100 5314/005/
April 201_

address?

5 Brunswick Close, Hove

post code?

BN3 1NA

thank you/flight GOR345/booking reference
GOR8YT5/send confirmation/tickets/
forgot – aisle or window?

window seat

OK/anything else?

recommend hotel?

Yes/XYZ Hotel good/make reservation?

No/book online

OK. Goodbye

OK. Thank you/choose Great Oriental/
goodbye

8 Your boss asks you to check out times and prices of business class flights to New Delhi, India (direct flights from the nearest airport). Search the internet and make notes on the options.

9 Work with a partner. Act out the following dialogue with the help of the role cards. If necessary, use a dictionary for help.

→ **ROLE CARD B:** page 260

Role card A

Sie sind Pedro de la Fuente von der Mietwagenfirma Luxurious Limos in San Francisco und erhalten einen Anruf von Ethan Taylor von der britischen Firma Zooks.

Nehmen Sie den Anruf entgegen:
- Mietwagen verschiedener Kategorien (Kompakt- bis Luxusklasse) zur Abholung am Flughafen.
- Kompakt ist der kleinste Wagen
- Preis für Kompaktklasse 200 $ pro Woche, Preis pro Tag 50 $
- keine Beschränkung der Zahl der gefahrenen Meilen (unlimited mileage)
- Versicherung im Preis inbegriffen, bei Unfall muss der Kunde 10 % der Kosten tragen.
- Zusatzversicherung zur Deckung der 10 % Beteiligung (excess coverage): 60 $ pro Woche
- 20 % Rabatt für Kunden der Airlines of the Americas
- Gesamtpreis: 200 $ minus 20 % Rabatt plus 60 $ Zusatzversicherung = 220 $
- Zahlung per Kreditkarte: Kreditkartennummer, Sicherheitscode, Gültigkeitsdatum, Anschrift des Kunden

B | Appointments

Jason Sanders von Unikonline Internet ADz wird am kommenden Montag in Berlin sein und möchte gern einen Termin mit Julius Braun.
Die Sekretärin von Herrn Braun, Elena Markovics, telefoniert mit Emma Holmes und fragt sie nach einem Termin.

1 Übernehmen Sie die Rollen von Emma und Elena im folgenden Rollenspiel.

KMK

Emma	Elena
	11.30 wäre am Montag möglich.
Leider klappt 11.30 bei Jason nicht. Er ist frei bis 10.30.	
	Julius Braun hat einen Termin bis 11.30.
Wie wäre es mit 12 Uhr?	
	12 Uhr geht leider auch nicht.
Hat Julius Braun vielleicht nachmittags einen Termin?	
	Eventuell um 17 Uhr. Einen Moment, bitte. Ich frage eben nach. Ja, 17 Uhr geht auch. Ist das OK für Jason?
Ja, das ist OK. Vielen Dank.	
	Prima! Also Montag um 17 Uhr. Ich bestätige den Termin noch einmal per E-Mail.
Vielen Dank! Auf Wiederhören!	

I **2** Elena Markovics' boss, Julius Braun, is planning a trip to the USA in connection with Brandenburg Mechatronics' plans to have a number of their products manufactured by a small family-owned American engineering company in Santa Barbara, California. It is Elena's job to arrange appointments with the managing director and the proprietor as well as with a firm of lawyers who are advising them. Julius Braun is planning to spend a day inspecting the company and on the second day meet with a firm of lawyers.

Elena rings Madeleine Collins, secretary to the managing director Gregory Johnson. They both have their bosses' calendars in front of them.

Sit back to back with your partner and act out the dialogue between them in which they discuss the arrangements and the schedule for the meeting. Use the role cards.

→ **ROLE CARD B:** page 260

Role card A

Terminkalender von Julius Braun	
Montag:	
9:00	Termin mit Leiter der Berliner Sparkasse
11:00	Termin bei Anwaltskanzlei von Richter
12:00	
14:30	Treffen mit Kunden in Potsdam
17:00	
Dienstag:	
8:40	Flug Berlin-Los Angeles. Ankunft c. 16.10 Ortszeit
	Kann mich jemand am Flughafen LA abholen
	(Flug BE27G) und zum Hotel Malibu Heights bringen?
Mittwoch:	
Geschäftliche Termine:	
Was steht beim Meeting in USA auf dem Programm?	
Donnerstag:	
Geschäftliche Termine:	
Was steht beim Meeting in USA auf dem Programm?	
Freitag:	
Venice Beach, Santa Monica / Hotel in Santa Monica gebucht.	
Samstag:	
Rückflug nach Berlin 18:10 Ortszeit LA	

TIPS FOR VISITORS TO THE UK

Trains:
There is no supplementary charge added to the ticket price for faster trains (the Eurostar trains to Brussels and Paris are more expensive). Trains that stop at many stations are obviously slower than those that rarely stop. How often and where they stop is given on the indicators and timetables. It is very important to check that the train stops where you want to get off! Do not just assume that the train will stop at the station where you got on on your outward journey. Each train may stop at a different selection of stations.

Pubs:
Pubs are an important institution in Britain and are a popular venue for an informal meal. Many provide food at lunchtime, less often in the evening. As a rule there is no waiter service. You go to the bar to buy drinks where turn-taking is observed although the queue is not always visible. People may express their annoyance if you push in. If the pub is crowded it may be a good idea to discreetly wave a 10 pound note to let the barman / barmaid know you are waiting to buy a drink. Often English people buy rounds, saying things like "What's yours?" or "What are you having". If it's your turn you say "It's my round." Everybody is in principle expected to by a round – if you don't, there may be an embarrassed silence. Food is also ordered and paid for at the bar and is brought to the table where you are sitting. All food and drink is paid for straight away and there is no tipping.

Tipping (taxis and restaurants):
In Germany you frequently tip by rounding up the amount of the bill.
If the taxi fare is € 8.10 you might just say 8.50 or 9. In Britain a taxi driver would not know what you mean. If the fare is £6.30 you could give the driver a 10 pound note and say "Please give me change for £7. In restaurants the bill is generally brought on a little tray. You put enough money on it to cover the bill. The waiter takes the tray and brings it back with your change. You then decide what to put on the tray as a tip – it doesn't have to be a percentage of the bill.

TASK:

3 Answer the following questions on the text.

1. Why can't you assume on your return journey that a train is scheduled to stop at the station where you got on?
2. How do you know whether a train is a slow train?
3. Why is it a good idea to display your money when waiting at a crowded bar?
4. Is it usual to leave a tip in a pub?
5. When do you decide what tip to leave in a restaurant?

M 4

KMK Ihr Vorgesetzter bittet Sie im Vorfeld seines ersten Geschäftsbesuchs in Großbritannien, Informationen zu den örtlichen Gepflogenheiten zusammenzustellen.
Lesen Sie die Tipps (oben) für Besucher in Großbritannien und fertigen Sie Notizen zu den wichtigsten Punkten für Ihren Vorgesetzten auf Deutsch an.

C | Booking an exhibition stand

R/M **1** Elena now has to ring the exhibition authorities in Shanghai to check that their order for a stand is OK. After checking her records she sees that she returned the application over a month ago.

Lesen Sie den Dialog, decken Sie den Text ab und drücken Sie Folgendes auf Englisch aus:

1. Ich möchte unsere Standreservierung überprüfen.
2. Wir haben keine Bestätigung erhalten.
3. Wann schicken Sie die Bestätigungen heraus?
4. Wir haben einen Stand von 40 m² mit Teeküche und Besprechungsraum gebucht.
5. Ich schicke Ihnen eine Broschüre mit Informationen über den Dolmetscher-Service zu.
6. Ich glaube, damit ist alles erledigt.

Elena:	Good morning, Elena Markovics from Brandenburg Mechatronics in Berlin speaking. Do you speak English or German?
Exhibition authorities:	I speak English. How can I help you?
Elena:	I'd like to check our stand reservation for the mechatronics exhibition.
Exhibition authorities:	I'll put you through to the department that deals with stand bookings.
Wang Tingting:	Good morning. Wang Tingting speaking, reservations department.
Elena:	Good morning. My name's Elena Markovics from Brandenburg Mechatronics in Berlin, Germany. I want to check that our stand reservation has gone through. I didn't receive any confirmation.
Wang Tingting:	Oh, I'm sorry about that. Just a second, I'll bring it up on my monitor. Yes, here it is. Brandenburg Mechatronics – a corner stand, 40 m², with kitchenette and conference area. Is that OK?
Elena:	Yes, excellent. When will you be sending out confirmations?
Wang Tingting:	You should receive a confirmation any day now. But you can assume that everything is OK. Is there anything else I can help you with?
Elena:	We should like to book an interpreter. Can you recommend anyone?
Wang Tingting:	We have our own interpreter service. Shall I make a note on your reservation that you would like to book an interpreter through our service?
Elena:	Yes – that seems the easiest thing to do. I'm not sure at the moment how often we'll need one.
Wang Tingting:	I will send you a brochure with their hourly rates. You can book them from one day to the next.
Elena:	Brilliant. I think that's everything dealt with. Thank you very much.
Wang Tingting:	Thank you for ringing. Goodbye.

LANGUAGE AND GRAMMAR

PROGRESSIVE AND SIMPLE FORMS

Die Verlaufsform beschreibt eine gerade vor sich gehende Handlung oder einen Prozess, der häufig durch „now", just, „still", „when", „while", „since" und „for" markiert wird.

Our competitors are **now** trying to undercut our prices.	Unsere Konkurrenten versuchen jetzt unsere Preise zu unterbieten.
We are **still** waiting for his decision.	Wir warten immer noch auf seine Entscheidung.
Growth has been slowing **since** January.	Das Wachstum hat sich seit Januar verlangsamt.

Die einfache Verbform in der Gegenwart drückt aus, dass sich etwas wiederholt oder immer so ist. Sie wird häufig mit „always", „every", „usually", „sometimes", „never" usw. verwendet.

They change their suppliers **every year.**	Sie wechseln ihre Lieferanten jedes Jahr.
They **always** use the same suppliers.	Sie nehmen immer dieselben Lieferanten.

Einfache Form und Verlaufsform der Gegenwart:

I am living in Düsseldorf (= but I'm planning to move).	Ich wohne zurzeit in Düsseldorf.
I live in Dresden (= permanently).	Ich wohne in Dresden.

Die Verlaufsform wird auch als Zukunftsform verwendet, um feste Vereinbarungen oder Abmachungen zu bezeichnen.

He's giving a presentation at the conference next month.	Er hält nächsten Monat eine Präsentation auf der Konferenz.
I'm picking him up at the airport next Friday.	Ich hole ihn nächsten Freitag am Flughafen ab.

TASK:

2 Translate the following sentences.

1. Als Anhang senden wir Ihnen unsere neue Broschüre.
2. Pro Woche verkaufen wir über 500 Fahrräder.
3. Leider warten wir noch immer auf die Begleichung der Rechnung.
4. Zurzeit versuchen unsere Konkurrenten auf dem chinesischen Markt Fuß zu fassen.
5. Die Kupferpreise fallen weltweit wegen der Verlangsamung des chinesischen Wachstums.
6. Jedes Jahr investieren wir 10 % des Gewinns in neue Technologien.
7. Er organisiert die Konferenz in diesem Jahr und wir buchen die Hotelzimmer.
8. Wir warteten schon auf ihn, als seine Sekretärin den Termin absagte.

Office expert

D | Handling schedules

You work for an international company in Berlin and your boss, who is on a business trip, has asked you to arrange a meeting for the week of 9 to 13 May with Ms Link, head of the logistics department, and Mr Brunner, head of production. Your boss needs at least two hours and would prefer a meeting early in the week.

1 After looking at Ms Link's and Mr Brunner's schedules, write an e-mail to your boss (m.desai@mail . . . .com) proposing two alternative dates for the meeting and asking which she would prefer. Explain why a meeting early in the week is not possible.

Ms Link's calendar

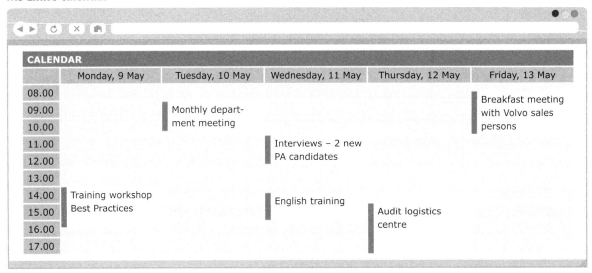

CALENDAR	Monday, 9 May	Tuesday, 10 May	Wednesday, 11 May	Thursday, 12 May	Friday, 13 May
08.00					Breakfast meeting with Volvo sales persons
09.00		Monthly department meeting			
10.00					
11.00			Interviews – 2 new PA candidates		
12.00					
13.00					
14.00	Training workshop Best Practices		English training		
15.00				Audit logistics centre	
16.00					
17.00					

Mr Brunner's calendar

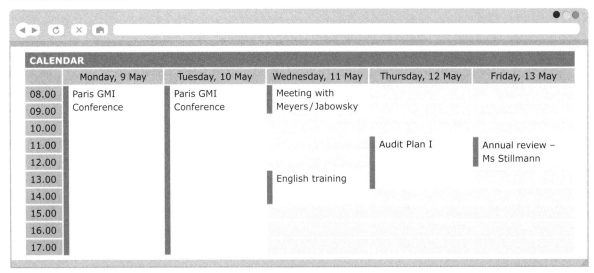

CALENDAR	Monday, 9 May	Tuesday, 10 May	Wednesday, 11 May	Thursday, 12 May	Friday, 13 May
08.00	Paris GMI Conference	Paris GMI Conference	Meeting with Meyers / Jabowsky		
09.00					
10.00					
11.00				Audit Plan I	Annual review – Ms Stillmann
12.00					
13.00			English training		
14.00					
15.00					
16.00					
17.00					

KMK Exam Training

1 Mediation (Englisch – Deutsch)

Stufe II Ihre Chefin hat an einer internationalen Besprechung aller Personalchefs der Firma teilgenommen. Sie bittet Sie das englische Protokoll der Besprechung ins Deutsche zu übertragen.

Minutes of Synchron Human Resources Meeting – 25th September 2016

Meeting called to order at 9:30 pm by meeting chair Jessie Bowens.

Members present:
Chair Jessie Bowens, USA
Shuo Li, China
Miranda Peres, Brazil
Beate Weiss, Germany
Harald Nicholson, England
Member Apologies:
Claude Demond, France

Reading and Approval of Minutes: 15th June 2016

Agenda item #1: measures	Report by Shuo Li concerning new English language training
Discussion:	Members interested in the measures but see need for better control of success
Action:	Shuo Li is to implement and report on improved success control at the next meeting
Agenda item #2:	Committee Report concerning the international standardization of job interview procedures
Discussion:	Opinions divided with some members, notably Miranda Peres, arguing that cultural differences would make such standardization difficult
Action:	Motion from Jessie Bowens: To approve the implementation of standardization procedures in a three-step process
Vote:	Motion carried, 4 in favour, 1 against
Future Agenda Items:	Planning of International Human Resources Day
Next meeting:	November 9th 2016
Approval of Minutes:	Motion to approve the minutes for September 25th 2016 carried unanimously

Meeting adjourned at **1:30 pm**

Phrases: Making arrangements

To book flights or trains

Please reserve a window / aisle seat **on** the 8.30 am flight to Munich.	Bitte reservieren Sie einen Platz am Fenster / Gang für den Flug um 8:30 Uhr nach München.
Are you travelling economy or business class?	Fliegen Sie Economy- oder Business-Class?
I would like to reserve a window seat on the 9.15 ICE train to Hamburg.	Ich möchte einen Fensterplatz im ICE um 9:15 Uhr nach Hamburg reservieren lassen.
Is that first or second class, one way or return?	Erster oder zweiter Klasse? Einfach oder hin und zurück?
Is there a supplementary charge for the InterCity to Edinburgh?	Muss für den Intercity nach Edinburgh ein Zuschlag bezahlt werden?
There is no supplementary charge.	Es wird kein Zuschlag erhoben.
You are booked **on** flight no ZY 652 **on** 23 March, departing London Gatwick **at** 7.30 am, arriving Munich 10.15 am.	Sie sind am 23. März für Flug Nr. ZY 652 gebucht, Abflug London Gatwick um 7:30 Uhr, Ankunft München 10:15 Uhr.
You should check in two hours before departure to allow **for** security.	Sie sollten wegen der Sicherheitsüberprüfung zwei Stunden vor Abflug einchecken.

To book hotel or conference rooms

We require a single / double room with **ensuite** bathroom.	Wir benötigen ein Einzel- / Doppelzimmer mit Bad.
I would like to book an executive suite for three nights **from** 3 **to** 6 March with Internet access.	Ich möchte eine Luxussuite mit Internetzugang für drei Nächte vom 3. bis 6. März buchen.
We require a conference room **to seat** 25 – 30 people.	Wir brauchen ein Besprechungszimmer für 25 – 30 Personen.
For our annual general meeting we need an assembly hall **of** at least 500 square metres equipped with a stage and a big screen.	Für unsere Jahreshauptversammlung brauchen wir einen Versammlungssaal von mindestens 500 Quadratmetern mit Bühne und Großbildschirm.
I should be grateful if you could confirm the booking **in** writing / **by** e-mail / **by** fax.	Wir wären für eine Bestätigung der Buchung per Brief / E-Mail / Fax dankbar.
Is it possible to order a buffet lunch?	Besteht die Möglichkeit ein Mittagsbuffet zu bestellen?
We regret that we have to cancel the reservation. We realise that it is very short notice.	Wir bedauern, diese Reservierung stornieren zu müssen. Wir sind uns dessen bewusst, dass dies sehr kurzfristig geschieht.

To make appointments

I'm afraid I'm engaged all day on Wednesday.	Leider bin ich am Mittwoch den ganzen Tag besetzt.
Friday would suit me fine.	Freitag würde mir gut passen.
I'd prefer Thursday morning.	Donnerstagmorgen wäre mir lieber.
It's Monday **at** 11 then.	Also bleibt es bei Montag um 11 Uhr.
Could we meet **on** Monday 17 at 10 am?	Könnten wir uns am Montag, den 17. um 10 Uhr vormittags treffen?
– Certainly. Monday at 10 am is fine.	– Ja, sicher. Montag 10 Uhr ist o.k.
Would Tuesday suit you?	Würde Ihnen Dienstag passen?
I'm free all day Wednesday.	Am Mittwoch geht es den ganzen Tag.

To book an exhibition stand

We are interested in displaying our products **at** the Madrid Motor Show.	Wir sind daran interessiert, unsere Produkte auf der Automobilmesse in Madrid auszustellen.
Our company wishes to reserve floor space for a stand **covering** 8 × 15 metres.	Unsere Firma möchte die für einen Stand von 8 × 15 Metern benötigte Ausstellungsfläche reservieren lassen.
We wish to book a stand in the main exhibition hall.	Wir möchten einen Stand in der Hauptausstellungshalle buchen.

To organise the necessary equipment

Our stand must have internet access and it must be equipped with telephone lines.	Unser Stand muss Internetzugang haben und er muss mit Telefonleitungen ausgestattet sein.
Catering services will also be required.	Wir benötigen ebenfalls Catering-Service.

To write invitations

The chairman will be pleased to welcome you **at** our annual dinner **at** the Park Hotel.	Der Vorsitzende gibt sich die Ehre, Sie zu unserem alljährlichen festlichen Abendessen im Park Hotel begrüßen.
The reception will be held in our main hall **between** 10 am **and** 3 pm.	Der Empfang findet zwischen 10 und 15 Uhr in unserer Haupthalle statt.

To have a stand built and dismantled

Are you in a position to design an eye-catching stand for us and erect it before 15 March?	Sind Sie in der Lage, für uns einen ins Auge fallenden Stand zu entwerfen und vor dem 15. März aufzubauen?
Can you help us remove the heavy exhibits and dismantle the stand?	Können Sie uns dabei helfen, die schweren Ausstellungsstücke zu entfernen und den Stand abzubauen?

07

What are the uses of presentations and meetings?

Presentations and meetings

The ability to make good oral presentations is a key skill. There are many situations where it is necessary to provide information about a new development or introduce a new product, either within the company or to an outside audience. Most of us probably feel a bit scared about standing up in front of an audience. However, it is a skill that can be acquired and improved with practice. Above all, it is important to be aware that the way you deliver a presentation is as important as its content.

It may also be part of your role as a PA or administrative assistant to arrange meetings and conferences both within your own company and with business associates from other companies. In the case of more formal conferences you may be asked to be present and take the minutes.

M **1** Translate the following sentences into German.

1. Making a good oral presentation is a key skill.
2. You may feel scared of standing in front of an audience.
3. This skill can be acquired and improved.
4. Style of delivery is as important as content.
5. You may be required to make a presentation on your company and its products.
6. You may be asked to be present at a meeting or conference and take the minutes.

WORD BANK

- *absentees*
- *to account for*
- *bar chart*
- *body language*
- *chair / chairman / chairperson*
- *conclusion*
- *content*
- *degree*
- *to deliver / delivery*
- *diagrams*
- *eye contact*
- *to fluctuate*
- *graphs*
- *item*
- *line graph*
- *main body*
- *percentage*
- *pie chart*
- *prompt cards*
- *rankings*
- *to rehearse*
- *to remain unchanged*
- *slight*
- *steady*
- *to take / keep the minutes*
- *to visualise*
- *visual aids*
- *vote*

A | Preparing a presentation

You have been asked to give a presentation on your company and its products. You have a maximum of 5 minutes at your disposal.

1 Read the following helpful hints.

How to make a presentation
- Start by deciding what you need to include and what you want to achieve.
- Imagine yourself in the audience – how many facts could you absorb before your attention starts to wander? Limit the facts and figures.
- Do not write out your presentation in full. Use numbered prompt cards with key words.
- Your presentation should have a structure – introduction, main body and conclusion.
- At the beginning say briefly what you are going to talk about.
- What are the main points in the body of the presentation? Make clear which one you are dealing with.
- Finally, the conclusion. This should be a brief summary of your main ideas and contain no new material.

Use expressions like:

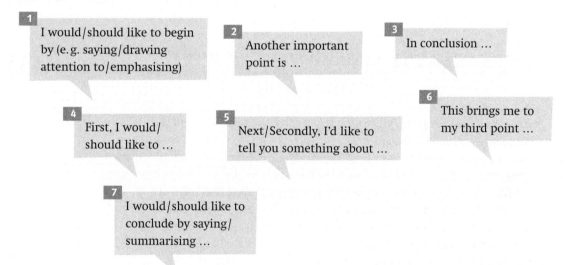

1 I would/should like to begin by (e.g. saying/drawing attention to/emphasising)

2 Another important point is …

3 In conclusion …

4 First, I would/should like to …

5 Next/Secondly, I'd like to tell you something about …

6 This brings me to my third point …

7 I would/should like to conclude by saying/summarising …

Use visual aids
Visual aids such as powerpoint slides make your presentation more lively and graphs, pictures, flowcharts or the keywords on your prompt cards make your presentation easier to understand. However, put a minimum of information on each slide – a maximum of four or five short lines of a maximum of six words.

Do not
- spend your time looking at them.
- turn your back on the audience.
- read them out.

Use colours which give a good contrast and which are easy to read for the audience. The slides may be printed out and used as a handout, but it is better to prepare a separate, more detailed handout.

M **2**
KMK Fassen Sie den Text über die Vorbereitung einer Präsentation unter Einbeziehung folgender Fragen auf Deutsch zusammen.

1. Mit welchen Überlegungen sollten Sie Ihre Präsentations-vorbereitung beginnen?
2. Wie soll eine Präsentation gegliedert werden?
3. Welche Vorteile bietet Anschauungsmaterial?
4. Wie sollen „powerpoint slides" aussehen, damit sie wirken?

R **3**
⊙ A2.1 Now listen to a presentation by Emma Hetherington from TopGuys Fashions Ltd and complete the text below.

Good morning, ladies and gentlemen. I'd like **1** saying a few words about our company. We founded TopGuys six years ago as a start-up and are meanwhile marketing our fashions throughout the EU and beyond. First I am pleased to mention that this year we have formed a joint venture with the German fashion company Cosmo-Mode GmbH in Berlin. **2** to market our products **3** , at first in Germany and the UK and later in Turkey and the Middle East. We are also planning joint ventures at leading fashion fairs worldwide.

This joint venture **4** the range of fashion that we are able to offer, combines distinctive British and German creativity, and should over time enable us to **5** marketing costs.

Second, I think it is important to underline the fact that we **6** the market segment for high-end fashion for young twenty-somethings. In the UK this market segment has benefited from the strong growth in the economy and low rate of unemployment over the past three years. Last year, our sales in the UK market increased **7** 11 percent (please see the graph on the slide) and profits before tax grew by 15%. Please see the handout for details of our **8** in our other markets. We are confident that this success will be matched in the present year.

I'd like to **9** that we look forward to continued growth in most of our EU markets and that we enjoy the **10** of working in this highly competitive and creative sector which requires us to constantly adapt to new trends. It certainly keeps us on our toes.

R **4**
⊙ A2.1 Emma Hetherington used the following prompt cards for her presentation. Listen to the presentation again and put the jumbled prompt cards into the right order.

1	**2**	**3**
Conclusion: continued growth / creative sector / constant adaptation to new trends	Market segment buoyant / strong economic growth / low unemployment	Sales figures / profits / see graph and handout

4	**5**	**6**
Joint venture with Cosmo / reduce marketing costs	Introduction: brief remark about history of company	Target group: twenty-somethings

P **5** You have now studied the above information, hints and examples. Prepare a similar presentation on your own company and its products. Write your prompt cards and decide what visual aids you wish to use.

Content of your presentation:

- size, type, location of your company
- when it was founded
- products and / or services
- main markets / domestic / export
- sales figures
- special features of products e.g. environment-friendly, cutting-edge technology, any other information that you think is important

---

6 Your English-speaking boss has asked you to research the latest computer projectors for the office within the price range of $500 to $1,000. Use the internet to find this information and make notes in English on one cheap and one expensive model.

B | Delivering a presentation

Useful tips

- Look at the audience – establish eye contact.
- Do not read out a text that you have written out in full – this tends to sound monotonous.
- Spoken language rather than written language.
- You make a much more lively impression if you speak freely using prompt cards and slides as reminders.
- This also helps to ensure that your body language and gestures are natural.
- Do not speak too quickly – pause before any new point.
- Emphasise important information. This dramatizes your talk – makes it more interesting
- Smile – where appropriate!
- Make sure that you know how to operate any equipment you plan to use.
- Practise and rehearse your presentation with your friends or other students as an audience

It is very helpful for the person giving the presentation to be given constructive, concrete and detailed feedback. Only in this way can they become aware of how they come across and how this might be changed. This is a prerequisite for developing skills in oral presentation.

1 Choose task a, b or c.

○ a. Which are the most important tips given on the previous page?

◐ b. Give a short summary of the points on the previous page. Why is it more effective to give greater emphasis to important points?

● c. Give a short summary of the points on the previous page and explain why reading out a written text is likely to bore your audience. Use your own ideas if you wish.

M **2**
KMK Ein Kollege muss eine Präsentation halten und hat Sie um Rat gebeten. Schreiben Sie ihm eine E-Mail auf Deutsch und geben Sie ihm Hinweise für eine Präsentation unter Verwendung der Informationen in „Useful tips".

P **3** Now give your presentation on your company to your fellow students. Do not go over the five minute limit! The other students listen and assess it according to the following evaluation scheme. They should award points out of 10 under each heading (on a separate sheet of paper).

Evaluation of presentation/checklist:		Points
Preparation	evidence of careful preparation	▪
Structure	introduction, main body – clear emphasis on small number of important points – conclusion	▪
Content	relevance, well-substantiated with facts and figures	▪
Visual aids	appropriate use of simple, easy-to-understand visual aids	▪
Delivery	not too fast, eye contact, appropriate body language, confident, relaxed	▪
Language	no jargon, straightforward, use of signalling expressions like: "I would/should like to begin/conclude by …"	▪
Overall impression	lively, humorous, easy to follow, right length	▪

LANGUAGE AND GRAMMAR

DESCRIBING GRAPHS AND DIAGRAMS

Statistics are easier to read if they are presented in the form of bar charts, line graphs or pie charts, pictographs or flow charts. When making a presentation, you may have to describe graphs. The expressions given on the following pages will be helpful.

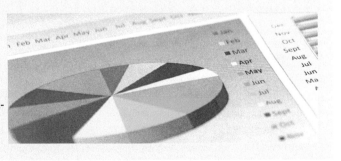

C | Line graphs

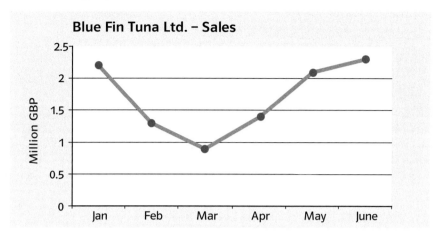

Blue Fin Tuna Ltd. – Sales

1 At a meeting, June Lalaurie from Blue Fin Tuna Ltd in Bristol presents her company to a gathering of potential customers. She refers to the last half year's sales and to the line graph above. Read her description and find the correct prepositions from the box.

at · by · from · of (2×) · to (3×)

In January sales stood **1** 2.2 million pounds. Then there was a dramatic decline **2** GBP 1.3 m in February. Sales continued to fall steadily and reached the minimum **3** 0.9 m in March. Between March and May, however, sales jumped **4** 0.9 m **5** 2.1 m. In June sales had risen **6** around 9 % **7** the peak **8** 2.3 million pounds.

To describe developments	
1. upwards	
to rise / increase / go up / jump by … from … to …	Between May and July exports rose by 5 % from 10,000 units to 10,050 units.
to reach a peak / maximum of …	In June prices reached a peak of €75.
2. unchanged	
to remain / stay unchanged / stable / flat at …	Sales remained unchanged at 750 m units.
to fluctuate between … and …	In the second quarter oil prices fluctuated between 42 and 61 dollars per barrel.
3. downwards	
to fall / decline / go down / drop / slump by … from … to …	Last year the average price dropped by 2 % from €100 to €98.
to reach a low / minimum of … / the lowest point at …	In March the lowest point was reached at 28 dollars.

2 Choose the correct adjective or adverb.

1. In January imports fell (sharp/sharply).
2. Sales remained (constant/constantly) for three months.
3. A (slight/slightly) increase in prices had been expected.
4. There was a (gradual/gradually) fall in turnover.
5. Oil prices have been rising (dramatic/dramatically).

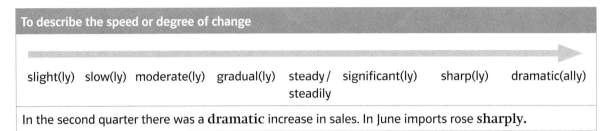

To describe the speed or degree of change
slight(ly) slow(ly) moderate(ly) gradual(ly) steady/ significant(ly) sharp(ly) dramatic(ally)
steadily
In the second quarter there was a **dramatic** increase in sales. In June imports rose **sharply.**

D | Bar charts

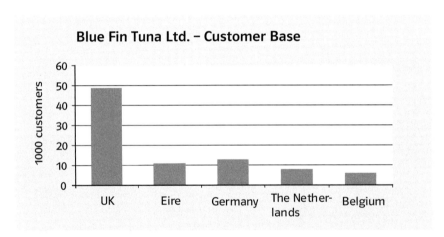

Blue Fin Tuna Ltd. – Customer Base

1 Study the bar chart above and June Lalaurie's description below and complete the description as appropriate.

Naturally most of our **1** are based in the UK, close to 50,000. Our next biggest **2** is Germany, where we have approx. 13,000 customers, closely **3** by The Irish Republic with more **4** 10,000 customers. The Netherlands and Belgium are **5** fourth and fifth place **6** around 8,000 and 6,000 customers, respectively.

To describe comparisons and rankings	
to be higher / lower / bigger / smaller / more / less expensive **than** …	Petrol prices in Germany are higher than in Austria.
to be **as** high / low / expensive **as** …	French cars are just as expensive as German cars.
to be the biggest / lowest / most expensive **of** …	This is the most expensive model of all.
to be / come first / second / last **with** …	Spain comes first with 45 million tourists.
to be / follow **in** first / fifth / last place	Norway is in fourth place behind France and the UK.
to be followed **by** …	Sweden is followed by Denmark which exports 56 % of its production.
to be **at** the bottom / top / of the list / table	Germany is at the bottom of the table with just 17 %.

E | Pie charts

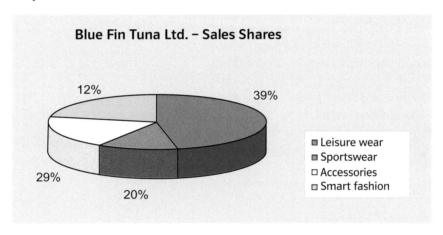

Blue Fin Tuna Ltd. – Sales Shares

39%
12%
29%
20%

■ Leisure wear
■ Sportswear
□ Accessories
□ Smart fashion

P **1** Write down what June Lalaurie might say to describe the above pie chart on Blue Fin Tuna's sales shares.

To describe shares (percentages)	
to make up … / to account for	Shoes make up 10 % and hand bags account for half of the total.
to have a share / percentage / slice of …	Schoolbags have a share of 40 %.

F | Meetings

Formal meetings usually have a defined structure. There is a chair / chairman or chairperson who chairs the meeting. He / She presents the minutes of the previous meeting for approval or amendment and appoints someone to keep the minutes of the present meeting. The chairperson welcomes those present and notes absentees (with or without apology) – it is important to know who was present if a vote and decision are taken. The chairperson also presents the agenda. He / She manages the meeting by calling on participants who wish to speak, making sure that no-one monopolises the meeting, saying when it is time to move on to the next item on the agenda and deciding whether to take a vote. The chairperson concludes by giving a brief summary of the results of the meeting and thanking the participants. Of course, meetings may also be held via video-conferencing.

M **1** Jayden Flaherty from Topguys Fashions is scheduling a meeting between key staff from the marketing department, Mme Yvette Beniguet from France and Moritz Pfeiffer, head of design at Cosmo Fashions Berlin. He gives the following draft agenda to his PA Emily Hobson and asks her to send it as an email attachment to mailto: y.beniguet@topguys . . . .fr and mailto: m.pfeiffer@cosmo-berlin . . . .de and to the mailing list from the previous meeting.
Übertragen Sie die Tagesordnung ins Deutsche.

Agenda
1. Welcoming participants
2. Minutes of the last conference in London
3. Report on the progress of the joint venture with Cosmo Mode GmbH by Moritz Pfeiffer
4. Report on the feasibility of setting up a sales organisation in Turkey
5. How do we ensure that the design and quality of our products reflect current trends and the expectations of young fashionistas in the target group at an affordable price?
6. Conclusions and recommendations

P **2** Take the role of Emily Hobson and send an email to Yvette Beniguet at TopGuys France (y.b@topguys . . . .fr) and Moritz Pfeiffer at Cosmo Mode Berlin (cosmo-mode . . . .de). Ask them to let you know if they would like to suggest any additions or changes to the agenda.

3 Preparing a meeting

As PA to Jayden Flaherty Emily Hobson has been asked to assist at the conference at Shoreditch, London. This involves supervising the preparation of the room, making sure that there is an adequate supply of tea, coffee, soft drinks and mineral water (still and sparkling) available.
Any equipment required such as a computer projector, interactive white-board or flip chart with board markers must be available and in working order. Her boss may require files, the minutes of the previous meeting, ad-ditional (e. g. statistical) information, or he may need her to make telephone calls etc. She must be present to provide any assistance that may be neces-sary. She may be asked to do some informal interpreting if a participant's command of English is not so good. She must also order a buffet lunch including vegetarian options from the catering company which TopGuys always uses for these occasions.

Read the text above, then choose task a, b, or c.
- a. Say briefly what you think are the three most important points for Emily.
- b. Say what you think are the most important points for Emily. Give a detailed account of Emily's various duties.
- c. Say what you think are Emily's main duties. Explain in detail why it is important for Emily's boss to be able to rely on all these things being taken care of.

4 Taking the minutes

It is important to have an accurate written record of the transactions of a meeting or conference. It must be possible for those involved to refer back to the minutes to see what was said and especially what decisions were taken. The minutes are evidence in law of the proceedings of a meeting. The names of those present or absent (with or without apology) must be recorded. In a discussion it is difficult to keep a word for word account of what is being said. The person taking the minutes may be able to note down only the most important points. It is essential to record dates and figures accurately. The minutes must be presented to those present at a later date for approval or corrections.

Wählen Sie Aufgabe a, b oder c.
- a. Übertragen Sie den obigen Text in Stichpunkten ins Deutsche. Benutzen Sie ein Wörterbuch, falls nötig.
- b. Übertragen Sie den obigen Text zusammenfassend ins Deutsche.
- c. Übersetzen Sie den obigen Text vollständig ins Deutsche.

R **5** The participants are discussing item 5 on the agenda. Listen to an extract
○ A2.2 from the meeting itself and answer the following questions.

1. How does Felicity express her disagreement with Ricky?
2. How does she support what Moritz says?
3. What words does Jayden use to ask Mme Beniguet for her opinion?
4. How does Ricky signal that he still disagrees with Yvette and Felicity?
5. How does Ricky ask Jayden for his opinion?

R **6** Choose task a, b or c.

A2.2 a. Listen to the CD and find 6 English idioms for the following German expressions.

> einen Vorteil haben · ein (gutes) Argument haben · Das kann man wohl sagen! · über die Runden kommen · Feierabend/Schluss machen · einer Meinung sein (bis zu einem gewissen Punkt)

b. Listen to the CD and find the corresponding idioms for the following English expressions.

> to be right about something · to be partly of the same opinion · to have an advantage over · to decide to stop work for the day · first-class · to get by

c. Listen to the CD and write down all the idioms. Then use some of these idioms to create a new dialogue.

COMMUNICATION ACROSS CULTURES

MEETINGS AND PRESENTATIONS

Presentations and business meetings naturally reflect cultural differences. The British or American presenter will make eye-contact with the audience since it is interpreted positively in Anglo-Saxon or German culture, signalling honesty or sincerity. In other cultures it may be seen as an invasion of privacy. British or American audiences enjoy (and expect!) a joke even when the topic is deadly serious. However, in other cultures (including possibly German?) a joke might suggest that the speaker doesn't take matters seriously enough. Attitudes to time also differ widely between cultures. In Britain, Germany or America meetings and presentations start more or less punctually as scheduled. In countries where personal relationships are regarded as the most important thing in business the participants may expect time to socialise before the presentation or meeting begins. Punctuality is less of a priority. Although behaviour varies a lot, in British culture there is a tendency to avoid direct confrontation. This is why expressions of disagreement are usually toned down using expressions such as: "I'm afraid I disagree" or "I agree with you up to a point, but in my opinion …" It's also important not to make a habit of interrupting others.

TASK:

7 Answer the following questions on the text.

1. Why do some cultures avoid eye-contact?
2. How might a joke be interpreted in some cultures?
3. Why may participants in some countries want to socialise before the meeting or presentation begins?
4. What is their attitude to punctuality?
5. What do many British people feel uncomfortable about in discussions?

Office expert

G | The structure and design of presentations

M **1** Read the following guideline and summarise the main points in German as

The first step in preparing a talk or presentation is to think about what you want to achieve. Is the point to share
5 information, convince your audience of something or motivate them? Once you have set your goals, you have to think about your
10 audience so you can customise your presentation to their needs. Will you be talking to experts or will your audience have little knowledge or
15 experience about your topic? What are their expectations? What kind of questions might they ask?

After determining the focus of your presentation, you will need to line up the facts to support your point of view. Your data –
20 whether as text or in graphical form – should be accurate and complete to portray you as a reliable source of information. You have to consider your priorities, your key points and just how much detail you want to include. Finding the right balance here isn't always easy; too much information and you'll overwhelm
25 your audience, too little will leave them feeling they haven't been adequately informed. As any successful speaker will tell you, rehearsing your presentation is an absolute must. Experts often recommend practising out loud in front of a mirror or even videotaping your practice sessions, keeping eye contact, body
30 language and pace in mind.

Last but not least, it's not a good idea to leave anything to chance. Make sure you know how to use the equipment without any problems and that it is set up and ready to run when you need it.

KMK Exam Training

1 Produktion

Stufe II   Verwenden Sie die Informationen des Tortendiagramms und der Tabelle, um Werbemethoden zu vergleichen. Fassen Sie auf Englisch die Informationen für eine Präsentation stichpunktartig zusammen.

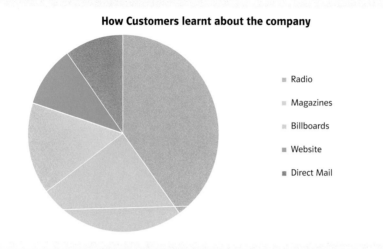

How Customers learnt about the company

- Radio
- Magazines
- Billboards
- Website
- Direct Mail

Advertising method	Annual cost
Radio	£ 120,000
Magazines	£ 45,000
Billboards	£ 105,000
Website	£ 25,000
Direct Mail	£ 40,000

Stufe II   Beschreiben Sie auf Englisch die Entwicklung der Verkaufszahlen für die drei Produkte (A, B, C) über den Zeitraum eines Jahres.

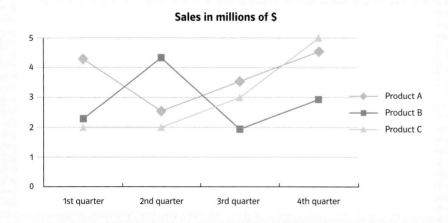

Sales in millions of $

Product A
Product B
Product C

Phrases: Presentations

To give a presentation

I would / should like to start **by** telling you something about my company / organisation.	Zunächst möchte ich Ihnen etwas über meine Firma / mein Unternehmen sagen.
First, I would / should like to introduce my company briefly.	Als Erstes möchte ich Ihnen mein Unternehmen kurz vorstellen.
My presentation will deal **with** …	Meine Präsentation behandelt …
I intend to keep my presentation as brief as possible.	Ich möchte meine Präsentation so kurz wie möglich halten.
I would like to focus **on** the following points / areas / products / services:	Ich möchte mich auf folgende Punkte / Gebiete / Produkte / Dienstleistungen konzentrieren:
I would welcome any questions **at** the end of my presentation.	Ich wäre gern bereit, etwaige Fragen am Ende meiner Präsentation zu beantworten.
Did everyone get a copy of the handout?	Haben alle das Handout bekommen?
The handout summarises the main points and gives an overview of the relevant figures.	Das Handout enthält die Hauptpunkte und gibt einen Überblick über die entsprechenden Zahlen.

To structure the main part of your presentation

Now my second point is …	Ich komme nun zu Punkt 2 …
Thirdly, let me give you some basic statistics.	Drittens darf ich Ihnen ein paar grundlegende Statistiken zeigen.
The gist of the matter / central issue is …	Der Kernpunkt / die zentrale Frage ist …
I would / should now like to move **on** to the next topic.	Ich möchte nun gern zum nächsten Thema kommen.
An excellent example **of** this is …	Ein hervorragendes Beispiel dafür ist …
I would / should like to give you an example to illustrate this point.	Ich möchte diesen Punkt mit einem Beispiel erläutern.
A distinct trend emerges **from** the figures.	Aus den Zahlen geht ein deutlicher Trend hervor.
In this connection it is worth mentioning …	In diesem Zusammenhang sollte man erwähnen, …

To conclude your presentation

To sum **up** we can say that …	Zusammenfassend kann man sagen, dass …
I would / should like to finish **by** saying / thanking the organisers / pointing out …	Ich möchte schließen mit der Bemerkung / dem Dank an die Organisatoren / dem Hinweis …

Phrases: Meetings

To prepare the agenda	
A draft agenda has already been drawn up.	Ein Entwurf für die Tagesordnung ist bereits erstellt worden.
Notification of any additions or changes is requested within a week.	Es wird gebeten, eventuelle Zusätze oder Änderungen innerhalb einer Woche anzugeben.

To prepare and assist at a meeting	
He / She is chairing the meeting.	Er / Sie leitet die Sitzung.
He / She is the chairperson.	Er / Sie ist der / die Vorsitzende.
Perhaps you could each introduce **yourself** briefly indicating your role in the company.	Vielleicht könnten Sie sich kurz vorstellen und dabei auf Ihre Stellung in der Firma eingehen.
Has everyone got a copy of the agenda?	Haben alle die Tagesordnung bekommen?
We shall adjourn **for** lunch **at** …	Um … unterbrechen wir für das Mittagessen.
Are there any further comments?	Gibt es noch Wortmeldungen?
Shall we take a vote?	Sollen wir nun abstimmen?
The proposal is accepted.	Damit ist der Vorschlag angenommen.

Stating an opinion	
In my opinion / view …	Meiner Meinung / Ansicht nach …
As far as I'm concerned …	Soweit es mich betrifft …

To ask for the other person's view	
How do you feel about this?	Was halten Sie davon?
What are your thoughts on this?	Was denken Sie darüber?
How do you see it?	Wie sehen Sie es?

To express agreement / disagreement	
I agree with you up to a point but …	Bis zu einem gewissen Punkt stimme ich Ihnen zu, aber …
You're absolutely right.	Sie haben vollkommen Recht.
Absolutely!	Unbedingt! / Auf jeden Fall!
You have a point there.	Da ist etwas dran. / Sie mögen hier Recht haben.
I'm afraid I (totally) disagree.	Ich stimme leider (überhaupt) nicht zu.

08

Do you ever write letters? When do you write an email rather than a text message?

Forms of written communication

Written communication plays an important role in business, especially where some form of documentation is required. It may also be used to rule out any possibility of misunderstanding. However, the traditional formal letter has been increasingly replaced by emails – a much quicker and often less formal medium of written communication.

This does not mean that the letter is dead. A disadvantage of emails is that it is difficult to ensure that they are read only by the addressee. Letters are regularly used where it is necessary to ensure confidentiality. They are also used in legal contexts, for instance, in connection with contracts or formal complaints. Often an email may be sent first for speed of communication with a letter sent by post or messenger confirming the content.

A PA or office administrator must be familiar with the language and form of a letter. Business emails generally follow the same structure and may be almost as formal as traditional letters. This is especially the case when sender and addressee are not on familiar terms. Of course personal emails are usually written in a much more informal style.

1 Discuss the following statement in class:
"Letters have been increasingly replaced by emails."

WORD BANK

- *addressee*
- *to attach*
- *attachment*
- *attention*
- *complimentary close*
- *covering page*
- *date*
- *to delete*
- *e-mail*
- *enclosure*
- *facsimile message*
- *to forward*
- *initials*
- *letter*
- *letterhead*
- *line*
- *linking words*
- *paragraph*
- *recipient*
- *reference line*
- *salutation*
- *sender*
- *signature*
- *structure*
- *style*
- *subject*

2 Choose task a, b or c.

○ a. Read the following text and list the advantages of emails.

◑ b. Read the following text and explain advantages and potential
disadvantages of emails.

● c. Give a detailed summary of the following text in German.

Emails

The strength of emails – speed, brevity and informality – may at
the same time be a source of weakness. It is always tempting to
react immediately to an email, especially if you're angry. In business,
5 it is obviously important to give yourself time to produce a more
considered reply. It is also easy to skip the small talk in an email
and get down to business straight away. But for the person on the
receiving end, it may sound like an abrupt list of demands. Emails
are notoriously easy to misunderstand – it is very difficult for the
10 recipient to fill in the gaps in communication and see what the writer's
intention was. You should try to make your intention clear. It is also
wrong to assume that emails are always informal. You often read
letters in the newspaper from business people complaining about all
the informal emails they get from people they don't know.
15 So, if in doubt, stick to a more formal style.

A | E-Mails*

1 Search the Internet and find out about "netiquette". Make notes and share
your findings with the group.

INFO: How to write e-mails

- Keep messages short and to the point.
- Focus on one subject per message and include a relevant subject title for the
  message.
- Include your signature footer when communicating with persons who may
  not know you personally.
- Capitalize words only to highlight an important point. Capitalizing is gener-
  ally felt to be like SHOUTING!
- Be sparing in your use of exclamation marks.
- Never send chain letters through the Internet.
- Be professional and be careful what you say. E-mails are easily forwarded.
- Be careful when using sarcasm and humour.
- Never assume that your e-mails will be read only by you and the recipient.
- Emoticons like :-) for "happy" or ;-) for "only joking" should be reserved for
  communication with business partners with whom you are on a familiar
  footing.
- Use abbreviations sparingly as you cannot be sure that your partner in a
  foreign country is familiar with them.

---

*both ways of spelling are acceptable, **e-mail** and **email**

INFO: E-mails

From:	h.eisenhof@koernertiefbau... .de
To:	lisa@albioncolleges... .co.uk **Cc:** s.maurer@koernertiefbau... .de
Sent:	13.08.20___ 14:23 **Attachments:**
Subject:	enquiry for group tuition

Dear Albion Colleges — salutation

Our company is planning to book a one-week all-day language course for four members of staff with intermediate knowledge of English. The course should be in October or November. Could you please let us know if that would be possible for you and how much the total cost of such a course would be.

body of e-mail

Kind regards — complimentary close

Hannelore Eisenhof
Human Resources — signature block

Koerner Hoch- und Tiefbau GmbH
An der Laake 39
44891 Bochum
Tel (+49)(0)2342638891 — signature footer

To: Make absolutely sure the recipient's address is spelt correctly, or else the email will be returned.

Cc: This stands for "carbon copy" and is where you enter the address of the person(s) you wish the message to be forwarded to.

Bcc: Addresses listed under "blind carbon copy" do not appear in the message header of the other recipients.

Attachments: You can attach any type of file such as Word documents (.doc / .docx), Excel sheets (.xls), pictures (.jpg) or Adobe Acrobat files (.pdf).

Subject: You should always mention the precise subject matter as this will help the recipient deal with your email. If you leave the subject box blank you run the risk of your message being deleted or ending up in the spam folder.

Salutation: Avoid very formal salutations such as "Dear Sir or Madam" or "Gentlemen". Instead, use "Dear Lisa" or "Dear Ms Blackwood". If you don't know the name of the addressee you may write "Dear…" plus the name of the firm, as in the example above.

Body: Whether you put a comma or a colon or no punctuation after the salutation, the first word of the text starts with a capital letter.

Complimentary close: There is a wide range of expressions you can choose from. The most common are: With best / kind regards
Kind / Best regards
Best wishes

Signature block: Write your title or department below your name. In Britain women often add "(Miss)" or "(Mrs)" in brackets after their name if they wish to be addressed in this way. If the marital status of the woman you are addressing is unknown, use "Ms" as in the example above.

Special characters such as "ß, ü, ö, ä" should be avoided as they may come out very strangely at the other end. Use "**ss, ue, oe, ae**" instead.

B | Business letters

1 Match the numbers (1–11) in the following business letter with the letters A–K below and on the following pages.

Albion Colleges **1**
122 Marine Parade · Bournemouth · BH1 2EY
www.albioncolleges….co.uk · (+44)(0)1202 766 392 8…
info@albioncolleges….co.uk

LM/ob-cn **2**   18 Aug 201_ **3**

Koerner Hoch- und Tiefbau GmbH **4**
An der Laake 39
44891 BOCHUM
GERMANY

Attn. Hannelore Eisenhof **5**

Booking confirmation **6**

Dear Hannelore, **7**

I'm very pleased to confirm your booking of an all-day English
language immersion course for four people from 15 to 20 October
201_.
I enclose a brochure of our college with some useful tips for
students as well as a statement of your account with Albion
Colleges.
We look forward to welcoming your group and thank you for
choosing Albion Colleges. **8**

Kindest regards, **9**
Albion Colleges **10**

Lisa Morelli

Lisa Morelli
Product Manager

Encs **11**

A **Reference line** may show the initials of the signatory and the secretary or references to files or departments.

B **Letterhead** shows a company's logo, name and address, its telephone, fax and e-mail numbers and its Internet address.

C **Attention** line ensures that the letter is dealt with by a specific person. You may write "Attention:", "For the attention of …:", or (less formal) "FAO:"

As an alternative the person's name may be included in the inside address. This is a must if the recipient is addressed by name in the salutation.

Global Catering 17 Nelson Square Manchester MA17 3DF UK Attention: Ms Susan Cole	Ms Susan Cole Global Catering 17 Nelson Square Manchester MA17 3DF UK

D **Inside address**

British usage	North American usage
Messrs J. McDream & Co. 91 Malvern Road Ashford Kent CA3 6AH UK	Samantha Duvet The Mattress Corporation 1386 Munras Avenue Monterey, CA 93940 USA

Note that in British business letters *Messrs*, *Mr*, *Mrs*, *Ms* and *Miss* are written on the same line as the name. In the USA they are often omitted altogether. *Messrs* is only used for smaller firms, such as partnerships. Do not write *Messrs* if the company's name is followed by "Ltd", Plc", "Inc." or "Corp.". *Ms* should be used whenever the marital status of the female addressee is not known.

Note that in Great Britain the postal code is written on its own line below the place name, whereas in USA and Canada it is placed after the place name on the same line.

When letters are written to foreign countries, the name of the country should be shown on the final line of the inside address in capital letters.

E **Date**

As 07/08/12 would mean 7 August 2017 for an Englishman and 8 July 2012 for an American, it is advisable to write out the month.

The following ways of writing the date are recommended:

7 August 2017   or   7 Aug 2017   or   August 7, 2017

Note that the year is written out in full.

Giving the year first, then the month and then the day is rapidly becoming accepted worldwide: 2017-08-07.

F Signature block

In the UK – but not in the USA – the signature block often begins with the company's name. The signatory's name and title (or department) are typed below the signature. If somebody signs the letter on behalf of another person, the other person's name is typed below the signature, preceded by the word **"for"** or by the abbreviation **"pp."** meaning "on behalf of".

NetOrbiter Ltd.

Maria Bertram

pp. Henry Crawford
Chief Information Officer

Fred Parry

for Betty Bickerton
Credit Manager

G Complimentary close (UK)

Yours faithfully/sincerely
(Yours faithfully is rarely used now)
Kind regards
Best regards
Best wishes

Complimentary close (USA and Canada)

Sincerely (yours), Very truly yours, Yours truly, Regards, Cordially

H Salutation (UK)

Dear Sir/Madam,
Dear Sir or Madam

Dear Ms Burnham
Dear Kemal Öztürk
Dear Customer
Dear Margaret

Salutation (USA and Canada)

(Ladies and) Gentlemen:
To whom it may concern:
Dear Mr O'Reilly:
Dear Anne Elliot
Dear Sean:

If at all possible you should address the person you are writing to by name.
"Dear Sir or Madam" or "(Ladies and) Gentlemen:" is only used when you do not have a name to write to. Traditionally salutation and complimentary close should be in line with each other.

I Enclosure

Whenever enclosures are sent with a letter, a reference to the enclosure is required at the bottom of the letter. You may write "Enclosure(s)" or "Enc(s)".

J Body of the letter

Note that in English the first word of a business letter starts with a capital letter.

K Subject line may be preceded by the words "Subject" or "Re" and should be as specific as possible. Do not just write "Your offer" but "Your offer for mouse pads of 23 May". In the UK subject lines are normally written below the salutation, in the USA above the salutation. They may be either underlined or typed in capital letters or bold type.

C | Structure and style of business correspondence

Beginning, main part and end

Business correspondence must be well organised. The body of the correspondence should consist of three separate parts: the beginning, the main part and the end.

The **beginning** is either a single sentence or a short paragraph that states the reason why you are writing the correspondence.
Example: I am going to be in Boston on May 20, and would like to meet you.

The **main part** contains the details. There should be a separate paragraph for every new idea.
Example: There are some issues with the new software which I would like to discuss with you personally. Would a 9 a. m. meeting be convenient for you?

In the **end section** the writer sums up and underlines what he / she would like the recipient to do. Alternatively he / she may add a remark designed to create goodwill.
Example: If this fits in with your schedule, please leave a message with my secretary. I look forward to seeing you in Boston.

Especially when you are writing to a customer it is advisable to end the communication on a friendly note.

Business correspondence should meet the so-called ABC specifications:
Accurate correct and complete as to facts
Brief short sentences, simple expressions, plain English
Clear easy, natural style, without formality or familiarity

1 Read the information above and choose task a, b or c.

○ a. Look at the following letter / email and rewrite it. Make sure it is well structured. Its three different parts should be clearly visible. If you think that the main part consists of more than one idea, use a separate paragraph.

◑ b. Rewrite the following letter / email in a structured form and then write a response thanking the sender, expressing interest in their products and promising to get in touch once the offer has been discussed with your boss.

● c. Rewrite the following letter / email in a structured form. Then, using its layout and structure as a template, write an offer of the products / services of your company to a prospective customer.

Dear Anita Johannsen. Your enquiry of 25 September. Thank you for your interest in our range of customised jacuzzis. As an attachment we are sending you our latest catalogue and price list. The prices include a 25 % trade discount. We also offer quantity discounts for major orders. Our terms of payment are 30 days net. Should you need any further information do not hesitate to contact our customer care department. We look forward to receiving your first order which will be given top priority. Kind regards. Grayson Flinders.

2 Read the text below.

Linking words

Business correspondence is often made up of standard phrases.
In order for the correspondence to read smoothly such individual text-building blocks ought to be connected by linking words like **also**, **as well as**, **both … and**, **in addition**, **moreover**, **further**, **firstly**, **secondly**, **finally** etc. which suggest a list.
Example: Finally, we should like to confirm the date for next year's fashion show.

Other linking words imply a contrast: **whereas**, **while**, **in contrast to**, **however**, **although** etc.
Example: Last month sales of DVD players rose by 3.5 per cent whereas sales of TV sets fell by 2.8 percent.

The following linking words indicate that an explanation is being given: **this is why**, **therefore**, **thus**, **as**, **because** etc.
Example: We are most dissatisfied with your services. This is why we have decided to instruct a different company.

3 Now complete the following email using the linking words from the box below.

> although · and · as · both · finally · in addition · while

Dear Customer

1 the festive season is approaching, we would like to draw your attention to our wide range of delicious stocking-fillers **2** for chocoholics **3** lovers of premium wines and spirits.

Our popular range of gingerbread biscuits is always a brilliant gift idea for someone with a sweet tooth.
4 we have launched a sugar-free biscuit collection for diabetics.

Our prize-winning New World wines are ideal partners for candle-light dinners or BBQs, **5** our French and Spanish sparkling wines are just the right thing for celebrations or a romantic evening.

6 our wide range of Belgian luxury chocolates has always meant that customers are really spoilt for choice, we have decided to add even more lines including hand-crafted chocolates made using select cocoa beans from Guatemala and Ecuador.

7 we would like to thank you for being among our most faithful customers and look forward to serving you very soon.

Best wishes

LANGUAGE AND GRAMMAR

BUSINESS CORRESPONDENCE (TYPICAL MISTAKES)

Wer diese Verben korrekt verwendet, vermeidet typische Fehler beim Verfassen englischer Geschäftskorrespondenz.

suggest (vorschlagen)

We suggest repeating the test.	Wir schlagen vor den Test zu wiederholen.
We suggest that you (we) repeat the test.	Wir schlagen vor, dass Sie (wir) den Test wiederholen.

Falsch: We suggest ~~to repeat~~ the test.

appreciate (schätzen, begrüßen, dankbar sein, anerkennen)

We would appreciate **it** if you could assist us.	Wir würden es begrüßen, wenn Sie uns unterstützen könnten.
We would appreciate receiving the units as soon as possible.	Wir hätten die Einheiten gern so bald wie möglich.

Falsch: We would ~~appreciate to~~ receive the units as soon as possible.

apologize (sich entschuldigen)

We apologize for the delay.	Wir entschuldigen uns für die Verspätung.

Falsch: We excuse us for the delay.

excuse (verzeihen, entschuldigen)

Please excuse the delay.	Bitte entschuldigen Sie die Verzögerung.

Falsch: Please ~~apologize~~ the delay.

look forward to (entgegensehen, sich freuen auf)

We look forward to hearing from you soon.	Wir freuen uns darauf, bald von Ihnen zu hören.

Falsch: We look forward ~~to hear~~ from you soon.

hope (hoffen)

We hope to hear from you soon.	Wir hoffen, bald von Ihnen zu hören.

Falsch: We hope ~~to hearing~~ from you soon.

TASKS:

4

Decide which of the alternatives in brackets is correct.

1. Please (apologize / excuse) the delay in delivery.
2. We would appreciate (to receive / receiving) the shipment before the summer break.
3. I look forward (to hearing / to hear) from you soon.
4. We (apologize / excuse) for the late delivery of the goods.
5. We hope (to establish / establishing) good business relations.
6. I would suggest (to contact / contacting) the local chamber of commerce.
7. We would appreciate (it if you settled / if you settled) your account by week 15.
8. We would appreciate (hearing / to hear) from you at your earliest convenience.
9. May we suggest (that you reset / to reset) the appliance to factory settings.
10. I (excuse myself / apologize) for the mix-up in our accounts department.

COMMUNICATION ACROSS CULTURES

THE TONE OF ENGLISH BUSINESS CORRESPONDENCE

What is considered polite differs from culture to culture. For example, one-word answers such as "ja" or "nein" are not impolite in German. If I say: „Sollen wir heute abend chinesisch essen gehen?", you could just answer "ja" in German. In English people tend to say things like "Yes, that would be nice / great". Similarly, German business correspondence tends to be factual and to the point. Polite phrases are often considered superfluous. This may come across as rather abrupt in English and may seem rude or signalling a lack of interest. If you wish to refuse something, you should at the very least say "No, thank you" and possibly add (I think I'd rather....). You also need to make frequent use of expressions like: **We would like to** (inform you....), **I would be grateful if** (you could assist in this matter), **I am afraid** (our systems crashed last Friday), **We are very sorry** (to inform you), **Would you be so kind as to** (pass on this message to...). Do not forget to insert the word **please** whenever you make a request, e.g.: If we can be of further assistance, please do not hesitate to contact us.

Note:
Do not say: "We kindly ask you to..." (it does NOT sound polite).
Say: "We would like to ask you", "Please be so kind as to..."

TASKS:

5 How could you make the following sentences sound more polite?

1. There's a problem with your order.
2. Would you like scrambled eggs for breakfast? Yes.
3. We have to inform you that delivery will be delayed by two weeks.
4. Pass the message on to Ryan Jones.
5. Would you like to go for a drink this evening? No.

6 Rewrite the following email to produce a less abrupt, more polite tone:

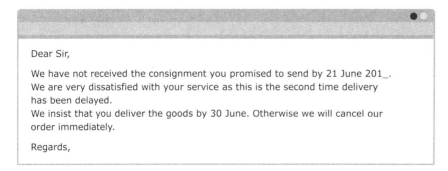

Dear Sir,

We have not received the consignment you promised to send by 21 June 201_.
We are very dissatisfied with your service as this is the second time delivery has been delayed.
We insist that you deliver the goods by 30 June. Otherwise we will cancel our order immediately.

Regards,

Office expert

D | Word processing

1 Complete the following text with the terms in the box.

> cut and paste · hard copies · hyphenation · insert ·
> justification · margins · search · word processor ·
> word wrap

With a **1** you can not only create and store documents, but also change them. Though there are different word processors, they all support a row of basic features. Probably the most useful one is their ability to delete or **2** characters, words, paragraphs or even whole sections of a text. If you make a typo, you just back up the cursor and correct it. **3** allows you to cut out or remove part of the text from one place in the document and insert or paste it in where you want to have it. You can also copy a section of the text by simply highlighting it. With a printer you can make **4** of your text.

With a word processor you can also determine different page sizes and **5** so that the text fits the page. **6** and replace is another useful feature that has the software look through the whole text for a certain word or phrase to either delete or replace it. With **7** the word processor moves from one line to the next as they are filled with text. To give your document a professional appearance, word processors also generally feature automatic hyphenation and justification. Using a comprehensive dictionary, the automatic **8** constantly checks words as you input them. If a word is too long when you come to the end of a line, it is split, a hyphen is added and the rest of the word is placed on the next line. **9** spaces your words evenly across a line so that the text is in line with the margin.

2 Match the word processing terms (1.–8.) to the descriptions (a.–h.).

1. graphics	a.	lets you insert text from one file into another for mass mailings
2. headers and footers	b.	finds words with similar meaning
3. mail merging	c.	highlights misspelt words and offers alternatives
4. page numbering	d.	the right one automatically appears on each page
5. spell checker	e.	finishes longer words
6. thesaurus	f.	let a text or graphic appear at the top or bottom of each page
7. windows	g.	allow you to work on two documents at a time
8. word completion	h.	lets you insert or create your own illustrations

KMK Exam Training

1 Rezeption: Leseverstehen

Stufe II   Spam oder unerwünschte Werbe-E-Mails sind lästig und zeitraubend. Eine Gegenmaßnahme, der Anti-Spam-Filter, wird im folgenden Text beschrieben. Lesen Sie den Text und bearbeiten Sie die anschließenden Aufgaben.

Spam Filtering

The main aim of spam filtering is to identify email messages which are probably spam, i.e. unwanted junk mail. The filter transfers
5 such messages into a separate mailbox called "spam" that you don't need to check as frequently as your main inbox.
The Spam Service mail switch is a scheme to support your spam filtering. It does not filter
10 out spam centrally but instead awards every message with a "spam score". By choosing a certain score level, you can decide how much of your incoming mail to filter out or install more detailed filters if you want. Remember
15 that even the best filter may let junk mail slip through or wrongly identify regular emails as junk mail and can never be 100% successful.

The spam score is made on the basis of tests.
20 These tests identify typical features of spam mail and non-spam mail and assign points to an email's score. An email message that scores 5 or above is almost always spam. It is recommended that you set your threshold to 5 to start with and adjust it 25 later if needed. If you set your threshold to less than 5 you run the risk of misclassifying normal emails as junk mail. Setting the threshold higher, on the other hand, can let too much spam through. 30
The filtered mail is automatically put in the special spam mailbox. To begin with you should check this mailbox regularly to be sure none of your regular mail lands there. From time to time you have to empty the 35 spam folder so that you do not reach your filespace quota and mail can still be delivered to you. By default, messages in your spam folder will be deleted automatically after 60 days, though you can change this time limit 40 on the same page that you used to set up and enable filtering.   **312 words**

Stufe II   Entscheiden Sie, ob die folgenden Aussagen zutreffen oder nicht zutreffen.

1. The purpose of a spam filter is to identify and delete junk mail.
2. How strictly you filter your incoming messages can be adjusted to your needs.
3. Spam filters are not very effective and often let through junk mail.
4. Spam mail has certain characteristics.

Stufe II   Beantworten Sie die Fragen auf Englisch.

1. What setting is recommended for your spam filter and why?
2. Why should you regularly check your spam mailbox?
3. What will happen if you neglect to empty out your spam folder?
4. What is the default setting for messages in your spam folder?

Phrases: Correspondence

To refer to previous communication	
Thank you very much for your letter / e-mail **of** …	Wir danken Ihnen für Ihren Brief vom …
We refer to your email / fax **of** …	Wir nehmen Bezug auf Ihr E-Mail / Fax vom …
Further to our discussion **on** 2 May …	Im Anschluss an unser Gespräch am 2. Mai …

To ask for something	
Please be so kind **as** to send us …	Wir bitten Sie höflich uns … zu schicken.
We **would** like to ask you for …	Wir möchten Sie um … bitten.

To refuse something	
I'm afraid I cannot agree **to** this proposal.	Leider muss ich diesen Vorschlag ablehnen.
I'm afraid that sounds quite unacceptable **to** us.	Das ist für uns leider völlig inakzeptabel.
We regret that we are unable to assist you.	Wir bedauern, Ihnen nicht behilflich sein zu können.

To apologize	
We are very sorry but …	Es tut uns sehr leid, aber …
We **would** like to apologize for the delay.	Wir möchten uns für die Verspätung entschuldigen.
Please accept our apologies for this.	Wir entschuldigen uns dafür.

To make a suggestion	
We would suggest that you send us a copy.	Wir schlagen Ihnen vor, uns eine Kopie zu schicken.
It would be advisable to send the details **by** email.	Es wäre gut, wenn Sie uns die näheren Angaben per E-Mail schicken könnten.

To request that something is done by a certain date	
We need the goods **by** Friday **at** the very latest.	Wir benötigen die Waren spätestens Freitag.
Monday, 31 July, is the final deadline.	Montag, der 31. Juli, ist der letzte Termin.

To end a correspondence on a friendly note	
We **look forward to hearing** from you.	Wir sehen Ihrer Antwort mit Interesse entgegen.
We **hope to hear** from you soon.	Wir hoffen, bald von Ihnen zu hören.
We hope this information **will** help you.	Wir hoffen, dass diese Auskunft hilfreich für Sie ist.
Thank you for your assistance.	Wir danken Ihnen für Ihre Bemühungen.

09

How would you make an enquiry about a product? What would you need to know?

Enquiries

A business transaction often starts off with an enquiry. **General enquiries** involve requests for things such as sales literature, pricelists and information about business terms. **Specific enquiries** give particulars about the goods / services required and request detailed **quotations**. These will usually also include terms of payment, delivery periods and details of any discounts.

The internet is often the most convenient way of locating suppliers and requesting information by email. Traditional sources of information such as chambers of commerce and trade associations have their own websites providing links to potential suppliers. Trade fairs and exhibitions provide information on the latest products in a given field.

1 Find the English equivalents for the following German words in the text above.

1. der/die/das Neueste
2. bequem, praktisch
3. beginnen
4. beinhalten
5. Preisangebot
6. Einzelheiten

2 Work in groups. Use the internet to research suppliers of an electronic device of your choice. If you were to make an enquiry, what questions would you ask the supplier(s)?

WORD BANK

- *brochure*
- *cash discount*
- *cost estimate*
- *early order discount*
- *enquiries*
- *initial order*
- *introductory discount*
- *price list*
- *quantity discount*
- *quotation*
- *samples*
- *source of information*
- *supplier*
- *terms and conditions*
- *trade discount*
- *transactions*
- *volume orders*
- *website*

A | Enquiries in writing

Tim Gordon, purchasing manager at Toytown, a British retail chain specialising in model aircraft, cars and railways, is interested in the latest range of vintage locomotives presented by Fächter & Suhr, the German manufacturers, on their website. He decides to make further enquiries by email.

1 Study Tim's email enquiry and say which of the prepositions in brackets are correct.

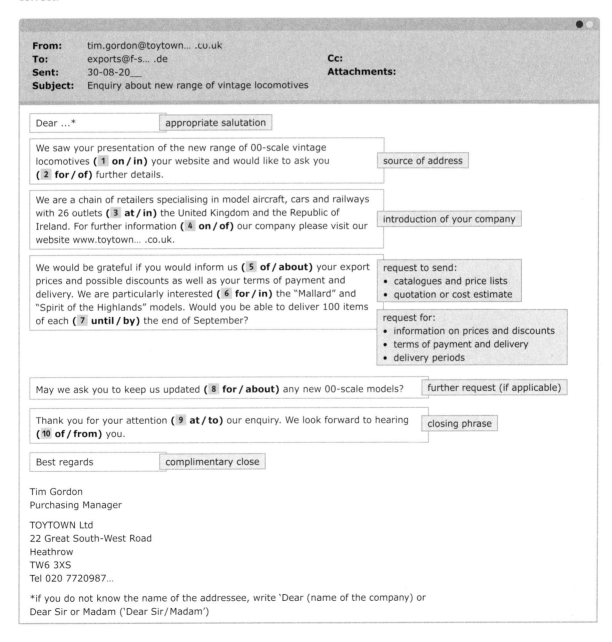

From:	tim.gordon@toytown... .co.uk	
To:	exports@f-s... .de	Cc:
Sent:	30-08-20__	Attachments:
Subject:	Enquiry about new range of vintage locomotives	

Dear ...* | appropriate salutation |

We saw your presentation of the new range of 00-scale vintage locomotives (**1 on / in**) your website and would like to ask you (**2 for / of**) further details. | source of address |

We are a chain of retailers specialising in model aircraft, cars and railways with 26 outlets (**3 at / in**) the United Kingdom and the Republic of Ireland. For further information (**4 on / of**) our company please visit our website www.toytown... .co.uk. | introduction of your company |

We would be grateful if you would inform us (**5 of / about**) your export prices and possible discounts as well as your terms of payment and delivery. We are particularly interested (**6 for / in**) the "Mallard" and "Spirit of the Highlands" models. Would you be able to deliver 100 items of each (**7 until / by**) the end of September?

> request to send:
> • catalogues and price lists
> • quotation or cost estimate

> request for:
> • information on prices and discounts
> • terms of payment and delivery
> • delivery periods

May we ask you to keep us updated (**8 for / about**) any new 00-scale models? | further request (if applicable) |

Thank you for your attention (**9 at / to**) our enquiry. We look forward to hearing (**10 of / from**) you. | closing phrase |

Best regards | complimentary close |

Tim Gordon
Purchasing Manager

TOYTOWN Ltd
22 Great South-West Road
Heathrow
TW6 3XS
Tel 020 7720987...

*if you do not know the name of the addressee, write 'Dear (name of the company) or Dear Sir or Madam ('Dear Sir/Madam')

2 Cover up Tim Gordon's email and complete the sentences below on your own sheet of paper.

1. Tim Gordon saw a presentation of …
2. Toytown Ltd is …
3. They would like to be informed about …
4. They are particularly interested in ..
5. They would need the locomotives by …
6. They would like to be updated about …

P **3** Copy the email form below. Use the example on the previous page and the phrases at the end of the Unit to write a detailed enquiry by email on a new range of leather laptop bags in different sizes and leather tablet cases. You recently saw the firm's online advertisement. If prices and terms are right, you would probably place a trial order. Address your email to accessories@cityfolks.yahoo….com. Use your imagination for any other details.

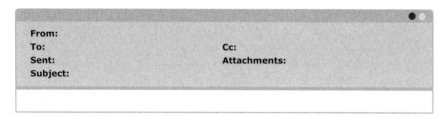

From:
To: Cc:
Sent: Attachments:
Subject:

P **4** Sie arbeiten bei Gebäudereinigung Schultz, Am Halleschen Tor 3, 10117 Berlin, service@schultz-gr….de, im Einkauf. Zum Neuen Jahr möchte Ihre Firma ihre guten Kunden mit einer ganz persönlichen elektronischen Grußkarte überraschen. Das Firmenlogo mit dem Cartooncharakter "Mr. S" soll dabei in einer Kurzanimation eine Rolle spielen. Ihre Chefin, Ilona Pollnow, hat auf der Homepage des indischen Webdesigners Animate-U, 22nd floor, No. 144 Bannerghatta Road, Bangalore, 560-035, contact@animate-u….in, India, ein entsprechendes Angebot gesehen.
Sie bittet Sie eine Anfrage zu verfassen und dabei folgende Punkte zu berücksichtigen:

- Datum 1. September
- Betreff
- Bezug auf Internetseiten von Animate-U
- Vorstellung Ihrer Firma als eine der größten Gebäudereinigungs-firmen im Raum Berlin-Brandenburg; Firmenbroschüre als Anhang
- Grund Ihrer Anfrage
- Bitte um Information über Preis für eine 1-minütige Animations-grußkarte
- Bitte um Angabe der Lieferzeit und der Zahlungsbedingungen
- Sonderwunsch: Integration von Grußbotschaft und animiertem Logo; beides als Anhang
- Bei Zufriedenheit mögliche langfristige Zusammenarbeit
- Bitte um baldige Antwort
- Anhang: Firmenbroschüre, Logo, mp-3 Datei mit Grußbotschaft

P **5** Your stressed out boss, an American, feels he is in desperate need of a
🌐 wellness holiday. He is very demanding and only the best is good enough
for him. Check out wellness holidays in Europe and make notes for him in
English.

B | Enquiries by phone

R **1** Listen to the dialogue and fill in the missing words or expressions.
⊙ A2.3

Amanda Jones:	Good morning. Chelsea Sofabeds Ltd, Amanda Jones speaking. How can I help you?
Russell Blanding:	Hello, my name is Russell Blanding. I'm interested in your new **1** of modern compact sofa beds. Could you send me a catalogue?
Amanda Jones:	Certainly. Could you give me your address, please?
Russell Blanding:	Yes. It's 127 Woodside Lane, Rawdon, Leeds LS19 6LR
Amanda Jones:	Thank you. I'll post it **2** .
Russell Blanding:	I **3** the catalogue includes a price list for the **4** .
Amanda Jones:	Definitely. It also gives details of the discounts we grant. For instance, we grant a 10% **5** on any initial order.
Russell Blanding:	Is it possible to order **6** from you?
Amanda Jones:	Certainly. We can deliver most models within 2 weeks from **7** .
Russell Blanding:	Great. Thank you.
Amanda Jones:	**8** . Is there anything else I can help you with today?
Russell Blanding:	No thank you – not at present. Goodbye.
Amanda Jones:	Goodbye. Thank you for calling.

I **2** Working with a partner now create and act out a similar dialogue along the
following lines.

A	B
Sarah/Martin Freedman from Albion Tours in Dover gets a call.	The caller introduces him/herself as Jonas/Janine Wels from Rostock, Germany. He/she is interested in guided tours to cultural highlights in Britain in the summer.
Sarah/Martin Freedman offers to send a detailed brochure and asks for the caller's address.	Jonas/Janine Wels spells his/her name and address, Ostseeallee 27, 66123 Rostock, Germany.
Sarah/Martin Freedman promises to send the brochure by post the next morning and thanks the caller for his/her interest in their tours programme. He/she adds that he/she is convinced that the caller will find a tour that suits her/his interests.	Jonas/Janine Wels thanks Sarah/Martin Freedman and says goodbye.

I **3** Work with a partner, sit back to back and act out the following telephone conversation with the help of the role cards.

→ **ROLE CARD B:** page 261

Role card A

Katja / Ben Schneider, Auszubildende/r bei Feinkostgroßhandel Messner, Düsseldorf, ruft auf Bitte der Chefin bei Bellheather Distilleries Ltd, Inverness, Schottland, an. Katja / Ben bittet um Auskunft über die Single Malt Whiskies der Brennerei.
Die E-Mail-Adresse lautet: imports@feinkostmessner... .de.
Vor allem möchte die Chefin Näheres über Lieferzeiten, Mengen-rabatte und spezielle Geschenkkartons erfahren.
Katja / Ben beendet das Gespräch und dankt für die Bemühungen.

R **4** Study the info box below. Then copy the sentences and complete them on your own sheet of paper inserting the appropriate type of discount.

INFO: Discounts

Granting discounts is an effective means of winning new or retaining old customers.
Trade discounts are granted to retailers.
Introductory discounts are granted to facilitate the introduction of new products or services.
Quantity discounts are granted for volume orders.
Early order discounts are granted for bookings / purchases made well in advance.
Cash discount is granted for early payment.

---

1. We'd be happy to launch your new range of vitamin supplements on the Irish market if you are prepared to grant us a substantial **1** .
2. Book your tickets up to 2 months in advance to profit from our attractive **2** .
3. As your order exceeds 250 items we are prepared to grant you a **3** of 15 %.
4. We grant 3 % **4** for payment within 7 days of receipt of invoice.
5. As you are a business registered in the UK you qualify for **5** .
6. Would you be prepared to grant us a **6** if we raised our order to 1000 units?

5 You are planning to organise a one-day seminar on setting up an online company which will take place in 3 months' time. How can you encourage potential participants to sign up well in advance?

I **6** Work with a partner. Your company – a manufacturer of hand-knitted scarves and gloves – has received an enquiry from a retailer who is likely to place a substantial first order. Discuss what discount(s) you would offer to close the deal.

7 Work with a partner. Partner A wishes to place an order with partner B, provided he / she is granted a discount. Use the ideas from the following example to negotiate the discount in the four situations below. Then change roles.

Person A

Person B

We would really love to introduce your new desktop loudspeakers to the German market. But as there is an enormous amount of competition this won't be easy without offering customers an attractive incentive. I was thinking of an introductory discount of 20 %.

I see your point, but we invested a lot of money into R&D* to arrive at this truly innovative HiFi solution. As we are a relatively small firm, we just don't have the same financial clout as big multinational companies. So I'm afraid a 20 % discount would not be feasible for us.

I understand your position and the quality of your product is really stunning, but in view of the stiff competition from other manufacturers we will have to offer some incentive. Do you think that a 10 % discount would be an option for you?

I will have to discuss this with my boss before I commit myself. Can I get back to you tomorrow?

*research and development

Situation 1:
You want to negotiate an early booking discount for conference facilities. Your boss was thinking of 20 %. The booking is for a conference that will take place in two months' time. The discount is normally only granted for bookings made 3 months in advance.

Situation 2:
Your firm would like to order 100 kg of Isle of Skye knitting wool. You want to negotiate a 10 % quantity discount as the price is rather high compared to that of competitors. The supplier points out that the production costs are high and the quality significantly better than that of most other producers.

Situation 3:
You are a sole trader with a medium-sized shop for glassware and kitchen utensils. You are interested in crystal glass decanters from an Irish firm. You would like to order 20 items and were thinking of a 25 % trade discount. The Irish firm points out that the quantity is too small to qualify for a trade discount.

Situation 4:
Your firm wants to order 150 desktop printers and as payment will be made within 14 days you ask for a 3 % cash discount. The supplier informs you that they normally only grant a discount of 2 %.

LANGUAGE AND GRAMMAR

ADJECTIVES AND ADVERBS

Mit Adjektiven werden Substantive und das Verb „to be" näher bestimmt.

We expect to place **regular** orders in the future.	Wir erwarten, in Zukunft regelmäßige Bestellungen aufgeben zu können.

Erklärung: „regular" ist ein Adjektiv und kennzeichnet das Substantiv „orders".

We will be **glad** to help you in any way we can.	Wir sind froh, wenn wir Ihnen irgendwie helfen können.

Erklärung: „glad" ist ein Adjektiv und kennzeichnet „we" in Verbindung mit „will be", einer Form von „to be".

Mit Adverbien (Adjectiv + ly) werden Verben, andere Adjektive und Adverbien näher bestimmt.

We assure you that your order will be delivered **promptly**.	Wir versichern Ihnen, dass ihre Bestellung umgehend geliefert wird.

Erklärung: „promptly" ist ein Adverb und kennzeichnet das Verb „to deliver".

There is a **rapidly** growing market for pharmaceutical products worldwide.	Es gibt weltweit einen schnell wachsenden Markt für pharmazeutische Produkte.

Erklärung: „rapidly" ist ein Adverb und kennzeichnet das Adjektiv „growing".

There is an **extremely** rapidly shrinking market for raw materials at present.	Gegenwärtig haben wir einen extrem schnell schrumpfenden Markt für Rohstoffe.

Erklärung: „extremely" ist ein Adverb und kennzeichnet das Adverb „rapidly".

Unregelmäßige Formen: fast, hard, good

He's a **fast** driver.	Er ist ein schneller Fahrer.

Erklärung: „fast" ist hier ein Adjektiv und beschreibt das Substantiv „driver".

He drives **fast**.	Er fährt schnell.

Erklärung: „fast" ist hier ein Adverb und beschreibt das Verb „to drive".

He's been working very **hard** lately.	Er arbeitet in letzter Zeit sehr hart.

Erklärung: „hard" ist hier ein Adverb und beschreibt das Verb „to work".

She's been given a number of extremely **hard** cases to deal with.	Sie hat eine Reihe von sehr harten Fällen zur Bearbeitung bekommen.

Erklärung: „hard" ist hier ein Adjektiv und beschreibt das Substantiv „cases".

He's **hardly** expecting to be promoted at this stage.	Er erwartet es zum gegenwärtigen Zeitpunkt kaum befördert zu werden.

Erklärung: „hardly" ist ein Adverb und bedeutet „kaum".

He's a **good** team player.	Er ist sehr teamfähig.

Erklärung: „good" ist ein Adjektiv und beschreibt hier das Substantiv „team player".

Can you work **well** under pressure?	Können Sie gut unter Zeitdruck arbeiten?

Erklärung: „well" ist das Adverb zu „good" und beschreibt hier das Verb „to work".

TASK:

8

Copy the sentences below and fill in the correct form, either the adjective or the adverb.

1. (prompt) Thank you for your 1 response to our enquiry.
2. (prompt) Thank you for replying 2 to my request for information.
3. (strict) This information is given in 3 confidence.
4. (relative) This is a 4 cheap manufacturing process.

Office expert

C | Negotiating in trade

The world of trade is about buying and selling at the best price. In order to ensure your company gets a good deal, you need to be a confident and competent negotiator. Having good negotiating skills in English is essential when dealing with people from around the world, especially face-to-face.

R **1** Work with a partner and match the descriptions (1–12) with the most suitable negotiating phrases (a–l).

1. a polite way of saying that sth. is impossible
2. a phrase that asks so. what they are prepared to pay
3. a phrase where one side suggests to the other side that they both make a compromise
4. a polite way to inform sb. that they haven't understood what you want
5. a phrase where one side says that there is a possibility of a compromise
6. a phrase that means you can't accept the offer they have made
7. a way of saying that you can't offer the same price or conditions another company has given
8. a different way to say, "We have an offer from another company."
9. a phrase where one party sets a limit on what it is willing to pay
10. the price that is normally paid in the market for sth.
11. a polite way to say, "It's pointless continuing."
12. a phrase that shows you appreciate the other party's point or situation

a. I understand what you're saying.
b. I don't think we could go that far.
c. We have received another quote.
d. I'm afraid we can't match that.
e. I'm afraid there is nothing else we can do.
f. Which price did you have in mind?
g. We wouldn't expect to pay more than …
h. the going rate
i. There may be some room for manoeuvre.
j. There seems to have been a slight misunderstanding.
k. Could you meet us halfway?
l. I'm afraid this is out of the question.

KMK Exam Training

1 Rezeption: Leseverstehen

Stufe II Sie arbeiten für eine Zeitarbeitsfirma, die auf Dienstleistungen im Bereich von Reinigungs- und Hausmeistertätigkeiten spezialisiert ist. Sie erhalten folgende E-Mail von einer internationalen Schule. Lesen Sie die Anfrage und beantworten Sie die Fragen.

From:	hilary.cooper@globalschools... .org
To:	www.cleanpower....de
Cc:	
Sent:	201_-07-13
Subject:	Enquiry about cleaning and janitorial services
Attachment(s):	

Dear Sir / Madam,

We visited your website and would like to enquire into further details about your housekeeping and janitorial services. We are a member of Global Schools with over 60 locations world-wide providing English language schooling from pre-school through to grade 12.

This coming autumn we will be opening a new school in Berlin near Humboldt University. To start we will be offering schooling for grades 1 – 6 but plan to expand. The school premises consist of a two-winged, three-story house built around a courtyard which will serve as a recess playground with a bike parking area and tool shed. Twenty classrooms, two staircases, six restrooms and 10 office spaces covering approximately 1,500 m² will require daily cleaning weekdays. In addition, there is general maintenance and grounds keeping.

Please inform us as to your fees. Do you charge by the hour or can you make us a flat fee offer? In such a case, we need to agree on what tasks would be included. For example, would your firm be willing and able to take on general caretaking jobs such as snow shoveling, waste management and minor repairs? Does your firm also provide cleaning materials and equipment?

We assume an adequate number of staff is available so that the general cleaning tasks can be completed after school hours, i.e. between 4 p.m. and 6 p.m. It would also be convenient, if not absolutely necessary, that some members of your staff speak English, especially in the case of janitorial workers.

We would be willing to offer you a limited contract period for one school year with the possibility of extending the contract should your services prove satisfactory.

Since we are a UN affiliated non-profit organization we would hope you can offer us a substantial discount of 15 % or more. We look forward to hearing from you as soon as possible.

Yours sincerely,

1. Welche Dienstleistungen benötigt Global Schools?
2. Welche Dienstleistungen bietet Global Schools an?
3. Wie ist das Schulgelände aufgebaut?
4. Wie ist das Schulgebäude aufgebaut?
5. Welche Alternative hinsichtlich der Art der Abrechnung gibt es?
6. Welche Hausmeistertätigkeiten sind erwünscht?
7. Wann sollen die Reinigungsarbeiten durchgeführt werden und warum?
8. Was ist für einige Mitarbeiter im Hausmeisterteam unerlässlich?
9. Welche Laufzeit soll der Dienstleistungsvertrag haben?
10. Warum erhofft sich die Schule einen Rabatt?

Phrases: Enquiries

To mention the source of address	
We have seen your advertisement for copiers in the computer journal *IT.News!*	Wir haben Ihre Anzeige für Kopiergeräte in der Computer-Zeitschrift *IT.News!* gesehen.
We have obtained your address **from** the Anglo-German Chamber of Commerce.	Wir haben Ihre Anschrift von der Deutsch-Britischen Handelskammer erhalten.
Your services have been recommended to us by a business partner, …	Ihre Dienstleistungen wurden uns von einem Geschäftspartner empfohlen, …

To introduce your company	
We are a young and rapidly growing firm **specialising** in …	Wir sind ein junges, rasch wachsendes Unternehmen und sind auf … spezialisiert.
We are well-established manufacturers of …	Wir sind ein gut eingeführter Hersteller von …
Our firm is a leading importer of … with excellent contacts all over the EU.	Unsere Firma ist ein führender Importeur von … mit ausgezeichneten Kontakten in der gesamten EU.

To say what you require	
Could you please let us have a brochure and a price list **for** the services you offer.	Wir bitten um einen Prospekt und eine Preisliste für die von Ihnen angebotenen Dienstleistungen.
Please enclose a catalogue **of** your products.	Bitte fügen Sie einen Produktkatalog bei.
Please send us a quotation / cost estimate **for** …	Bitte machen Sie uns ein (Preis-) Angebot / einen Kostenvoranschlag über …
We need a further shipment of …	Wir benötigen eine weitere Lieferung …

To ask for further information	
We would be grateful for information on your terms of payment and delivery.	Wir bitten um nähere Angaben zu Ihren Liefer- und Zahlungsbedingungen.
Do you grant any quantity discounts / early order discount / trade discount / introductory discount / cash discount?	Gewähren Sie Mengenrabatt / Frühbucherrabatt / Wiederverkaufsrabatt / Einführungsrabatt / Skonto?
Can you deliver ex stock?	Können Sie ab Lager liefern?

To close the communication with a standard phrase	
We look forward to **hearing** from you soon.	Wir freuen uns darauf, bald von Ihnen zu hören.
If your prices are competitive, we may be able to place substantial orders in future.	Wenn Ihre Preise konkurrenzfähig sind, werden wir Ihnen bald größere Aufträge erteilen können.

10

In what way might offers from various suppliers differ?

Offers

According to English law if you make an offer it is **legally binding** whether it is a solicited offer, i.e. made in response to a specific request from another person or company or unsolicited – sent on your own initiative to companies which might be interested in the products or services you offer.

It is possible to limit the legally binding nature of your offer to supply certain goods or carry out specified services at a certain price and on certain terms by stating in the offer that

- prices are subject to change without notice
- the offer is without engagement or
- valid until a certain date or
- valid as long as stocks last.

The word quotation is also often used to designate detailed specific offers. Offers for work to be carried out (e.g. redecoration of company premises) take the form of cost estimates.

1 Are the following statements true or false?

1. Only solicited offers are legally binding.
2. You are free to change the terms of any offer as you wish.

2 What is the point of sending out offers that have not been requested?

3 Study the text and find equivalents for these German terms: freibleibend, solange der Vorrat reicht, Preisänderungen vorbehalten.

WORD BANK

- to attach
- brochure
- catalogue
- cost estimate
- to enclose
- INCOTERMS
- offer
- options
- price list
- to process
- quotation
- sample
- solicited
- stock
- terms of delivery
- terms of payment
- to quote
- unsolicited
- valid

4 Complete the following text with a suitable word or phrase from the box below.

> legally binding · cost estimate · as long as stocks last · solicited offer ·
> without engagement · unsolicited · subject to change without notice

With a view to generating business HandbagsGalore Ltd send offers to their customers without being asked to do so. These are **1** offers. They are careful to emphasise that these offers do not represent a legal commitment and they reserve the right to change the prices without warning. The offer is thus **2** and prices are **3** . They further stipulate that the offer is only valid until the goods in their warehouse run out, or **4** . Emily's Beauty Emporium Ltd has asked ABC Construction to tell her how much it would cost to have the façade of her shop re-painted and the lettering re-done. She asks for a **5** . Felicity Jones Interiors asks Sarl Elegance Parisienne for a firm offer to supply 24 French-style "Bergère" armchairs. Elegance Parisienne's offer is a **6** and specifies a period of three months for which it is **7** .

M **5** Ihr Vorgesetzter bittet Sie, folgende Sätze ins Englische zu übersetzen.
KMK

1. Solange der Vorrat reicht, bieten wir Ihnen die neue Produktreihe zu Sonderkonditionen.
2. Viele Firmen schicken unverlangte Angebote an Firmen, die sich möglicherweise für ihre Produkte interessieren.
3. Dieses Angebot ist freibleibend.
4. Ich brauche einen Kostenvoranschlag für die Renovierung der Büroräume.
5. Diese Preise gelten nur bis 30. Juni 201_.
6. Ein verlangtes Angebot wird als Reaktion auf eine Anfrage abgegeben.
7. Preisänderungen bleiben vorbehalten.

INFO: Successful offers

Effective offers are decisive for the success of your business. When making an offer you should

- answer an enquiry promptly
- whenever possible personalise the salutation
- thank the enquirer for his interest in your goods or services
- let the prospective customer know that his enquiry will be processed as soon as possible if you cannot provide all the information right away
- be as helpful and polite as possible
- give all the information required
- provide additional information that might be useful
- refrain from making promises you cannot keep
- say something positive about your firm and / or your products
- conclude your offer with a phrase designed to make the customer feel positive towards your firm

6   Refer to the info-box on the previous page and choose task a, b or c.
○   a.   Give examples for the last 2 bullet points.
◖   b.   In your view which of the bullet points are the most important?
        Explain your decision.
●   c.   Rank the bullet points and give detailed reasons for your decision.

A | Offers in writing

In reply to her enquiry about cast iron cookware sets Annisa Bhatnagar from Chefland Ltd has received the following email offer from Arthäuser & Brinck.

1   Study the email offer and find the missing nouns from the box below.

> account · attachment · delivery period · discount · enquiry · orders ·
> regards · relations · satisfaction · stock

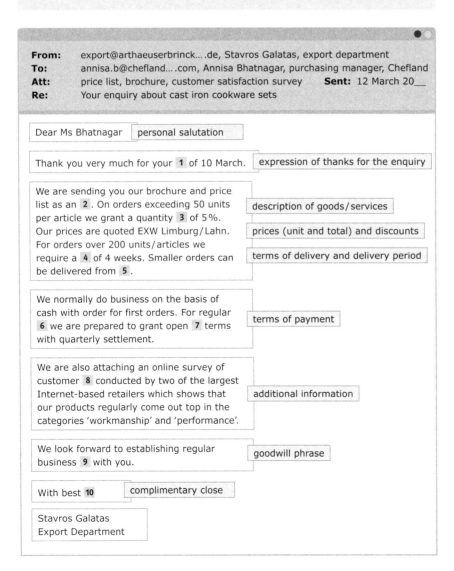

From:	export@arthaeuserbrinck….de, Stavros Galatas, export department
To:	annisa.b@chefland….com, Annisa Bhatnagar, purchasing manager, Chefland
Att:	price list, brochure, customer satisfaction survey **Sent:** 12 March 20__
Re:	Your enquiry about cast iron cookware sets

Dear Ms Bhatnagar │ personal salutation

Thank you very much for your **1** of 10 March. │ expression of thanks for the enquiry

We are sending you our brochure and price list as an **2**. On orders exceeding 50 units per article we grant a quantity **3** of 5%.
Our prices are quoted EXW Limburg/Lahn.
For orders over 200 units/articles we require a **4** of 4 weeks. Smaller orders can be delivered from **5**.

   description of goods/services
   prices (unit and total) and discounts
   terms of delivery and delivery period

We normally do business on the basis of cash with order for first orders. For regular **6** we are prepared to grant open **7** terms with quarterly settlement.

   terms of payment

We are also attaching an online survey of customer **8** conducted by two of the largest Internet-based retailers which shows that our products regularly come out top in the categories 'workmanship' and 'performance'.

   additional information

We look forward to establishing regular business **9** with you.

   goodwill phrase

With best **10**   │ complimentary close

Stavros Galatas
Export Department

2 You work in the export department of a German wholesaler for flooring and carpeting. Your boss, Andrea Kwasni, has received the following email enquiry. Reply to this enquiry taking your boss's note into account.

From: dylan.mcintyre@clydeside-home... .co.uk
To: a.kwasni@endura... .de
Sent: 02-08-201_
Subject: Enquiry about Endura's Welsh Slate loop-pile and woven fabric carpets

Dear Ms Kwasni,

Please quote us your best prices for the following products from the Welsh Slate range:

20 rolls	at 500 m² each of Welsh Slate woven, wool, width 4 m, article no. 2–66

2–66 in der gewünschten Menge vorrätig. Rollenpreis 8.100 Euro

Rollenpreis für 2–53: 7.700 Euro

15 rolls	at 350 m² each of Welsh Slate loop pile, wool, width 4 m, article no. 2–53

2–53: nur noch 7 Rollen auf Lager. Restlieferung in 6 Wochen möglich

Als möglichen Ersatz für 2–53 Granite (Art. Nr. 3–52) vorschlagen. Gleiche Qualität, gleicher Preis. Farbton etwas heller.

As we will be opening our new store in West Glasgow later this summer, we would need the goods as quickly as possible. Could you please let us know your earliest date of delivery.

Versand kann drei Tage nach Auftragseingang erfolgen. 10 % Mengenrabatt für den gesamten Auftrag einräumen.

We assume that the usual terms of payment and delivery will apply.

ja

Best regards,

Bitte meinen Namen unter die Antwort setzen. Danke. AK

Dylan McIntyre
Clydeside at Home Ltd
22 Glasgow International Business Park
Paisley
PA16 7JL
Tel: 01 41 80 96 87 3...

P **3**
KMK

Sie sind Caily / Cameron Fenton und arbeiten im Verkauf bei Male Space, 124 Burgess Rd, Southampton, SO21 8TU. Pia / Paul Heimholz von der Firma Euroland, Weidenauer Str. 7, 57088 Siegen, hat um eine schriftliche Bestätigung des Angebots gebeten, das Sie ihm / ihr heute früh gemacht haben. Verfassen Sie dieses Schreiben in englischer Sprache und berücksichtigen Sie dabei Folgendes:

- Datum von heute
- Betreff: Angebot Nr. D-103-171016
- Bezug auf Telefongespräch
- Angebot für 200 Stück 4-Rotor Helikopterdrohnen mit hochauflösender Kamera (high resolution camera), Artikel Nr. 103
- Listenpreis pro Stück: €49,00, FCA Southampton, Incoterms 2010, einschließlich Verpackung, abzüglich 30% Händlerrabatt
- Gesamtpreis nach Abzug des Händlerrabatts: €6.860,00
- Zahlungsbedingungen: innerhalb von 30 Tagen netto, innerhalb von 10 Tagen 2% Skonto
- Lieferzeit: 10 Tage
- 1 Muster-Drohne wird heute an Euroland zu Testzwecken geschickt
- Dank für das Interesse an den Produkten von Male Space
- Zusicherung sorgfältiger Ausführung des Auftrags

B | Offers by phone

Alistair Hewson from Havant Group Ltd in Portsmouth, UK gets a phone call from an overseas customer.

R **1**
⊚ A2.5
First read the following statements, then listen to the dialogue and note down whether the statements are true of false.
Choose task a, b or c.

- ○ a. 1. Jonathan Chin is calling from Hong Kong.
  2. He and Alistair know one another.
  3. He has run out of Havant group computers.

b. 1. Jonathan Chin is running out of computer Havant Group projectors.
2. Alistair doesn't have many in stock himself.
3. JC needs to order 500 units of Optima 2000 and the same number of X250 Home Projector.
4. Prices have stayed the same.
5. Prices are quoted CIF Singapore.

c. 1. Last year's model Optima 2000 cost £ 350.
2. Price rises are due to currency movements.
3. There is increasing competition from Japan.
4. 30 % discount will be granted on all future orders.
5. The customer asks for an offer in writing.
6. Delivery time is six weeks from receipt of order.

2 Copy Alistair Hewson's quotation and insert the missing expressions from the box.

> from receipt of order · look forward to · pleased to · Referring to · within 30 days

From: ah@havantgroup... .co.uk
To: jc@singaporeelectronics... .sp
Cc:
Sent:
Subject: Optima 2000 and X250 computer projectors – Quotation no CP-2056
Attachments:

Hi Jonathan

1 your enquiry of 17 June 201_ I am **2** inform you that we can quote as follows:

Quantity	Description	Unit Price	Subtotal
500	Optima computer projector	£ 385.00	GBP 192,500.00
500	X250 Home Projector	£ 220.00	GBP 110,000.00
			GBP 302,500.00
	less 30 % trade discount		GBP 91,506.25
TOTAL			**GBP 210,993.75**

Delivery: within four weeks **3** , CIF Singapore
Payment: net cash **4** from receipt of invoice

We **5** receiving your order.

Kind regards
Alistair Hewson
Havant Group Ltd

C | Comparing options

 R **1** Sie wurden beauftragt, Angebote zu Intensiv-Sprachkursen in England
KMK einzuholen. Sie haben im Internet zwei interessante Angebote gefunden,
die Sie nun vergleichen. Kopieren Sie die Tabelle und füllen Sie sie aus.

	A	B
Veranstalter	**The Holywell College of Languages**	**Brighthelm Language College**
Kursort		
Verkehrsanbindung		
Teilnehmerkreis und -zahl		
Werden spezielle Kurs-wünsche berücksichtigt?		
Unterrichtsstunden pro Tag		
Unterbringung		
Ausflüge		
Freizeitangebot		
Kurstermine		
Unterkunft		
Verpflegung		
Kursgebühren		
Ermäßigungen		
Anzahlung		
Kontakt		

Anbieter A

The Holywell College of Languages / Eastbourne

The Holywell College of Languages offers programmes in Business English tailored to the
requirements of your staff. Our offer includes a one-
week course, five hours of tuition a day focusing on
general business English and any specialised area
you may require.

Our language school is located in Eastbourne, a
traditional resort situated on the English Channel,
which has good transport links to Brighton and
London. For nature lovers there is the South Downs
National Park only a few minutes from the centre
of Eastbourne which includes the spectacular white
cliffs known as the Seven Sisters.

Your staff will be placed with English business and professional families. We ensure that we do not
place two native speakers of the same language in the same family.

We organise a programme of excursions and sports including tennis, swimming, surfing and sailing.

Tuition fees: £650
For a group of ten or more participants from one company we offer a 10% discount.
Accommodation and full board in host families: £520
Booking fee, to be paid when booking: £100. Payment in full: 6 weeks before the course begins.
Contact: Dylan Masterman, dm@holywellcol… .co.uk

Anbieter B

Brighthelm Language College / Brighton

Brighthelm Language College is an international language school specialising in courses for business people, located in Brighton on the South Coast of England. Brighton is a vibrant forward-looking seaside resort and conference centre.

Our business English intensive courses take place throughout the year, last from 1 to 2 weeks and are designed specially to meet your requirements. These intensive courses consist of 5 hours of tuition per day with a programme of study visits to British firms in the afternoons.

Maximum number of participants per course: 8. Accommodation for our students is arranged either at an exclusive private hotel or with carefully selected English host families.

There is a wide range of sports activities available such as golf, riding, surfing, sailing and hang-gliding. Equipment can be hired at a reasonable charge.

Course fees: £600 per student per week

Accommodation with breakfast:

Private hotel: £75 per night

Host family: £480 per week

To confirm a booking a deposit of £100 per person is required payable online either by credit / debit card or bank transfer. The balance is due no later than 8 days before the course commencement date.

Contact: Antonia Lazenby (Mrs):
al@brighthelmlanguagecollege... .yahoo.com
or tel.: + 44 1273 729 4810...
Address: Brighthelm Language College, 135 Montpelier Drive, Hove BN3 1NA

P **2** Decide which of the two offers you would prefer. Then write a brief memo for your Swedish parent company's HR department (company language English), giving at least two reasons for your choice.

P **3** Your boss has asked you to research business English courses in Lyme Regis and Poole in the South West of England.
Make notes on a couple of courses that seem suitable and write a memo in English giving names and details.

P **4** A business associate has recommended the Pavilion Language School in Brighton (info@pavilionlsb... .com) to your boss.
Send them an email and enquire about their courses and fees, accommodation, after-class activities, public transport etc. The contact person for enquiries is Karen Wills.

P **5** Your firm is going to send you to a one-week language course to Malta.
Write an email to antonia.laurini@malta-lingo... .mt specifiying your requirements and wishes as to language teaching and leisure activities.

D | INCOTERMS® (Terms of delivery)

The Incoterms are a set of nationally and internationally accepted rules defining the obligations of the seller and the buyer as regards the tasks, costs and risks involved in the transport of goods. They were first drawn up by the International Chamber of Commerce in Paris in 1936 and were last updated in 2010.

The Incoterms 2010 are grouped in two categories:
- rules for any mode or modes of transport
- rules for sea and inland waterway transport

The Incoterms 2010 consist of 11 rules, two of which are new:
- DAT (Delivered at Terminal) replaces the former DEQ rule
- DAP (Delivered at Place) replaces the former rules DAF, DES and DDU

Incoterms® 2010

I. Any mode or modes of transport

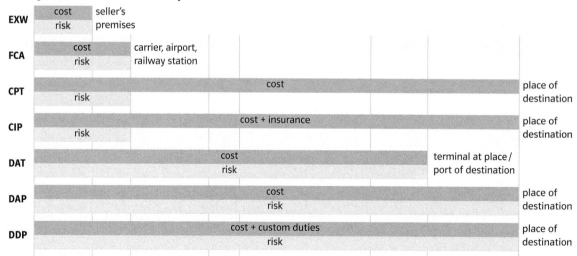

	cost / risk range	location
EXW	cost / risk	seller's premises
FCA	cost / risk	carrier, airport, railway station
CPT	cost (full) / risk (to carrier)	place of destination
CIP	cost + insurance (full) / risk (to carrier)	place of destination
DAT	cost / risk (full)	terminal at place / port of destination
DAP	cost / risk (full)	place of destination
DDP	cost + custom duties / risk (full)	place of destination

II. Sea and inland waterway transport

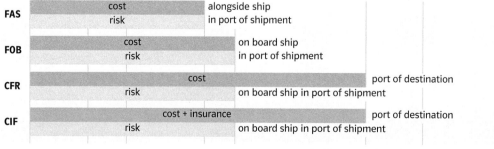

	cost / risk range	location
FAS	cost / risk	alongside ship in port of shipment
FOB	cost / risk	on board ship in port of shipment
CFR	cost / risk	port of destination / on board ship in port of shipment
CIF	cost + insurance / risk	port of destination / on board ship in port of shipment

nach: International Chamber of Commerce, (ICC)

Rules for any mode or modes of transport Incoterms® 2010

Inco-term	Designation	Seller's obligations	Passing of risk from seller to buyer
EXW	**Ex Works** Ab Werk	place the goods at the disposal of the buyer at the seller's premises (factory, warehouse etc.)	at the seller's premises
FCA	**Free Carrier** Frei Frachtführer	deliver the goods to the carrier named by the buyer	when the goods are handed over to the carrier
CPT	**Carriage Paid to** Frachtfrei	deliver the goods to the carrier and pay the cost of carriage to the named place of destination	when the goods are handed over to the carrier
CIP	**Carriage and Insurance Paid to** Frachtfrei versichert	deliver the goods to the carrier, pay the cost of carriage and take out insurance to the named place of destination	when the goods are handed over to the carrier
DAT	**Delivered at Terminal** Geliefert Terminal	place the goods at the buyer's disposal, unloaded, at a named terminal at a named place/port	when the goods have been unloaded at the terminal
DAP	**Delivered at Place** Geliefert benannter Ort	place the goods at the buyer's disposal, ready for unloading, at the named place of destination	at the place of destination
DDP	**Delivered Duty Paid** Geliefert verzollt	place the goods at the buyer's disposal, ready for unloading, at the named place of destination, carry out all customs formalities and pay import duty, if any	at the place of destination

Rules for sea and inland waterway transport Incoterms® 2010

Inco-term	Designation	Seller's obligations	Passing of risk from seller to buyer
FAS	**Free Alongside Ship** Frei Längsseite Schiff	deliver the goods alongside the ship named by the buyer at the named port of shipment	when the goods are alongside the ship in the port of shipment
FOB	**Free on Board** Frei an Bord	deliver the goods on board the ship named by the buyer at the named port of shipment	when the goods are on board the ship in the port of shipment
CFR	**Cost and Freight** Kosten und Fracht	deliver the goods on board the ship and pay the costs and freight to the named port of destination	when the goods are on board the ship in the port of shipment
CIF	**Cost, Insurance and Freight** Kosten, Versicherung und Fracht	deliver the goods on board the ship; pay the costs and freight to the named port of destination and take out insurance for the transport	when the goods are on board the ship in the port of shipment

Under all clauses the seller must deliver the goods to the buyer at the named place and the buyer must take delivery of the goods *(Ware abnehmen)*. The seller must procure *(beschaffen)* or help to procure the transport documents and pack the goods, if customary *(handelsüblich)*.

Note that under the Incoterms CPT, CIP, CFR and CIF the seller bears the risks only up to the place of delivery, i.e. until the goods are handed over to the (first) carrier or have been loaded on board a ship in the port of shipment. Under these terms the seller must, in addition, contract *(Vertrag abschließen)* and pay for the carriage to the place or port of destination.

1 Read the business transactions and complete them with the right Incoterms.

1. Amberley Real Estate has bought five document shredders from Tyneside Security. Amberley's driver picks the shreddders up from Tyneside Security's production plant. The shredders were sold on the basis of …?

2. Male Space Ltd have received a large export order from a Canadian customer. Male Space pays for the goods to be taken to the docks in Southampton and for loading on board the vessel "Hugh Dundas". The terms of delivery are …?

3. Blauhelm GmbH, a German manufacturer of electric tools, usually deliver their goods by lorry to DIY-World's premises in Croydon, assuming all costs and risks for the entire transport and dealing with any border formalities that may arise. Their terms of delivery are most likely …?

4. Endura is processing a major order for high-quality carpeting from a Kuweiti customer. Endura arrange and pay for the transport of two 20 ft containers to the container terminal at the port of Kuweit. Endura deliver on the basis of …?

M **2** Study the Incoterms on the previous pages and find the English equivalents for the following German expressions:

1. Spediteur/Frachtführer
2. verzollt
3. Bestimmungshafen
4. ab Werk
5. Einfuhrzoll
6. Versicherung abschließen
7. handelsüblich
8. angegebener Bestimmungsort
9. Frachtdokumente beschaffen
10. Transport per Binnenschifffahrt
11. entladebereit
12. Gefahrenübergang

LANGUAGE AND GRAMMAR

SOME AND ANY

„Some" steht in bejahten Aussagen.

Here are **some** interesting replies to our survey.

Hier sind einige interessante Rückmeldungen zu unserer Umfrage.

„Some" steht in Fragen, auf die eine positive Antwort erwartet wird.

Could I have **some** of these folders?

Könnte ich einige von diesen Ordnern haben?

„Any" steht in verneinten Aussagen.

I'm afraid there aren't **any** details available.

Es sind leider keine Einzelheiten erhältlich.

„Any" steht in Fragen, auf die eine negative Antwort erwartet wird.

Have we received **any** responses to our ad?

Haben wir (überhaupt) Rückmeldungen zu unserer Anzeige bekommen?

„Any" steht bei „hardly", „scarcely" oder „barely" (deutsch: kaum).

We've hardly had **any** opportunity to socialize with customers.

Wir hatten kaum Gelegenheit mit Kunden Kontakte zu knüpfen.

„Any" steht in Bedingungssatzen.

If there are **any** problems, please let me know.

Wenn es (irgendwelche) Probleme gibt, lassen Sie es mich wissen.

„Any" steht nach Ausdrucken des Zweifels.

I wonder whether **any** of these products have been adequately tested.

Ich frage mich, ob (überhaupt) irgendwelche von diesen Produkten ordentlich geprüft wurden.

TASK:

3

Complete the following sentences using "some" or "any".

1. He says he's been thinking of changing jobs for … time now.
2. We didn't have … difficulties obtaining the necessary spare parts.
3. There is hardly … time left before the lease expires.
4. We will send you … samples by post.
5. When we got to the garden party there was scarcely … food left.
6. Could you give me … help with this report?
7. I couldn't think of … leaving present he might like.
8. Would you like … refreshments?
9. I doubt that … body would have been able to deal with that angry customer.
10. … of these parts may not arrive before the deadline.
11. Could you bring in … chairs from the room next door?
12. I wonder if … members will bother to turn up for the meeting.

4 Choose task a, b or c.

○ a. Find 5 English idioms in the box below for the following German expressions. Use a dictionary or the internet if necessary.

> ein Thema, das keiner ansprechen möchte · den Vorsprung vor der Konkurrenz halten · bürokratische Regeln · alles auf eine Karte setzen · bahnbrechend/innovativ

◐ b. Find the English idioms in the box below that correspond to the following paraphrases:

> a generous offer with no hidden conditions · to stick to one's point of view in spite of criticism · to be forced to go back to the beginning · to be making a profit · to have a controlling position in the market

● c. Make sentences or dialogues in English using the idioms in the box below.

> **Idioms**
>
> 1. to corner the market
> 2. an elephant in the room
> 3. to stand one's ground
> 4. to keep ahead of the pack
> 5. red tape
> 6. to put all your eggs in one basket
> 7. ground-breaking
> 8. to be in the black
> 9. to go back to square one
> 10. an offer with no strings attached

INFO: Idioms

Idioms sind bildhafte Ausdrücke und Wendungen, deren Sinn sich oft durch einfache Übersetzung nicht erschließen lässt. Muttersprachler wissen natürlich genau, wann, wie und wo sie solche Idioms einfließen lassen können. Doch Vorsicht! Selbst jemand mit sehr guten Fremdsprachenkenntnissen hat nicht unbedingt diesen muttersprachlichen Instinkt. Idioms sind abhängig von Region, Alter, Sozialschicht, Geschlecht und vielen anderen Faktoren. Eine idiomatische Wendung, die in einem Pub in Yorkshire Lachsalven auslöst, ist möglicherweise eine Quelle von Missverständnissen oder gar eine Beleidigung in einem Londoner Büro.

Man sollte häufig benutzte Idioms auf jeden Fall kennen, da sie eben von Muttersprachlern und auch gern in der englischen Presse benutzt werden. Bei der eigenen Verwendung von Idioms sollte man allerdings eher zurückhaltend sein und ein Idiom nur dann verwenden, wenn man sich sicher ist, dass es richtig und passend ist und in einer gegebenen Situation auch wirklich von allen verstanden wird.

Im Zweifelsfall gilt die Regel: Auf Nummer sicher gehen und auf idiomatische Ausdrücke verzichten!

Office expert

E | Evaluating services

P **1** You work for an office that requires new cleaning services. Work in pairs and discuss the pros and cons of the different options below. Discuss not just costs but also reliability and fairness to the cleaners. Take notes and present your results to the class.

Options	Pros	Cons
one full-time worker		
outsourcing to cleaning firm		
several part-time workers		

F | Office supplies fair

1
KMK Lesen Sie die Website zur Office Expo und beantworten Sie die Fragen auf Deutsch.

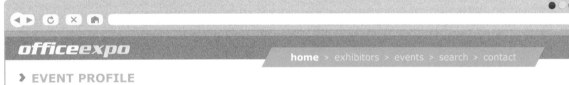

officeexpo home > exhibitors > events > search > contact

❯ EVENT PROFILE
Organized by Media Expos at New Delhi, India, the Office Expo in Mumbai is a pioneer show providing a platform for office equipment and supplies. It is an annual mega event offering enormous opportunities for exhibiting various products and trends in making office environments more efficient and effective.

❯ VISITORS' PROFILE
- architects and interior designers
- communication managers
- CEOs and presidents
- administrators
- secretaries
- purchasers, importers and exporters
- department stores

❯ EXHIBITORS' PROFILE
The exhibition is focused on the following segments of office improvement: office automation, equipment, office furniture, office security, office stationery, services, audio visual equipment and IT products.

Business timing: 10:00 am – 07:00 pm

Public timing: 12:00 am – 07:00 pm

1. Was ist die Office Expo?
2. Wie oft und wo findet die Office Expo statt?
3. Aus welchen Berufsgruppen stammen die Messebesucher?
4. Welche Produktarten werden auf der Messe ausgestellt?
5. Wie sind die Öffnungszeiten für
   a. Geschäftsleute?   b. die Öffentlichkeit?

KMK Exam Training

1 Mediation (Englisch – Deutsch)

Stufe II Lesen Sie die Beschreibung der drei Stühle von Topchairs und fassen Sie die wichtigsten Punkte für eine Kundin auf Deutsch zusammen.

STILLA €295.00 €147.50

Conference chair made in shiny welded aluminum with a fixed base and a fabric covered seat. Combining aesthetics and functionality, STILLA measures 55 cm (width), 100 cm (height) and 47 cm (depth). Due to radical price reduction, no further discounts are available. Free delivery for orders over 100 and easy credit terms.

ARCO €549.00

Heavy-duty office chair made of aluminum with a reclining, hydraulic controlled leather seat. Thanks to its gas piston system, both the height and armrests are adjustable for customized use. It is 65 cm wide, 120 cm high and has a depth of 58 cm. We offer an initial order discount of 5% for orders over €2,000 with payment per credit card. Delivery is ex works.

SIMPLEX €115.00

This practical chair is made of sturdy plastic with a wheeled steel base. Due to its gas piston system, the height is adjustable and it measures 60 cm × 110 cm × 60 cm. We offer a 6% discount for orders over 20 with payment in advance. Price does not include packaging and shipping costs.

2 Produktion

Stufe II Schreiben Sie per E-Mail eine Anfrage an die Firma Topchairs (info@topchairs....com) und berücksichtigen Sie dabei die folgenden Punkte:

- Erwähnen Sie, wie Sie die Firma in Erfahrung gebracht haben.
- Bringen Sie Ihr Interesse an dem Bürostuhl Arco zum Ausdruck.
- Fragen Sie, ob die Stühle in Ihrer Firmenfarbe (grün) erhältlich sind.
- Fragen Sie nach möglichen Rabatten und den Zahlungs- und Lieferbedingungen.
- Beenden Sie die E-Mail in angemessener Form.

Phrases: Offers

To say thank you for an enquiry	
Many thanks for your enquiry **of** 2 October **about** our new range of ...	Wir danken Ihnen vielmals für Ihre Anfrage vom 2. Oktober wegen unseres neuen Sortiments von ...
We **were** pleased to hear that you are interested in our ...	Wir freuen uns über Ihr Interesse an unseren ...

To make an offer and to refer to prices and discounts	
As requested, we are sending you enclosed our latest catalogue and price list.	Wie gewünscht, fügen wir unseren neuesten Katalog und unsere Preisliste bei.
We are pleased to quote **as** follows:	Wir freuen uns, Ihnen hiermit folgendes Angebot machen zu können:
We would now like to make the following quotation:	Wir möchten Ihnen nun folgendes Angebot unterbreiten:
... **at** a unit price of € ..., including packing. ...	zum Stückpreis von € ... einschließlich Verpackung.
... less 30 % trade discount. ...	abzüglich 30 % Händlerrabatt.
We can offer a 10 % quantity discount **on** orders **for** at least 500 units.	Für Aufträge über mindestens 500 Stück wird 10 % Mengenrabatt gewährt.
May we draw your attention **to** our special offer for ...?	Dürfen wir Sie auf unser Sonderangebot für ... aufmerksam machen?
We grant 2 % cash discount **for** payment within 10 days.	Für Barzahlung innerhalb von 10 Tagen gewähren wir 2 % Skonto.
We take pleasure **in** submitting the following cost estimate:	Wir freuen uns Ihnen folgenden Kostenvoranschlag zu unterbreiten:

To state your terms of delivery and payment	
Our prices are quoted CIF Singapore.	Unsere Preise verstehen sich CIF Singapur.
Terms of delivery: EXW Neustadt	Lieferbedingungen: EXW (Ab Werk) Neustadt
Our terms of payment are: cash **with** order cash **on** delivery 30 days net, 10 days 2 % **by** irrevocable and confirmed letter of credit	Unsere Zahlungsbedingungen lauten: Barzahlung bei Auftragserteilung Barzahlung bei Lieferung 30 Tage netto, 10 Tage 2 % Skonto durch unwiderrufliches und bestätigtes Akkreditiv
Regular customers are granted open account terms.	Unseren Stammkunden gewähren wir offenes Zahlungsziel.
We would request payment **by** bank transfer **to** our account **with** ABC bank.	Wir bitten um Zahlung per Banküberweisung auf unser Konto bei der ABC Bank.

To refer to the delivery time	
The delivery period is 6 weeks.	Die Lieferzeit beträgt 6 Wochen.
Delivery can be made ex stock.	Die Lieferung kann ab Lager erfolgen.

To inform the customer how long the offer is valid	
The offer is – firm **until** 31 March. – without engagement. – valid **as long as** stocks last.	Das Angebot ist – fest bis 31. März. – unverbindlich. – gültig solange der Vorrat reicht.
The prices are **subject to** change without notice.	Preisänderungen bleiben vorbehalten.
The offer is **subject to** prior sale.	Zwischenverkauf vorbehalten.

To create goodwill	
I hope this quotation will find your approval.	Ich hoffe, dieses Angebot sagt Ihnen zu.
We look forward to welcoming you as our customers.	Wir freuen uns darauf, Sie als Kunden begrüßen zu dürfen.
We assure you that your order **will be** dealt with promptly and carefully.	Wir sichern Ihnen eine rasche und sorgfältige Erledigung Ihres Auftrags zu.
Should you have any further queries, our staff **will be** pleased to assist you **at any** time.	Sollten Sie nun weitere Fragen haben, stehen Ihnen unsere Mitarbeiter jederzeit gerne zur Verfügung.

11

In what ways can you place an order?

Orders

The duties of an administrative assistant may involve dealing with incoming orders or the company's own orders to suppliers for products for resale if the company is a retailer or wholesaler, or orders for materials and parts if it is a manufacturer. The latter process is often known as procurement, which in large companies will be dealt with by a separate department. Dealing with an order also involves agreeing delivery dates, transportation, establishing payment terms and possibly granting discounts. In the case of procurement it also involves comparing alternative suppliers, their products and terms. Sometimes a trial order is placed to test the product and service. In the case of an initial order from a new customer it is important to stipulate a secure payment method.

1 Answer the following questions on the text.

1. What is meant by the term procurement?
2. Why is it important to be particularly careful with initial orders?
3. What other arrangements are part of the process of dealing with an order?
4. Why is a trial order often placed when using a new supplier?
5. What word is often used to refer to first orders?

2 Why is it advisable to be cautious as regards method of payment with a new customer?

WORD BANK

- *article*
- *to choose*
- *to deliver*
- *description*
- *initial order*
- *item*
- *to order*
- *order form*
- *order on call*
- *pattern*
- *to place an order*
- *to process*
- *quantity*
- *repeat order*
- *sample*
- *terms and conditions*
- *total price*
- *trial order*
- *unit price*
- *standing order*

A | Orders in writing

Tim Gordon from Toytown has studied Fächter & Suhr's offer for 00-scale vintage locomotives and has read an e-mail update about the German company's new models that have been added to their range. This e-mail also contained a link to the product test results published by a leading German consumer safety group. As the test results are very positive and Fächter & Suhr's offer attractive and competitive, he decides to place a trial order.

1 Use the correct prepositions from the box on the right and complete Tim Gordon's order letter and the order form on the next page.

by (2×) · for · from · of · to · with (2×)

TOYTOWN Ltd   22 Great South-West Road · Heathrow TW6 3XS
www.toytown.....co.uk · info@toytown.....co.uk

pi / TG   6 Sept 201_

Johannes Weisshaupt
Fächter & Suhr
Industriepark Mittelfranken
90762 Fürth
Germany

Dear Mr Weisshaupt | appropriate salutation

Order for 00-scale Mallard, Spirit of the Highlands and Isambard Brunel

Thank you for your e-mail offer **1** 2 September and your separate e-mail update regarding the launch of your Isambard Brunel model and the test results of your products.   reference to offer etc.

We are favourably impressed **2** the positive test results and your company's attention to detail and quality of design. We therefore wish to place a trial order **3** a total of 300 items as per our attached Order Form No. 3980.   order on relevant form

Please confirm this order indicating the bank account **4** which you wish to have the sum in question transferred so that we can settle the account immediately.

The goods will be collected **5** Freightmasters Ltd who will contact you shortly.   instructions, if necessary

We look forward to receiving the consignment soon. If the models find our customers' approval we will be pleased to place further orders **6** you.   appropriate ending

Best regards | complimentary close
TOYTOWN

Tim Gordon
Tim Gordon
Purchasing Manager

Encl Order Form No. 3980 | Enclosure, if applicable

Order form

TOYTOWN Ltd

22 Great South-West Road · Heathrow TW6 3XS
www.toytown... .co.uk · info@toytown... .co.uk

ORDER NO. 3980   5 October 201_

Fächter & Suhr
Industriepark Mittelfranken
90762 Fürth

Please supply

> order (on order form, if appropriate)
> * quantity
> * description (article No.)
> * unit price, total price
> * terms of delivery and payment
> * delivery time

Quantity	Item	Product No	Unit Price	Total Price
100	Mallard	BV-0-12	€ 82.40	€ 8240.00
100	Spirit of the Highlds.	BV-0-18	€ 82.40	€ 8240.00
100	Isambard Brunel	BV-0-27	€ 78.00	€ 7800.00

Terms of delivery: EXW Fürth

Terms of payment: Cash 7 order

Delivery: 8 stock

Tim Gordon

Tim Gordon
for Toytown Ltd

P **2** You work in the purchasing department of a chain of German stationery shops, Schreibwaren Petersen mit Zentrale in 19053 Schwerin, email: a.petersen@schreibwarenpetersen....de.
Your boss, Anton Petersen, has put this leaflet on your desk with his handwritten notes asking you to email an order to qualexstationery....com.

Qualex-stationery

proudly presents its new multilingual architectural calendar range with superb new photography

Great buildings of Europe *besonders beliebt*
12" × 12" wall calendar   *100 Stück bestellen*

Magnificent architecture of India
9" × 9" wall calendar   *fragen, ob auch in 12"×12" erhältlich.*
Wenn ja 100 Stück bestellen kleineres Format verkauft sich nicht hierzulande

Beautiful Buildings of Mexico and South America spectacular new photos!
12" × 12" wall calendar   *besonders schöne Aufnahmen! 150 Stück bestellen*

Highlights of Asian architecture
12" × 12" wall calendar
Romance of the old Silk Road

ungewöhnliche Ansichten! 100 Stück bestellen

Qualex Stationery
1783 Manatee Creek
San Sebastian, CA 94901
mg@qualexstationery...com
www.qualexstationery...com

Special rates for orders of 200 + items

an Matt Granger adressieren
auf sofortige Lieferung per Luftpost drängen
an „special rates" für Bestellungen von mehr als 200 Stück erinnern!
Zahlung, wie üblich, per Banktransfer bei Erhalt der Rechnung
um kurze Auftragsbestätigung bitten
E-Mail in meinem Namen an Matt Granger senden: mg@qualexstationery...com

P **3**
KMK Sie arbeiten bei GAIA, Chemnitzer Str. 189, 10405 Berlin, import@gaia....de im Einkauf. Ihre Chefin, Annabel Frahsa, hat am 5.September von der schottischen Bee Farmers' Association in Stirling (29 Alloa Rd, Stirling, FK18 6TR, Great Britain, sales@sbfa....co.uk) ein Angebot über naturreinen Hochland Heidehonig* erhalten. Der Ansprechpartner ist Ian Bradshaw. Wählen Sie Aufgabe a, b oder c.

○ a. Das Angebot enthält keine Angaben zum Mengenrabatt bei einer Abnahme von mehr als 1.000 Gläsern. Ihre Chefin bittet Sie eine kurze E-Mail nach Stirling zu schicken und um die nötige Information zu bitten. Machen Sie den Empfänger darauf aufmerksam, dass Sie möglichst schnell eine Antwort benötigen. Heute ist der 06.09.

◐ b. Das Angebot enthält keine Angaben zum Mengenrabatt bei einer Abnahme von mehr als 1.000 Gläsern. Ihre Chefin bittet Sie eine kurze E-Mail nach Stirling zu schicken und um die nötige Information zu bitten. Fragen Sie auch nach, ob garantiert werden kann, dass die Produkte 100 % biologisch sind, da GAIA nur Naturprodukte verkauft. Machen Sie den Empfänger darauf aufmerksam, dass Sie möglichst schnell eine Antwort benötigen. Heute ist der 06.09.

● c. Ihre Chefin bittet Sie, das Auftragsschreiben, das sie selbst unterschreiben wird, zu verfassen und dabei folgende Punkte zu berücksichtigen:

- Datum 10. September
- Betreff
- Dank für Angebot vom 5. September
- Bestellung: je 600 Gläser Heidehonig*, 435g und 225g
- Preis: € 3,25 (435 g) und € 2,50 (225 g)
- Mengenrabatt: 10 %
- Lieferungsbedingung: DAP Chemnitzer Str. 189, 10405 Berlin, Germany, Incoterms 2010
- Zahlung: bei Erhalt der Ware per Banküberweisung auf das Konto bei der Strathclyde Bank
- Bitte um strikte Einhaltung der versprochenen Lieferfrist von 2 Wochen.
- Bestellung wird auf Grund unserer beiliegenden allgemeinen Geschäftsbedingungen erteilt.
- Anlage: Geschäftsbedingungen

*heather honey

B | Orders by phone

The Lion and Lobster Catering Company in the City of London has received an enquiry from a German professional association in London to supply a range of German specialities for an annual event. Your boss asks his PA Andrea Smith to email International Snacks GmbH in Düsseldorf (info@ internationalsnacksgmbh....de)

R/P **1**   Choose task a, b or c.

○   a.   Take the role of Andrea Smith and write an email to International Snacks GmbH in Düsseldorf Germany asking them to send an order form and a list of their products asap by email (catering@lionandlobster....com).

◖   b.   Meanwhile International Snacks have sent their order form and list of specialities. Her boss asks Andrea to ring the German company and place an order. Listen to their conversation, then answer the following questions.

⊙ A2.6

    1.   Who are Lion and Lobster Catering organising an event for?
    2.   What is the event?
    3.   What kind of meal are they planning to serve?
    4.   How many people are they catering for?
    5.   What sort of specialities does the customer want?
    6.   How much does Niko propose to charge per head?
    7.   What does this include?
    8.   What special requirements does Andrea feel they should cater for?
    9.   What kind of wines does Niko suggest?
  10.   Why would it be best to send the articles ordered by airfreight?

●   c.   Hören Sie das Gespräch und schreiben Sie als Niko Dahlke die im Telefonat mit Andrea Smith angekündigte E-Mail als Auftragsbestätigung mit Versandanzeige. Kopieren Sie vorher das Bestellformular und kreuzen Sie die bestellten Gerichte an. Notieren Sie ggf. auch Sonderwünsche und Mengenangaben. Sie hören das Telefonat zweimal.

⊙ A2.6

From: nm@internationalsnacksgmbh....de
To: catering@lionandlobster....com
Subject: Auftrag-Nr. 357G vom 10. Juni 201_

Sie bestätigen den Auftrag: Kaltes Buffet „Deutsche Spezialitäten" für 60 Personen mit einer Auswahl deutscher Qualitätsweine zum Preis von 25€ pro Person: Gesamtpreis 1.500,00€ (Luftfrachtkosten inbegriffen). Sie haben inzwischen folgende Einzelheiten zum Versand geklärt:
Versand per Luftfracht durch Spedition Fuhrmann und Söhne, Düsseldorf
Flug-Nr. PH 3954, Abflug: Flughafen Düsseldorf, 13:50 Uhr deutsche Zeit
Ankunft: London City Airport, Freight Terminal, 13:20 Uhr britische Zeit

---

Bestellformular		
Portionen	Code-Nr.	Artikel
	PSF 135	Schwäbischer Wurstsalat
	PSF 136	Schinkenröllchen mit Spargel
	PSF 137	Salami-Aufschnitt auf Roggentaler
	PSF 138	Kartoffelsalat mit kleinen Frankfurter Würstchen und Mini-Frikadellen
	PSG 235	Salat Nicoise mit Anchovies
	PSM 311	Räucherlachs auf Pumpernickel mit Meerrettich
	PSM 312	Weißer Spargel mit Sauce Hollandaise
	PSM 313	Bismarckhering, gerollt mit Gürkchen
	PSM 315	Früchtequark
	PSD 408	Rote Grütze mit Vanillecreme
Transportart:		
Liefertag und -zeitpunkt:		
Lieferort:	Rechnung an:	

I **2** Work with a partner and act out the following telephone conversation. Then change roles.

A	B

A

Sie sind Kirsten/Kevin Böttger und arbeiten bei Heim & Bau in Bremerhaven. Sie hatten ihren schwedischen Lieferanten Isfisk gestern in einer E-Mail gebeten, einen Auftrag über 500 Robotersauger, Modell X33, eine Woche früher auszuliefern.

B

You are Birte/Björn Staargard from Isfisk Elektronik in Malmö, Sweden. Yesterday you received a message from a German customer, Heim & Bau, Bremerhaven, requesting you to bring delivery of their order for 500 robot *vacuum cleaners* forward by one week. You ring them up. Begin the conversation with a few friendly remarks e.g. asking how the person *taking the call* is doing.

Sie nehmen den Anruf entgegen. Reagieren Sie angemessen auf die Frage, wie es Ihnen geht.

Refer to yesterday's email and tell your partner that you *regret* that it is absolutely impossible to *dispatch* this *particular* model earlier.

Drücken Sie Ihre Enttäuschung aus und erklären Sie, dass Sie wegen der Robotik-Messe, die nächste Woche in Bremen eröffnet wird, eine starke Nachfrage nach dem Modell erwarten.

Suggest that you send a *substitute*, model X34, which is very similar to the X33.

Fragen Sie nach dem Preis des Alternativmodells.

Tell your partner that you are sorry to inform them that the price per item is €20 higher than the model originally ordered as it has an improved battery life.

Machen Sie Ihrem Gesprächspartner klar, dass Sie nicht in der Lage sind so viel zu bezahlen.

To accommodate the customer offer a 2.5% introductory offer on this particular order.

Zeigen Sie sich erfreut über dieses Entgegenkommen und fragen Sie, wann die 500 Robotersauger abgeschickt werden können.

Reply that the consignment will be handed over to the *forwarders* tomorrow morning and should reach the customer the day after tomorrow.

Danken Sie Ihrem Gesprächspartner für seine Bemühungen und beenden Sie das Gespräch.

Close the call.

LANGUAGE AND GRAMMAR

USE OF CAPITAL LETTERS

Geographische Eigennamen werden großgeschrieben.

We have customers in **New South Wales** in Australia.	Wir haben Kunden in New South Wales in Australien.

Im Gegensatz zum Deutschen werden im Englischen auch geographische Adjektive großgeschrieben.

Our **British** and **Italian** subsidiaries are expanding rapidly.	Unsere britischen und italienischen Tochtergesellschaften expandieren rasant.

Wochentage, Monate und Feiertage werden großgeschrieben.

The meeting will be held next **Friday** / in **September** / before **Christmas**.	Das Treffen wird nächsten Freitag / im September / vor Weihnachten stattfinden.

Vorangestellte Titel, die Teil des Namens bilden, schreibt man groß.

The report was presented by **Vice-President** Charles Amory.	Der Bericht wurde vom Vizepräsidenten Charles Amory präsentiert.

Nachgestellte Titel werden meist kleingeschrieben.

James Critchley, **chairman** of Mediatiq, announced his resignation.	James Critchley, Vorstand der Mediatiq, hat seinen Rücktritt angekündigt.

Die Namen von Ministerien, Behörden etc. werden großgeschrieben.

Revenue and Customs	Finanzamt
Foreign Office	Außenministerium
European Commission	Europäische Kommission

Bei Überschriften und Schlagzeilen wird meistens nur das erste Wort großgeschrieben.

Report on the US economy in the first quarter **Chancellor** meets Turkish prime minister for discussions	Bericht zur US-Wirtschaft im ersten Quartal Die Kanzlerin / Der Kanzler trifft den türkischen Ministerpräsidenten / die türkische Ministerpräsidentin zu Gesprächen

TASK:

3 Rewrite the following text using capital letters where necessary.

the european economic community was founded in 1957 by the treaties of rome. the signatories were france, germany, italy, belgium, holland, and luxembourg. british governments were in favour of european integration but were originally not interested in joining. the first british applications for membership were unsuccessful due to french opposition. denmark, ireland and britain finally joined in 1973 after the resignation of the french president, general de gaulle, bringing the total number of member states to nine. this initiated a development in which more and more european countries applied to join. first elections to the european parliament took place in 1979. the maastricht treaty signed in 1992 by the then twelve member states brought into being the european union.

Office expert

C | Ordering over the phone

Despite the widespread introduction of high-speed internet connection and mobile email devices, the telephone remains a vital part of business communication. With advancements in both hardware and telecommunications, conversations can be had wherever you are.

P 1 Why do you think the telephone is still an important tool for business communication even though the internet and email are widely available? Work with a partner and make a list of pros and cons for telephoning and emails, giving examples of when you would use them.

R 2 Listen to the conversation between Peaks Ltd., a wholesaler for outdoor
⊙ A3.21 equipment, in Cardiff and Outdoor Welt in Stuttgart. Note down the missing parts of the conversation on a separate sheet of paper.

Ebru: Outdoor Welt, Özalan. Was kann ich für Sie tun?

Diane: Good morning. My name is Diane Riley, calling from Peaks Ltd. in Cardiff. Do you 1 ?

Ebru: Yes, of course Ms Riley. My name is Ebru Özalan. How can I help?

Diane: I'd like to 2 , please.

Ebru: Certainly, Ms Riley. Could I have your 3 ?

Diane: Yes, it's P2807UK.

Ebru: Thank you, Ms Riley. Could I have the first 4 , please?

Diane: Yes, it's AE 332.

Ebru: OK, that's the Arctic Explorer sleeping bag.

Diane: That's right. 12 please, in green. Then, article number 5 , the Gipfel 3000 tent. 36, please.

Ebru: Is that the two-man or the four-man version?

Diane: Oh yes, of course. The two-man version, please.

Ebru: OK, 6 ?

Diane: Yes, article number MT 003, the men's 7 , 20 pairs. Article number FCG 061, the climbing gloves, 16 pairs. Article number CT 821, the foldable table and chairs, two 8 and four in orange. And finally, 24 of article number 9 , the Junior rucksack, eight each in the colours red and green. Thanks.

Ebru: Let me 10 . Article number AE 332, 12 items, article GU 228, 36 items, article MT 003, 20 pairs, 11 of article FCG 061. OK, then we have article CT 821, two in green and four in orange, and 24 of article JR 559 – eight in red and eight in green.

Diane: Yes, that's correct. What is the 12 ?

Ebru: The total is € 4.266,89 plus € 78,50 13 .

Diane: OK, and when can I 14 ?

Ebru: Your order will be 15 in two to three working days, Ms Riley.

Diane: OK, that's fine. Thank you for your help. Goodbye.

Ebru: 16 . Goodbye.

KMK Exam Training

1 Mediation (Englisch – Deutsch)

Stufe II Ihre Chefin plant eine Geschäftsreise nach Japan und will gut vorbereitet sein. Sie finden folgende Hinweise zur Visitenkartenetikette in Japan im Internet. Erklären Sie Ihrer Chefin die Hinweise auf Deutsch.

Tips for Using Business Cards in Japan

- In Japan business cards are called meishi (may-shi) and are essential for establishing business as well as personal contacts.
- If you plan a visit to Japan consider having new cards made with one side printed in Japanese. Printing cards nowadays is so inexpensive and it's well worth the effort.
- When handing someone your card present it with the Japanese side face up.
- Present and receive business cards with both hands as a sign of respect.
- Don't forget to bow and introduce yourself after presenting your card. Say your name, company and title.
- When someone hands you their card it is important to look at it for a moment before putting it carefully away in a case, for example, – don't just stuff it in your pocket.
- Rank is important in Japan so have any titles printed prominently.
- You should also present your card to the highest ranking person first.
- Don't play with, fold or write anything on another person's business card.

2 Interaktion

Stufe II Führen Sie in Partnerarbeit mithilfe der Rollenkarten einen Dialog.

→ **ROLE CARD B:** page 261

Role card A

Sie besuchen die Messe *Office Expo* in Manchester und führen dort ein Gespräch mit einem Vertreter / einer Vertreterin von *Better Business Cards*.
- Stellen Sie sich vor und bekunden Sie Interesse am Kauf von Visitenkarten.
- Erkundigen Sie sich, ob die Karten mit der Farbe und dem Logo Ihrer Firma versehen werden können.
- Fragen Sie, ob die Karten zweisprachig (Deutsch / Englisch) bedruckt werden können und welche Papierqualitäten zur Auswahl stehen.
- Erkundigen Sie sich nach möglichen Rabatten.
- Fragen Sie nach den Zahlungs- und Lieferbedingungen.
- Bedanken Sie sich für das Gespräch und verabschieden Sie sich.

Phrases: Orders

To refer to previous contacts and place an order	
We have studied your quotation and enclose Purchase Order No. ...	Wir haben Ihr Angebot genau durchgesehen und fügen unsere Bestellung Nr. ... bei.
Please supply the following items **on** the terms stated below:	Bitte liefern Sie uns folgende Positionen zu den unten genannten Bedingungen:

To confirm prices and discounts	
We would like to order model AC **at** the price of € ... less 5% introductory discount.	Wir möchten Modell AC zum Preis von € ..., abzüglich 5% Einführungsrabatt, bestellen.
We would like to confirm that the prices are taken **from** your price list **of** 1 September.	Wir möchten bestätigen, dass die Preise Ihrer Preisliste vom 1. September entnommen sind.

To confirm the method of payment and the terms of delivery and the delivery time	
As agreed, we will effect payment **by** bank transfer 30 days **from** date of invoice.	Wie vereinbart werden wir die Zahlung 30 Tage nach Rechnungsdatum per Banküberweisung vornehmen lassen.
Payment will be made **by** irrevocable and confirmed letter of credit.	Die Zahlung erfolgt durch unwiderrufliches und bestätigtes Akkreditiv.
Your above-mentioned prices are quoted CIF Hamburg.	Ihre oben genannten Preise verstehen sich CIF Hamburg.
Delivery **is to** be made DAP Stuttgart.	Die Lieferung soll DAP Stuttgart erfolgen.
Complete delivery **by** ... is a firm condition of this order.	Vollständige Lieferung bis ... stellt eine feste Bedingung für diesen Auftrag dar.
Please note that the goods must reach us **by** 1 March at the latest.	Wir weisen darauf hin, dass die Ware bis spätestens 1. März hier eintreffen muss.

To give instructions and ask for confirmation	
Please arrange for transportation **by** Eurotrans Ltd.	Bitte veranlassen Sie, dass der Transport von Eurotrans Ltd. durchgeführt wird.
Please make sure that the figurines are packed with the utmost care.	Bitte sorgen Sie dafür, dass die Figürchen äußerst sorgfältig verpackt werden.
Please acknowledge this order promptly.	Bitte bestätigen Sie diesen Auftrag umgehend.

To close the correspondence	
We look forward to receiving the goods and to doing further business with you.	Wir sehen dem Eintreffen der Ware entgegen und freuen uns auf weitere Geschäfte mit Ihnen.

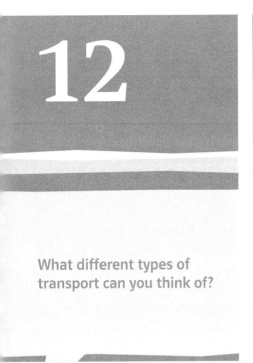

12

What different types of transport can you think of?

Transport and logistics

As a sector transport and logistics is of fundamental importance to the economy and both national and international trade. The sector includes freight logistics, freight and passenger transport systems and transport planning and management. Freight logistics is considered to have a significant impact on a manufacturing company's performance. Some large companies run their own logistics operations while most outsource these functions to logistics service providers, also known as freight forwarders, who generally offer multiple services under one umbrella including land transportation, warehousing, sea and airfreight, dealing with export formalities and documentation. One of the biggest and most far-reaching innovations of the last few decades has been the growth of containerisation. Today, more than 90 % of non-bulk cargo is transported in standardised containers which can be loaded on to ships, goods trains and lorries.

WORD BANK

- *to acknowledge*
- *bill of lading*
- *cargo*
- *certificate of origin*
- *to confirm*
- *consignment note*
- *to deliver*
- *dispatch advice*
- *door-to-door delivery*
- *forwarding*
- *freight*
- *insurance policy / certificate*
- *logistics*
- *modes of transport*
- *to pack*
- *packing list*
- *to send*
- *to ship*
- *shipping*
- *to transport*
- *transport*
- *types of packing*
- *waybill*
- *to wrap*

1 Using the internet research the 5 biggest logistics providers worldwide.

⊕

2 What percentage of goods is transported a) by road b) by rail c) by air within the EU?

3 What are the main inland waterways in Germany, France and Austria?

4 How does containerisation facilitate the transportation of goods? (Use the internet for inspiration if necessary.)

A | Modes of transport

Andrew Bell from the trade journal "Transport and Logistics Today" interviews the journalist Samantha Forrester on the various modes of transport and recent developments in logistics.

1
⊙ A2.7   Listen to the interview twice and complete the grid below on a separate sheet of paper. Then add whatever advantages, disadvantages and suitable cargoes you can think of. Compare notes with your neighbour.

	Road	Rail	Air	Sea/Inland Waterways
Advantages	door-to-door delivery; flexible timetables			
Disadvantages		goods must be transported to and collected from the station		slow; seaworthy packing required
Suitable cargoes			light, urgently required, perishable or valuable goods	

2   Work in groups. Choose one of the goods mentioned below and decide which mode of transport you would use. Give reasons for your choice. Use the expressions in the bubbles below.

Example: I'd send the office furniture from Aachen to Antwerp by road because door-to-door delivery is the easiest option in this case and faster than road/rail/road.

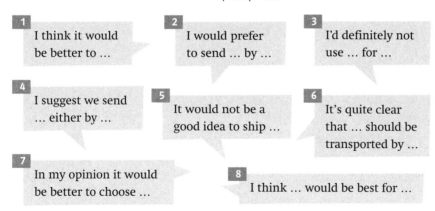

1 I think it would be better to …

2 I would prefer to send … by …

3 I'd definitely not use … for …

4 I suggest we send … either by …

5 It would not be a good idea to ship …

6 It's quite clear that … should be transported by …

7 In my opinion it would be better to choose …

8 I think … would be best for …

- Urgent medical supplies from London to Athens
- Bottled olive oil from Italy to the UK
- Smart phones from Hong Kong to Hamburg
- A bulky generator from Bochum to Saudi Arabia
- Orchids from Brazil to Denmark
- Designer handbags from Milan to Paris
- A consignment of gravel from Belgium to Switzerland
- Steel girders from Newcastle to Morocco
- A consignment of cars from Stuttgart to Buenos Aires (Argentina)

B | Packing

Adequate packing is essential to ensure that goods arrive in perfect condition, regardless of the distance they have travelled.

1 Match the German terms (see photos above) with their English equivalents.

1. Eisenfass, Trommel	a. bale
2. Holzkiste	b. bundle with steel strapping
3. Fass	c. coil on euro-pallet
4. folienumwickelter Karton	d. container
5. Rolle, Coil auf Europalette	e. crate
6. Kunststoffbox mit Formeinlagen	f. drum
7. Container	g. foil-wrapped cardboard box
8. Ballen	h. plastic box with mouldings
9. Bündel mit Stahlbandumreifung	i. one-way pallet
10. Lattenkiste, -verschlag	j. sack
11. Einwegpalette	k. wooden case
12. Sack	l. barrel

R/P **2** The following sentences do not make much sense. Rearrange the words to form meaningful sentences.

1. The fruit will be packed in 15 bundles with steel strapping.
2. The pure new wool will be sent in a crate.
3. The steel rods will be shipped in bales.
4. The replacement Mp3 player will come on a reusable pallet.
5. The printing machine will be packed in a cardboard box.
6. The engine will be sent in a plastic gift box with mouldings.

C | Dispatch advice

As soon as the goods are ready for dispatch it may be necessary to let the customer know that they can either be collected at the seller's premises or that they have been handed over to the carrier. This depends on the Incoterms agreed upon in the sales contract. Always bear in mind that you are dealing with a customer and be as polite and helpful as possible.

1 Maybaum Motoren has received an order for 200 outboard engines from the Irish company Atlantic Yachting in Spanish Point. Christine Metzinger, head of sales at Maybaum, informs Ian Dorking that the goods have now been shipped to the Republic of Ireland. Complete Christine's email using the verbs from the box.

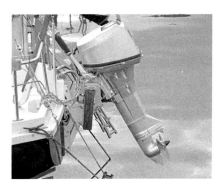

accompanied · arrive · attached · serving · delivered · given · packed · picked up · pleased · reach

---

From: christine.metzinger@maybaum... .de
To: ian.dorking@atlanticyachting... .ie
Cc:
Sent: 14-08-201_
Attachments: invoice No. 298/01/IR
Subject: your order No. 667 D dated 7 AUG for 200 outboard engines

Good morning Mr Dorking

We are **1** to inform you that the consignment has today been **2** by our hauliers, Frans ten Bosch, to be **3** by road to your warehouse in Spanish Point, County Clare.
The forwarders have **4** us the assurance that the goods will **5** you by Thursday afternoon, 16 Aug, at the latest.

The outboard engines are **6** in 20 crates on two pallets.
The consignment is **7** by the required documents (consignment note, packing list and commercial invoice). A copy of the invoice is **8** .

Thank you once again for you order. We are confident that the goods will **9** safely and in good time.
We look forward to **10** you again soon.

Kind regards

Christine Metzinger
Maybaum Motoren
Niederrhein-Park C34
46446 Emmerich
Tel +49 28 22 87 79 56 3...

P **2** Ms Hiruni Heladveepa, export manager at Lanka Garments, has been processing an order for tennis shoes from the German firm Krokodil. She now sends them a dispatch advice. Write her email using the following prompts:

- reference to their order of 20 January and their letter of 1 February
- consignment packed in one 20 ft container
- markings on the container KKL, 896B, Antwerp
- loaded yesterday on board the container ship Colombo in the port of Hambantota
- expected time of arrival at Antwerp: on or about 12 March
- polite closing phrase

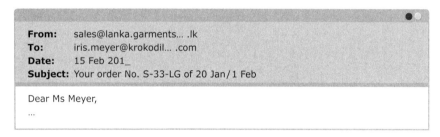

> **From:** sales@lanka.garments... .lk
> **To:** iris.meyer@krokodil... .com
> **Date:** 15 Feb 201_
> **Subject:** Your order No. S-33-LG of 20 Jan / 1 Feb
>
> Dear Ms Meyer,
> ...

P **3**
KMK Sie (eigener Name) arbeiten bei der Fürther Firma Fächter & Suhr (E-Mail: exports@f-s... .de). Ein norwegischer Kunde, Ole Gunnarson, Einkäufer bei der Warenhauskette Storgard (E-Mail: ole.g@storgard... .com), hatte bei Ihnen eine Sendung Spur-N (N-gauge) Modelllokomotiven bestellt, die dringend für die Eröffnung der ‚Weihnachtswelt' in den Häusern in Oslo und Bergen benötigt werden.
Wählen Sie Aufgabe a, b oder c.

○ a. Schreiben Sie eine kurze E-Mail, in der Sie mitteilen, dass die bestellte Ware abgeschickt worden ist und am 22.10. an die Firmenadresse von Storgard weitergeleitet wird.

◑ b. Schreiben Sie eine E-Mail als Versandanzeige und berücksichtigen Sie dabei Folgendes:

- Bezug auf den Auftrag vom 18. Oktober
- Sendung heute der Spedition Holzmann zum Transport per Luftfracht übergeben
- Scandair Flug Nr. SR 968
- Abflug: Flughafen Frankfurt, 22 Oktober, 11:35 Uhr
- Ankunft: Flughafen Oslo, 12:55 Uhr
- Sendung wird automatisch von Holzmann an Firmenadresse zugestellt

● c. Schreiben Sie eine E-Mail als Versandanzeige und berücksichtigen Sie dabei Folgendes:

- Bezug auf den Auftrag vom 18. Oktober
- Sendung heute der Spedition Holzmann zum Transport per Luftfracht übergeben
- Scandair Flug Nr. SR 968
- Abflug: Flughafen Frankfurt, 22 Oktober, 11:35 Uhr
- Ankunft: Flughafen Oslo, 12:55 Uhr

- Sendung wird automatisch von Holzmann an Firmenadresse zugestellt
- Erwartung, dass Ware rechtzeitig für die Arbeiten an „Weihnachtswelt" eintreffen
- Nochmaliger Dank für den Auftrag
- Hoffnung auf weitere Aufträge

D | Order confirmation and inquiry by phone concerning transport

R **1** Daniel Friedel from Kandesca Designs GmbH has received an order from
⊙ A2.8 a British customer. He confirms the order and transport arrangements by phone. Listen to the dialogue and answer the following questions.

1. What is the name of Miranda Cooke's firm?
2. Have Daniel and Miranda spoken before?
3. How and when did Miranda place the order?
4. When is the order expected to arrive?
5. What does Miranda expect to come with the consignment?
6. How does she expect their loyalty as a customer to be honoured?

2 Christine Metzinger from Maybaum Motoren in Emmerich had promised Ian Dorking from Atlantic Yachting in Spanish Point, Republic of Ireland, that the outboard engines he had ordered would arrive by Thursday afternoon, 16 August, at the latest. It is now Friday morning, 9pm GMT, and the lorry has not yet arrived. Ian Dorking rings Christine Metzinger.
Act out their dialogue in pairs using the prompts below.

Christine Metzinger: Ian Dorking:

Maybaum Motoren, Metzinger

Ian Dorking, Atlantic Yachting/outboard engines/not yet arrived/now Friday 17/9am

Try to reach driver on his mobile/hold line?/ring back?

hold/urgent

Spoken to driver/on his way to Spanish Point/35 km away/reason for delay/held up in Calais/security issue at entrance to Channel Tunnel/several shuttles cancelled

here next half hour?

driver confident/arrive by 10am

glad to hear/thanks

sorry for inconvenience

email as soon as goods arrive/good weekend/bye

too/bye

E | Documents in foreign trade

Waybills, also called **consignment notes, (Frachtbriefe)** are used in road, rail or air transport. They are contracts between the sender of the goods and the carrier (Frachtführer) and provide detailed information about the consignment and the transportation.

The **Bill of Lading** (B/L) **(Konnossement)** is the freight document in sea transport and when the transportation involves several modes of transport. It is a document of title (Eigentumsurkunde) , which means that any lawful holder of the B/L is the rightful owner of the goods. Bills of Lading must be **clean (rein)**, that is to say the carrier (e.g. the captain of the ship) must have signed the B/L **without** making a note on it that the consignment shows signs of a defect or damage from the outside.

A **Certificate of Origin (Ursprungszeugnis)** shows the country of origin of the goods or the country where they were mainly produced. There is a common EU Certificate of Origin. Certificates of Origin are usually legalized by a chamber of commerce.

The **Packing List (Packliste)** is a detailed statement of the goods supplied in a particular consignment.

Commercial Invoice (Handelsrechnung) and Proforma Invoice (Proforma-Rechnung) see Unit 13.

Insurance Policy / Certificate (Versicherungspolice /-schein)
Export documents are available as standard paper forms. Nowadays, however, such documents are almost exclusively created by computer software and forwarded via the internet.

R **1** Compare the translation with the above text on the Bill of Lading and find the missing words from the box.

> Beschädigung · Eigentümer · Kapitän · Seetransport · Sendung

Das Konnossement (B/L) ist das Frachtpapier für den **1** und für Transporte, bei denen mehrere Transportarten zum Einsatz kommen. Es ist eine Eigentumsurkunde, d. h. jeder rechtmäßige Inhaber der B/L ist rechtmäßiger **2** der Ware. Konnossemente müssen rein sein, das heißt, der Frachtführer (z. B. der **3** des Schiffes) muss die B/L unterschrieben haben, ohne einen Vermerk anzubringen, der besagt, dass die **4** äußerlich Zeichen eines Mangels oder einer **5** aufweist.

INFO: Insurance Policy / Certificate

Exports shipments are usually insured **"against all risks"**, which covers a wide range of risks, from sinking to theft. The contract between the sender and the insurance company is called a **policy**. Whenever an open policy, covering a certain lump sum or valid for a certain period, has been taken out, the insurance company issues an insurance **certificate** for an individual shipment. The **premium** is the sum payable by the insured to the insurance company at regular intervals.

Office expert

F | Just in time

R **1** Read the text and answer the questions below.

What is JIT?

JIT stands for just-in-time and is a strategy to make companies more efficient. With just-in-time delivery goods are supplied just when,
5 not before or after, they are actually needed. What is the advantage? Previously, businesses had to keep a large stock of goods, i.e. high inventories, available at all times. Warehousing costs money, though, and ties
10 up resources. In addition, retailers run the risk of overestimating sales and piling up inventory they have to sell at reduced prices. Underestimating sales, though, results in
15 empty shelves and frustrated customers. For manufacturers there is the danger of running out of required supplies, bringing production to a halt: the finished products cannot be delivered as promised.
20 The challenge in JIT is to accurately predict what goods and supplies will be needed exactly when. This calls for a continuous and accurate monitoring of product demand. One method to achieve this is "Kanban" which
25 means signboard or billboard in Japanese. It is a scheduling and inventory system which signals when the next part or product is needed. Electronic systems also help support JIT
30 inventory management. They enable business to monitor inventory and to react

quickly to demands. Some systems are so good that the product is not even made before the customer actually buys it. This
35 has the added advantage of customers being able to tailor their product requirements, i.e. choose a particular color or special feature in a new car, for example.
Are there any drawbacks? Aside from the
40 need for constant monitoring, some take a negative view of the increased volume of traffic the smooth running of JIT delivery requires. A train of trucks oscillating back and forth from supplier to customer, they
45 claim, have simply taken over the function of warehouses.

1. What is JIT?
2. What is meant by high inventories?
3. How can retailers profit from JIT?
4. How can manufacturers profit from JIT?
5. What is the biggest problem in connection with JIT?
6. What is Kanban?
7. Aside from saving costs, what is a side benefit of JIT?
8. Why do some critics view JIT negatively?

KMK Exam Training

→ **VOCABULARY**
Cabinet Office – Büro des Premier-
   ministers
burgeoning – wachsend, aufkeimend
blip – Bildmarke, kurzer Signalton
deluge – Flut
to clog up – verstopfen
to implement – einführen,
   installieren

1 Mediation (Englisch-Deutsch)

Ihr Ausbildungsunternehmen will den Umgang mit E-Mails verbessern.

Stufe III **Im Rahmen Ihrer Recherche zur *Corporate Communication* stoßen Sie auf diesen Artikel, den Sie abschnittsweise auf Deutsch zusammenfassen.**

How to manage your emails efficiently

The average worker misses a third of emails. How can you boost productivity and avoid distractions from correspondence?
5 Before sending that email, consider your e-etiquette: does it need to go at all? A few months ago I read that officials at the Cabinet Office had been ordered not to send internal emails for a day because they'd
10 become "overwhelmed and bombarded" by unnecessary messages. (…) I'm sure this is something every professional can relate to, not least of all those who are running burgeoning small businesses.
15 As someone whose job involves develop- ing new and more efficient ways of communicating in the workplace, it seems crazy to me that the first method that still springs to mind for most is email. (…) While
20 I'm not labelling it as the root of all evil, we all know it can be hard to stay on top of that overflowing inbox and it's easy to ignore other, more efficient ways of communicating and collaborating effectively in the
25 workplace. (…)

The problem with email

Our own research has found that 18 % of employees feel that inefficient communi- cation holds them back, so if you're a
30 company of 10 that's two people who could be missing important information. Just one blip (or missed email) can all too quickly lead to a delay or harm the relationship you have with one of your customers.
35 Sometimes, the number of emails we receive means that we simply can't keep up with what's going on. The average UK worker only deals with 36 emails a day, but still manages to miss one third of those. So it's definitely
40 time to take a step back and think about other ways to get your message across.

Reviewing the alternatives

Is email really the best way to brief someone on a complex and detailed task? More often than not, it's far easier to explain something
45 in person if you can. Face-to-face communi- cation allows you to engage fully with your team and quickly see whether they under- stand what you're asking of them. In today's digital world it's important not to forget how
50 effective seeing people in person can be. Emails are just a small part of the communi- cation process in a business. Think about all the workflows, documents and figures that are involved. Trying to juggle all this within
55 an email chain is just impractical. Using more visual project management tools which integrate emails, Outlook diaries, messaging tools and all the Word, Excel and PowerPoint documents you use on a daily basis is far more
60 effective. It allows you to get past the data deluge, clearly map out tasks for people, spot priorities, avoid obstacles and generally help you work smarter as a team.
Professional social networks are another
65 excellent way to share information, ideas and documents without clogging up people's inboxes. Some of these solutions allow you to set up specific project groups, tag key phrases, message instantly and search
70 back through for relevant information. Some of the companies we work with have implemented these as a way to reduce internal emails with great success.

517 words

© 2014, Guardian News & Media Ltd.

Phrases: Transport and logistics

To give particulars about packing	
The goods are packed in …	Die Ware ist verpackt in …
• polythene bags.	• Plastikbeutel.
• 20 bales weighing 50 kgs per bale.	• 20 Ballen zu je 50 kg.
• one 20 ft container.	• einem 20-Fuß-Container.
• fibreboard boxes with steel bands.	• Hartfaserkisten mit Stahlbändern.
The goods will be shipped …	Die Ware wird versandt …
• **in** sturdy crates.	• in stabilen Lattenkisten.
• **on** reusable pallets.	• auf Mehrwegpaletten.

To say that the goods are ready for collection	
We are pleased to inform you that the keyboards can now be collected **at** our plant in Leeds.	Wir freuen uns Ihnen mitteilen zu können, dass die Keyboards jetzt in unserem Werk in Leeds abgeholt werden können.

To give particulars about the transport	
The consignment has today been handed over to the freight forwarders **for** transportation **to** Warsaw by lorry.	Die Sendung wurde heute der Spedition zur Beförderung nach Warschau per LKW übergeben.
Yesterday the machine was loaded **on board** MS Seagull in Bremerhaven.	Die Maschine wurde gestern in Bremerhaven auf die MS Seagull verladen.
The spare parts will be sent **by** air freight **on** Air Canada flight No. AC 442, arriving **at** Toronto airport at 11:55 **on** 25 September.	Die Ersatzteile werden per Luftfracht mit Air Canada, Flug Nr. AC 442 verschickt. Ankunft: Flughafen Toronto, 25. Sept., 11:55 Uhr.

To close on a friendly note	
We hope the goods will arrive punctually and in good condition.	Wir hoffen, die Ware kommt pünktlich und in gutem Zustand bei Ihnen an.
We trust that the quality of our garments will meet your expectations.	Wir sind überzeugt, dass die Qualität unserer Bekleidungsartikel Ihren Erwartungen entspricht.
We feel sure that your customers will be pleased with our new range of …	Wir sind sicher, dass unser neues Sortiment von … Ihren Kunden gefallen wird.

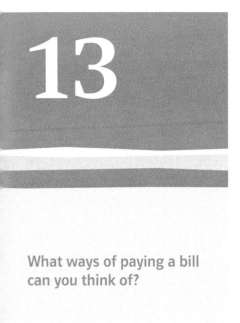

13

What ways of paying a bill can you think of?

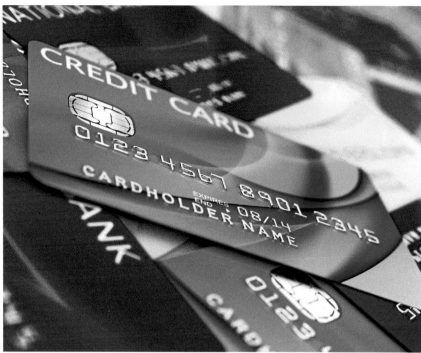

Payment and reminders

Making and receiving payments is a vital part of business. This involves monitoring incoming payments and taking action promptly when an invoice is overdue. In this case the first step is often to telephone the company to check whether an invoice has been overlooked or whether there is some other explanation. However, if the matter cannot be settled by a telephone call, it will be necessary to send written reminders. It is also necessary to ensure that outgoing payments are made promptly.

As Germany trades with many countries outside the Eurozone – the USA and the UK are among its four main export markets, for instance – payments frequently involve foreign currency transfers.

WORD BANK

- *amount due*
- *bank account*
- *BIC*
- *bill of exchange*
- *to break even*
- *cash on delivery*
- *to collect*
- *commercial invoice*
- *commission charges*
- *contactless payment*
- *credit card*
- *currency*
- *debit card*
- *finger print recognition*
- *IBAN*
- *letter of credit*
- *mobile banking*
- *to make out an invoice*
- *open account*
- *open credit*
- *payment in advance*
- *proforma invoice*
- *reminder*
- *settlement*
- *statement of account*
- *subtotal*
- *to take legal steps*
- *to transfer*
- *unit price*

1 Use the internet to answer the following questions.

1. Which is the oldest currency: Euro, Dollar, or Pound Sterling?
2. When was the Dollar introduced?
3. What is the name of the Chinese currency?
4. When was the Euro introduced?
5. Are Euro, Dollar and Sterling exchange rates fixed or floating?
6. What effect does this have on prices of goods and invoices?
7. Which EU countries do not use the Euro?
8. What are the advantages of the euro zone for individuals?

A | The invoice

The **commercial invoice** (Handelsrechnung) is sent by the seller to the buyer and provides full details of the transaction, including names, dates, numbers, descriptions, quantities, prices, discounts, terms, taxes (VAT) etc. When making out an invoice you should ensure that it includes the IBAN and BIC for your company's account.

A **proforma invoice** (Proformarechnung) contains all the details of the subsequent commercial invoice. It may serve as a quotation or be required in the buyer's country to apply for an import licence.

1 What do the abbreviations VAT, IBAN and BIC stand for?

2 Johannes Weisshaupt is processing the trial order for gauge 00 locomotives which his company, Fächter & Suhr, has received from Toytown Ltd, a British chain of scale modelling and toy shops . The necessary arrangements for transportation have been made and Johannes now confirms the order by email and sends the invoice as an attachment.
Study his email and decide which of the tenses is correct.

Dear Mr Gordon,

Thank you very much for your order No. 3980.

We are pleased to inform you that the consignment **1** is picked up / will be picked up by Freightmasters Ltd for transportation to the UK on Tuesday, 12 September. The forwarders **2** have given / had given us the assurance that the goods **3** will be delivered / will have been delivered to your premises in Heathrow on Wednesday, 13 September, between 10 am and 1 pm GMT.

Since this is a first order, we **4** are sending / have been sending you our invoice No GB / 187-9 as an attachment and would appreciate it if you could **5** instructed / instruct your bank at your earliest convenience to remit the sum of € 24,280.00 to our account with Frankenbank. Please see the attached invoice for details.

We **6** are feeling / feel sure that your customers **7** will be pleased / are pleased with our scale models as they combine excellent craftsmanship and love of detail with our usual high technical standards. We look forward to receiving further orders from you in the near future.

Kind regards,

Johannes Weisshaupt
Fächter & Suhr

Fächter & Suhr

Industriepark Mittelfranken
90762 Fürth, Germany
www.f-s….de

USt. ID DE 907 778 026

INVOICE No. GB / 187-9

Your order No. 3980 of 2 September

Toytown Ltd
22 Great South-West Road
Heathrow
TW6 3XS
Great Britain

VAT No. 231 889 032

Customer No. GB 21051

Date: 11 September 20_

for any queries contact:
Ilse Schroeder
Tel +49 911 9 88 29 01…
accounts@f-s….de

Quantity	Item	Product No	Unit Price	Subtotal
100	Mallard	BV-0-12	€ 82.40	€ 8240.00
100	Spirit of the Highlds.	BV-0-18	€ 82.40	€ 8240.00
100	Isambard Brunel	BV-0-27	€ 78.00	€ 7800.00

Total sum payable: € 24,280.00

Tax-exempt intra-EU delivery
Terms of delivery: EXW Fürth
Terms of payment: cash on receipt of invoice
Please credit our account with: Frankenbank AG
                                        Account No. 9035 990 776
                                        BIC: FNBADE TS28
                                        IBAN: DE49 9897 2296 6125 3339 66

3 Choose task a, b or c.

○ a. Study the invoice and find words and expressions for the following German equivalents.

1. zahlbar
2. Stückpreis
3. Zahlungsbedingungen
4. unserem Konto gutschreiben
5. Kundennummer
6. bei Erhalt
7. Menge
8. Zwischensumme
9. bei Rückfragen
10. Artikel

◐ b. Study the invoice and draw up the invoice Christine Metzinger sent Ian Dorking on 14 August. Refer back to the dispatch advice (see Unit 12, C) and use your imagination for any details you want to include.

● c. Study the invoice and draw up an invoice. Refer back to the dispatch advice (see Unit 12, C). Make up details of products / terms of payment and delivery / prices / bank details etc.

B | Means of payment in trade

A **credit card** (Kreditkarte) issued by a major credit card company is widely accepted as a means of payment all over the world. The amount to be paid is advanced by the credit card company and debited to the cardholder's account at a later date.

A **debit (or bank card)** (Bankkarte) is issued by a bank. The account-holder may use it to pay for goods and services in shops without handling cash. It differs from credit cards in that the customer's account is immediately debited with the amount of the transaction. Debit cards can also be used to withdraw money from cashpoints (ATMs). The German EC card is a debit card.

A cheque (Scheck) is a written order to a bank to pay a sum of money to a named person or to the bearer (Überbringer) of the cheque. Crossed cheques (Verrechnungs-schecks) require the sum to be paid into a bank account. In the UK cheques are still widely used in private and business transactions.

A **bill of exchange** (Wechsel) is a written order instructing one person to pay a certain sum of money to a named person on demand or at a specified time in the future. If the exporter wishes payment to be made immediately, he instructs the importer to pay the invoice amount on demand, or "at sight", which means on presentation of the bill of exchange (B / E). If the exporter is prepared to grant the importer credit, he will order him to pay the invoice amount at a specified time in the future, e.g. 60 days after the date of the B / E. It is used nowadays only in foreign trade.

1 Choose task a, b or c.

a. Match the following expressions with their German equivalents.

1.	to debit an account with an amount/to debit an amount to an account	a.	eine Girocard ausstellen
		b.	Kreditkarten akzeptieren
		c.	Kredit gewähren
2.	to advance an amount	d.	einen Betrag vorschießen
3.	to grant credit	e.	Geld abheben
4.	to issue a debit card	f.	einen Betrag einem Konto gutschreiben
5.	to withdraw money		
6.	to credit an amount to an account	g.	ein Konto belasten
7.	to accept credit cards		

b. Match the expressions above with their German equivalents.
Explain the difference between credit cards and debit cards in German.

c. Match the expressions above with their German equivalents.
Explain the difference between the different means and terms of payment according to the text above in German.

C | Payment by plastic cards

R **1** Read this text on the use of credit and debit cards in the UK and then answer the questions that follow.

Credit and debit cards in the UK

The UK accounts for about 30% of all card spending in the EU and 73% of the EU credit card market. At the same time 75% of all spending in the UK retail market was by plastic card. The vast majority of retail outlets in the UK accept cards as a matter of
5 course and many, especially supermarkets, offer cashback. Double-digit annual growth in online retail is also driving the use of credit and debit cards which are essential for online purchases. The introduction of "contactless" payment for purchases up to a certain amount will presumably give a further boost to the use of cards.

10 The introduction of the debit card in 2005 to a large extent ousted the use of cash and cheques revolutionising the way we pay for goods and services. Nevertheless, cheques are still popular with small traders including such professions as plumbers, electricians and painters and decorators as a way of obtaining payment on the
15 spot.

Given the popularity in the UK of credit cards, fears periodically resurface that consumers are losing control of their finances and becoming over-indebted.
Credit card providers argue that they carefully vet credit card
20 applications and that over-indebtedness is a problem in only 4% of households.

1. What factors are seen as boosting the use of plastic cards?
2. Why do some professions prefer to be paid by cheque?
3. Why are banks keen to phase out cheques?
4. What do the credit card companies say they do in order to exclude people who are not creditworthy.
5. What is the downside to the widespread availability of credit cards?

2 Use the internet to find similar statistics on preferred payment methods – cash, debit card, credit card, bank transfer – in Germany.

D | Terms of payment in foreign trade

The terms of payment chosen in an international transaction will depend on the size of the order, the creditworthiness of the customer and the banking system and political situation in the customer's country.

Payment in advance (Vorauszahlung) provides maximum security for the seller, e.g. when the goods have to be manufactured to the buyer's specifications. Payment in advance may also be part of staggered payment, e.g. 1/3 with order, 1/3 on delivery, 1/3 30 days after delivery.

If **Cash on delivery (COD)** (Zahlung durch Nachnahme) has been agreed upon, the carrier (e.g. the postman) will hand over the goods to the buyer against payment or against written proof by the bank that payment has been effected.

Open credit (Zahlung gegen einfache Rechnung) terms are terms like "30 days net, 10 days 2 %", which means that the buyer has to remit the invoice amount within 30 days. If he pays the amount within 10 days he will be entitled to deduct 2 % cash discount from the invoice amount. Open credit terms provide little security for the seller but are widely used in transactions involving comparatively small sums and / or trusted customers.

In long-standing business relations it is customary to trade on **open account** terms (offenes Zahlungsziel). This means that the buyer does not pay individual invoices, but waits for the monthly or quarterly statement of account.

A **letter of credit (L / C)** (Akkreditiv) is a promise made by the importer's bank to pay a certain sum to the exporter on presentation of specified documents, the most important of which is a clean bill of lading (see Unit 12). Nowadays L / Cs are irrevocable (unwiderruflich) that means they cannot be revoked without the consent of all parties concerned. As the L / C offers maximum security for both buyer and seller it has become one of the most widely used methods of payment in foreign trade. The exporter can be sure to receive payment as he can rely on the promise made by the importer's bank (the opening bank) – and in the case of a confirmed (bestätigtes) L / C – also on the promise of a bank in his own country (the confirming bank). The importer can be sure to receive the goods as the bank(s) will only advance the money against presentation of the shipping documents which prove that shipment has been effected.

R/M **1** Study the paragraph on the Letter of Credit above and choose the correct prepositions from the box below for the following text. Then translate the text into German.

> at · by · in · until

In a major export transaction the terms of payment may read as follows: Terms of payment: Payment **1** irrevocable and confirmed letter of credit, to be opened **2** our favour, payable **3** a German bank and valid **4** 31 July.

2 Complete the following business transactions by matching the terms of payment from the box with the numbers in the text.

> payment in advance · open account terms · cash on delivery · open credit · letter of credit

Pumpentechnik Hecht GmbH has received an enquiry from a Canadian manufacturer of marine diesel engines who wishes to have 200 high-pressure fuel pumps manufactured to the Canadian firm's specifications. As Hecht would be unable to sell these pumps to another customer if the deal broke down, Hecht will insist on **1** .

Maybaum Motoren made an offer for diesel generators to the Karakul Farming Cooperative in Keetmanshoop, Namibia. The terms of payment stipulated were: net cash within 30 days from receipt of invoice. This is referred to as **2** .

The Giggling Squid, a British party catering firm, usually takes orders online and payment is by credit or debit card. Some customers, however, prefer a different option, where orders are made over the telephone and the amount due is paid to the driver of the delivery van. In this option, the terms of payment are **3** .

GAIA GmbH in Berlin have a long-standing business relationship with a manufacturer of Shetland Wool knitware on the Isle of Skye, Scotland. GAIA decide to order 300 sweaters from the manufacturers new range. These two business partners will probably be doing trade on **4** .

Arthäuser & Brinck, manufacturers of high-quality cookware, have received an enquiry for a substantial order for cast-iron sets from a firm in Brazil they have not yet done business with. The export manager decides to stipulate payment by **5** .

E | Mobile online banking

Caixabank launches mobile-only banking service

Banks are poor at serving "millennials" and must innovate or risk losing their younger customers, the head of the biggest retail lender in Spain said as he launched a new mobile-only service aimed at twentysomethings.

Gonzalo Gortázar, chief executive of Caixabank, told the Financial Times that its launch on Thursday of imaginBank – a cheaper banking service only available through a mobile app or social media – would help it attract more customers aged 18 to 35. "We started a year-and-a-half ago looking at our clients and the way they interact with the bank using their mobiles and we decided that, particularly for millennials, the traditional banking product doesn't correspondent to their needs," he said.

Millennials, (...) born between the early 1980s and early 2000s, are much less likely to visit a bank branch or even to call a helpline than older generations and they are more comfortable doing most of their banking via a mobile app. In response, traditional banks have been closing branches and launching more mobile services to compete with a fast-growing array of digital start-ups. They also face moves into the financial sector by big technology groups such as Apple and Google. Kevin Burrowes, global banking and capital markets leader at PwC, said: "This war for the customer is getting more intense and the big banks are starting to ask: how do we react?" (...)

"This is not replacing, it is additive," said Mr Gortázar. "What we have seen is that many millennials will only deal with us through mobile. This segment of the population is not being offered what they want by banks." (...)

Customers of imaginBank will have access to customer services through a live chat option in the mobile app as well as via social media, such as Twitter and WhatsApp, and a call-centre.

It will offer current accounts, transfers and contactless digital payments without commission charges as well as preapproved personal loans of up to € 15,000 with no arrangement fee. But it will not offer credit cards or mortgages. Caixabank is the main account provider for more than a quarter of Spanish people and has 5,253 branches in the country. Mr Gortázar expects a big chunk of its 2.9 m customers aged between 18 and 35 to switch to the new service.

But after the first year he says more of its new customers will come from rival banks or be opening their first account. (...)

ImaginBank's customers will be insured against electronic fraud for free and be able to use fingerprint recognition to sign into their account. "People love innovation, but when it comes to money they love the security that a large financial institution brings," he said.

"Even for non-millennials, things are changing fast and I find myself doing financial transactions on my mobile that I would not have done a few years ago," he added.

Martin Arnold, Banking Editor   **486 words**

© 2015, Financial Times

R **1** Read the text on the previous page and answer the following questions.

1. Why has Caixa launched imaginbank?
2. Who is it intended to appeal to?
3. Why are traditional banks under pressure to offer a mobile banking service?
4. How will Caixa customers sign into their account?
5. What services will the bank provide?
6. What service will it not offer?
7. How will account holders access customer services?

2 Explain the meaning of the following words used in the text:

1. millennials
2. to launch a service
3. contactless payments
4. transfers
5. commission charges
6. finger print recognition

F | Reminders

Sometimes bills are not paid by the due date. Steps must then be taken to collect the invoice amount. One or several reminders may have to be sent, with the request for payment becoming increasingly insistent. At first a copy of the invoice or statement of account may be enclosed or attached in case the invoice has been overlooked or mislaid. If further reminders by telephone, email or letter fail to produce the desired response, the seller may threaten to charge interest on the amount outstanding or to take legal steps unless payment is received by a specified deadline.

1 On 5 July, Lakeland Inc, an American manufacturer of engines for airboats in Tampa, Florida, placed an order for fuel pumps with Pumpentechnik Hecht GmbH in Cuxhaven. The two companies agreed on payment to be effected 30 days after date of invoice. The goods were shipped by air and were scheduled to arrive at Tampa International Airport on 25 July. It is now 13 September and no communication from Lakeland has been received. Max Grauke, who is in charge of accounts at Hecht, decides to send a first polite reminder by email. Complete Max Grauke's email on the next page using the words from the box.

above · appreciate · aware · dated · due · settle

From: grauke@hecht-pumpen....de
To: ben.snyder@lakeland-tampa....com
Date: 20__-09-13
Re: Our invoice No. 5997-09 **1** July 22 | reference to invoice and due date

Hello Ben:

I just checked our records and noticed that the **2** invoice which was **3** on 21 August has not been settled.

I wonder whether the invoice has been overlooked or if there has been an issue with the order of which we are not **4** ? | request for explanation

I would **5** it if you could doublecheck your files and **6** the account asap. | request for settlement

Hope everything is fine at your end and you have not been affected by hurricane Lousia.

Talk soon, all the best.

Max

Max Grauke
Accounts
Pumpentechnik Hecht GmbH
Cuxhaven, Germany

---

2 Choose task a, b or c.

○ a. Translate the above email into German. Use a dictionary if necessary.

◑ b. You are Ben Snyder, purchasing manager at Lakeland (ben.snyder@ lakeland-tampa....com). You have just received Max Grauke's email. Send Max (grauke@hecht-pumpen....de) an email and include the following elements:

  - thanks for email
  - apologize for the delay in payment
  - reason: new software in accounts department faulty
  - operations now running smoothly
  - bank instructed to remit invoice amount
  - further orders probably next month

● c. Think of a situation that may occur in your company and which may lead to a delay in payment. Write an email – which may or may not be in response to a reminder – and include as many details as necessary. Be apologetic and explain why payment was delayed. End your email with a few polite phrases.

P Sie arbeiten bei der Solarion GmbH München in der Exportabteilung. Ihre Chefin hat gestern nachstehende E-Mail eines lettischen Kunden erhalten. Bitte beantworten Sie die E-Mail und berücksichtigen Sie dabei die handschriftlichen Anweisungen Ihrer Chefin.

An:	raimonds.murniece@terrahanseatica….lv
Von:	nicola.pollnow@solarion….eu
Gesendet:	25-01-20__
Betreff:	Your Invoice No. LV-0502-H

Dear Ms Pollnow

We have received your email of 18 January concerning the above invoice and would like to apologise for the delay in payment.

Today we have instructed our bank to transfer € 28,000 to your account. Much to our regret we will have to ask you to grant us a respite of six weeks for the rest of the invoice amount. *Dank für Überweisung*

You will have been aware of the severe spell of cold weather and snow storms that caused considerable problems throughout the country and led to power cuts.
Our premises were also affected and some of our stock was damaged. Unfortunately, our insurance company will take some time to assess the damage and compensate us. In the meantime, we are having to advance considerable sums for repairs to our electrical system and for the replacement of damaged stock. This is why we must ask you for the extension.
Bedauern über Schäden. Bilder im Internet gesehen

We hope your will understand our difficulties and grant us this respite.
Mit Aufschub grundsätzlich einverstanden

We are very sorry for any inconvenience caused and look forward to your comments.
Dennoch Bitte um Überweisung sobald T.H. dazu in der Lage

Yours sincerely

Raimonds Murniece
Terra Hanseatica
Riga • Latvia

P Sie (eigener Name) arbeiten im Rechnungswesen der Firma Irigio GmbH, Darmstadt (xxx@irigio….de) . Ihre Firma hatte der italienischen Gartencenter-Kette Primaverde in Verona (lado@primaverde….it) Bewässerungssysteme geliefert. Der Rechnungsbetrag hierfür ist seit 6 Wochen überfällig. Eine erste Erinnerung war ohne Reaktion geblieben. Schreiben Sie eine Mahnung unter Berücksichtigung folgender Punkte:

- Datum: 18. Mai
- Ansprechpartner: Giovanni Lado
- Bezug auf Rechnung Nr. 7-1189 vom 25. März
- Verweis auf Ihr Schreiben vom 4. Mai
- Rechnung inzwischen 6 Wochen überfällig
- Frage nach möglichen Gründen, da bisher immer pünktlich gezahlt wurde
- Bitte um umgehende Überweisung des Betrags, sonst Rücknahme der günstigen Zahlungsbedingungen
- umgehende Reaktion erwartet

G | Reminders and replies to reminders by telephone

Lea Haverkamp from Digitalimage GmbH in Magdeburg rings their French customer SARL Publicité La Rochelle, France.

R **1**
⊙ A2.9

Listen to the dialogue and decide whether the following statements are true or false.

1. Frédéric Dupont is the best person to speak to.
2. Amanda Diquero works in accounts.
3. The reference number is AC10 5XY
4. The amount of the invoice is € 7.950
5. The invoice is 4 weeks overdue.
6. For some reason the online transfer was unsuccessful.
7. Amanda is going to transfer the sum immediately.
8. This is the first time there has been a delay in payment.

M **2**
KMK
⊙ A2.9

Sie sind Lea Haverkamp und überwachen bei Digitalimage GmbH in Magdeburg den Zahlungseingang. Sie haben soeben einen französischen Kunden wegen einer überfälligen Rechnung angerufen und das Gespräch aufgezeichnet.

Hören Sie sich das Gespräch noch einmal an und verfassen Sie darüber eine Aktennotiz für die Abteilungsleiterin Frau Nielsen.

MEMO

Für:	
Von:	
Datum:	
Betreff:	

LANGUAGE AND GRAMMAR

HOW TO TRANSLATE THE GERMAN WORD „SOLLEN"

Es gibt mehrere Entsprechungen, je nachdem was mit „sollen" mitgeteilt werden soll.
Die Entsprechung „shall" passt nur bei

a) **Fragen:**

Shall I help you?	Soll ich Dir / Ihnen helfen?

b) **juristischen Texten:**

The parties to this contract **shall** notify the administrator within 24 hours.	Die Vertragsparteien haben den Verwalter innerhalb von 24 Stunden zu benachrichtigen.

„should" bedeutet „sollte", manchmal „muss / müssen"

You **should** bring out this point more clearly.	Sie sollten diesen Punkt deutlicher machen.
Applications **should** reach this office by 21 October, 201_.	Bewerbungen müssen bis zum 21. Oktober 201_ diesem Büro vorliegen.

„ought to" bedeutet „sollte eigentlich"

You really **ought to** apologise for your behaviour (= but I doubt whether you will).	Du solltest dich / Sie sollten sich (eigentlich) für dein / Ihr Verhalten entschuldigen.

„sollen" kann in Fragen mit „do you want me / us to?" übersetzt werden.

Do you want us to return these parts?	Sollen wir diese Teile zurückschicken?

„to be to" ist eine passende Übersetzung für „sollen", wenn es um

a) **eine Anordnung geht:**

You are to report to Frau Meyer immediately.	Sie sollen sich sofort bei Frau Meyer melden.

b) **einen festen Plan geht:**

Building work **is** (scheduled) **to start** on 1 June.	Die Bauarbeiten sollen am 1. Juni anfangen.

Wenn es sich um eine Absicht handelt, wird sollen mit „to be intended to" wiedergegeben:

The increase in prices **is intended to** cover rising costs.	Die Erhöhung der Preise soll die steigenden Kosten decken.

„to be said to" bedeutet „sollen" im Sinne von „es heißt", „man sagt":

The company **is said to** be in difficulty.	Die Firma soll sich in Schwierigkeiten befinden.

„sollen" kann in bestimmten Situationen mit „to be supposed to" übersetzt werden.
Eine skeptische Haltung seitens des Sprechers schwingt immer mit:

We're supposed to be there at five o' clock.	Wir sollen (eigentlich) um 17 Uhr dort sein.
He's supposed to be very intelligent.	Er soll (angeblich) sehr intelligent sein.

Office expert

H | An ATM

1 Choose task a, b or c.

a. Find the English equivalents in the instructions below for the following German terms:

> Einzahlungsbeleg · abheben · Umschlag · Quittung · Öffnung ·
> Geschäftsvorgang · Bargeld · wählen · Bankkarte

b. Put the following instructions (A.–L.) for using an ATM into the correct order.

A. Select a language.
B. Or if you want to deposit money, enter the amount, confirm and then insert the envelope/deposit slip into the slot when the machine opens it.
C. Enter your PIN (Personal Identification Number), then press Enter.
D. Wait while the system processes your transaction.
E. Once you arrive at the bank, insert your ATM card into the machine.
F. If you want to withdraw money, enter the amount, confirm and then put the cash directly into your wallet.
G. First of all, always be alert, especially at night or in an unfamiliar area.
H. Remember to take an envelope and prepare deposits ahead of time.
I. Choose whether you want a receipt by selecting Yes or No.
J. Select a transaction.
K. Use the receipt to record the transaction in your passbook.
L. Choose whether to do an additional transaction.

c. Put the instructions above for using an ATM into the correct order. Then translate the instructions into German.

KMK Exam Training

1 Rezeption: Leseverstehen

Stufe II Lesen Sie den Text über *Village Banking* und entscheiden Sie, ob die folgenden Aussagen richtig sind (T), nicht richtig sind (F) oder anhand des Textes nicht beantwortet werden können (NT).

Village banking

Village banking is a microcredit methodology which means that money lending is organized locally rather than by an established bank. The aim is to help poor people, especially female heads of household in underdeveloped countries, to get credit or small loans.

5 An early innovator of this methodology was John Hatch who worked in Bolivia in the 1980s.. He saw that the lack of funds was keeping the farmers there poor. Traditional banks would not lend them money because they had no collateral. Collateral is property, e.g. a house that the bank is willing to accept as security for a loan but many poor people don't own a house or anything else of value. That is why he established FINCA International, a so-called MFI or 10 microfinance institution for supporting village banks.

How does a village bank work? It is a self-help group of some 20 to 30 people, usually women who have to support their families. Normally, a majority of new members are quite poor with a daily per-capita expenditure of less than $2, sometimes as little as $1. This means, for example, that a mother of four might have just $5 a day to pay for everything she needs for 15 her family: rent , food, clothes, medicine, schooling etc.

The members of a village bank meet weekly to get loans for projects or small businesses, train their skills and support and motivate each other. First loans are usually between $50-$100 and for a period of four months with repayment in 16 weekly installments. Village banks are democratic and self-managing. The members elect their own leaders, decide who 20 can become a member, do their own paperwork and manage all the funds themselves. They also levy fines, i.e. make members pay a penalty if they come late, miss meetings or don't pay back their loans on time.

The main difference between regular banks and village banks is that those wanting a loan don't need collateral. Village banks instead rely on a system of cross-guarantees. That means each 25 member of the village bank ensures the loan of every other member. This leads, of course, to members exerting social pressure on other members to repay their loans in full. The method is surprisingly effective with FINCA having a repayment rate of over 97% worldwide.   388 words

1. Village Banking aims to help people in poor countries , especially women, to save money.
2. The first village bank was established in South America in the 1980s.
3. Banks in Bolivia thought lending money to poor farmers would be risky.
4. FINCA helps poor people all over the world to get loans.
5. You have to be poor with a PCE of less than $2 to be a member of a village bank.
6. Loans from village banks are limited to a maximum of $100.
7. The repayment period for loans from village banks is usually quite short.
8. Members of a village bank are self-governing.

Phrases: Invoices and reminders

To write a first reminder	
We are sending you our invoice No. 43-298 **amounting to** € 304.75 as an attachment.	Als Anhang senden wir Ihnen unsere Rechnung Nr. 43-298 in Höhe von 304,75 €.
The enclosed statement of account shows a balance of € 5,402.90 **in** our favour.	Der beiliegende Kontoauszug weist einen Saldo von 5.402,90 € zu unseren Gunsten auf.
I wonder whether the invoice has been overlooked.	Ich frage mich, ob die Rechnung übersehen wurde.
We should be grateful for an early settlement of the statement of account.	Für einen baldigen Ausgleich unseres Kontoauszugs wären wir dankbar.
If payment has been effected in the meantime, please disregard this email.	Sollte die Zahlung inzwischen erfolgt sein, betrachten Sie diesen Brief bitte als gegenstandslos.

To write a second reminder	
We refer to our letter of 12 May asking you to settle the above invoice in the amount of $ 4445.60.	Wir beziehen uns auf unser Schreiben vom 12. Mai, in dem wir Sie um Begleichung obiger Rechnung in Höhe von 4445,60 $ baten.
The invoice was due on 31 July.	Die Rechnung war am 31. Juli fällig.
The invoice amount is now six weeks overdue.	Der Rechnungsbetrag ist nun sechs Wochen überfällig.
So far you have not given us any explanation for the delay in payment.	Sie haben uns keinerlei Erklärung für den Zahlungsverzug gegeben.
Please remit the amount due immediately.	Bitte überweisen Sie den fälligen Betrag umgehend.
We would ask you to clear the balance without further delay.	Wir möchten Sie bitten, den Saldo unverzüglich auszugleichen.
We should be sorry to lose a long-standing customer and would ask you to contact us immediately.	Wir würden einen langjährigen Kunden nur ungern verlieren, setzen Sie sich deshalb bitte sofort mit uns in Verbindung.

To write a third reminder	
We regret to inform you that we have not received a reply to our requests for payment of 8 July and 13 August.	Wir bedauern Ihnen mitteilen zu müssen, dass wir noch keine Antwort auf unsere Zahlungsaufforderungen vom 8. Juli und 13. August erhalten haben.
We must insist that you make payment **by** 5 April **at the latest**.	Wir müssen darauf bestehen, dass Sie die Zahlung bis spätestens 5. April vornehmen.

Should you fail to meet this deadline we shall have no option **but** to change our terms of payment.	Sollten Sie diese Frist nicht einhalten, bleibt uns keine andere Wahl als unsere Zahlungsbedingungen zu ändern.
If we do not receive payment **by** the end of the week, we will have to stop further deliveries.	Wenn Ihre Zahlung nicht bis Ende der Woche hier eingeht, müssen wir die Belieferung einstellen.
I will have to take legal steps if you do not settle the account within 7 days.	Ich werde juristische Schritte einleiten müssen, falls Sie die Rechnung nicht innerhalb von 7 Tagen begleichen.
Unless you remit the amount in time, we will hand the matter over to a collection agency.	Wenn Sie den Betrag nicht rechtzeitig überweisen, übergeben wir die Angelegenheit einem Inkassounternehmen.

To reply to a reminder	
We have instructed our bank to transfer the sum of €7,455 **to** your account **with** Sachsenbank.	Wir haben unsere Bank angewiesen, den Betrag von 7.455 € auf Ihr Konto bei der Sachsenbank zu überweisen.
We have received your letter **of** 2 July and thank you for your patience.	Wir haben Ihr Schreiben vom 2. Juli erhalten und danken Ihnen für Ihre Geduld.
We assure you that payment will be effected in full as soon as our computers are operational again.	Wir versichern Ihnen, dass die Zahlung in voller Höhe erfolgt, sobald unsere Rechner wieder funktionieren.
We are deeply sorry that the invoice has become overdue.	Es tut uns sehr leid, dass die Rechnung überfällig wurde.
We apologize for the delay **in** payment.	Wir entschuldigen uns für den Zahlungsverzug.
The delay was due to • an oversight. • a breakdown of our computer system. • an error **by** our bank.	Der Grund für den Zahlungsverzug war • ein Versehen. • eine Störung unserer EDV-Anlage. • ein Irrtum unserer Bank.
We are afraid we must ask you **for** an extension of 4 weeks.	Wir müssen Sie leider um einen Aufschub von 4 Wochen bitten.
We suggest that we pay **in** 3 instalments **of** $30,330.	Wir schlagen vor, dass wir in 3 Raten von 30.330 $ zahlen.
We are prepared to pay 7% interest on arrears.	Wir erklären uns bereit, Verzugszinsen in Höhe von 7% zu entrichten.
We hope you will understand our difficult situation and grant us this concession.	Wir hoffen, Sie haben Verständnis für unsere schwierige Lage und machen uns dieses Zugeständnis.

What do you need to take into account when making or dealing with a complaint?

Complaints and adjustments

Things do not always go right in business transactions with the result that it is necessary to make a complaint. It may be about goods or services being supplied late, goods that are faulty or damaged, unsatisfactory services, delivery of the wrong goods or the wrong quantities. In such cases the customer must promptly notify the seller of the problem in writing, especially if a complaint by telephone has not produced the desired result. A complaint should not be written to express anger but to get results. It should be calm and polite but also firm. It is also important to realise that the way a complaint is made differs considerably from culture to culture.

WORD BANK

- *adjustment*
- *complaint*
- *compromise*
- *damaged*
- *defective*
- *discount*
- *explanation*
- *faulty*
- *inconvenience*
- *justified*
- *replacement*
- *solution*
- *substitute*
- *to apologize*
- *to cancel*
- *to complain*
- *to grant*
- *to insist on*
- *to repair*
- *to replace*
- *to return*
- *to take back*
- *too late*
- *transaction*
- *unjustified*
- *wrong*

1 Explain the following words taken from the text in English.

1. faulty
2. unsatisfactory
3. anger
4. firm
5. considerably

M **2** Summarise the above text in German.

3 Why might the way a complaint is made differ from culture to culture? Discuss in class.

A | Making complaints

In your written complaint you should
- give all the necessary details of the transaction (order no, date of delivery, etc.)
- describe the problem clearly (wine different from that ordered, surface of coffee machines badly scratched, etc.)
- stress the inconvenience caused
- suggest a solution (replacement, discount, repair, etc.)
- ask for immediate action.

1 Match the causes for complaint on the left with suggested solutions on the right. Sometimes more than one solution may be appropriate.

1.	delay in delivery	a.	grant a reduction in price
2.	faulty/defective goods	b.	improve the service rendered
3.	goods damaged	c.	send replacements by airfreight
4.	service unsatisfactory	d.	make up the missing quantity
5.	the wrong goods	e.	repair the goods
6.	the wrong quantity	f.	replace the goods
		g.	take the goods back
		h.	take back the surplus goods
		i.	send a credit note

P **2** Describe orally a recent experience when you had reason to complain or actually complained. If you can't think of one use the prompts below.

distance to beach much greater than stated in the advertising material

wasp in glass of orange juice

food served that you hadn't ordered

bank debited your account with wrong amount

delay in crediting a refund for returned purchases to your account

food not hot enough in restaurant

stitching inside new shoes defective

service very slow in a restaurant

botched haircut at hairdresser's

jacket bought online wrong size

B | Complaints in writing

The German chain of leisure fashion, Just Relax GmbH, has just received a consignment of tennis shoes from a supplier in Bangladesh. On inspecting the goods, the company's quality control team found that the consignment includes a large number of defective shoes. Marie Bilker, the purchasing manager, decides to write a complaint by email.

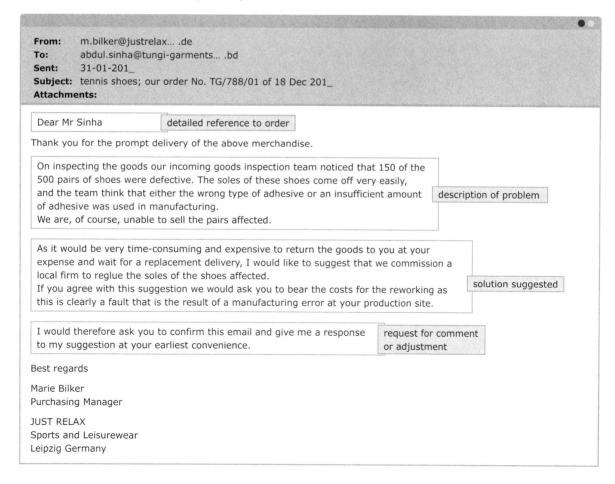

From: m.bilker@justrelax... .de
To: abdul.sinha@tungi-garments... .bd
Sent: 31-01-201_
Subject: tennis shoes; our order No. TG/788/01 of 18 Dec 201_
Attachments:

Dear Mr Sinha   detailed reference to order

Thank you for the prompt delivery of the above merchandise.

On inspecting the goods our incoming goods inspection team noticed that 150 of the 500 pairs of shoes were defective. The soles of these shoes come off very easily, and the team think that either the wrong type of adhesive or an insufficient amount of adhesive was used in manufacturing.
We are, of course, unable to sell the pairs affected.   description of problem

As it would be very time-consuming and expensive to return the goods to you at your expense and wait for a replacement delivery, I would like to suggest that we commission a local firm to reglue the soles of the shoes affected.
If you agree with this suggestion we would ask you to bear the costs for the reworking as this is clearly a fault that is the result of a manufacturing error at your production site.   solution suggested

I would therefore ask you to confirm this email and give me a response to my suggestion at your earliest convenience.   request for comment or adjustment

Best regards

Marie Bilker
Purchasing Manager

JUST RELAX
Sports and Leisurewear
Leipzig Germany

1 Read the email on the previous page carefully (you may need to read it several times), then cover it up and complete the following sentences:

1. Thank you for the **1** delivery of the merchandise.
2. **2** inspecting the merchandise, our goods inward inspection noticed that some of the shoes were **3** .
3. We are unable to sell the pairs **4** .
4. I would like to **5** that we commission a local firm to reglue the soles.
5. If you agree with this suggestion we would ask you to **6** the costs for the reworking.
6. I would ask you to give a comment on my suggestion at your earliest **7** .

P **2** You work in Human Ressources at HSC GmbH (hr@hsc. . . .de), a major supplier to the aviation industry. Your firm has been sending junior executives to a language school in London for several years for intensive coaching in Business English. Although participants have usually been very positive about the experience, this year's group (3 participants) was not entirely satisfied with the services offered. They attended the course from 2 to 10 May 201_. Send an email to the school's principal (trevor.chase@hawthorne. international. . . .co.uk) and mention the following points:

*   new school premises in noisy business park
*   classrooms without adequate noise insulation
*   classrooms overheated
*   participants' needs – language of export procedures – not properly taken into account
*   on last two days class was merged with another student group (5 participants) with different needs

Ask for comments and refund of part of the course fees.
Bear in mind that your company has a long, largely positive, business relationship with the school.

P **3** Think of a situation at the company you work for and write a complaint (email or letter) to a supplier from whom you have received faulty goods / inadequate services. Describe the problem and suggest a solution.

I **4** You have just arrived at the 4-star hotel you booked for a one-week holiday. Unfortunately you discover that next to your hotel another hotel is under construction and the noise from the building site will prevent you from enjoying the hotel pool.
Discuss with your group your options in this situation.

P **5** Think of a situation that you experienced personally as a tourist/ private customer and where you were unhappy with the services/goods provided. Describe the problem and suggest a solution.

Sie sind Lea Bruckner und arbeiten bei der Firma Tangerine Dreams (An der Alster 225, 20099 Hamburg) in der Importabteilung. Ihre Firma bezieht seit 3 Jahren in regelmäßigen Abständen Kosmetikartikel der Firma Goodwood of Chelsea (133 King's Road, London, SW5 7HL, England). In letzter Zeit hat Ihnen dieser Lieferant wiederholt Anlass zur Unzufriedenheit gegeben. Schreiben Sie einen förmlichen Beschwerdebrief an den Geschäftsführer (Robert Clarkson), und führen Sie dabei Folgendes an:

- Datum: 2. September 201_
- anfänglich guter Service, aber seit letztem Jahr Häufung von Problemen:
  - Ware oft nicht vorrätig
  - immer längere Lieferzeiten
  - keine prompte Reaktion auf E-Mails und oft telefonisch nicht erreichbar
  - 2 Lieferungen mit falscher Menge innerhalb von 8 Monaten
- heutige Lieferung mit falscher Ware (200×125 ml Aftershave Lotion, Art. Nr. 77-09 statt 200×100 ml Eau de Toilette, Art. Nr. 76-56; Auftr. Nr. 1-779 vom 10. August)
- Bitte um baldmöglichste Abholung der beanstandeten Ware durch übliche Spedition
- sofortiger Ersatz erforderlich
- drei Monate Frist für Verbesserung des Service, ansonsten keine Verlängerung des Liefervertrags

C | Complaints by telephone

Sophia Corelli (SC) from Gartencenter Auwald OHG has placed an order for flower bulbs and tubers with the Dutch firm Roderbosch BV. As the consignment is now 5 days overdue, she decides to ring Tim De Beer (TD) at Roderbosch whom she has contacted in connection with numerous other transactions.

1 Read the following dialogue. Then choose task a, b or c.

TD: Roderbosch, Tim speaking. How may I help?

SC: Hi Tim. This is Sophia from Gartencenter Auwald. How are things with you?

TD: Thanks, Sophia. Everything's fine here. I hope you're not calling about a problem with one of your orders.

SC: I am, actually. Could you do me a favour and check if our order No. 335-9 has already been dispatched? The consignment was due 5 days ago.

TD: Bear with me, I'm just bringing your account up. Here we are, order No. 335-9 placed on 20 August for bulbs and tubers. Is that correct?

SC: Yes, that's the order I'm talking about.

TD: That's strange. The order has been marked as 'dispatched'. The dispatch date was 22 August.

SC: Well, all I can say is that the consignment never arrived at our warehouse.

TD: Oh, dear, I'm terribly sorry, Sophia. There must have been a serious mix-up somewhere. This has never happened before.

SC: No, I know. You've always been very reliable. But the problem is that we need the goods urgently. You know that the bulb-planting season is almost here and we want everything ready in our stores. What do you suggest we do?

TD: Don't worry. I'll look into this matter personally and make sure that you receive the consignment by tomorrow late afternoon. Would that be okay for you?

SC: You're a star, Tim. Thanks ever so much.

TD: You're more than welcome. Sorry again for the trouble caused.

SC: That's alright. Have a good weekend. Take care.

TD: And you. Bye now.

SC: Bye

a. Answer the following questions in English.

1. Why does Sophia ring Tim?
2. When was the delivery scheduled to arrive?
3. What goods did the garden centre order?
4. Why is Tim surprised?
5. Why is the consignment needed urgently?
6. What does Tim promise Sophia?

b. Sophia waits until the evening of the following day, but the goods still haven't arrived. She decides to contact Tim again. Act out the dialogue with a partner.

c. Work with a partner. Draw up a similar dialogue about delay in delivery. Then act it out with your partner.

I Esma Akgül from Geschenke Dohmke in Stuttgart had ordered a total of
300 glass paperweights from the Mosta Workshops in Valletta, Malta. The
consignment arrived on time, but on inspecting the goods, quality control
staff detected chips in 50 of the paperweights. Shape and size of the
300 items do not seem to be 100 % uniform. Esma rings Lorenza Albertis at
Mosta Workshops.
Act out their dialogue with another student, using the prompts below:

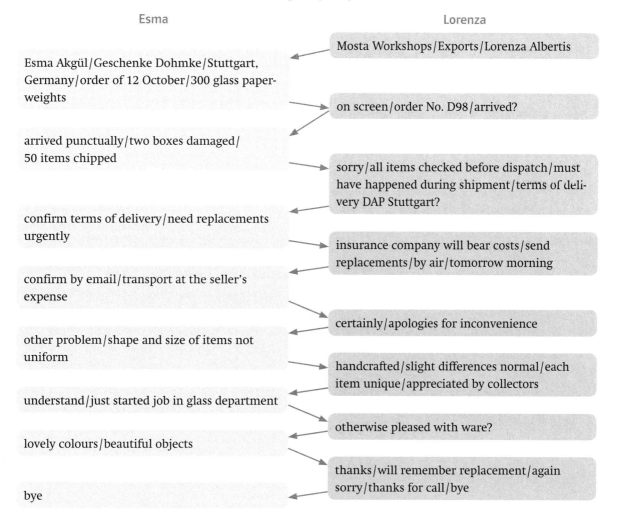

Esma / Lorenza

Mosta Workshops/Exports/Lorenza Albertis

Esma Akgül/Geschenke Dohmke/Stuttgart, Germany/order of 12 October/300 glass paperweights

on screen/order No. D98/arrived?

arrived punctually/two boxes damaged/50 items chipped

sorry/all items checked before dispatch/must have happened during shipment/terms of delivery DAP Stuttgart?

confirm terms of delivery/need replacements urgently

insurance company will bear costs/send replacements/by air/tomorrow morning

confirm by email/transport at the seller's expense

certainly/apologies for inconvenience

other problem/shape and size of items not uniform

handcrafted/slight differences normal/each item unique/appreciated by collectors

understand/just started job in glass department

otherwise pleased with ware?

lovely colours/beautiful objects

thanks/will remember replacement/again sorry/thanks for call/bye

bye

R Ethan Carrington of Chelsea Interiors London has received a consignment of
A2.11 designer furniture from the Italian manufacturer Desegno dei Laghi srl.
As there are a number of discrepancies he decides to ring the Italian firm.
Listen to the dialogue and answer the following questions.

1. What firm does Ethan work for?
2. What is Claudia Mezzanotte's role in the Italian company?
3. What is the problem with the Lucca dining table and some of the chairs?
4. Why wouldn't a generous discount help with the problem?
5. Why do you think Claudia offers a discount anyway?
6. How is Claudia planning to send the replacements?

P **4** You are Ethan Carrington. Copy the form below and then write a telephone message for your boss Victoria Hancock.

TELEPHONE MESSAGE

Message for: _____

Message taken by: _____ Date: _____

Caller: _____

Subject: _____

_____

COMMUNICATION ACROSS CULTURES

COMPLAINTS

Making a complaint is an area where unwritten rules differ considerably between cultures. The issue is basically one of "losing face" – how much loss of face can the complainer expect the complainee to accept in a given culture? While there are differences between individual speakers, most Germans go for a direct strategy, stating clearly – and, from an English point of view, often bluntly – the reasons for their dissatisfaction. This is the accepted norm and nobody takes offence at the no-nonsense style of German complaints.

However, in the English-speaking world the usual strategy is far more indirect, conciliatory and even apologetic. The complainee must not be subjected to a loss of face. The style of complaining usual in Germany would cause offence and would not get the desired result. The other person would feel antagonised and would probably become quietly uncooperative.

Direct	**Indirect**
My food is cold.	I'm afraid my food is not very hot.
We've been waiting for at least 30 minutes	I can see that you're terribly busy but we have been waiting rather a long time.
You're wrong.	I'm afraid I cannot quite agree / or: Do you really think so?
The noise is dreadful. Turn the music down.	I'm awfully sorry but could you possibly turn the music down a bit. I'm sure you don't realise how much sound carries.

The same goes for written complaints:

We expect you to send replacements.	We would be grateful if you could send replacements.
We are not satisfied with your service.	I'm afraid that we are not entirely satisfied with your service.
You have made a mistake.	I'm afraid there must be a mistake somewhere.

Make the following complaints sound more indirect.

1. The goods were damaged in transit.
2. Please remit payment by Friday at the latest.
3. We are dissatisfied with the way our orders are executed.
4. I have been waiting for half an hour. When will I get my food?
5. You're wrong. I don't agree.

Use the internet to find other examples of cultural differences which may lead to problems of intercultural communication. Make notes and discuss your findings with the group.

D | Adjusting complaints

It is much easier to keep existing customers than to get new ones. This is why it is important to take customer complaints seriously and deal with them satisfactorily. Dissatisfied customers are twice as likely as satisfied ones to tell others about their experience with your company.

- Do not fob the customer off.
- Thank the customer for bringing the problem to your attention.
- Treat him / her with courtesy and patience.
- Say that you are sorry about the inconvenience caused.
- Respond to the complaint quickly and tell the customer what will happen next.
- If possible, give an explanation for how the problem arose.
- Involve the customer in the process of finding a solution.
- Suggest a compromise that meets the customer half way if the complaint is not entirely justified.
- Make sure that whatever action you promise is carried out straight away.
- Explain the reasons for saying "no" if the complaint is unjustified. It may be possible to offer a sweetener such as a discount voucher.

M 1 Use the text above to help you translate the following recommendations.

Reklamationen

Die Erledigung von Reklamationen muss mit großer Sorgfalt geschehen, um den Kunden nicht zu verlieren. Zunächst sollten Sie dem Kunden dafür danken, dass er Sie auf ein Problem aufmerksam gemacht hat, und ihn dann in die Suche nach einer Lösung einbeziehen.

Beschwerden müssen umgehend beantwortet und der Kunde über den Fortgang der Erledigung auf dem Laufenden gehalten werden. Wenn möglich, sollten Sie dem Kunden erklären, wie es zu der für ihn unbefriedigenden Situation kommen konnte.

Zudem müssen Sie den Kunden davon überzeugen, dass Sie Maßnahmen treffen werden oder schon eingeleitet haben, die sicherstellen, dass sich solche Vorfälle nicht wiederholen.

Falls die Reklamation nur teilweise begründet ist, sollten Sie versuchen, sich mit dem Kunden auf einen Kompromiss zu einigen. Sind Sie gezwungen, die Reklamation als völlig unbegründet zurückzuweisen, empfiehlt es sich zuerst die Gründe zu erläutern, bevor die Absage erteilt wird.

| 2 | Work in pairs with student A making a complaint by email or text message and student B giving an appropriate explanation / offering a solution. Use the prompts below:

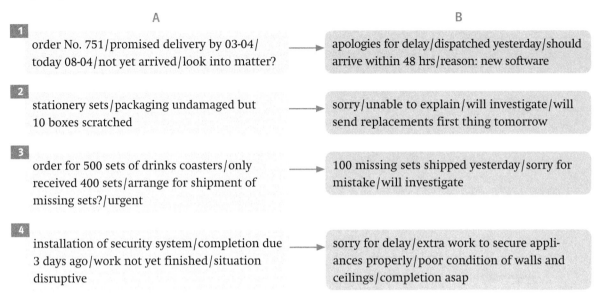

A

1
order No. 751 / promised delivery by 03-04 / today 08-04 / not yet arrived / look into matter?

2
stationery sets / packaging undamaged but 10 boxes scratched

3
order for 500 sets of drinks coasters / only received 400 sets / arrange for shipment of missing sets? / urgent

4
installation of security system / completion due 3 days ago / work not yet finished / situation disruptive

B

apologies for delay / dispatched yesterday / should arrive within 48 hrs / reason: new software

sorry / unable to explain / will investigate / will send replacements first thing tomorrow

100 missing sets shipped yesterday / sorry for mistake / will investigate

sorry for delay / extra work to secure appliances properly / poor condition of walls and ceilings / completion asap

3 Mr Sinha's PA answers Ms Bilker's email (see B) concerning the faulty tennis shoes that Just Relax GmbH received from Tungi Garments. Complete the body of his email using the expressions from the box.

assured · bear · dispatched · faulty · inconvenience

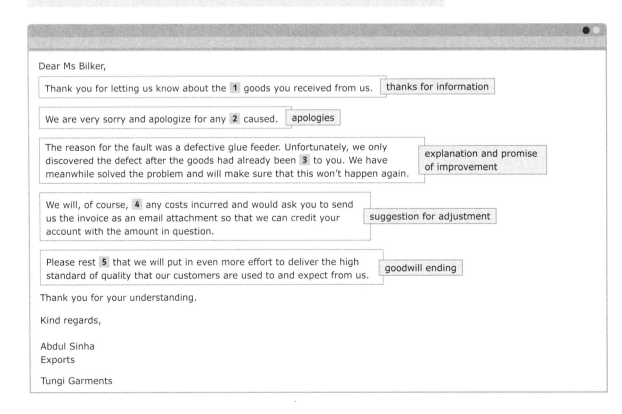

Dear Ms Bilker,

Thank you for letting us know about the **1** goods you received from us. | thanks for information

We are very sorry and apologize for any **2** caused. | apologies

The reason for the fault was a defective glue feeder. Unfortunately, we only discovered the defect after the goods had already been **3** to you. We have meanwhile solved the problem and will make sure that this won't happen again. | explanation and promise of improvement

We will, of course, **4** any costs incurred and would ask you to send us the invoice as an email attachment so that we can credit your account with the amount in question. | suggestion for adjustment

Please rest **5** that we will put in even more effort to deliver the high standard of quality that our customers are used to and expect from us. | goodwill ending

Thank you for your understanding.

Kind regards,

Abdul Sinha
Exports

Tungi Garments

P **4** You are Trevor Chase, principal at Hawthorne International School London. Three members of staff from HSC GmbH, Germany, attended a Business English course from 2 to 10 May. You have received an email from their human resources department complaining about a number of problems regarding the course:

- new school premises in noisy business park;
- classrooms without adequate noise insulation
- classrooms overheated
- participants' needs – language of export procedures – not properly taken into account
- on last two days class was merged with another student group (5 participants) with different needs

Reply by email and bear in mind that HSC is a long-standing customer. Use the following prompts:

- sorry to hear that students were not happy
- premises usually quiet; construction works nearby at the time of the course; works now completed
- contacted firm that installed heating; problem solved
- apologies for the inconvenience caused
- checked class register; language of export procedures dealt with; additional text material on that topic area attached as pdf file
- merger of classes administrative mistake; fees for these days will be refunded
- offer a 25 % refund for the first seven days
- hope that good relations will not be affected

P **5**
KMK Sie sind Robert Clarkson, Geschäftsführer bei Goodwood of Chelsea, 133 King's Road, London SW5 7HL. Die deutsche Firma Tangerine Dreams, An der Alster 225, 20099 Hamburg, ist seit Jahren mit Ihnen in Geschäftskontakt. Lea Bruckner, zuständig für den Einkauf, ist zunehmend unzufrieden mit dem Service, den Goodwood bietet und hat sich bei Ihnen in einem förmlichen Brief beschwert (siehe Seite 185).
Beantworten Sie den Brief und beachten Sie dabei folgende Punkte:

- Datum: 5. September 201_
- vor einem Jahr Übernahme durch eine australische Investmentfirma
- organisatorische und personelle Änderungen
- neue Lieferanten
- jetzt ausschließlich zertifizierte Lieferanten
- Entschuldigung
- radikale Maßnahmen eingeleitet
- Service in Kürze wieder einwandfrei
- Ersatzlieferung bereits unterwegs
- 20 % Rabatt auf diesen Auftrag (Auftrag Nr. 1-779)
- Beanstandete Ware wird vom Spediteur bei Ersatzlieferung abgeholt
- Hoffnung auf weiterhin gute Geschäftsbeziehungen
- Schluss-/Grußformel

LANGUAGE AND GRAMMAR

CONDITIONAL CLAUSES

Bedingungssätze (conditional clauses) werden im Englischen nach einem relativ festen Schema gestaltet. Es gibt drei Grundtypen von Bedingungssätzen:

	Hauptsatz	Nebensatz der Bedingung
1	We **will** take the goods back (Future)	if you **return** them at your expense. (Present tense)
2	We **would** grant you a discount (Conditional)	if you **increased** your order. (Simple past)
3	He **would have taken** part in the meeting. (Conditional perfect)	if he **had not been** away on a business trip. (Past perfect)

Das Schema gilt auch dann, wenn der Nebensatz der Bedingung vor dem Hauptsatz steht:

If it **is** fine on Friday, we **will** have the office party in the park.

Wenn es am Freitag schön ist, werden wir die Büroparty im Park feiern.

If you **applied**, you **would** get the job.

Wenn Sie sich bewerben würden, würden Sie die Stelle bekommen.

If you **had applied**, you **would have got** the job.

Wenn Sie sich beworben hätten, hätten Sie die Stelle bekommen.

Ferner gilt das Schema, wenn der Nebensatz durch eine andere Konjunktion eingeleitet wird wie z. B. „unless" (wenn nicht, außer wenn), „provided (that)" (vorausgesetzt, dass), „on condition (that)" (unter der Bedingung, dass):

They will not place any further orders unless you offer a satisfactory solution.

Sie werden keine weiteren Bestellungen aufgeben, wenn Sie keine zufriedenstellende Lösung anbieten.

Employees may smoke provided they go out into the courtyard.

Die Angestellten dürfen rauchen, vorausgesetzt sie gehen raus in den Hof.

Eine besondere Form stellt der Bedingungssatz ohne Konjunktion dar:

Should you have any further questions, please do not hesitate to contact us.

Sollten Sie weitere Fragen haben, zögern Sie bitte nicht sich an uns zu wenden.

But for John helping out (If John had not helped out …), we would never have coped with the sudden demand.

Wenn John nicht ausgeholfen hätte, hätten wir die plötzliche Nachfrage niemals bewältigen können.

Eine Ausnahme von diesem Schema bildet die höfliche Bitte in der Geschäftskorrespondenz:

We would be grateful if you would grant us a respite of 4 weeks.

Wir wären dankbar, wenn Sie uns 4 Wochen Zahlungsaufschub gewähren würden.

TASK:

6   **Choose the correct form of the verbs in brackets.**

1. We will guarantee next day delivery if you (order) by Monday.
2. We would place an order immediately if you (grant) a 15 % discount.
3. We would not have ordered the goods if you (not promise) delivery within one week.
4. We (be grateful) if you (settle) the invoice without delay.
5. Unless you instruct us otherwise, we (ship) the regular consignment at the end of this month as usual.

Office expert

E | The five R's of complaints

1 The point of a complaint is not just to criticize but to achieve compensation in some form. Match the following Five R's to keep in mind when making complaints (1.–5.) to their definitions (a.–e.).

1.	redress	a.	to fix something and restore to a good condition
2.	refund	b.	to make up for a loss
3.	reimburse	c.	to provide a substitute
4.	repair	d.	to pay money back
5.	replace	e.	to right a wrong (legal term)

F | Key account management

1 Sie arbeiten als Assistent/in einer Großkundenberaterin. Lesen Sie den Text über Ihr Arbeitsfeld und beantworten Sie die Fragen dazu auf Deutsch.

A key account manager deals with the customers that are most important to a company. They are usually the customers with whom the company has the largest volume of business or the most profit. Developing customer relations to such key accounts and making sure they remain loyal customers is the job of the key account manager. On a day to day basis, sales proposals need to be prepared and the market analysed. A key account manager's job is similar to that of a sales manager but they usually only have a limited number of accounts. This means they can get to know their customers well to be able to better meet their needs. A good understanding of the customer's business as well as factors such as prices, delivery times and forms of payment is important. The job calls for a high degree of negotiation and communication skills.

The assistant of a key account manager is responsible for administrative tasks such as filing reports, answering the phone, coordinating appointments and dealing with customer correspondence. An accounts assistant should be familiar with standard software programmes and be friendly and outgoing.

1. Was ist mit *key accounts* gemeint?
2. Worin besteht die Aufgabe eines Großkundenberaters im Allgemeinen?
3. Welche Aufgaben fallen einem Großkundenberater konkret zu?
4. Was unterscheidet einen Verkaufsberater von einem Großkundenberater?
5. Welche Kenntnisse und Fähigkeiten sollte ein Großkundenberater haben?
6. Welche Aufgaben hat der/die Assistent/in eines Großkundenberaters?
7. Welche Qualifikationen sollte der/die Assistent/in mitbringen?

G | Coping with the copy machine

R **1**
A3.22
Matthew aus den USA bittet seine Kollegin Karin um Hilfe mit dem Kopierer. Hören Sie sich das Gespräch zweimal an und beantworten Sie die folgenden Fragen auf Deutsch.

1. Wobei benötigt Matthew Hilfe?
2. Wo befindet sich das Kartuschenfach und wie lässt es sich öffnen?
3. Womit sollte man Tonerflecken auf Kleidung auf keinen Fall entfernen?
4. Wo befindet sich die Anweisung zum Kartuschenwechsel?
5. Beschreiben Sie die Schritte zum Einsatz der neuen Kartusche.
6. Was geschieht mit der alten Kartusche?

H | Licence agreements

R **1**
You would like to buy a library of templates from Boxed Business. Before you can download the software you have to agree to an End User Licence Agreement (EULA). Read the extract from the EULA and choose the right options below.

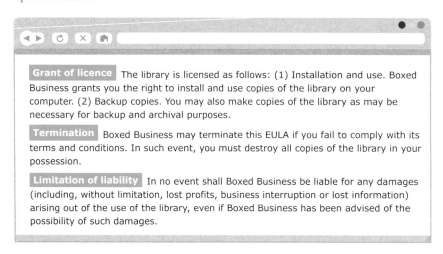

Grant of licence The library is licensed as follows: (1) Installation and use. Boxed Business grants you the right to install and use copies of the library on your computer. (2) Backup copies. You may also make copies of the library as may be necessary for backup and archival purposes.

Termination Boxed Business may terminate this EULA if you fail to comply with its terms and conditions. In such event, you must destroy all copies of the library in your possession.

Limitation of liability In no event shall Boxed Business be liable for any damages (including, without limitation, lost profits, business interruption or lost information) arising out of the use of the library, even if Boxed Business has been advised of the possibility of such damages.

1. The EULA gives you permission to do the following with the library:
   a. install and use it; b. install it and make backup copies; c. install and resell it.
2. Boxed Business can cancel the EULA if you
   a. destroy your copies; b. violate the contract; c. misuse the library.
3. Boxed Business is not responsible for damages
   a. without limitation; b. of lost profits or data; c. if they warn you.
4. May you cancel the EULA with Boxed Business?
   a. Yes, if you suffer damages. b. Yes, if you lose money or business.
   c. No reasons are given.

KMK Exam Training

1 Rezeption: Leseverstehen

Stufe II **Lesen Sie den Text und beantworten Sie die nachfolgenden Verständnisfragen in Stichwörtern auf Deutsch.**

1. Was unterscheidet eine konstruktive von einer nicht konstruktiven Beschwerde?
2. Wann und wie sollten Sie sich beschweren?
3. Was sollte man auch bei einer berechtigten Beschwerde nicht vergessen und warum?
4. Was sollte der Leitfaden bei einer Beschwerde sein?

Stufe II **Lesen Sie den folgenden Text und entscheiden Sie bei den unten stehenden Aussagen, ob sie richtig oder falsch sind. Begründen Sie Ihre Entscheidung auf Deutsch. Beginnen Sie Ihre Begründung mit „Richtig / Falsch, weil ..."**

1. Sich bei der Arbeit zu beschweren, ist immer zwecklos. Für eine Beschwerde gibt es nie berechtigte Gründe.
2. Man sollte keine Zeit verlieren und sich möglichst zeitnah beschweren.
3. Es ist nicht zu empfehlen, jemanden direkt mit einer Beschwerde anzusprechen.
4. Manchmal sollte man den Grund für eine Beschwerde genauer prüfen.
5. Es ist keine gute Idee, immer den anderen die Schuld zuzuweisen.
6. Der Zweck einer Beschwerde sollte darin liegen, eine Lösung oder Verbesserung herbeizuführen und nicht darin, jemandem die Schuld für den Beschwerdegrund zuzuschieben.

Constructive complaining at work

Things don't always go the way you would like at work and there are certainly legitimate reasons for complaining – the boss only criticizes never praises you, some team members always
5 come late to meetings, the copy machine doesn't work right, a promised report is three days late etc. Just as in everyday life, complaining plays a role in business and is a way to let others know that you are dissatisfied with a situation.
But how can you go about complaining in a way that will lead
10 to positive change? The key here is to distinguish between constructive complaining which is effective and can change things for the better and unconstructive complaining which can even worsen the situation by creating a negative atmosphere. What is the difference?
15 As with many things, choosing the right time is also important when complaining. While the temptation is to complain at the moment you are feeling most annoyed that is not always a

good idea for a number of reasons. First of all, emotions can be
running high and secondly, you probably don't have the time,
20 patience and will to deal constructively with the matter at that
moment. For example, after waiting for a colleague to finally
show up with some important papers you urgently need for a
meeting, is not the time to launch into a litany of complaints
about their tardiness. Wait and choose a time when you are not
25 rushed and can talk in a calm manner with your coworker.
Griping to colleagues about the boss or to colleague A about
colleague B's bad habit of pinching your pencils might make you
feel momentarily better but will it change anything? Hardly. In
fact, it can even have an adverse effect if word gets back- as it so
30 often does - that you have been complaining about them behind
their backs. It is a much better policy to complain directly to the
person who is the reason for the complaint or someone who can
do something about the problem. For example, if your boss is
unfair and won't listen to you, you might have to talk to their boss.
35 When complaining, always ask yourself what the real issue at
hand is. It is not constructive to complain about the symptoms
without thinking about the underlying problem. After being
promoted to the position of office supervisor, for example, you
have noticed that an older colleague very often calls in sick,
40 comes late and makes a lot of mistakes. You have complained
to him but the situation hasn't improved. Is the real problem
perhaps that he feels he was overlooked for the supervisory
position or are there health issues? Try and find out.
In this connection, it is also important to keep in mind another
45 principle of constructive complaining: Don't only just complain
but also appreciate and praise what's good. In the case of the
older colleague you might say that you always admired the
careful attention to detail in his work or that you were counting
on him with all his experience to help you lead the team.
50 Finally, the golden rule of constructive complaining is to seek a
solution and not just point your fingers and blame others. Trying
to get someone to admit they're to blame is counter-productive.
They'll only feel bad and want to justify themselves. And who
knows? Perhaps you yourself are at least part of the problem. And
55 does it matter who's at fault? It makes more sense to try and find
a solution to the problem or conflict.

593 words

Phrases:
Complaints and adjustments

To start a complaint	
We are writing **with** reference to our order no …	Wir nehmen Bezug auf unseren Auftrag Nr. …
We regret to report that we have not yet received the goods ordered **on** 18 May.	Wir bedauern Ihnen mitteilen zu müssen, dass wir die am 18. Mai bestellten Waren noch nicht erhalten haben.

To give reasons for your complaint	
On unpacking the cases our Incoming Goods Control discovered that 15 items are missing.	Beim Auspacken der Kisten stellte unsere Warenannahme fest, dass 15 Positionen fehlen.
We are afraid that several units are – seriously damaged / defective. – broken / badly scratched / stained.	Leider sind mehrere Teile – schwer beschädigt / schadhaft. – zerbrochen / stark zerkratzt / verschmutzt.
The goods should have arrived a week **ago**.	Die Waren hätten schon vor einer Woche eintreffen sollen.
We are sorry to point out that the repair work has been poorly executed.	Wir müssen leider darauf hinweisen, dass die Reparatur schlecht ausgeführt wurde.

To mention likely reasons for the problem	
We believe that the damage may be due to rough handling **in** transit.	Wir glauben, dass der Schaden auf unsachgemäße Behandlung beim Transport zurückzuführen ist.
Apparently, our order was **mixed up** with another customer's order.	Unser Auftrag wurde anscheinend mit einem anderen verwechselt.

To inform the seller what you expect him to do and what steps you are taking	
Please arrange for the immediate dispatch of the missing items.	Bitte sorgen Sie dafür, dass die fehlenden Artikel sofort abgeschickt werden.
We would ask you to – replace the faulty goods at your expense. – have the defective articles collected at our warehouse. – grant us a price reduction of 20 %. – cut the price to €780.	Wir möchten Sie bitten, – die mangelhafte Ware auf Ihre Kosten zu ersetzen. – die schadhaften Artikel von unserem Lager abholen zu lassen. – uns einen Preisnachlass von 20 % zu gewähren. – den Preis auf €780 zu senken.

To demand prompt adjustment

We expect that you will settle this matter speedily and **to** our entire satisfaction.	Wir erwarten, dass Sie die Sache rasch und zu unserer vollen Zufriedenheit regeln.

To refer to a complaint received

Thank you for your e-mail drawing a serious problem **to** our attention.	Danke für Ihre E-Mail, mit der Sie uns auf ein ernstes Problem aufmerksam gemacht haben.

To apologize

We wish to apologize **for** this mistake.	Wir bitten für diesen Fehler um Entschuldigung.
We are extremely sorry **for** the poor service you have received.	Es tut uns außerordentlich leid, dass Sie so schlecht bedient wurden.

To explain the problem or promise to investigate it

The damage was caused **by** a software failure.	Der Schaden wurde durch fehlerhafte Software verursacht.
We will investigate the matter thoroughly and inform you of the steps taken.	Wir werden die Angelegenheit gründlich untersuchen und Sie über die Schritte informieren, die wir unternommen haben.

To suggest a solution and inform the buyer what you expect him to do

We are pleased to say that replacements are now on their way to you.	Wir freuen uns, Ihnen mitteilen zu können, dass Ersatz bereits unterwegs ist.
Please return the faulty items at our expense.	Bitte senden Sie die mangelhaften Artikel auf unsere Kosten zurück.
We are prepared to reduce the price by 15 % if you decide to keep the goods.	Wir sind bereit, den Preis um 15 % zu senken, wenn Sie sich entschließen, die Ware zu behalten.

To reject an unfounded claim

After careful examination of the case we must say that the order was carried out in accordance with the contract.	Nach gründlicher Untersuchung des Falles müssen wir festhalten, dass der Auftrag vertragsgemäß ausgeführt wurde.
As we are in no way to blame we have no alternative but to reject your claim.	Da uns keinerlei Schuld trifft, bleibt uns nichts anderes übrig, als Ihre Reklamation zurückzuweisen.

To close on a note designed to promote goodwill

We hope that this proposal will find your approval.	Wir hoffen, dieser Vorschlag findet Ihre Zustimmung.
We trust that the solution suggested will help to settle the matter to the satisfaction of all parties concerned.	Wir hoffen, dass die vorgeschlagene Lösung dazu beiträgt, die Angelegenheit zur Zufriedenheit aller Beteiligten zu erledigen.

15

What in your opinion does marketing involve?

Marketing products and services

Marketing is the process by which a concept or idea is gradually transformed into a product or service. It includes a wide range of activities. Even at the concept stage a company will conduct market research to assess the potential demand for the proposed product or service. This is necessary because developing a new product is extremely costly. In addition, marketing includes co-ordination of the so-called 4Ps – product, price, place, promotion – i.e. what kind of a product to develop, what price to charge, what channels to sell it through – e.g. exclusive dealers or retail outlets appealing to a mass-market and whether to include a digital dimension. Finally, the company has to develop and implement a promotional strategy which includes advertising. Both marketing and advertising have been revolutionised by the internet and mobile telephony.

1 Why does market research begin even before a company has a product?

2 What is meant by the "four Ps"?

3 What is your experience of mobile marketing?

4 Search the internet and give examples of successful / unsuccessful
⊕ marketing campaigns.

WORD BANK

- *to advertise*
- *advertisements*
- *advertising*
- *agent*
- *to aim at*
- *to break bulk*
- *commercials*
- *commission*
- *to conduct research*
- *consumer goods*
- *distribution*
- *E-commerce*
- *internet advertising*
- *interview*
- *life cycle*
- *mail shots*
- *manufacturer*
- *market research*
- *marketing*
- *marketing mix*
- *media*
- *posters*
- *to promote*
- *public relations*
- *to represent*
- *retail outlets*
- *retailer*
- *slogans*
- *sponsoring*
- *target group*
- *trade fairs*
- *trade journals*
- *warehouse*
- *wholesaler*

A | Life cycle of a product

Products are generally considered to have a life cycle consisting of five phases:

1. introduction to the market
2. a growth phase in which sales expand
3. a maturity phase where sales reach a plateau
4. decline when sales start to drop off
5. phasing out where a product is gradually removed from the market.

A company may try to extend the life of the product by devising a life cycle extension strategy which may consist in updating the packaging, adding new features or lowering the price.

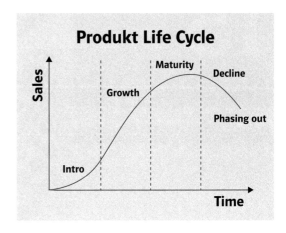

Produkt Life Cycle

1. Study the information above and answer the following questions.

1. How many phases is the life cycle of a product said to have?
2. What happens after sales peak?
3. What happens during the growth phase?
4. What is meant by "phasing out"?
5. How do companies try to extend a product's life cycle?

B | Branding and USP

Companies attempt to create brands or products with a distinct identity that marks them off from similar products. The company itself may function as a brand. When customers buy a brand they buy the values it represents. Branding is a key tool for creating and maintaining competitive advantage by encouraging loyalty to the company or product.

A unique selling proposition (USP) makes your business stand out from the competition. It tells your customers what makes your product(s) different and better in comparison with the competition.

P **1** Is the brand important to you (e.g. shoes or clothes) or are you happy to buy generic products (i.e. non-branded products)? Why? Give examples.

I **2** Work in groups. Choose a couple of UK or US brands and discuss the features of the brands. How does the company make the brand seem special? Refer to online or offline advertising to indicate how the brand image is created and maintained. Present your ideas to the class.

P **3** Work in pairs. Search the internet and find definitions and examples of USPs. Present your results to the class.

C | Market research

Companies conduct market research either to find out what new products or services might be profitable or to find out whether their products are meeting customer needs and expectations. This may involve primary research where original data is gathered by interviews or surveys and secondary research where data is analysed that has already been published elsewhere (e.g. statistics).

The internet has presented companies with a wealth of additional resources to conduct free or low-cost research online and thus obtain primary data. The internet is also an excellent way of researching the competition. In addition, there are websites that assist companies in creating and carrying out surveys.

R **1** Cosmopolis Business Research Ltd have been commissioned by a major
A2.12 supermarket chain to conduct a survey on online shopping habits. They plan to do a mixture of online questionnaires and telephone interviews. Listen to the interview and answer the questions that follow. Choose task a, b or c.

a. **Answer the following questions.**

1. What is the survey investigating?
2. What age group does the participant belong to?
3. How many members of her household are there?

b. **Answer the following questions.**

1. Where and when does the interviewee generally place her order?
2. How many days does she aim to shop for?
3. What reasons does she give for shopping for groceries online?
4. How much does she usually spend?

c. **Answer the following questions.**

1. What does the interviewee reveal about her living conditions?
2. What is her attitude towards shopping for groceries online?
3. In what way does she benefit?
4. What might change her shopping habits?
5. How might she react to the introduction of a £50 minimum?
6. Does she have any other criticisms to make of this service?

D | Distribution channels

Deciding on how a product is to be distributed is one of the key elements of marketing – the fourth of the classic 4 Ps. Traditionally, wholesalers were the link between manufacturers of a product and retailers. Nowadays, thanks to the internet, many manufacturers have become their own retailers, selling directly either B2B (business to business) or B2C (business to consumer), depending on the type of product (industrial or consumer). Large retailers have always been able to bypass the wholesaler and the internet has opened up new chains of supply for online retailers.

Retailers
The retail sector provides a range of goods to the end-user. This sector has been radically shaken up by the internet. In the UK the proportion of e-commerce of total retail sales is roughly 15 % (excluding tickets and holidays) and online sales are expected to increase by 10 % pa over the next few years. It is the fastest growing retail segment. This is putting considerable pressure on so-called "bricks and mortar" retailers who have a physical presence on the High Street. Many have set up their own online operation.
Nevertheless, there is still a wide variety of retailers – small specialist shops such as independent pharmacies, opticians, mobile phone outlets and exclusive fashion boutiques etc. Most High Street stores, including supermarkets and department stores which offer different types of goods under one roof, are branches of major chains.

Wholesalers

Traditionally, manufacturers sold goods in large quantities to wholesalers, who sold them on in smaller quantities to retailers (= breaking bulk), who sold to the end-user. Wholesalers are still important in that they provide services which benefit both manufacturers and retailers. They may have a sales force that has close contact with retailers and can provide useful feedback on demand, product satisfaction etc. They still repack large lots of goods into smaller quantities thus performing their traditional function. They have warehousing facilities, offer credit lines plus training and advisory services. They may provide a one-stop-shop for retailers in that they are likely to stock a range of similar goods from a number of manufacturers. However, they are under pressure as they are a big cost factor which many retailers and manufacturers would like to eliminate. Large retailers were always able to bypass the wholesaler.

Agents

Manufacturers frequently appoint agents to cover important export markets. There are a number of advantages: the agents speak the language, they are familiar with the market and any cultural peculiarities. They will also have a network of contacts, an office and possibly warehousing facilities. An agent is a much cheaper option for a company than setting up its own sales organisation as the agent is usually paid on a commission basis receiving a commission (say 3%) on sales. The manufacturer may also help with the cost of advertising and participation at trade fairs.

1 Say whether the following statements are true or false.

1. "Bricks and mortar" retailers are the fastest growing retail segment.
2. Traditionally, wholesalers were the link between the manufacturer and the retailer.
3. In the past manufacturers generally sold to the end-user.
4. Wholesalers are under pressure because they are a big cost factor.
5. Small retailers have always been able to bypass the wholesaler.
6. The traditional function of wholesalers is to break bulk.
7. Many retailers with stores on the High Street also have online operations.
8. Wholesalers usually have warehousing facilities.

M **2**
KMK
Übertragen Sie die wichtigsten Inhalte zu „Retailers", „Wholesalers" und „Agents" ins Deutsche.

3 Choose task a, b or c.
○ a. Explain the traditional role of the wholesaler.
◔ b. What are the advantages of appointing an agent in a foreign export market?
● c. In what ways are large retailers undermining the traditional role of the wholesaler? What is the impact of e-commerce on stores with a physical presence on the High Street?

R

A2.13

Listen to the following statements and make brief notes. Then answer the following questions.

1. What type of company does speaker 1 work for?
2. What kind of company is speaker 2's employer?
3. What kind of customers does speaker 3 sell to?
4. Why is the company of speaker 4 able to sell their cosmetics more cheaply?
5. Where does the firm of speaker 5 buy its products?
6. What kind of a company is that of speaker 6? Where do they get their goods from?
7. What companies sell their products through speaker 7's company?
8. Speaker 8's firm sells to the end-user. Is it a retailer? How do they sell their products?

COMMUNICATION ACROSS CULTURES

STANDARDISATION VERSUS LOCALISATION

It has long been debated whether the marketing of products in a globalised market can be standardised, or whether marketing and advertising has to be customised to reflect local culture (localisation). Multinationals would prefer to standardise their marketing strategy across international markets to deliver a consistent message and identity worldwide. However, this has often led to marketing flops which may do considerable damage to a successful brand. Attempting naively to reproduce the sound of its product name in Chinese characters (which do not represent individual sounds), Coca-Cola, for example ended up with something that sounded like Coca-Cola but meant "Bite the wax tadpole"!

Every aspect of a marketing campaign must be checked for cultural differences. A well-known international manufacturer of baby diapers retained the image of a stork delivering a baby on its packaging in Japan. As this popular myth does not exist in Japan, Japanese consumers were mystified about what the image meant.

Similarly, like "13" in the West, in Japan the unlucky numbers are "4" and "9", which explains why a manufacturer of golfballs selling in packs of four was not very successful. Likewise, the meaning attributed to colours may be different. In Eastern cultures, for instance, "white" may be associated with death and mourning.

Flops are also often due to a lack of awareness of what the words used might imply on a slang level. Thus the inventors of the slogan "Nothing sucks like an Electrolux" (vacuum cleaner) were tragically unaware of the slang expression "it sucks" = "it's useless".

Thus despite the development of a global market it is essential in marketing to be aware of the many potential pitfalls caused by inadequate sensitivity to cultural differences and to the often unforeseen associations which words have that on the surface may seem quite harmless. It is essential to assess how any aspect of a marketing strategy is impacted by culture.

TASK:

Work in groups. Use the internet to find other examples of marketing flops caused by lack of cultural or linguistic awareness. Discuss your findings with the class.

E | Advertising

Advertising includes both the more traditional print and screen media and also online advertising. In the UK at the present time half of all ad spend goes on digital media. Annual growth rates are above 10%.

This surge in digital advertising is being partly fuelled by the explosion in the popularity of portable devices (smartphones and tablets). A big advantage of online marketing is that it immediately generates market data (i.e. how many click on to a site and register and how many just bounce off). Thus, it is much easier to track effectiveness. This also means that it is more difficult to make a clear distinction between marketing and advertising online, especially as advertising and selling often take place through the same channel.

Print and screen media:

Direct mail / mail shots: These now tend to be carried out by email, which is much cheaper. There is still a role for postal mail shots where a seller is targeting a well-defined group of better-off clients in the context of more valuable products. The mail shot may contain a personalised letter and brochure and involve such products as private health insurance, exclusive and expensive educational holidays etc.

Newspapers and magazines: These media are under intense pressure from digital advertising. An advantage of magazines is that they generally appeal to a particular readership so that the advertiser can target a specific group – e.g. men's fashion for high-earning males between late 20s and early 40s, keen gardeners, yachting enthusiasts etc.

Posters, hoardings, billboards: This advertising reaches large numbers of people in public places.

TV advertising / commercials: This is very expensive and affordable only for consumer goods with a very wide appeal. Like cinema ads it can associate an attractive lifestyle with the product. High visual quality compared with the internet.

Digital advertising:

Advertising by email: Sending promotional email messages was one of the earliest forms of digital marketing. Companies send promotional emails to potential customers. Effectiveness depends on the quality of the consumer database, i.e. to what extent it is sorted according to specific target groups. Companies with established online operations send emails that are bespoke to each user and reflect their buying patterns.

SEO (search engine optimization) / **SEM** (search engine marketing): This is the technique of increasing a website's visibility or increasing the number of keywords that a site ranks for. Search engines auction desirable keywords with companies paying per click (up to £50 per click). The advertisement appears above or next to the 'generic' information searched for.

PPC (pay per click)**:** Using others' websites – buying banner space to advertise on a website belonging to a third party. The website owner is paid per number of clicks.

Affiliate **marketing:** Many companies opt to use an experienced "affiliate network" which has already built a large base of affiliates and which generates a flow of visitors to their websites. The advertising company pays website owners a commission (say 5 %) on sales.
An example would be e-commerce operations with products such as fashion, accessories, leather goods from a range of manufacturers. Payment based on sales (rather than clicks) will be higher incentivising the website host to display ads more prominently. Affiliate marketing also uses links and email-marketing.

Advertising in podcasts: Ads can be inserted and updated at any point in a popular audio show or in digital audio programmes, often series.

Mobile advertising / text messaging: This is the communication of advertising material to mobile devices such as smartphones. It includes short message service (SMS) texts and interactive advertisements.

Social media: Social media involve all forms of electronic communication with the aim of sharing information and other content among friends or within a social group or community.

M Listen Sie die wesentlichen Informationen aus den einzelnen oben genannten Punkten („Print and screen media" und „Digital advertising") stichwortartig auf Deutsch auf.

2 Explain the following words and terms taken from the texts above. Use a dictionary if necessary.

1. surge
2. fuelled
3. to bounce off
4. to track
5. better-off clients
6. educational holidays
7. to target
8. bespoke
9. generic information
10. affiliate marketing

I **3** Work in groups. Discuss TV, cinema or magazine ads you have seen recently. Say what you liked or disliked about them and whether you think they are effective.

R **4** Listen to Seth Adamson from Adnovatrix, an online PR and marketing
⊙ A2.14 consultancy, talking to Angelina Jones from the magazine Digital Native about marketing and social media and new trends in mobile advertising. Choose task a, b or c.

○ a. How does Seth explain people's need to form virtual communities or "tribes"?

◖ b. Why are companies so eager to engage with groups of consumers via social media?

● c. How do the social media change the relationship between companies and their customers?

F | Public Relations (PR)

In PR the focus is on the company rather than specific products with a view to projecting and maintaining an image or identity. A company may emphasise its environmental credentials, sponsor sports events, make large donations to educational establishments or charities. A PR department attempts to influence and interpret the flow of information from the organisation to the public. Especially in political contexts this is known as "putting a positive spin on something" and the experts are somewhat disrespectfully known as "spin doctors". The PR department attempts to engage with its public and to foresee and analyse any issues that may impact on the company. PR departments will also attempt to engage with the media by issuing press releases and making sure they are aware of events or charities the company is sponsoring etc. Of course, the PR department will engage with web communities on a daily basis. While larger companies have PR departments, in smaller companies there will be at least one person responsible for PR. Companies both large and small take advice from outside PR consultancies.

1 Answer the following questions on the text.

1. What does PR involve according to the text?
2. What are the main tasks of a PR department?

2 Explain the term "spin doctors"?

3 Work in groups. Choose a major company and investigate what image it seeks to project and how it does this. Has there recently been any news coverage of the company's activities?

G | Advertising industrial goods – B2B advertising

For manufacturers of industrial goods it is generally easier to identify potential customers (there will not be so many of them), though the buying or selling process may be more complex than for consumer goods. Many industrial companies now market their products via a company website and search engine marketing or by placing ads on other related websites. They may also use emails to make likely companies aware of their product range. Companies also place advertisements in the specialised trade journal for their sector. These still exist in print form but many also have an online presence. For manufacturers of industrial products the relevant trade fairs are an important forum in which to present their latest innovations and an opportunity to meet and exchange views with competitors. Trade fairs are an important advertising and marketing medium.

M **1** Summarize the above text in German.

H | Language and techniques of advertising

Advertising is generally divided into two broad categories – informative and persuasive. The first is used to inform potential buyers about the specifications of a product and as a result is more text-oriented. The second is used to persuade consumers to buy a particular brand and uses language and the techniques listed below to appeal to or awaken desires, wishes and dreams on a more subjective level.

Logos	Logos need to be simple, attractive and immediately recognisable. They are important as they imprint themselves on our visual memory.
Company/product name	Companies often try to create a memorable name – Zooks!
Images	Images are of key importance in ads and commercials. Everything (light, angle, colour and symbolism) is carefully calibrated for the right effect.
Text	Nowadays text is kept to a minimum but it is still important.
Slogan or motto	The motto of one of the worldwide biggest banks is "Your local bank".
USP	Get your pizza in 20 minutes or it's free!
Jingle	A diamond is forever. Think Big.
Puns	"poultrygeist" = poultry (i.e. turkey or chicken) and poltergeist – a fanciful name of a sandwich on a menu in New Orleans.
Alliteration	Sensuously seductive silk saris.
Exaggeration	Wow your guests with this exciting sushi!
Dramatisation	Indulge in the luxury of real leather luggage!
Emotionally charged language	Jewellery lovingly handcrafted by dedicated artists.

1 Choose task a, b or c.

○ a. Why it is important to have a good logo and company name?

◐ b. Explain how persuasive advertising works.

● c. Explain how advertising, branding and PR work together to make a product attractive.

P **2** Work in groups. Design your own advertising campaign. Use the internet for inspiration if you wish. Present your group's results to the class.

- Think of a product or service.
- Create a company name.
- Design a logo.
- Create a slogan and think of a USP.
- Think about images, colours, fonts and text for ads, promotions and offers.

LANGUAGE AND GRAMMAR

COMPARATIVES AND SUPERLATIVES

Adjektive, meist in Form von Komparativen oder Superlativen, spielen in der Werbung eine große Rolle.

Einsilbige Adjektive bilden Komparativ und Superlativ durch Anhängen von -er, -est.

This car has **faster** acceleration than comparable models.	Dieses Auto hat eine schnellere Beschleunigung als vergleichbare Modelle.

Drei – oder mehrsilbige Adjektive bilden Komparativ und Superlativ durch Voranstellen von „more" oder „most" vor das Adjektiv:

This is the **most** intelligent article I've read on the subject.	Dies ist der intelligenteste Artikel, den ich zu diesem Thema gelesen habe.

Zweisilbige Adjektive werden entweder wie einsilbige oder wie mehrsilbige gesteigert: Adjektive, die auf -er, -ow, -y oder -le enden, hängen -er, -est an. Vor Adjektive, die auf -ful oder -re enden, wird „more" oder „most" gesetzt:

It was the **most awful** journey we had experienced for a long time.	Es war seit langer Zeit die schrecklichste Reise, die wir gemacht haben.

Manche englische Adjektive haben die Wirkung von Superlativen:

cutting-edge technology	Spitzentechnologie
a must-have	ein Muss
state-of-the-art	neuester Stand (der Technik)

Adverbien können ebenfalls gesteigert werden. Komparativ und Superlativ werden durch Voranstellen von „more" und „most" gebildet:

They replied **more promptly** than I had expected.	Sie antworteten schneller, als ich es erwartet hatte.
The internet has changed our lives **most profoundly.**	Das Internet hat unser Leben am tiefgreifendsten verändert.

TASK:

3   **Choose the correct form of the adverb or adjective in brackets.**

1. This is the (fascinating) holiday I have ever spent.
2. The company has survived because it reacted (flexible) to changing markets than its competitors.
3. The roads seem to be getting (narrow) and (narrow).
4. The changes to company structure went (smooth) than we had envisaged.
5. Could you send us sales literature on your (late) models.
6. He was one of the (able) administrators the company had ever employed.

4   Choose task a, b or c.

○ a. Match the English idioms below with the explanations in German.

◔ b. Find the English idioms below that correspond to the following paraphrases:

    a. gradually get launched
    b. to find ways of doing things quicker, easier, cheaper
    c. to make unsolicited telephone calls for marketing purposes
    d. a market suddenly goes dead/demand disappears
    e. to do the calculations

● c. Match the English idioms below with the explanations in German and make sentences or dialogues in English using the idioms.

1. to be in the market for something	a. zur Sache kommen
	b. verschiedene Angebote prüfen
2. to bounce off	c. die Nachfrage bleibt plötzlich aus
3. to cut corners	d. etwas kaufen wollen
4. to get down to business	e. mündlich weitergeben
5. to pass on by word of mouth	f. eine Webseite anklicken und
6. to shop around	verlassen ohne sich anzumelden.
7. to crunch numbers	g. Telefonwerbung machen
8. to get off the ground	h. alles durchkalkulieren
9. to make cold calls	i. Wege finden, um etwas leichter
10. the bottom drops out of the market	und billiger zu machen
	j. in Schwung kommen

Office expert

I | Incentives and customer satisfaction

1 Match the buying incentives (1.–8.) to their German equivalents (a.–h.).

1.	cash discount	a.	Geschenk
2.	contest	b.	Gutschein
3.	coupon	c.	Preisausschreiben, Wettbewerb
4.	discount	d.	Rückzahlung
5.	freebie	e.	Preisnachlass
6.	gift	f.	Skonto
7.	rebate	g.	Warenprobe
8.	sample	h.	Werbegeschenk

P **2** You work for an office supplier which would like to determine how satisfied customers are with their current equipment. Your boss has made some notes and asks you to rewrite them as survey questions. Then use the questions to interview your classmates or colleagues at work. Report back your findings in class.

Example: Which features of your office chair should be adjustable?
a. seat height   b. armrests   c. backrests   d. seat inclination

Adjustable features:

chair:	seat height · armrests · backrests · seat inclination
desk:	keyboard tray · height adjustable · standing · extra writing space
keyboard:	built-in palm rest · wireless · zoom function · 4-way scrolling
mouse:	wireless · joystick design · programmable buttons · palm rest
monitor:	wide-screen · tilt function · flat screen · high-quality resolution

3 Complete the text about the office of the future with the words from the box.

available · collect · displays · freedom · happier · in tandem · lower · phrases · productivity · sensors · technology

Visions of the office of the future are being developed at research labs of **1** and office-equipment companies. Ideas include **2** that detect when you get to the office to inform colleagues that you're **3** to talk. There are also micro-electromechanical systems that produce super-sharp images on **4** the size of a wall. They work **5** with tablet computers that network to a shared-team display. Business software can help users find and **6** information by learning relationships among the words and **7** people use. Some companies are experimenting with doing away with dedicated desks and offices to give employees the **8** to choose where, when and how they work. Results indicate a **9** workforce, improved staff retention rates, increased **10** and **11** building costs.

KMK Exam Training

1 Produktion

Stufe II Sie arbeiten in der Marketingabteilung eines Herstellers von Elektrowaren. Um die Effektivität der eingesetzten Werbemethoden zu überprüfen, hat Ihre Abteilung neulich eine Umfrage durchgeführt, in der die Kunden befragt wurden, auf welchem Weg sie von der Firma und deren Produktangebot erfahren hatten. Verwenden Sie die unten dargestellten Diagramme, die die Ergebnisse der Umfrage zeigen, und schreiben Sie einen Bericht auf Englisch, der die folgenden Punkte berücksichtigt:

- Anlass der Umfrage bzw. des Berichts
- Kurze Einleitung der Thematik
- Alle relevanten Fakten und Ergebnisse der Umfrage
- Ihre Empfehlungen bezüglich des zukünftigen Einsatzes von Werbemitteln (mit Begründungen)

Advertising Methods

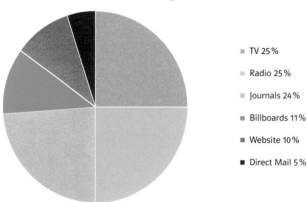

- TV 25 %
- Radio 25 %
- Journals 24 %
- Billboards 11 %
- Website 10 %
- Direct Mail 5 %

Advertising Methods	Annual Costs
TV	150,000 €
Radio	80,000 €
Journals	50,000 €
Billboards	105,000 €
Website	25,000 €
Direct Mail	40,000 €

Phrases: Advertising

Advertising products and services	
This state-of-the-art mobile phone is easy to operate with its simple slide-out keyboard.	Dieses Handy, das auf dem neuesten technischen Stand ist, hat eine leicht zu bedienende ausziehbare Tastatur.
It has an easy to use touch screen.	Es hat einen leicht zu bedienenden Touch-Screen.
This must-have versatile gizmo includes all the latest features.	Dieses vielseitige Hi-Tech-Spielzeug, das man unbedingt haben muss, hat all die neuesten Funktionen.
You'll love its slim compact shape.	Die schlanke, kompakte Form wird Sie begeistern.
You'll be bewitched by the dazzling designs of our new collection.	Lassen Sie sich verführen von den bestechenden Designs unserer neuen Kollektion.
The ultimate **in** costume jewellery.	Der ultimative Modeschmuck.
We use a minimum of packaging to minimise the environmental impact.	Wir verwenden ein Minimum an Verpackung, um die Auswirkungen auf die Umwelt so gering wie möglich zu halten.
Your finger-nails will look flawless and perfectly cared **for**.	Ihre Fingernägel sehen makellos und perfekt gepflegt aus.
… subdued autumnal colours …	… dezente Herbstfarben …
This is a portable stereo-system **of** truly diminutive dimensions.	Es handelt sich um eine tragbare Super-Mini-Stereoanlage.
This hand-crafted leather bag combines perfect chic with amazing capacity.	Diese handgearbeitete Ledertasche ist superschick und dabei unglaublich geräumig.
We rely **on** tried and tested craftsmanship.	Wir verlassen uns auf unser erprobtes handwerkliches Können.
Weekends feel simply wonderful in our silky soft-touch tops.	Erleben Sie romantische Wochenenden mit unseren flauschig-kuscheligen Tops.
This downy soft luxury scarf will go with all your winter garments. … ideal for sensitive skins …	Dieser daunenweiche Luxusschal passt zu Ihrer gesamten Wintergarderobe. … ideal für die empfindliche Haut …

16

Would you be prepared to work in another EU country? Why? / Why not?

Job applications in Germany and the EU

WORD BANK

- *to advertise*
- *to apply*
- *commissioners*
- *Council of Ministers*
- *CV*
- *education*
- *to employ*
- *European Commission*
- *European Parliament*
- *European Union*
- *experience*
- *free movement*
- *interview*
- *to invite*
- *job application*
- *job centre*
- *job exchange*
- *letter of application*
- *member countries*
- *opening*
- *to paraphrase*
- *to recruit*
- *recruitment agencies*
- *references*
- *research facilities*
- *to shortlist*
- *skills*
- *strengths*
- *training*
- *vacancy*

The principle of free movement of labour within the EU and recognition of national qualifications has potentially opened up a huge job market, of which more and more people take advantage. Working abroad may be an important building block in your career. There is evidence that a majority of employers believe global experience makes employees more adaptable, more inquisitive and more open-minded. Working in a different country and culture makes you realise that there are different ways of thinking and different ways of doing things. With the globalisation of business and trade there is a pressing need to understand how other cultures work.

At the same time, the internet has contributed to the internationalisation of the job market, making it relatively easy to find out what jobs are available in your field in a given location and whether you fulfill the requirements. On a national level newspapers carry job advertisements and job centres can help with information, directories and internet access.

M **1** Summarize the above text in German.

2 In what way has the internet contributed to the globalisation of the job market?

3 How did you find your job / apprenticeship?

A | Job advertisements

1 Study these three advertisements.

Advertisement 1

Bilingual PA / Secretary – English / German

Salary: £ 25 – 27,000   **Reference: A857302**

Aspirion plc is looking to recruit a bilingual PA / secretary with a minimum of 2 years' experience for their vibrant and cosmopolitan office in Central London. This is an excellent opportunity to work in a fast paced and varied role with plenty of opportunity for personal development and training.

Duties will comprise a wide range of administrative tasks including coordinating international meetings (plus minute taking), coordinating travel, supporting managerial staff with diary management, database management and dealing with statistical data.

Please send your CV in Word format (other formats will not be accepted) and covering letter to arnojarvis@aspirion… .com. If you do not hear from us within 5 working days, please assume that your application has not been successful. We may consider you for similar positions in the future.

Advertisement 2

German-speaking freight forwarder
Britfreight Ltd
Ashford Way
Folkestone
CT19 1FA

Reference: 23472G
Salary: £ 25 – 30,000 per annum
We, a leading logistics company, are seeking to employ a German-speaking freight forwarder to join our team in Folkestone, Kent.

- Fluent English and near-native German are essential.
- Previous experience as a logistics planner, freight forwarder and sales administrator is required.
- Accuracy, ability to work in a team under pressure dealing with a high volume of client enquiries is also a must.

Please send your CV and a covering letter to Alicia Daco at Britfreight.

Advertisement 3

Mundia Recruitment

Export Administrator / Wales

Salary: £ 23,000 – 27,000 pa
Reference: 4732000

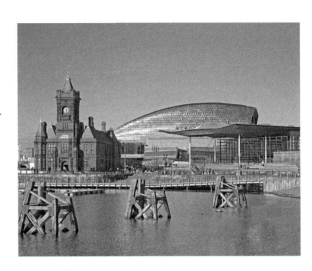

Our client is looking to appoint an export administrator who will report to the Export Manager.

Key duties will be
- maintaining and processing orders and invoices for the export department.
- dealing with customer questions via email and telephone.
- liaising with the warehouse and stock control departments.

The successful applicant will in addition be required to deal with foreign agents and give them any assistance they may require.
You will also liaise with the credit controller re overdue accounts etc.
Knowledge of Excel and SAGE would be an advantage.

Please send your CV to richardashley@clandonfitnessequipment… .co.uk

I **2** What German qualifications would equip you to apply for the jobs advertised? Discuss this in groups and then present your ideas to the class.

P **3** Describe your (future) qualifications in English and state what kind of job you would like. Do you have any idea of a career objective? For job titles refer back to Unit 1.

M **4** Beschreiben Sie mit einem Partner eine der ausgeschriebenen Stellen auf Deutsch. Besprechen Sie das Ergebnis mit der Klasse.

B | Letter of application (covering letter)

A good covering letter is essential when you are looking for work. However, it needs to be brief and attention-grabbing . Before writing the letter you should do some research on the company as your letter (and your CV) should be tailored to that company. If the job ad gives a name, you should use it. The company advertising the position may instruct you to send the covering letter by email or as an attachment. The text should still be written like a letter (and with the same care!). If they do not ask for a covering letter you should not send one.

Your letter of application, whether sent as a letter or email depending on the instructions of the potential employer, should be set out clearly and include the points below. It should be as brief as possible – not more than 1 side.

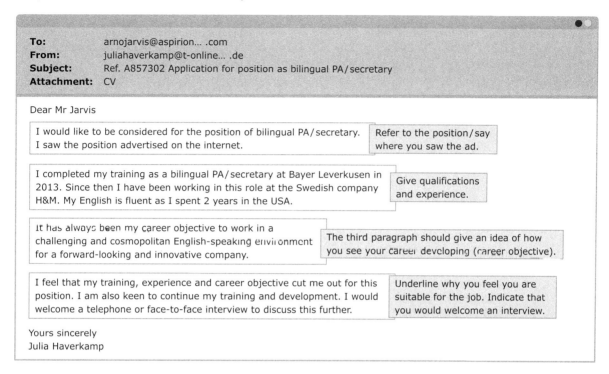

To: arnojarvis@aspirion... .com
From: juliahaverkamp@t-online... .de
Subject: Ref. A857302 Application for position as bilingual PA / secretary
Attachment: CV

Dear Mr Jarvis

I would like to be considered for the position of bilingual PA / secretary. I saw the position advertised on the internet.
Refer to the position / say where you saw the ad.

I completed my training as a bilingual PA / secretary at Bayer Leverkusen in 2013. Since then I have been working in this role at the Swedish company H&M. My English is fluent as I spent 2 years in the USA.
Give qualifications and experience.

It has always been my career objective to work in a challenging and cosmopolitan English-speaking environment for a forward-looking and innovative company.
The third paragraph should give an idea of how you see your career developing (career objective).

I feel that my training, experience and career objective cut me out for this position. I am also keen to continue my training and development. I would welcome a telephone or face-to-face interview to discuss this further.
Underline why you feel you are suitable for the job. Indicate that you would welcome an interview.

Yours sincerely
Julia Haverkamp

1 Now complete this covering letter using the word from the box.

> grateful · apply · as advertised · apprenticeship · bilingual · German-speaking · administrator · experience

Reference 783582G

Dear Ms Daco

I would like to **1** for the position of a **2** freight forwarder **3** on your website yesterday.

I completed a 3 year **4** at a well-known German freight forwarder in Bremen four years ago and am still working for this company. I have the required **5** as a logistics planner, freight forwarder and sales **6**. I am also used to working under pressure.

I am **7** and fluent in both German and English and am planning to move to England.

I would be **8** if you would consider me for this position.

Yours sincerely
Jonathan Maier

Encl. CV

P **2** Write a letter of application (covering letter) for one of the three jobs advertised on the previous pages. Use your own name and address.

C | CV (Curriculum Vitae)

A carefully arranged CV is a prerequisite for any application. The following are two standard German Lebensläufe with paraphrases in English. They are relatively brief because the subjects are at the beginning of their careers and have very little job experience. It should be emphasised that it is only possible to give an approximate equivalent for German schools, examinations and professions. It is important to remember that a foreign employer will probably not be familiar with the German education and vocational training systems. When applying for a job in English – and there are more and more companies in continental Europe whose company language is English – it is also important to be aware of differences. See the text under Intercultural Communication.

1 Study the following German CVs with a paraphrase in English.

German CV 1

Tabellarischer Lebenslauf

Persönliche Angaben

Name	Melek Aydogan
Adresse	Kalkumer Platz 21
	50667 Köln
	Tel.: 01 70 525 39 63,
	E-Mail: melekaydogan@t-online… .de
Staatsangehörigkeit	deutsch
Geburtstag	23.01.1995
Geburtsort	Köln
Familienstand	ledig

Schulbildung

2001–2005	Grundschule Niederkassel
2005–2013	Rahel-Varnhagen-Gymnasium, Köln
2013	Abitur (Leistungskurse: Englisch, Mathematik, Grundkurse: Sozialwissenschaften, Türkisch, Gesamtnote: 2,2)

Tätigkeiten

August 2011–Juli 2012	Hausaufgabenhilfe im „Lernzentrum", Köln
August 2012–Juni 2013	Aushilfstätigkeit im Reisebüro „Evren", Düsseldorf
seit September 2013	Ausbildung zur Kauffrau für Büromanagement im Reisebüro „Evren"

Sprachkenntnisse

Deutsch: wie Muttersprache
Türkisch: Muttersprache
Englisch: gut in Wort und Schrift
Italienisch: Grundkenntnisse

PC-Kenntnisse

Microsoft Office, Excel, Powerpoint

Interessen

Musik, Kanufahren, Volleyball

English paraphrase CV1

Curriculum Vitae

Personal details

Name	Melek Aydogan
Address	Kalkumer Platz 21
	50667 Köln
	Tel.: 01 70 525 39 63
	Email: melekaydogan@t-online… .de
Nationality	German
Date of birth	23 January 1995
Place of birth	Cologne, Germany
Marital status	single

Education

2001 – 2005	Primary school Niederkassel
2005 – 2013	Rahel Varnhagen-Gymnasium, Cologne (grammar school)
2013	Abitur (= A-Levels) Major subjects: English, Mathematics. Subsidiary courses: Social sciences, Turkish. Overall grade: 2.2 (= good = B)

Job experience and other activities

August 2011 – July 2012	Assisting pupils with homework at the „Lernzentrum" (Learning Centre),Cologne
August 2011 – June 2013	Temporary employment at the „Evren" travel agency in Düsseldorf
From September 2013	Traineeship as an office management clerk/assistant at the „Evren" travel agency

Languages	German: native command
	Turkish: mother tongue
	English: good command of both spoken and written English
	Italian: basic knowledge
Computer skills	Microsoft Office, Excel, Powerpoint
Hobbies	Music, canoeing, volleyball

German CV2

Tabellarischer Lebenslauf

Persönliche Angaben

Name	Niko Pfeiffer
Adresse	44894 Bochum
	Montanusstr. 42
	Tel.: 02 34 466 98 34
	E-Mail: nikopfeiffer@aol… .com
Staatsangehörigkeit	deutsch
Geburtstag	10.05.1995
Geburtsort	Dortmund
Familienstand	ledig

Schulbildung

2001 – 2005	Grundschule Bochum-Langendreer
2005 – 2009	Albert-Einstein-Realschule Bochum
2009 – 2011	Gesamtschule am Teich, Dortmund
2011 – 2013	Höhere Handelsschule, Kaufmännische Schule II, Dortmund

Ausbildung

2014 – 2017	Ausbildung zum Industriekaufmann bei Kabel AG, Leverkusen Schwerpunkte: Rechnungswesen, Einkauf
2016	KMK – Fremdsprachenzertifikat Englisch für kaufmännische und verwaltende Berufe, Stufe II
voraussichtlich Mai 2017	Abschlussprüfung

Tätigkeiten

2011 – 2013	Aushilfstätigkeit als Fahrradkurier
2013 – 2014	Bundesfreiwilligendienst in einer Behindertenwerkstatt

Sonstige Kenntnisse	MS Office, Linux
	Englisch fließend, Spanisch ausbaufähig
Interessen	Fitness, Fußball, Science-Fiction

English paraphrase CV 2

Curriculum Vitae

Personal details

Name	Niko Pfeiffer
Address	44894 Bochum
	Montanusstr. 42
	Tel.: 02 34 466 98 34
	E-Mail: nikopfeiffer@aol… .com
Nationality	German
Date of birth	10 May 1995
Place of birth	Dortmund
Marital status	single

Education/Training

2001–2005	Primary School Bochum-Langendreer
2005–2009	Albert-Einstein-Realschule (= higher secondary school), Bochum
2009–2011	Gesamtschule am Teich (comprehensive) Dortmund, School-leaving certificate "Fachoberschulreife" enabling student to continue education at a higher vocational college
2011–2013	Höhere Handelsschule, Kaufmännische Schule II (= higher commercial college), Dortmund Final examination: Fachhochschulreife enabling student to enrol at a polytechnic university
2014–2017	Traineeship as an industrial clerk/industrial business management assistant at Kabel AG, Leverkusen Focus: accounting, purchasing
2016	KMK-foreign language certificate in English for commercial and administrative professions, Level 2
scheduled May 2017	Final examination traineeship

Job experience

2011–2013	Temporary employment as a cycle courier
2013–2014	Voluntary social service in a workshop for disabled people

Other skills	MS Office, Linux, fluent English, basic Spanish
Personal Interests	Working out, football, science fiction

P/M **2**   Now produce a paraphrase of your own CV using one of these models.

COMMUNICATION ACROSS CULTURES

JOB APPLICATION IN THE EU

Even within the EU ideas about what makes for a good CV differ. If you are applying for a job in one of the member countries, it is important to find out about any requirements that differ from the norm in your own country. In English CVs it is now not usual to give details of age or marital status. Nor is it usual to include a photo. Often a "career objective" – i.e. where you would eventually like to be careerwise – is mentioned in the CV. Employers in Britain do not generally hand out testimonials. When applying for a job you will be asked to give the names of referees whom the potential employer then approaches independently. If this is what the job advert says, you should not include testimonials. CVs should be no longer than one side of a page (like the two models given here). However, if you have a lot of relevant job experience, you could use a second side – but not more. American CVs should not be longer than 1 side. American employers will not read beyond the first page. Generally, (unlike the German "Lebensläufe" given here) CVs in English-speaking countries are arranged in reverse chronological order. The usual order is: name + address; employment history starting from the present; secondary education (not necessary to give details of primary schools etc); other skills. Again you are not required to disclose your personal interests although you may do so if you wish. Remember also that the person reading your CV will probably not be familiar with the education system in your country. So it is important to say clearly which school is a secondary school and what is the final examination.

TASK:

3 List the main differences between German and English CVs.

P **4** Now rewrite your paraphrased CV in the English format as described above.

I **5** Moritz Sinhuber plans to apply for a job with Trendissimo, a London men's fashion and accessories company, which he saw advertised in a German newspaper. The advertisement gives no name to address the covering letter to so he decides to ring the company.
Roleplay the following dialogue using the prompts.

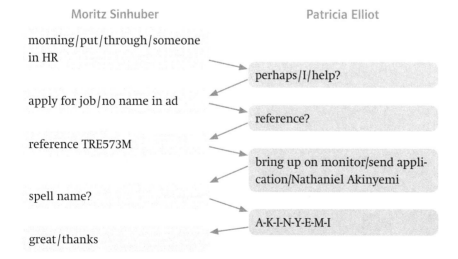

Moritz Sinhuber	Patricia Elliot
morning/put/through/someone in HR	
	perhaps/I/help?
apply for job/no name in ad	
	reference?
reference TRE573M	
	bring up on monitor/send application/Nathaniel Akinyemi
spell name?	
	A-K-I-N-Y-E-M-I
great/thanks	

D | Interviews

Julia Haverkamp has received an email from Aron Jarvis to say that he wishes to conduct a telephone interview with her on the coming Tuesday at 10 am her time. She has clearly been shortlisted. She has a few days to prepare.
Tuesday comes and Julia's mobile rings.

R **1** Listen to the interview and answer the questions below.

A2.15
1. How does Arno Jarvis put Julia at her ease?
2. What kind of a working environment does Julia ideally want to work in?
3. What does Arno want to know about her role in her present office?
4. What does she know about Aspirion? Why does he ask her about this?
5. How does Julia turn the question about the gap in her CV to her advantage?
6. Where are Aspirion's offices located?

2 Read the following text and answer the questions on the next page.

If you are invited to an interview:
- Do some research. Find out as much as you can about the company, its products or services and the image it projects so that you can make an informed impression and demonstrate that you are interested in the company. Check out the company's website and social media profiles. Has the company been mentioned in the press recently?
- Re-visit the ad. Refresh your memory as to what exactly they are looking for.
- Think about any questions you would like to ask about points that are not covered by the interviewer. How big is the office you'll be working in? Finding accommodation in London? Exact location of the office?
- Be prepared for any embarrassing questions the interviewer might ask. Gaps in your CV? Reasons for wanting to change jobs?
- What are your other interests? Think carefully about this. If you say you like films, expect to be asked what was the last film you saw.
- Do not underestimate the importance of so-called "soft skills". In a face-to-face or video interview it is important to be dressed smartly and not too informally (no jeans or T-shirts!). In Britain women should go for a skirt and jacket top. Men should wear a business suit.

1. Why is it important to do some research on the company (or companies) you are applying to?
2. What is meant by "soft skills"?
3. What sort of things in a CV might be embarrassing?
4. Why do you think it is a good idea for the interviewee to ask a question?

3 You have applied for a job in the purchasing department of Waitrose, a British supermarket chain. Use the internet to do some research on the company.

4 Read the following text and decide which of the statements below are true or false.

Things that employers say make a negative impression in interviews:
- poor personal appearance (clothes, hair, shoes etc)
- lack of interest and enthusiasm – passive
- lack of confidence – obvious nervousness
- failure to ask questions about the job
- underlying attitude of "What can you do for me?"
- lack of preparation for the interview
- lack of planning for career – no purpose or goals
- over-emphasis on money
- inability to express thoughts clearly
- failure to look the interviewer in the eye

Statements:
1. People are more relaxed nowadays – it's OK to wear jeans and a T-shirt to an interview.
2. You can't really be expected to know much about the firm – after all you might not get the job.
3. You should make eye contact with the interviewer, smile and nod to indicate agreement or enthusiasm.
4. It's not fair to expect you to know where you want to end up careerwise – if you haven't even finished your traineeship.
5. You should be prepared to talk about any interests you mention.
6. If you find talking about some interests in English too difficult, it's OK not to mention them.
7. It's very important that you find out what your holiday entitlement is.
8. It makes a good impression if you express your thoughts clearly and confidently.

5 Interviewers often ask difficult or unexpected questions.
Match the following questions with the replies.

1.	Why do you want to leave your present job?	a.	I enjoy working with people and always have a good rapport with customers.
2.	How would you like to see your career develop. Do you have an objective in mind?	b.	I like the work and the people but the company is very small and I don't have much scope to use my languages. I'd like to gain some experience working for a big company.
3.	Why would you like to work for this company?	c.	From the job ads I've seen € 2,200 to 2,500 seems to be the going rate. I'd be happy with a salary somewhere in that range.
4.	What did you find most satisfying about your previous job?	d.	I am very motivated and enjoy challenges. I'm good at working to deadlines – they don't faze me. I've got a good sense of humour.
5.	What would you say were your strengths?	e.	I'm very interested in the company's products and services and the values it projects – especially re cultural and ethnic diversity. I like its profile on social media. It think it would allow me to expand my interest and competence in IT.
6.	What are your expectations re salary?	f.	I'd like to continue my training and when I've got sufficient experience I'd like to go for a job in management. I also toy with the idea of setting up my own company eventually.

6 Using the above questions as a guideline, act out an interview situation with a partner. Practise giving your own answers to the above questions (plus any others you think are relevant).

7 A friend rings you to tell you he's got an interview. As you've had more experience of interviews, he asks you for a few tips. (Refer back to the section on interviews.)
Choose task a, b or c.

○ a. Text him a few tips about what to wear.

◐ b. Text him a few tips about his appearance, body language and knowing something about the company.

● c. Send him a text regarding appearance, body language, career objective and passivity.

8 Jonathan Maier sent off his application to Alicia Daco at Britfreight Ltd and
⊙ A2.16 has been invited to a face-to-face interview. He presents himself at 9 am looking very smart wearing a grey business suit, shirt and tie.
Listen to the interview and choose task a, b or c.

○ a. Answer the following questions.

1. Where has Jonathan come from to attend the interview?
2. Why does he want to move to South East England?
3. What are Jonathan's duties in Bremen?

◐ b. Answer the following questions.

1. Why is there such a lot of freight traffic near Folkestone?
2. Why is the atmosphere so competitive?
3. What is meant by being "proactive about getting new accounts"?

●   c.   Answer the following questions.

     1. How will Jonathan be involved with the sales team?
     2. How does he answer the question about his customer service skills?
     3. Why do you think Alicia suggests that Jonathan should meet the team he'd be working with?

| **9** Work with a partner. Prepare and act out the following interview in a role play in English using the prompts on the role cards.

→ **ROLE CARD B:** page 262

Role card A (interviewer)

Sie sind Richard Ashley (oder seine Kollegin Emilia Chadwicke) von der HR-Abteilung der Clandon Fitness Equipment Ltd.
Über die Mundia Online-Recruitment Agency suchen Sie eine/n zweisprachige/n Mitarbeiter/in für die Exportabteilung. Sie haben mehrere Bewerber zu einem Vorstellungsgespräch eingeladen.

Beginnen Sie das Gespräch mit allgemeinen Fragen z. B. nach:
* Flug
* Heimatstadt des Bewerbers
* Wetter

Fassen Sie die Anforderungen kurz zusammen:
* zweisprachig
* Erfahrung in einer Exportabteilung
* Zusammenarbeit mit den anderen betroffenen Abteilungen
* teamfähig
* Kontakt halten mit Vertretern im Ausland

Fragen Sie nach der Berufserfahrung.
* Erkundigen Sie sich nach den Gründen , warum der Bewerber in GB arbeiten möchte.
* Versprechen Sie innerhalb von 10 Arbeitstagen Bescheid zu geben.
* Verabschieden Sie den Bewerber.

E | The European Union

The free movement of labour was and is one of the central principles in the creation of a unified single market in Europe. The free movement of goods and services is the second and the free movement of capital the third. The free movement of goods and capital are furthest advanced. Problems of language, cultural differences and tradition make it more difficult for people to move to other countries in the European Union to work than say, to move from New York to San Francisco in the USA. Despite its imperfections as a single market, the EU does offer immense opportunities and the number of people taking advantage of their right to look for employment and take up residence in other EU countries is increasing.

It has been estimated that sixty per cent of the laws and regulations that affect our lives no longer originate in Berlin, Paris or London, but in Brussels, the seat of the European Commission. This is why it is important to have a basic understanding of EU institutions.

European Commission
At the present time each of the 28 members nominates one commissioner. They are appointed and not elected. Each commissioner has a portfolio, e.g. transport, trade, competition, environment.
The President of the Commission is also nominated by the 28 member countries. Both the president and the commissioners have to be endorsed by the European Parliament.
What is the role of the Commission?
- It ensures that the various treaties signed by the member states are not violated. It may impose fines.
- It introduces regulations (directives).
- It makes proposals for new legislation.
- It spends the budget agreed upon by the 28 member states which also decide how it is to be spent.

Council of Ministers
Political decisions are taken by the Council of Ministers. This council is made up of 1 minister from each of the 28 member states. When financial or fiscal issues are involved the ministers of finance meet, when agricultural issues are to be dealt with ministers of agriculture meet etc. They have indirect democratic legitimacy as they are elected in their country of origin. The European Council consisting of the prime ministers or presidents of the member countries meet up to four times a year to resolve issues which could not be dealt with at a lower level.

European Parliament

Members of the European Parliament are elected in all 28 member states. It's prestige suffers from low participation in the European elections. It does, however, have powers to monitor the work of the commission and even to reject individual commissioners or the commission as a whole.

President

The president is appointed by the 28 member countries for a once-renewable term of 2½ years.

Foreign Affairs

and EU "embassies" abroad are the responsibility of the High Representative of the Union for Foreign Affairs and Security Policy (also appointed by the 28 member countries.)

1 Answer the following questions.

1. What employment advantages does the EU offer the citizens of the 28 member countries?
2. How great is the impact of the EU on our everyday life?
3. What is the role of the European Commission?
4. Which of the EU institutions takes the political decisions?
5. What powers does the EU parliament have?

2 Work in groups. Use the internet to research current developments in the EU. What problems does the EU face at the present time? Present your findings to the class.

3 What is the Schengen Agreement? Which countries are signatories, which are not? Use the internet as a source of information.

4 Which EU countries do not use the Euro as their national currency? What currencies do they use. Use the Internet to check this out.

INFO: EU-Facts and figures

EU member countries (28 at present):
Austria, Belgium, Bulgaria, Croatia, Cyprus, Czech Republic, Denmark, Estonia, Finland, France, Germany, Greece, Hungary, Ireland, Italy, Latvia, Lithuania, Luxemburg, Malta, The Netherlands, Poland, Portugal, Romania, Slovakia, Slovenia, Spain, Sweden, United Kingdom*.

Total area: 4,423,147 sq.km.

Total population: c. 505.73 million

Total GDP: between $18 and $20 trillion

Languages: There are over 24 official languages. English is spoken by 51% of European citizens – the most widely spoken foreign language.

---

*In June 2016 the UK voted to leave the EU ("Brexit").

Office expert

F | Office jobs

WILLING TO WORK IN A MULTICULTURAL OFFICE ENVIRONMENT?

Take a big step forward with our internship program! At Studios Limited we offer you the chance to gain hands-on office work experience to give you an advantage over future competitors in the job market. Our interns come from different companies, cultures and countries, from all over Europe. Our program runs all through the year, lasting from two weeks up to a year, so you can choose your start and end dates yourself.

Join our team of young and motivated people. The program includes the practical application of all aspects of office work, as well as the opportunity to advance your communication and foreign language skills. Experience learning to live and work within a multicultural office setting.

INTERNATIONAL PARTICIPATION

We are seeking international organizations able to provide us with a source of qualified, enthusiastic trainees. Internship4America provides domestic and international internships for students and young professionals from around the world. Our USA internships, summer internships, hospitality internships and international internships provide housing, transportation and a stipend for qualified trainees. We develop corporate internship programs. Our programs are designed to meet the US State Department Exchange Visitors Program criteria. Submit your résumé and application to be considered for our program.

R **1** Read the texts above and decide if these statements are
a. TRUE of both texts, b. TRUE of text 1 only, c. TRUE of text 2 only.

1. The programme is targeted towards college students/graduates.
2. The programme gives young people the chance to work abroad.
3. It would be possible to do an internship during holiday break.
4. Applicants are invited to send in their curriculum vitae.
5. The programme arranges for a place to live and a small salary.
6. The programme is in keeping with government regulations.
7. People from all over the world participate in the programme.
8. The programme promises to improve your career opportunities.

P **2** Write a letter / an email of enquiry to one of the two job ads above. Include the following points:

- A brief personal introduction stating your current position
- Reason why you want to do an internship
- Preferences concerning country, length and time frame for the internship
- At least one question concerning costs (e. g. housing, transportation) or payment
- Reference to attached CV
- Express hope to receive a positive answer soon.

KMK Exam Training

1 Mediation (Englisch – Deutsch)

Stufe II   Sie suchen eine neue Herausforderung und finden die folgende Stellenanzeige im Internet. Fassen Sie die Hauptanforderungen und Aufgaben der Stelle auf Deutsch zusammen.

Promotional Events Assistant

The Modern Music Academy in Munich is looking for an experienced and dynamic assistant for our promotional events manager. The candidate must be an outstanding communicator with sales and public speaking experience and speak fluent English and German. The position involves a wide range of duties to achieve our goal of recruiting the desired number of talented students.

Key qualifications

- Sales-focused and goal orientated
- Able to communicate (internal and external) at all levels
- Outstanding presentation and promotional skills
- Willingness to learn about all our courses and admissions processes.
- Can work flexibly and calmly under pressure
- Willing to work evenings and weekends as required
- Strong communication skills: face to face and in front of groups
- Fluent in English and German Language
- Feeling for music and an understanding of the modern music industry

Principal tasks

- Assist the manager of Promotional Event in the goal of enrolling 175 new students
- Deliver course offers to all potential applicants promptly and correctly
- Assist with organizing and implementing Open House Days and workshops
- Assist with organizing promotional events all over Germany
- Liaise with the Events team concerning schools tours, recruitment events, education fairs etc.
- Liaise with the central marketing team regarding events, PR activities, website content and social media

In addition to the above, it is also desirable that the candidate is willing and able to support the administration in processing applications, audition bookings and enquiries when required.   **238 words**

2 Produktion

Stufe II   Verfassen Sie eine E-Mail auf Englisch, um sich auf die Stellenanzeige oben zu bewerben. Folgende Punkte sollten enthalten sein (die Angaben können frei erfunden sein):

- Erwähnen Sie, wie Sie auf die Stelle aufmerksam geworden sind.
- Stellen Sie sich kurz vor und geben Sie an, in welcher Position Sie derzeit tätig sind.
- Geben Sie relevante Informationen bezüglich Ihrer Ausbildung und Berufserfahrung.
- Heben Sie Qualifikationen (Softskills) hervor, die Sie besonders auszeichnen und ideal zur ausgeschriebenen Stelle passen.
- Sagen Sie, warum Sie besonders an dieser Stelle interessiert sind.
- Bringen Sie zum Ausdruck, dass Sie für ein Interview zur Verfügung stehen und sich freuen würden von der Schule zu hören.

Phrases: Applications

To refer to the source of address	
I saw your advertisement **in** …	Ich habe Ihre Anzeige in … gesehen.
I saw this vacancy advertised **on** the … website.	Ich habe diese Stellenanzeige auf der … Webseite gefunden.
I would like to apply for the position advertised in the …	Ich möchte mich für den in der … ausgeschriebenen Posten bewerben.
I am applying on the off-chance that you may have a vacancy.	Ich erlaube mir, Ihnen eine Initiativbewerbung zu schicken, für den Fall, dass bei Ihnen eine Stelle frei ist.

To give reasons for applying	
I am particularly attracted **to** this position as …	Ich bin an dieser Stelle besonders interessiert, …
I have just completed a traineeship **at** …	Ich habe gerade meine Ausbildung bei … abgeschlossen.
I completed an apprenticeship two years ago.	Vor zwei Jahren haben ich meine Ausbildung abgeschlossen.
I have some experience in the export trade.	Ich habe Erfahrungen im Außenhandel.
I am familiar **with** this kind of work.	Mit dieser Tätigkeit bin ich vertraut.
I enjoy working in a team.	Ich arbeite gern im Team.
I would welcome the opportunity to …	Ich würde mich über die Möglichkeit freuen …
I am keen to use my knowledge **of** English and French.	Ich möchte sehr gerne meine Englisch- und Französischkenntnisse anwenden.

To refer to your German school career	
From … to … I attended … comparable **to** • primary school • grammar school (UK) • higher secondary school • secondary modern school • comprehensive (school) • high school (USA) • vocational school • commercial school • business college • polytechnic university, university of applied sciences	Von … bis … besuchte ich … vergleichbar mit • Grundschule • Gymnasium • Realschule • Hauptschule • Gesamtschule • (Einheitsschule für die Sekundarstufe) • Berufsschule • Höhere Handelsschule • Berufskolleg • Fachhochschule

To refer to your German school career

In ... I obtained the • certificate enabling a student to continue education at higher vocational school • German higher education entrance qualification • German university entrance qualification	Im Jahre ... erwarb ich das Zeugnis der • Fachoberschulreife • Fachhochschulreife • allgemeine Hochschulreife (Abitur)

In ... I passed the
• state examination in English for clerical and administrative professions
• Chamber of Commerce examination
   – "Certified Foreign Language Correspondent"
   – "English for Commercial Trainees"
	Im Jahre ... legte ich die ...
	• Zertifikatsprüfung Englisch für kaufmännische und verwaltende Berufe (KMK-Zertifikat)
	• IHK-Prüfung
	   – „Geprüfte/r Fremdsprachenkorrespondent/in"
	   – „Zusatzqualifikation Englisch für kaufmännische Auszubildende" ab.

To refer to qualifications

I **took** my Abitur two years ago.	Vor zwei Jahren habe ich das Abitur gemacht.
My main subjects included English and Maths.	Meine Leistungskurse waren Englisch und Mathematik.
I have trained **as a** ...	Ich bin gelernte/r ...
I have completed an apprenticeship **in** ...	Ich habe eine Ausbildung als ... abgeschlossen.
I did my apprenticeship **with** the ... company.	Ich habe eine Ausbildung bei der Firma ... gemacht.
I spent two months in Bath **on** a placement.	Ich war zwei Monate zu einem Praktikum in Bath.
I have good admin and bookkeeping skills.	Ich verfüge über gute Kenntnisse und Fertigkeiten, was Organisation und Buchhaltung angeht.

To refer to certificates and references

I enclose certified copies of my certificates / translations of ...	Als Anlage übersende ich Ihnen beglaubigte Zeugniskopien / Übersetzungen von ...
I would be happy to provide the names of referees.	Ich würde Ihnen gerne Referenzen angeben.

To refer to starting date and relocation

I would be able to start **at** short notice.	Ich kann kurzfristig anfangen.
I could start **on** 1 August.	Ich könnte am 1. August anfangen.
I would be prepared to move **to** ...	Ich wäre bereit nach ... umzuziehen.

To close the letter

I look forward **to hearing** from you.	Ich sehe Ihrer Antwort mit Interesse entgegen.
I hope that you will consider my application suitable and give me the opportunity to present myself **at** an interview.	Ich hoffe, dass Sie meine Bewerbung in Betracht ziehen und mir die Möglichkeit geben, mich Ihnen persönlich vorzustellen.

Mock Exam

Stufe II

Schriftliche Prüfung

Zeit:	90 Minuten
Hilfsmittel:	allgemeines zweisprachiges Wörterbuch
Maximale Punkte:	100 Punkte

Die Aufgabenteile der schriftlichen Prüfung werden wie folgt gewichtet:
- Rezeption   40 %
- Produktion   30 %
- Mediation   30 %

Die vorgelegte Musterprüfung besteht aus vier Aufgaben. Die ersten zwei Aufgaben gehören zum Bereich Rezeption und prüfen Ihre Fähigkeit, sowohl gesprochene als auch geschriebene englische Texte zu verstehen. Bei der dritten Aufgabe (Produktion) soll ein Schriftstück in Englisch erstellt werden. Für die vierte Aufgabe müssen Sie Texte von der deutschen oder englischen in die jeweils andere Sprache übertragen = Mediation.

Aufgabe 1 – Rezeption: Hörverstehen | 20 VP |

⊚ A2.17   **Teil 1 (Anrufbeantworter)** | 8 VP |

Ihre Firma hat bei einem Hersteller in Dänemark eine Abfüllmaschine für medizinische Produkte bestellt und erwartet die Lieferung durch einen dänischen Spediteur.

Ihre Vorgesetzte bittet Sie, folgende Nachricht auf dem Anrufbeantworter abzuhören und ihr die nötigen Details auf dem Formular der Telefonnotiz auf Deutsch mitzuteilen. Sie hören die Nachricht zweimal.

MEDICARE GMBH STUTTGART
TELEFONNOTIZ

Datum: _12.06.20..._   Uhrzeit: _08:15 Uhr_

Anrufer: _____ (1 VP)

Grund des Anrufs: _____ (1 VP)

Inhalt des Anrufs: _____ (5 VP)

E-Mail: _____ (1 VP)

⊙ A2.18   **Teil 2 (Dialog)**   12 VP

Sie sind am Ende Ihrer Ausbildung und haben sich bei einer neuen Firma
beworben. Diese hat Sie zum Vorstellungsgespräch eingeladen. Ihr Kollege
hat zu diesem Thema einen Podcast gefunden, den er Ihnen zumailt.

Beantworten Sie die Fragen stichwortartig auf Deutsch.
Sie hören den folgenden Podcast zweimal.

1. Warum sind so viele Leute vor dem Vorstellungsgespräch
   nervös? *(1 VP)*
2. Wie kann man seine Chancen bei einem Vorstellungsgespräch
   verbessern? *(2 VP)*
3. Warum ist es wichtig, dem Interviewer Fragen zu stellen? *(1 VP)*
4. Nach welchen zwei Dingen sollte man am besten nicht
   fragen? *(1 VP)*
5. Was machen immer mehr Firmen im Vorstellungsgespräch
   und wozu? *(2 VP)*
6. Welche Ratschläge hat Herr Loader für das Vorstellungsgespräch selbst? (3 Nennungen) *(3 VP)*
7. Welche Dinge sollten bei einem Videointerview beachtet
   werden? (2 Nennungen) *(2 VP)*

Aufgabe 2 – Rezeption: Leseverstehen   20 VP

Lesen Sie den folgenden Text durch und beantworten Sie bitte die
nachfolgenden Verständnisfragen in Stichworten auf Deutsch. Sie erhalten
pro Antwort 1 – 4 Verrechnungspunkte.

1. Warum kann das Arbeiten in einer multikulturellen
   Umgebung problematisch sein? *(2 VP)*
2. Was ist mit dem Terminus „lingua franca" gemeint? *(2 VP)*
3. Welche vier Elemente spielen bei der sprachlichen
   Kommunikation eine Rolle? *(4 VP)*
4. Wodurch entstehen oft Missverständnisse in der inter-
   kulturellen Kommunikation? *(2 VP)*
5. Was ist mit dem Begriff „stereotypes" gemeint? *(2 VP)*
6. Worin besteht die Gefahr, wenn man zu sehr in „Stereotypen"
   denkt? *(2 VP)*
7. Welche weiteren individuellen und kulturellen Unterschiede
   führen oft zu Missverständnissen oder sogar Konflikten? *(2 VP)*
8. Welche Unterschiede gibt es zwischen den verschiedenen
   Kulturen in Bezug auf Small Talk? *(2 VP)*
9. Wie stehen verschiedene Kulturen dazu, Gefühle zu zeigen?
   (2 VP)

Textgrundlage zu Aufgabe 2

Barriers in Intercultural Communication

In today's business world we are increasingly required to communicate with people from different cultural backgrounds. Living and
5 working in a multicultural environment is not always easy or free of conflict. The problems can be complex and create barriers that have to be overcome.

10 Obviously, language is the first hurdle. In order to talk to someone, you must first find a common language. Today, English is generally the lingua franca for business communication. This means that two people
15 who both speak a different native language will end up speaking a third language, English, if they need to communicate with each other.

How does that affect their interaction?
20 Languages are complex and learning to communicate in a foreign language is challenging. It is not a matter of simply learning the right phrases. Speaking a language involves gestures, body language,
25 facial expressions and tone of voice. Such communication elements are used to convey complex emotions and concepts and vary widely from culture to culture. This can easily lead to misunderstandings.

30 Aside from language, stereotyping can also create communication barriers. Stereotypes are assumptions we make about the characteristics and behaviour of people of another group or culture. Typical stereotypes
35 are: Americans are impatient, Spanish-speaking people are always late, the Japanese are very polite and so on. Whether there is an element of truth in such stereotypes

is not the point. The danger is in assuming that each and every person belonging to a 40 given group possesses the characteristics that are ascribed to that group and, even worse, acting on those assumptions.

Also, there are differences between individuals and between cultures, like 45 differences in tastes, habits and behaviour patterns. Such differences can lead to misunderstandings and even conflicts. Cultures as well as people have different ideas about what is the right way to act and 50 what is considered rude or inappropriate. For example, people from some cultures feel more comfortable if they can make small talk before a negotiation, while others feel it's a waste of time and want to get straight 55 to business. Such differences can cause conflicts and be barriers to communication if they are ignored.

Another important point and something that differs greatly from culture to culture, 60 is how people display emotions. For some, notably North American and Western European cultures, showing anger or other strong emotions in a business environment is generally considered taboo while other 65 cultures tolerate or even expect emotional engagement in discussions. Being unaware of such differences can easily lead to misunderstandings.

If you are unsure about cultural differences 70 between you and your business partner, find out before you take up communication. It is not just what you communicate, but also how you do it that can make all the difference. **457 Wörter** 75

Aufgabe 3 – Produktion: Schriftstücke erstellen

30 VP

Sie arbeiten in der Einkaufsabteilung der Firma MediCare GmbH in Stuttgart. Ihr Unternehmen bestellt regelmäßig Büromaterial bei der Firma Office4You Ltd. In letzter Zeit allerdings gab es einige Probleme. Sie haben sich bereits mehrmals telefonisch bei der Firma beschwert, aber leider ohne Erfolg. Da die Waren von Office4You äußerst günstig sind und ihre Qualität sehr gut ist, möchten Sie ungern Ihren Lieferanten wechseln.

Verfassen Sie einen Beschwerdebrief auf Englisch, einschließlich Anrede und Betreff. Bitte schreiben Sie vollständige Sätze und berücksichtigen Sie dabei folgende Punkte:

Office4You Ltd.

Ansprechpartner:	Emma Thornton
Straße:	Stocker Rd
Hausnummer:	28
Postleitzahl:	EX4 4PT
Ort:	Exeter
Land:	England

- Datum, Anrede, Betreff
- Als langjähriger Kunde schätzen Sie die Firma aufgrund ihrer guten Preise und der qualitativ hochwertigen Produkte.
- Dennoch gab es in letzter Zeit Grund zur Beschwerde:
  - Die letzten drei Lieferungen kamen zu spät und waren dazu auch noch unvollständig.
  - Die letzten zwei Rechnungen enthielten Fehler.
  - Sie haben den Kundenservice bereits mehrmals per Telefon kontaktiert – ohne Erfolg.
- Sie bitten um eine Erklärung.
- Sollten sich die Probleme wiederholen, sehen Sie sich gezwungen, den Lieferanten zu wechseln.
- Beenden Sie den Brief höflich und zuversichtlich.

Aufgabe 4 – Mediation: Übertragen eines Textes

30 VP

Sie vertreten eine Kollegin aus der Export- und Verkaufsabteilung der MediCare GmbH bei der monatlichen Verkaufsbesprechung und sind zuständig für die Erstellung des Protokolls. Sie haben das Protokoll bereits in deutscher Sprache verfasst. Übertragen Sie es nun stichwortartig ins Englische.

Protokoll

Monatliche Verkaufsbesprechung:
25. Januar 20…

Anwesend:
Julia Burrup, Louise Edwards, Anton Flossmann, Eric Foster, Theresa Gnamm, Tilman Hohlke, Stephen Myers, Jochen Rothaupt, Alexandra Smith, Karin Werner (Vorsitzende)

Entschuldigt abwesend:
Larissa Schwarz

Genehmigung:
Das Protokoll der Sitzung vom 18. Dezember 20… wird einstimmig angenommen.

Zu klärende Fragen:
keine

Verkäufe:
Julia berichtet, dass die Großbritannien-Verkäufe im Vergleich zum November um 5 % gesunken sind. Der November musste bereits einen Rückgang um 4 % gegenüber den Monaten August bis September verzeichnen.
→ Julia bereitet bis 30. Januar einen Verkaufsbericht über die letzten sechs Monate vor.

Werbebudget:
Eine Erhöhung des Werbebudgets für das nächste Halbjahr wird genehmigt. Eric schildert einzelne Probleme mit der Werbeagentur „Think Big" und empfiehlt einen Wechsel. Es wird zugestimmt, dass eine neue Werbeagentur gesucht werden soll.
→ Stephen stellt zum 15. Februar einen Überblick über die Werbeausgaben bereit.
→ Eric besucht am Mittwoch, den 3. Februar, die Werbeagentur „Think Big", um die Probleme der Werbeaktion zu besprechen und sie über den Wechsel zu einer anderen Agentur zu informieren.

Verkaufstagung:
Die Hotelkosten werden dieses Jahr beträchtlich höher sein im Vergleich zum letzten Jahr. Der bevorzugte Tagungsraum ist im Mai oder Juni nicht verfügbar.
→ Alexandra sucht nach Ausweichmöglichkeiten und liefert Preisinformationen bei der nächsten Sitzung.

Sonstiges:
Samuel Levine, Leiter der US-Verkäufe, wird am 19. März in der Niederlassung in London sein. Am 1. April gibt es einen Personalwechsel im deutschen Verkaufsteam. Karin Werner wechselt nach Frankreich, die neue Vertriebsleiterin heißt Janine Hörmann.

Nächste Sitzung:
Dienstag, 27. Februar 20…

246 Wörter

Mündliche Prüfung

Bei der mündlichen Prüfung sollen Sie persönliche wie fachliche Gespräche mit einem / einer Partner/in durchführen. Sie sollen sich situationsgerecht äußern und entsprechend reagieren, sich verständlich ausdrücken und gut zuhören.

Die Prüfung dauert insgesamt 40 Minuten, davon sind 20 Minuten für die Vorbereitung und 20 Minuten für die Durchführung. Die Prüfung besteht aus zwei Teilen:

Teil 1: Sie sollen einige Fragen zu persönlichen oder beruflichen Themen beantworten.

Teil 2: Zusammen mit einem anderen Prüfling führen Sie ein fach-bezogenes Rollenspiel durch.

Hilfsmittel: allgemeines zweisprachiges Wörterbuch (während der

Teil 1 – Tandemprüfung: Introducing yourself   30 VP

Partner A und Partner B:

Persönliche Vorstellung kann bestehen aus:
- Name, Alter, Wohnort
- Hobbys
- Ausbildungsunternehmen: Informationen zum Unternehmen wie Produkte / Dienstleistungen, Anzahl Mitarbeiter, Firmengeschichte, etc.
- Abteilung, in der der Prüfling momentan arbeitet und seine täglichen Aufgaben
- Berufliche Zukunftspläne

Teil 2 – Telephoning (back to back): Enquiry

Partner A

Situation:
Sie arbeiten für die Firma Bürohengst GmbH, einem Großhändler für Büro-
ausstattung in Köln. Sie erhalten einen Anruf von Ron/Ronda Fisher von der
Firma Baxter's Country Foods Ltd. aus Glasgow.
Führen Sie mithilfe der vorgegebenen Struktur ein englisches Telefon-
gespräch.

<table>
<tr><td>Partner A: Lieferant
(Bürohengst)</td><td>Partner B: Kunde
(Baxter's Country Foods)</td></tr>
</table>

1. Sie nehmen den Anruf entgegen (Firma, Name, Begrüßung).

2. …

3. Sie haben den Namen nicht genau verstanden und bitten
   darum, ihn zu buchstabieren. Außerdem fragen Sie nach der
   Kundennummer.

4. …

5. Sie haben nun alles verstanden. Sie fragen, welche Artikel
   angefragt werden sollen.

6. …

7. Sie erwidern, dass Sie kurz im System überprüfen müssen, ob
   die Stühle verfügbar sind. … 15 Stühle können kurzfristig geliefert werden, die anderen in zwei Wochen. Die Schreibtische
   sind auf Lager.

8. …

9. Sie nennen einen Stückpreis von 179,00 € für die Stühle und
   399,00 € für die Schreibtische. Bei dieser Menge gibt es einen
   Rabatt von 4 %. Sie fragen nach, ob der Kunde die Waren bestellen möchte.

10. …

11. Skonto ist möglich, Lieferung erfolgt ab Werk, die Kosten
    für die komplette Lieferung betragen 510,59 €. Die Lieferung
    erfolgt per LKW mit der Spedition "Euro Logistics", diese wird
    sich dann vor der Lieferung mit dem Kunden in Verbindung
    setzen.

12. …

13. Sie bestätigen die Bestellung, fassen noch einmal zusammen
    und sagen zu, einen Katalog zuzusenden. Dann weisen Sie noch
    darauf hin, dass im kommenden Monat die Firma auf der Büro-
    möbelmesse in Bonn vertreten ist.

14. …

15. Sie bedanken sich für die Bestellung und verabschieden sich.

Partner B

Situation:

Sie heißen Ron/Ronda Fisher und arbeiten für die Firma Baxter's Country Foods Ltd. in Glasgow. Sie möchten Büromöbel bei der Firma Bürohengst GmbH, einem Großhändler für Büroausstattung in Köln bestellen. Führen Sie mithilfe der vorgegebenen Struktur ein englisches Telefongespräch.

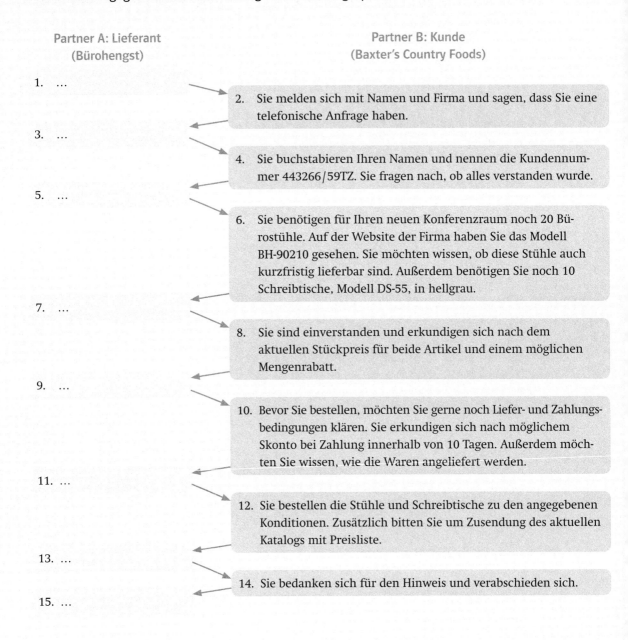

Partner A: Lieferant
(Bürohengst)

Partner B: Kunde
(Baxter's Country Foods)

1. …

2. Sie melden sich mit Namen und Firma und sagen, dass Sie eine telefonische Anfrage haben.

3. …

4. Sie buchstabieren Ihren Namen und nennen die Kundennummer 443266/59TZ. Sie fragen nach, ob alles verstanden wurde.

5. …

6. Sie benötigen für Ihren neuen Konferenzraum noch 20 Bürostühle. Auf der Website der Firma haben Sie das Modell BH-90210 gesehen. Sie möchten wissen, ob diese Stühle auch kurzfristig lieferbar sind. Außerdem benötigen Sie noch 10 Schreibtische, Modell DS-55, in hellgrau.

7. …

8. Sie sind einverstanden und erkundigen sich nach dem aktuellen Stückpreis für beide Artikel und einem möglichen Mengenrabatt.

9. …

10. Bevor Sie bestellen, möchten Sie gerne noch Liefer- und Zahlungsbedingungen klären. Sie erkundigen sich nach möglichem Skonto bei Zahlung innerhalb von 10 Tagen. Außerdem möchten Sie wissen, wie die Waren angeliefert werden.

11. …

12. Sie bestellen die Stühle und Schreibtische zu den angegebenen Konditionen. Zusätzlich bitten Sie um Zusendung des aktuellen Katalogs mit Preisliste.

13. …

14. Sie bedanken sich für den Hinweis und verabschieden sich.

15. …

Video Lounge

A2 **V1 At reception** (Collins)

Sally Smith is the receptionist at Lowis Engineering in London. John Carter and Paul Rogers are visiting the company today.

1 Watch the video and answer the questions.

1. What time is the appointment?
2. Which company are John and Paul from?
3. Why does Paul ask for a pen?
4. Complete Sally's sentences:
   a) Please could you wear …
   b) Someone will come down to …
   c) Please have …

A2 **V2 Company visitors** (Collins)

Jasmine Goodman is Diane Kennedy's personal assistant at Lowis Engineering.

1 Watch the video and decide whether the following statements are true or false. Correct the false statements.

1. John and Jasmine are colleagues.
2. Jasmine's boss asked her to meet the visitors.
3. The British say 'elevator' and the Americans say 'lift'.
4. Jasmine is taking the visitors to the third floor.
5. Jasmine doesn't like the building she works in.

A2 ⓕV3 Making visitors feel welcome (Collins)

Jasmine takes John and Paul to the meeting room.

1 Watch the video and do the tasks. Listen for the polite English equivalents of the German phrases.

1. Wollen Sie mir Ihren Mantel geben?
2. Möchten Sie Platz nehmen?
3. Leider ist Diane noch in einer Besprechung.
4. Möchten Sie eine Tasse Kaffee?
5. Wie ist es mit Ihnen, Mr Rogers?
6. Bitte nennen Sie mich Paul.
7. Es tut mir leid, dass Sie warten müssen.
8. Machen Sie sich keine Sorgen.

2 What phrase does Jasmine use when she hands Paul a cup of tea?

A2 ⓕV4 Small talk (Collins)

Jasmine is talking to John and Paul while they wait for Diane Kennedy, her boss.

1 Watch the video. Which of the following small talk phrases do you hear?

1. So how was the journey?
2. How's the hotel?
3. Is this your first time here?
4. How long are you staying?
5. Have you been here before?
6. What should we do at the weekend?
7. Would you like to see a tennis match?
8. That sounds great.

2 Watch the video again and complete the sentences.

1. We had to check in … (when? where?)
2. Airport security …
3. It's our first time to …
4. Do you like …?
5. Would you like …?
6. I've made a reservation for … for … at …
7. I'll find out … and … you're here.

A2 ⊙📹 V 5 How was your visit?

(Collins)

Jasmine asks John and Paul about their visit to the test facility yesterday.

1 Watch the video and decide whether the following statements are true or false. Correct the false statements.

1. John and Paul didn't have time to see much at the test facility.
2. Both John and Paul saw the new computer centre.
3. Jasmine tells John and Paul how much the facility cost.
4. John and Paul found the testing equipment for the pumps impressive.
5. John thinks the testing equipment will be useful for quality control.
6. John and Paul spent more than a couple of hours at the test facility.
7. The managing director took them to lunch.
8. They ate at a Chinese restaurant.

A2 ⊙📹 V 6 Goodbye

(Collins)

John and Paul have finished their visit to Lowis Engineering and are returning to Australia. Jasmine is saying goodbye.

1 Watch the video and answer the questions:

1. How will John and Paul travel to the airport?
2. How long does it normally take from Lowis Engineering to the airport?
3. What time is the flight?

2 What do they say in English?

1. Es war schön Sie wiederzusehen.
2. Ich freue mich, dass es Ihnen gefallen hat.
3. Ich hoffe, wir sehen uns bald wieder.
4. Passen Sie auf sich auf!
5. Guten Flug!

B1/B2 ☞ V7 Tata looks towards global market (BBC)

This video is about Tata, a major international company.

LAND ROVER & JAGUAR SALE
Indian manufacturer Tata to pay £1 billion

1 Look out for the answers to the following questions.

1. Which country is Tata based in?
2. What companies is it buying in the UK? Who from?
3. What type of vehicles did Tata traditionally produce?
4. What acquisition transformed Tata into the sixth biggest steel manufacturer worldwide?
5. Were the two UK companies profitable that Tata is buying?
6. What do the trade unions think about this development?

B1/B2 ☞ V8 New generation of Chinese consumers (BBC)

You are about to see a video on young Chinese consumers.

1 While watching the video, you should be on the look-out for the answers to the following questions.

1. What supermarket chain is celebrating "American products day"?
2. How many stores has it opened so far in China?
3. How have spending and saving patterns changed?
4. What does the video say about the salaries of young urban Chinese?
5. What effect has this had on the number of credit cards in circulation?
6. What is China's number 1 sports brand?
7. How are the eating habits of young Chinese changing?
8. How does an expert quoted in the video describe the Chinese market?

B1/B2 ⊙⥮V9 Business and Twitter (BBC)

This video is about companies' use of social media.

1 After watching it answer the following questions.

1. How is Kate's professional role described?
2. Name the benefits she lists for companies using social media?
3. What positive effect can a company's presence on social media have on its brand image?
4. What are the potential dangers for companies using social media?
5. How expensive is it for a company to engage with social media? Are there any costs involved?

B1/B2 ⊙⥮V10 Young entrepreneurs (BBC)

You are about to see a video on young business graduates starting their own companies.

1 Watch the video and then answer the following questions.

1. What event are these young graduates attending?
2. What is Jason hoping to achieve?
3. Why is he getting discouraged?
3. What business is John Campbell in? What exactly does he sell?
4. How did he start the business?
5. What is Scott telling his student audience about?
6. How does John think the job market has changed compared with 20 years ago?
7. What are the risks of entrepreneurship?

B1/B2 ⊙ᴳ V11 Soda companies to cut calories (BBC)

This video deals with an important health issue.

1 Listen carefully to the video and then answer the following questions.

1. What have three major American manufacturers of fizzy drinks announced?
2. In what ways do they plan to achieve their aim?
3. How long has soda consumption been declining?
4. How will these companies probably try to increase their share of the market as the consumption of soda continues to drop?

B1/B2 ⊙ᴳ V12 Job interview tips (BBC)

This video shows an interview with an expert on job interviews.

1 Listen carefully to her recommendations and then answer the questions below.

1. What does the expert say is the secret of a good job interview?
2. What questions are interviewers not supposed to ask?
3. How does she suggest the interviewee might react to such questions?
4. What does she say about the idea that it's the interviewer's job to get the best out of the candidate?
5. What does she have to say about doing some practising?
6. Which of the examples of interviewees' blunders do you find most amusing? How would you answer the question "What are your weaknesses?"

Role cards

Unit 5 C | Exercise 4

→ ROLE CARD A: page 71

Role card B

1. +33 (0)297 66 32 91
2. 14 Vanderbilt Avenue, New York, NY 10014, USA,
    Tel.: 001-213-242 24 66, mailto:info@uscyberlife ... .com
3. www.visitscotland ... .com
4. mailto:cheung@shanghai-cd ... .com
5. mailto:jonathan_chan@globaltrader ... .sg

Unit 5 C | Exercise 6

→ EXERCISE 6: page 73

Role card A / B

A	B
Persons for whom the message is intended:	Possible contents of message:
Ross Davidson	Jayden Flaherty would like to postpone Friday's appointment / next Wednesday / 2 pm / pressure of work
Export manager	Meeting in Istanbul on Thursday / scheduled 9 am to 1 pm / 10 participants
Miss Kaitlyn Peakman in purchasing	Proposal OK / suggest meeting next week / finalise details
Dr Josef von Richter	Draft contract ready / make appointment next week to discuss / sign
Frau Luisa Lorenz	Flight delayed / suggest meeting tomorrow / 11 am

Unit 6 A | Exercise 9

→ ROLE CARD A: page 90

Role card B

Sie sind Ethan Taylor von der Firma Zooks und wollen für Ihre Geschäftsreise nach San Francisco einen Wagen mieten. Ein Freund hat Ihnen die Mietwagenfirma Luxurious Limos empfohlen. Rufen Sie dort an:

- Wagen vom 25. bis 30. August benötigt
- Abholung und Rückgabe am Flughafen San Francisco
- Kleinwagen genügt / Preis für 6 Tage / Versicherung inbegriffen?
- Zusatzversicherung für Selbstbeteilung (excess coverage) erwünscht
- Rabatt für Kunden der Airlines of the Americas?
- Gesamtpreis für eine Woche?
- Zahlung per Kreditkarte?
- Visa Nr. 4731 5026 7100 5314, Sicherheitscode 275, gültig bis 7/201_
- Adresse: Hanover Avenue, Hove, BN3 1NA, UK

Unit 6 B | Exercise 2

→ ROLE CARD A: page 92

Role card B

Calendar of Gregory Johnson	
Monday:	
9:00	whole day visiting customers in LA
Tuesday:	
9:00	Janice Romero at Santa Barbara Investment Services
13:00	Lunch Larry Fernandez at Chamber of Commerce
16:00	Michael Herrera from Monterey Precision Engineering at our office
Do we need to arrange for a driver to pick up Julius Braun at LA Airport?	
Wednesday:	
10:30 – 13:00	Tour of company premises
13:30 – 15:00	Lunch at country club with Gregory Johnson and proprietor Madeleine McCain
15:30	Meeting with company engineers and IT specialists
19:00	Dinner with Gregory Johnson and wife Julia at their private residence.
Thursday:	
10:00	Meeting and discussion with company engineers and IT specialists.
13:00	Lunch in company cafeteria
14:00	Meeting with law firm Sagely and Sagely
Saturday:	
Return flight to Berlin	

Unit 9 B | Exercise 3

→ **ROLE CARD A:** page 132

Role card B

- Kirsty / Sean McDuff from Bellheather Distilleries Ltd, Inverness gets a call.
- She / he offers to send brochures and price lists by e-mail and asks for Messner's e-mail address.
- Details about delivery time, quantity discounts and information on special gift boxes are dealt with in the brochure.
- Kirsty / Sean thanks the caller for her / his interest in Bellheather's products.

Unit 11 KMK Exam Training | Exercise 2

→ **ROLE CARD A:** page 164

Role card B

Sie vertreten die Firma Better Business Cards auf der Messe Office Expo in Manchester. Dort führen Sie ein Gespräch mit einem potentiellen Kunden.
- Begrüßen Sie den Kunden und heben Sie zwei Vorzüge von Business Cards hervor.
- Beantworten Sie die Frage zur Auswahl einer bestimmten Farbe und dem Abdruck des Firmenlogos positiv.
- Visitenkarten können problemlos zweisprachig gedruckt werden.
- Sie bieten Visitenkarten in zwei Qualitäten an:
  1. Value Cards (Digitaldruck, hohe Festigkeit);
  2. Premium Cards (Offsetdruck, extrem hohe Festigkeit).
- Sie bieten ein Skonto von 2 % sowie 5 % Mengenrabatt ab 20 Stück.
- Bei einer Erstbestellung ist Vorkasse und Lieferung ab Werk üblich, danach Lieferung auf Rechnung.
- Bedanken Sie sich für das Gespräch und verabschieden Sie sich.

Unit 16 D | Exercise 9

→ ROLE CARD A: page 237

Role card B (Interviewee)

Sie (eigener Name) haben sich bei Clandon Fitness Equipment Ltd
in Chichester als zweisprachige/r Exportsachbeiter/in beworben
und sind zu einem Vorstellungsgespräch eingeladen worden. Sie
sind 24 Jahre alt und haben vor zwei Jahren ihre Ausbildung als
Kaufmann/frau im Groß- und Außenhandel abgeschlossen.

Beantworten Sie die allgemeinen Fragen nach Wunsch:

- Flug angenehm / unruhig / verspätet
- Wetter sonnig / regnerisch
- Sätze zu Ihrer Heimatstadt
- Sie kennen die Anforderungen und glauben sie zu erfüllen:
  - Deutsch Muttersprache
  - Englisch fließend, da 3-jähriger Schulbesuch in England.
    Vater arbeitete zeitweise in Manchester.
  - Sie arbeiten gern im Team.
  - mit allen Export- und Importverfahren vertraut

Berufserfahrung:

- Ausbildung in verschiedenen Abteilungen (Verkauf, Einkauf,
  Lagerhaltung, Rechnungs- und Personalwesen) bei einem
  exportstarken Unternehmen im Ruhrgebiet.
- Seit zwei Jahren in der Exportabteilung eines mittelständischen
  Maschinenbau- Unternehmens
- vertraut mit Excel und Sage
- Begründen Sie Ihren Wunsch in GB zu arbeiten.

Chronological word list

Abkürzungen und Zeichen

etw. = etwas	sth. = something
Pl. = Plural	BE = britisches Englisch
jmdn., jmdm. = jemanden, jemandem	AE = amerikanisches Englisch
sb. = somebody	◎ = Vokabeln zu den Hörtexten
so. = someone	

01 | Introducing yourself

to include [ɪnˈkluːd] einbeziehen; einschließen
for instance [fərˈɪnstəns] zum Beispiel
professional [prəˈfeʃnl] beruflich; professionell
duties [ˈdjuːtiz] Aufgaben
casual [ˈkæʒuəl] zwanglos; leger
to fancy doing sth. [ˌfænsi ˈduːɪŋ ˌsʌmθɪŋ] Lust auf etw.
 haben

A | Talking about yourself

placement [ˈpleɪsmənt] Praktikum
to act as [ˈækt ˌəz] *hier:* fungieren als
to look after [ˌlʊk ˈɑːftə] sich kümmern um
sector [ˈsektə] Branche
to start the ball rolling [ˌstɑːt ðə ˌbɔːl ˈrəʊlɪŋ]
 den Anfang machen
background [ˈbækgraʊnd] Hintergrund; beruflicher
 Hintergrund
mainly [ˈmeɪnli] hauptsächlich
freight forwarding and logistics services clerk [ˌfreɪt
 ˈfɔːwədɪŋ ˌənd ləˌdʒɪstɪks ˈsɜːvɪsɪz ˌklɑːk] Kaufmann/
 frau für Spedition und Logistikdienstleistung

canoeing club [kəˈnuːɪŋ ˌklʌb] Kanuverein
adventurous [ədˈventʃrəs] abenteuerlich
to move on to [ˌmuːv ˈɒn tə] weitergehen zu
apprenticeship [əˈprentɪʃɪp] Lehre; Ausbildung
management assistant in wholesale and foreign trade
 [ˈmænɪdʒmənt əˌsɪstnt ˌɪn ˌhəʊlseɪl ˌənd ˌfɒrɪn ˈtreɪd]
 Kaufmann/frau im Groß- und Außenhandel
to enjoy doing sth. [ɪnˌdʒɔɪ ˈduːɪŋ ˌsʌmθɪŋ] etw. gern tun
traineeship [ˌtreɪˈniːʃɪp] Ausbildung
event management [ɪˌvent ˈmænɪdʒmənt]
 Veranstaltungsmanagement
management assistant in advertising [ˈmænɪdʒmənt
 əˌsɪstnt ˌɪn ˈædvətaɪzɪŋ] Werbekaufmann/frau
eventually [ɪˈventʃuəli] letztendlich; schließlich;
 irgendwann
to turn [tɜːn] werden
foreign language secretary [ˌfɒrɪn ˌlæŋgwɪdʒ ˈsekrətri]
 Fremdsprachensekretär/in
vintage [ˈvɪntɪdʒ] klassisch; altmodisch
enterprising [ˈentəpraɪzɪŋ] unternehmungslustig;
 geschäftstüchtig
roughly [ˈrʌfli] ungefähr; in etwa
at the same stage [ət ðə ˌseɪm ˈsteɪdʒ] im gleichen
 Stadium

to line up [ˌlaɪnˈʌp] organisieren

to get off to a good start [getˌɒf tʊˌə ˌgʊd ˈstɑːt] einen guten Start erwischen; sich gut einführen

IT management assistant [aɪtiː ˈmænɪdʒmənt əˌsɪstnt] Informatikkaufmann/frau

insurance clerk [ɪnˈʃɔːrns ˌklɑːk] Versicherungskaufmann/frau

insurance business management assistant [ɪnʃɔːrns ˌbɪznɪs ˌmænɪdʒmənt əˈsɪstnt] Versicherungskaufmann/frau

office management assistant [ˌɒfɪs ˈmænɪdʒmənt əˌsɪstnt] Kaufmann/frau für Büromanagement; Bürokaufmann/frau

office administration clerk [ˌɒfɪs ədˌmɪnɪˈstreɪʃn ˌklɑːk] Bürokaufmann/frau

event management assistant [ɪˌvent ˈmænɪdʒmənt əˌsɪstnt] Veranstaltungskaufmann/frau

event consultant [ɪˈvent kənˌsʌltnt] Veranstaltungsberater/in

wholesale and export clerk [ˌhəʊlseɪl əndˈekspɔːt ˌklɑːk] Kaufmann/frau im Groß- und Außenhandel

management assistant in wholesale and foreign trade [ˈmænɪdʒmənt əˌsɪstnt ɪn ˌhəʊlseɪl ənd ˌfɒrɪn ˈtreɪd] Kaufmann/frau im Groß- und Außenhandel

bank clerk [ˈbæŋk ˌklɑːk] Bankangestellte/r

bank business management assistant [bæŋk ˌbɪznɪs ˌmænɪdʒmənt əˈsɪstnt] Bankkaufmann/frau

management assistant in advertising [ˈmænɪdʒmənt əˌsɪstnt ɪnˌædvətaɪzɪŋ] Werbekaufmann/frau

management assistant in freight forwarding [ˈmænɪdʒmənt əˌsɪstnt ɪn ˌfreɪt ˈfɔːwədɪŋ] Speditionskaufmann/frau

management assistant in retail business [ˈmænɪdʒmənt əˌsɪstnt ɪn ˌriːteɪl ˈbɪznɪs] Kaufmann/frau im Einzelhandel

publisher's assistant [ˈpʌblɪʃəz əˌsɪstnt] Verlagskaufmann/frau

industrial clerk [ɪnˈdʌstrɪəl ˌklɑːk] Industriekaufmann/frau

industrial business management assistant [ɪnˌdʌstrɪəl ˌbɪznɪs ˈmænɪdʒmənt əˌsɪstnt] Industriekaufmann/frau

hang-gliding [ˈhæŋˌglaɪdɪŋ] Drachenfliegen

to go clubbing [ˌgəʊ ˈklʌbɪŋ] in die Disko gehen

to chill out [ˌtʃɪlˈaʊt] sich entspannen; relaxen

to socialise [ˈsəʊʃlaɪz] Kontakte pflegen

volunteer work [ˌvɒlənˈtɪə ˌwɜːk] ehrenamtliche Arbeit; freiwillige Arbeit

IT practitioner [aɪtiː prækˈtɪʃnə] IT-Fachmann/frau

context [ˈkɒntekst] Zusammenhang; Kontext

surname [ˈsɜːneɪm] Familienname; Nachname

B | Young people talk about their future professions

to have in common [ˌhæv ɪn ˈkɒmən] gemeinsam haben

to grow up [ˌgrəʊˈʌp] aufwachsen

to jump at an offer [ˈdʒʌmp ət ən ˌɒfə] ein Angebot begeistert annehmen

to be into sth. [biˈɪntə ˌsʌmθɪŋ] etw. gerne machen; sich für etw. interessieren

to be dying to do sth. [bi ˌdaɪɪŋ tə ˈduː ˌsʌmθɪŋ] darauf brennen etw. zu tun

to get on well with so. [ˌget ɒn ˈwel wɪð ˌsʌmwʌn] sich gut mit jmdm. verstehen

management assistant for tourism and leisure [ˈmænɪdʒmənt əˌsɪstnt fə ˌtʊərɪzm ˌand ˈleʒə] Kaufmann/frau für Tourismus und Freizeit

automobile sales management assistant [ˌɔːtəməbiːl ˌseɪlz ˈmænɪdʒmənt əˌsɪstnt] Automobilkaufmann/frau

foreign language correspondent [ˌfɒrɪn ˌlæŋgwɪdʒ ˌkɒrɪˈspɒndnt] Fremdsprachenkorrespondent/in

prospects *(pl)* [ˈprɒspekts] Perspektiven ; Chancen

promotion [prəˈməʊʃn] Aufstieg; Beförderung

vocational education [vəˌkeɪʃnl ˌedʒʊˈkeɪʃn] Berufsausbildung

protected [prəˈtektɪd] geschützt

to prescribe [prɪˈskraɪb] verschreiben; vorschreiben

on the job training [ˌɒnðədʒɒb ˈtreɪnɪŋ] Ausbildung am Arbeitsplatz

to inspire [ɪnˈspaɪə] anregen; inspirieren

salary [ˈsælri] Gehalt

accounting [əˈkaʊntɪŋ] Buchhaltung; Rechnungswesen

Business Administration [ˌbɪznɪs ədˌmɪnɪˈstreɪʃn] Betriebswirtschaftslehre

hospitality and catering [hɒspɪˌtæləti ənd ˈkeɪtrɪŋ] Hotel- und Gaststättengewerbe

carpentry [ˈkɑːpntri] Zimmermannshandwerk

bricklaying [ˈbrɪkˌleɪɪŋ] Maurerhandwerk

plumbing [ˈplʌmɪŋ] Klempnerarbeit; Klempnerei

National Vocational Qualification [ˌnæʃnl vəˌkeɪʃnl ˌkwɒlɪfɪˈkeɪʃn] staatlich anerkannte berufliche Qualifikation

to sit an exam [ˌsɪt ən ɪgˈzæm] eine Prüfung machen

throughout [θruːˈaʊt] überall in

literally [ˈlɪtrli] wortwörtlich; buchstäblich

to paraphrase [ˈpærəfreɪz] umschreiben; paraphrasieren

to attend courses [əˌtend ˈkɔːsɪz] Kurse besuchen

various [ˈveəriəs] verschieden; unterschiedlich

Chamber of Commerce [ˌtʃeɪmbər əv ˈkɒmɜːs] Industrie- und Handelskammer

Office expert

C | Job profiles

to assign [əˈsaɪn] zuordnen; benennen
to apply to [əˈplaɪ tə] betreffen; zutreffen
to conduct [kənˈdʌkt] durchführen
to process [ˈprəʊsəs] bearbeiten
to screen [skriːn] überprüfen; aussondern
to balance an account [ˌbæləns ən əˈkaʊnt] ein Konto ausgleichen
to maintain [meɪnˈteɪn] pflegen; führen
refund [ˈriːfʌnd] Erstattung

D | Streamlining office procedures

to streamline [ˈstriːmlaɪn] optimieren
template [ˈtempleɪt] Dokumentvorlage; Schablone
to replicate [ˈreplɪkeɪt] nachbilden; reproduzieren
shortcut [ˈʃɔːtkʌt] Abkürzung; Tastenkombination

02 | Taking care of visitors

to take care of [ˌteɪk ˈkeər əv] aufpassen auf
to make s.o. feel at home [ˌmeɪkɪŋ sʌmwʌn ˌfiːl ət ˈhəʊm] dafür sorgen, dass sich jmnd. wohlfühlt
impression [ɪmˈpreʃn] Eindruck
to entertain [ˌentəˈteɪn] sich um jmdn. kümmern; unterhalten
lingua franca [ˌlɪŋgwə ˈfræŋkə] internationale Verkehrssprache

A | Greeting visitors

well-known [ˌwelˈnəʊn] bekannt
range [reɪndʒ] Spektrum; Palette; Angebot
twenty-somethings [ˈtwentiˌsʌmθɪŋgz] junge Leute in den Zwanzigern
high-end [ˌhaɪˈend] Luxus-; Nobel-
major [ˈmeɪdʒə] groß; wichtig; Haupt-
fashion chain [ˈfæʃn ˌtʃeɪn] Kette von Modegeschäften
joint venture [ˌdʒɔɪnt ˈventʃə] Gemeinschaftsunternehmen

⊙ **in charge of** [ɪn ˈtʃɑːdʒ əv] verantwortlich für; betraut mit
sparkling mineral water [ˌspɑːklɪŋ ˈmɪnrl ˌwɔːtə] Mineralwasser mit Kohlensäure
dehydrated [ˌdiːhaɪˈdreɪtɪd] ausgetrocknet
couldn't quite place you [ˌkʊdnt kwaɪt ˈpleɪs juː] wusste nicht genau, woher wir uns kennen

white coffee [ˌwaɪt ˈkɒfi] Kaffee mit Milch
to be ashamed [bi əˈʃeɪmd] sich schämen
rudimentary [ˌruːdɪˈmentri] rudimentär; einfach
to come along [ˌkʌm əˈlɒŋ] mitgehen

to accompany [əˈkʌmpəni] begleiten

B | Making conversation

⊙ **hitch** [hɪtʃ] Haken; Problem
bumpy [ˈbʌmpi] unruhig; holprig
anxious [ˈæŋkʃəs] besorgt; ängstlich
convinced [kənˈvɪnst] überzeugt
rag trade [ˈræg ˌtreɪd] Bekleidungsindustrie
reliable [rɪˈlaɪəbl] zuverlässig
boot [tə ˈbuːt] obendrein
anecdotal evidence [ˌænɪkdəʊtl ˈevɪdns] Anhaltspunkte

waste of time [ˌweɪst əv ˈtaɪm] Zeitverschwendung
to enable [ɪˈneɪbl] in die Lage versetzen; befähigen
bond [bɒnd] Bindung
offence [əˈfens] Anstoß; Beleidigung
permissible [pəˈmɪsəbl] zulässig; erlaubt
changeable [ˈtʃeɪndʒəbl] wechselhaft
due to [ˈdjuː tə] wegen; aufgrund
inexhaustible [ˌɪnɪgˈzɔːstəbl] unerschöpflich
convenience store [kənˈviːniəns ˌstɔː] kundenfreundlicher Laden in der Nähe
dreadful [ˈdredfəl] schrecklich
awful [ˈɔːfl] scheußlich; schrecklich
ghastly [ˈgɑːstli] entsetzlich
congestion [kənˈdʒestʃn] Verkehrsstau
tailback [ˈteɪlbæk] Stau
overcast [ˈəʊvəkɑːst] bedeckt; bezogen (Himmel)
drizzle [ˈdrɪzl] Nieselregen
sudden downpour [ˌsʌdn ˈdaʊnpɔː] plötzlicher Regenguss
convenient [kənˈviːniənt] praktisch; bequem; angenehm
vibrant [ˈvaɪbrənt] lebendig; pulsierend
prosperous [ˈprɒsprəs] wohlhabend

C | Giving directions

staircase [ˈsteəkeɪs] Treppe; Treppenhaus
monitor [ˈmɒnɪtə] Bildschirm; Monitor
itinerary [aɪˈtɪnərəri] Reiseroute
landmark [ˈlændmɑːk] Wahrzeichen
junction [ˈdʒʌŋkʃn] Kreuzung
bend [bend] Kurve

D | Taking the visitors on a tour of the premises

premises ['premɪsɪz] Geschäftsräume; Firmengelände

⊚ **ground floor** [ˌgraʊnd 'flɔ:] Parterre; Erdgeschoss

spacious ['speɪʃəs] geräumig

open-plan office [ˌəʊpnplæn_'ɒfɪs] Großraumbüro

sociable ['səʊʃəbl] gesellig; umgänglich

cooped up [ˌku:pt_'ʌp] eingepfercht

senior staff [ˌsi:niə 'stɑ:f] Führungskräfte; leitende Angestellte

alongside [əˌlɒŋ'saɪd] nebeneinander

deputy director [ˌdepjəti dɪ'rektə] stellvertretende/r Direktor/in

garments ['gɑ:mənts] Kleidung

actual ['æktʃuəl] tatsächlich

to outsource ['aʊtsɔ:s] auslagern

competitively [kəm'petətɪvli] konkurrierend; wetteifernd

produced ethically [prəˌdju:st_'eθɪkli] nach ethischen Maßstäben produziert

major concerns [ˌmeɪdʒə kən's3:nz] Hauptsorgen

to hatch [hætʃ] ausbrüten

freelance ['fri:lɑ:ns] freiberuflich

evidence ['evɪdns] Beweis; Nachweis

airy ['eəri] luftig

organic [ɔ:'gænɪk] biologisch; Bio-

humanely [hju:'meɪnli] menschenwürdig

free-range [ˌfri:'reɪndʒ] freilaufend

fusion cooking [ˌfju:ʒn 'kʊkɪŋ] Fusionsküche

now and again [ˌnaʊ_ənd_ə'gen] ab und zu

Currywurst brigade ['kʌriw3:st brɪˌgeɪd] Currywurst-Fraktion

pricey ['praɪsi] teuer

to charge for ['tʃɑ:dʒ fə] berechnen für

at cost [ət 'kɒst] zum Selbstkostenpreis

contribution [ˌkɒntrɪ'bju:ʃn] Beitrag

workforce ['w3:kfɔ:s] Belegschaft; Gesamtheit der Mitarbeiter

E | Taking foreign visitors to a restaurant

lengthy ['leŋkθi] lang; langwierig

scrubbed [skrʌbd] geschrubbt; gescheuert

by his own admission [baɪ hɪzˌəʊn_əd'mɪʃn] nach eigener Aussage

⊚ **cream of cauliflower soup** [ˌkri:m_əv ˌkɒliflaʊə 'su:p] Blumenkohlcremesuppe

wrapped [ræpt] eingewickelt

slice [slaɪs] Scheibe; Anteil

smoked ham [ˌsməʊkt 'hæm] geräucherter Schinken

black pudding [ˌblæk 'pʊdɪŋ] Blutwurst

mashed potatoes [ˌmæʃt_pə'teɪtəʊz] Kartoffelpüree

onion ['ʌnjən] Zwiebel

venison ['venɪsn] Hirsch; Rotwild (als Fleisch)

game [geɪm] Wild

red cabbage [ˌred 'kæbɪdʒ] Rotkohl

potato dumplings [pə'teɪtəʊ 'dʌmplɪŋz] Kartoffelklöße

fried potatoes [ˌfraɪd pə'teɪtəʊz] Bratkartoffeln

cucumber salad [ˌkju:kʌmbə 'sæləd] Gurkensalat

reasonably obvious [ˌri:znəbli_'ɒbviəs] ziemlich offen-sichtlich

asparagus [ə'spærəgəs] Spargel

to adore [ə'dɔ:] lieben; verrückt sein nach

red jelly [ˌred 'dʒeli] Rote Grütze

redcurrants ['redˌkʌrənts] rote Johannisbeeren

cheese board ['tʃi:z_ˌbɔ:d] Käseplatte

to do without [ˌdu: wɪ'ðaʊt] ohne etw. auskommen

dessert [dɪ'z3:t] Nachspeise

pike [paɪk] Hecht

grated ['greɪtɪd] gerieben; geraspelt

deer [dɪə] Rotwild

menu ['menju:] Speisekarte

starter ['stɑ:tə] Vorspeise

main course [ˌmeɪn 'kɔ:s] Hauptgericht; Hauptgang

research [rɪ's3:tʃ] (Nach)Forschung

inventive [ɪn'ventɪv] erfinderisch

ambitious [æm'bɪʃəs] ehrgeizig; anspruchsvoll

Office expert

F | Corporate entertainment

spouse [spaʊs] Ehegatte; Ehegattin

cordially ['kɔ:diəli] herzlich

hospitality package [ˌhɒspɪ'tæləti ˌpækɪdʒ] Besucher-paket; Bewirtungspaket

high-end [ˌhaɪ'end] Luxus-; Nobel-

kit [kɪt] Ausrüstung; Ausstattung

jersey ['dʒ3:zi] Trikot

on request [ɒn rɪ'kwest] auf Anfrage

Danube ['dænju:b] Donau

to treat sb. to sth. ['tri:t ˌsʌmbədi tə ˌsʌmθɪŋ] jmdn. mit etwas bewirten

corporate ['kɔ:prət] Firmen-

to experience [ɪk'spɪəriəns] erleben

03 | The company and its products and services

to project an image [prə͵dʒekt͵ən͵'ımıdʒ] einen Eindruck vermitteln

brand image [͵brænd͵'ımıdʒ] Markenimage

well-established [͵welı'stæblıʃt] gut eingeführt; fest etabliert

to prize [praız] schätzen; Gewicht legen auf

solidity [sə'lıdəti] Festigkeit; Stabilität

to emphasise ['emfəsaız] betonen; hervorheben

forward-looking [͵fɔ:wəd'lʊkıŋ] zukunftsorientiert

approach [ə'prəʊtʃ] Herangehensweise; Ansatz

to adapt to [ə'dæpt tə] (sich) anpassen an

trustworthy ['trʌst͵wɜ:ði] vertrauenswürdig

mature [mə'tʃʊə] reif; alteingesessen

quality-conscious [͵kwɒləti'kɒnʃəs] qualitätsbewusst

A | Introducing a firm and giving a brief history

sustainable [sə'steınə'bl] nachhaltig; umweltgerecht

committed [kə'mıtıd] engagiert

impact ['ımpækt] Auswirkung; Einfluss

large-scale [͵lɑ:dʒ'skeıl] im großen Maßstab; groß angelegt

processing ['prəʊsesıŋ] Bearbeitung; Verarbeitung

to grow [grəʊ] (Pflanze:) anbauen

environmentally-friendly [ın͵vaırnmənt'frendli] umweltfreundlich

hemp [hemp] Hanf

fertiliser ['fɜ:tılaızə] Dünger

pest-resistant [͵pestrı'zıstnt] schädlingsresistent

EU-funded loan [͵i:ju:͵fʌndıd 'ləʊn] EU-finanziertes Darlehen

grower ['grəʊə] Bauer; Bäuerin; Pflanzer; Pflanzerin

spinning mill ['spınıŋ ͵mıl] Spinnerei

up-and-coming [͵ʌpən'kʌmıŋ] aufstrebend

production facilities [prə'dʌkʃn fə͵sılətiz] Produktionseinrichtungen; Produktionsstätten

corporate ['kɔ:prət] Firmen-

to source sth. (from) ['sɔ:s ͵sʌmθıŋ frəm] etw. beziehen (von)

organically-grown [ɔ:͵gænıkli 'grəʊn] biologisch angebaut

linen ['lının] Leinen

beeswax ['bi:zwæks] Bienenwachs

bee keeper ['bi: ͵ki:pə] Imker/in

plant-based [͵plɑ:nt'beıst] auf pflanzlicher Basis

essential oils [ı͵senʃl͵'ɔılz] ätherische Öle

knitwear ['nıtweə] Strickwaren

sturdy ['stɜ:di] fest; stabil

practical ['præktıkl] Praktikum

◉ **low-interest loans** [͵ləʊ͵ıntrəst 'ləʊnz] Niedrigzinsdarlehen

to struggle ['strʌgl] kämpfen; sich abmühen

to sign up to [͵saın͵'ʌp tə] sich anmelden; sich registrieren

efficient [ı'fıʃnt] effizient

pop-ups ['pɒpʌps] Werbeeinblendungen

to spread [spred] verteilen

from the outset [frəm ðı͵'aʊtset] von Anfang an

to sign up to [͵saın͵'ʌp tə] sich anmelden; sich registrieren

comparable [kəm'pærəbl] vergleichbar

B | Describing products and services

to comply with [kəm'plaı wıð] einhalten; befolgen

strict [strıkt] streng

additive ['ædıtıv] Zusatzstoff; Zusatz

pesticides ['pestısaıdz] Pestizide

herbicides ['hɜ:bısaıdz] Unkrautvernichtungsmittel

lavender oil ['lævəndər͵ɔıl] Lavendelöl

bracket ['brækıt] Klammer

device [dı'vaıs] Gerät

start-up (business) ['stɑ:tʌp ͵bıznıs] Neugründung; junges Unternehmen

foldable bicycle [͵fəʊldəbl 'baısıkl] Klapprad

medium-sized company [͵mi:dıəmsaızd 'kʌmpəni] mittelständisches Unternehmen

wholesaler ['həʊl͵seılə] Großhändler

retailer ['ri:teılə] Einzelhändler/in

public limited company [͵pʌblık ͵lımıtıd 'kʌmpəni] in etwa vergleichbar einer AG

private limited company [͵praıvət ͵lımıtıd 'kʌmpəni] in etwa vergleichbar einer GmbH

household appliances [͵haʊshəʊld͵ə'plaıənsız] Haushaltsgeräte

removal services [rı'mu:vl ͵sɜ:vısız] Umzugsdienste

legal services ['li:gl ͵sɜ:vısız] Rechtsdienstleistungen

upmarket [͵ʌp'mɑ:kıt] gehoben; teuer; nobel

unique [ju:'ni:k] einzigartig

low-maintenance [͵ləʊ'meıntnəns] wartungsfreundlich

thorough ['θʌrə] umfassend; gründlich

state-of-the-art [͵steıtəvðı'ɑ:t] auf dem neuesten Stand (der Technik)

sophisticated [sə'fıstıkeıtıd] hoch entwickelt; technisch ausgefeilt elaborate [ɪ'læbrət] sorgfältig ausgeführt; gut durchdacht

bespoke [bɪ'spəʊk] maßgeschneidert

tailor-made [ˌteɪlə'meɪd] maßgeschneidert

customized ['kʌstəmaɪzd] maßgeschneidert

funding ['fʌndɪŋ] finanzielle Unterstützung

catchy ['kætʃi] griffig; einprägsam

04 | The Office

◎ spacious ['speɪʃəs] geräumig

purpose-built [ˌpɜːpəs'bɪlt] für bestimmten Zweck gebaut

to accommodate [ə'kɒmədeɪt] Unterkunft bieten; entgegenkommen; aufnehmen

prestigious [pres'tɪdʒəs] angesehen; renommiert

converted [kən'vɜːtɪd] umgebaut

back office [ˌbæk 'ɒfɪs] Büro ohne Publikumsverkehr

front office [ˌfrʌnt 'ɒfɪs] Büro mit Publikumsverkehr

fitted out with [ˌfɪtɪd 'aʊt wɪð] ausgestattet mit

dedicated ['dedɪkeɪtɪd] spezialisiert; engagiert

A | The office environment

◎ automotive parts [ɔːtəˌməʊtɪv 'pɑːts] Autoteile

computer projector [kəmˌpjuːtə prə'dʒektə] Beamer

gossip ['gɒsɪp] Klatsch

high-end [ˌhaɪ'end] Luxus-; Nobel-

accounts [ə'kaʊnts] Kunden; Buchhaltungsabteilung

detergent [dɪ'tɜːdʒnt] Waschmittel

to house [haʊz] unterbringen

millennial-born [mɪˌleniəl'bɔːn] um die Jahrtausendwende herum geboren

client base ['klaɪənt ʁbeɪs] Kundenstamm

B | Catering in the office

fridge [frɪdʒ] Kühlschrank

reasonably ['riːznəbli] halbwegs

nutrition-conscious [njuːˌtrɪʃn'kɒnʃəs] ernährungsbewusst

to go for ['gəʊ fə] sich entscheiden für

convenience food [kən'viːniəns ˌfuːd] Fertiggerichte

to microwave ['maɪkrəweɪv] im Mikrowellenherd erhitzen

upmarket [ˌʌp'mɑːkɪt] gehoben; teuer; nobel

panini [pə'niːni] italienisches Brötchen

wrap [ræp] gefüllte Fladenrolle

desperate ['desprət] hier: verzweifelt vor Hunger

set time [ˌset 'taɪm] feste Zeit

C | The company's organisation chart

family-owned company [ˌfæmliˌəʊnd 'kʌmpəni] Familienunternehmen

escalator ['eskəleɪtə] Rolltreppe

chartered accountant [ˌtʃɑːtəd ə'kaʊntnt] Wirtschaftsprüfer/in

to report to [rɪ'pɔːt tə] unterstehen

administration and finance [ədmɪnɪˌstreɪʃnˌənd 'faɪnæns] Verwaltung und Finanzen

customer service [ˌkʌstəmə 'sɜːvɪs] Kundendienst

◎ forklift truck ['fɔːklɪftˌtrʌk] Gabelstapler

luckily ['lʌkɪli] glücklicherweise

pressure ['preʃə] Druck

to take on [ˌteɪk 'ɒn] annehmen; einstellen

raw materials [ˌrɔː mə'tɪəriəlz] Rohstoffe

prospective suppliers [prəˌspektɪv sə'plaɪəz] potentielle Lieferanten

to pass on [ˌpɑːs 'ɒn] weitergeben; weiterleiten

Office expert

E | Office suite applications

database ['deɪtəbeɪs] Datenbank

at one time [ət ˌwʌn 'taɪm] zur gleichen Zeit

to retrieve [rɪ'triːv] abrufen

spreadsheet ['spredʃiːt] Tabellenkalkulation

width [wɪtθ] Breite; Weite

to edit ['edɪt] redigieren; bearbeiten

mail merge ['meɪlˌmɜːdʒ] Serienbrief

to compose [kəm'pəʊz] verfassen; zusammenstellen

record ['rekɔːd] Datensatz

item ['aɪtəm] Punkt; Artikel

folder ['fəʊldə] Ordner

certain ['sɜːtn] bestimmt

◎ to delete [dɪ'liːt] löschen

remainder [rɪ'meɪndə] Rest

reminder [rɪ'maɪndə] Zahlungserinnerung; Mahnung

protocol ['prəʊtəkɒl] Protokoll; Benimmregeln

05 | Telephoning

essential [ɪ'senʃl] wesentlich
to maintain [meɪn'teɪn] *hier:* aufrechterhalten
to afford [ə'fɔːd] sich leisten
access ['ækses] Zugang

A | Appliances and components

appliances [ə'plaɪənsɪz] Geräte
component [kəm'pəʊnənt] (Bestand-)Teil

B | Receiving and redirecting calls

engaged [ɪn'geɪdʒd] besetzt (Telefon)
to hold [həʊld] warten
to make a complaint [ˌmeɪk ə kəm'pleɪnt] sich
  beschweren; reklamieren
on the other line [ɒn ðiˌ ʌðə 'laɪn] am anderen Apparat
to catch [kætʃ] mitbekommen; verstehen; erreichen
digit ['dɪdʒɪt] Ziffer
solicitor [sə'lɪsɪtə] Rechtsanwalt; Rechtsanwältin
to look into sth. [ˌlʊkˌ'ɪntə ˌsʌmθɪŋ] einer Sache nachgehen
asap (as soon as possible) [ˌeɪeseɪ'piː] so bald wie
  möglich; schnellstmöglich

○ **I'm awfully sorry** [aɪmˌ'ɔːfli ˌsɒri] es tut mir schrecklich
  leid
to bother ['bɒðə] belästigen
No worries [nəʊ 'wʌriz] Kein Problem
to bear with so. [ˌbeə 'wɪð ˌsʌmwʌn] etw. Geduld
  haben; so lange warten (am Telefon)
to put so. through [ˌpʊt ˌsʌmwʌn 'θruː] durchstellen;
  verbinden

facial expression [ˌfeɪʃlˌɪk'spreʃn] Gesichtsausdruck
to frown [fraʊn] die Stirn runzeln
raised eyebrows [ˌreɪzdˌ'aɪbraʊz] hochgezogene
  Augenbrauen
to make a fool of oneself [ˌmeɪk ə 'fuːl əv ˌwʌn'self]
  sich blamieren
to wonder ['wʌndə] sich fragen
comeback ['kʌmbæk] Reaktion
all the more important [ˌɔːl ðə mɔːrˌɪm'pɔːtənt] umso
  wichtiger
set expression [ˌsetˌɪk'spreʃn] feststehende Redewendung
at your fingertips [ətˌjɔː 'fɪŋgətɪps] parat; verfügbar

○ **sweater** ['swetə] Pullover
undyed [ˌʌn'daɪd] ungefärbt
organic wool [ɔːˌgænɪk 'wʊl] Bio-Wolle
at short notice [ətˌʃɔːtˌ'nəʊtɪs] kurzfristig
to get [get] mitbekommen; verstehen
I didn't quite catch that [aɪˌdɪdnt kwaɪt 'kætʃ ðæt]
  Ich habe das nicht ganz verstanden
the line is bad [ðəˌlaɪnˌɪz 'bæd] die Verbindung ist
  schlecht (Telefon)
to make a note [ˌmeɪk ə 'nəʊt] notieren
upper-case letter [ˌʌpəkeɪs 'letə] Großbuchstabe
confirmation [ˌkɒnfə'meɪʃn] Bestätigung
patient ['peɪʃnt] geduldig

C | Taking messages

to take down [ˌteɪk 'daʊn] aufschreiben; notieren
accurate ['ækjərət] genau; präzise
to read back [ˌriːd 'bæk] wiederholen
consecutive [kən'sekjətɪv] aufeinanderfolgend
slight [slaɪt] leicht; gering(fügig); kaum merklich
to make up [ˌmeɪk 'ʌp] erfinden
as they go along [əz ðeɪ gəʊ ə'lɒŋ] im Laufe des
  Telefonats
form [fɔːm] Formular

○ **to leave a message** [ˌliːv ə 'mesɪdʒ] eine Nachricht
  hinterlassen
to take place [ˌteɪk 'pleɪs] stattfinden
accommodation [əˌkɒmə'deɪʃn] Unterkunft
to pass on [ˌpɑːs 'ɒn] weitergeben; weiterleiten
to be due back [biˌdjuː 'bæk] zurückerwartet werden
to be due to do sth. [biˌdjuː tə 'duː ˌsʌmθɪŋ] etw. tun
  sollen
to keep the appointment [ˌkiːp ðiˌə'pɔɪntmənt]
  den Termin halten
to stand in for so. [ˌstænd 'ɪn fə ˌsʌmwʌn] jmdn.
  vertreten
in good time [ɪnˌgʊd 'taɪm] rechtzeitig
to emphasise ['emfəsaɪz] betonen; hervorheben
to be keen to do sth. [biˌkiːn tə 'duː ˌsʌmθɪŋ] sehr
  daran interessiert sein, etw. zu tun; etw. unbedingt
  tun wollen
to go ahead [ˌgəʊ ə'hed] fortfahren

to finalise ['faɪnəlaɪz] zum Abschluss bringen
appropriate [ə'prəʊpriət] geeignet; passend;
  angebracht
to deliver [dɪ'lɪvə] (aus)liefern

D | Making telephone calls

suitable ['suːtəbl] geeignet; passend
request [rɪ'kwest] Bitte

◎ **picture frame** ['pɪktʃə ˌfreɪm] Bilderrahmen
to obtain [əb'teɪn] erhalten
catalogue ['kætlɒg] Katalog

though [ðəʊ] allerdings
corporate bonding [ˌkɔːprət 'bɒndɪŋ] Herstellen von Firmenkontakten
added benefit [ˌædɪd 'benəfɪt] Zusatznutzen
quote [kwəʊt] Kostenvoranschlag
deposit [dɪ'pɒzɪt] Anzahlung
mode of payment [ˌməʊd əv 'peɪmənt] Zahlungsart
rock climbing ['rɒk ˌklaɪmɪŋ] Klettern
caving ['keɪvɪŋ] Höhlenklettern; Höhlenwandern
canoeing [kə'nuːɪŋ] Kanufahren
raft-building ['rɑːft ˌbɪldɪŋ] Floßbau
rafting ['rɑːftɪŋ] Rafting
kayaking ['kaɪækɪŋ] Kajakfahren
archery ['ɑːtʃri] Bogenschießen
abseiling ['æbseɪlɪŋ] Abseilen
bush craft ['bʊʃ ˌkrɑːft] Überlebenstraining
log cabin [ˌlɒg 'kæbɪn] Blockhütte
self-catering [ˌself'keɪtrɪŋ] Selbstversorgung
on site [ˌɒn 'saɪt] vor Ort
precaution [prɪ'kɔːʃn] Vorsichtsmaßnahme
due [djuː] fällig
balance ['bæləns] Restbetrag; Saldo
bank transfer ['bæŋk ˌtrænsfɜː] Banküberweisung

E | Leaving messages on an answering service, answering machine or voicemail

addressee [ˌædres'iː] Adressat; Empfänger/in
It goes without saying [ɪt ˌgəʊz wɪˌðaʊt 'seɪɪŋ] Es versteht sich von selbst
inclusion [ɪn'kluːʒn] Einbeziehung; Aufnahme
predictive text [prɪˌdɪktɪv 'tekst] automatische Texterkennung
to tend [tend] tendieren; dazu neigen
nevertheless [ˌnevəðə'les] trotzdem; dennoch
over the top [ˌəʊvə ðə 'tɒp] übertrieben
to enclose [ɪn'kləʊz] beifügen

Office expert

F | Mobile madness

to modulate ['mɒdjəleɪt] *hier:* dämpfen; abschwächen
proximity [prɒk'sɪmɪti] Nähe
to outlaw ['aʊtˌlɔː] verbieten; für ungesetzlich erklären
place of worship [ˌpleɪs əv 'wɜːʃɪp] Gotteshaus
ringer ['rɪŋə] Telefonklingel
to flash [flæʃ] blinken

06 | Making arrangements

on behalf of [ɒn bɪ'hɑːf əv] im Namen von; im Auftrag von
to reschedule [ˌriː'ʃedjuːl] verlegen; neu terminieren
a good command of English [ə ˌgʊd kəˌmɑːnd əv 'ɪŋglɪʃ] gute Englischkenntnisse

A | Flights and accommodation

subsidiary [səb'sɪdiəri] Tochtergesellschaft
to schedule ['ʃedjuːl] zeitlich einplanen
opposite number [ˌɒpəzɪt 'nʌmbə] Gegenüber; Kollege; Kollegin

◎ **to cater for** ['keɪtə fə] etw. bieten für

single room [ˌsɪŋgl 'ruːm] Einzelzimmer

◎ **executive** [ɪg'zekjətɪv] leitende/r Angestellte/r
to man [mæn] besetzen; betreuen
vacant ['veɪknt] frei
adjacent [ə'dʒeɪsnt] angrenzend; daneben
firm booking [ˌfɜːm 'bʊkɪŋ] feste Buchung
to assume [ə'sjuːm] annehmen; von etw. ausgehen
dish [dɪʃ] Speise; Gericht; Schüssel

to cc so. [ˌsiː'siː ˌsʌmwʌn] jmdn. auf cc setzen
duration [djʊə'reɪʃn] Dauer
expiry date [ɪk'spaɪəri ˌdeɪt] Ablaufdatum; Verfallstermin
aisle [aɪl] Gang
option ['ɒpʃn] Alternative; Variante

B | Appointments

proprietor [prə'praɪətə] Inhaber/in
supplementary charge [ˌsʌplɪmentri 'tʃɑːdʒ] Zuschlag
rarely ['reəli] selten; kaum
indicator ['ɪndɪkeɪtə] Anzeigetafel
selection [sə'lekʃn] Auswahl

venue ['venju:] Veranstaltungsort; Treffpunkt

as a rule [əz ə 'ru:l] in der Regel

waiter service [ˌweɪtə 'sɜ:vɪs] Bedienung

turn-taking ['tɜ:nˌteɪkɪŋ] sich anstellen; warten, bis man dran ist; abwechseln

queue [kju:] Warteschlange

visible ['vɪzəbl] sichtbar

annoyance [ə'nɔɪəns] Unmut; Ärger

to push in [ˌpʊʃ 'ɪn] sich vordrängen

embarrassed silence [ɪmˌbærəst 'saɪləns] peinliche Stille

straight away [ˌstreɪt ə'weɪ] sofort

tipping ['tɪpɪŋ] Trinkgeld geben

to tip [tɪp] Trinkgeld geben

to round up [ˌraʊnd 'ʌp] aufrunden

amount [ə'maʊnt] Betrag; Summe

tray [treɪ] Tablett

to cover the bill [ˌkʌvə ðə 'bɪl] die Rechnung begleichen

to display [dɪ'spleɪ] zeigen

C | Booking an exhibition stand

records ['rekɔ:dz] Unterlagen; Dokumente

hourly rate [ˌaʊəli 'reɪt] Stundensatz

to undercut [ˌʌndə'kʌt] unterbieten

Office expert

D | Handling schedules

schedule ['ʃedju:l] Terminplan; Aufstellung

to propose [prə'pəʊz] vorschlagen

KMK Exam Training

to call to order [ˌkɔ:l tʊ 'ɔ:də] zur Ordnung aufrufen; um Ruhe bitten

apologies [ə'pɒlədʒiz] entschuldigte Abwesenheiten

to implement ['ɪmplɪment] einführen

notably ['nəʊtəbli] insbesondere

motion ['məʊʃn] Antrag

to approve [ə'pru:v] genehmigen; billigen

to carry a motion [ˌkæri ə 'məʊʃn] einen Antrag annehmen

unanimously [juː'nænɪməsli] einstimmig

to adjourn [ə'dʒɜ:n] verschieben; vertagen

Phrases

to remove [rɪ'mu:v] entfernen

to dismantle [dɪ'smæntl] auseinandernehmen

07 | Presentations and meetings

key skill [ˌki: 'skɪl] Schlüsselqualifikation

to acquire [ə'kwaɪə] sich aneignen

to be aware of sth. [bɪ ə'weər əv ˌsʌmθɪŋ] sich etw. bewusst sein

to deliver a presentation [dɪˌlɪvər ə prezn'teɪʃn] eine Präsentation halten

content ['kɒntent] Inhalt

A | Preparing a presentation

at your disposal [ət jɔ: dɪ'spəʊzl] zu Ihrer Verfügung

to achieve [ə'tʃi:v] erreichen; erzielen

to absorb [əb'zɔ:b] aufnehmen

to wander ['wɒndə] umherschweifen

prompt cards ['prɒmt ˌkɑ:dz] Stichwortkarten

conclusion [kən'klu:ʒn] Schluss

to draw attention to [ˌdrɔ: ə'tenʃn tə] Aufmerksamkeit lenken auf

to turn your back on [ˌtɜ:n jɔ: 'bæk ɒn] jmdm. den Rücken zuwenden

jointly ['dʒɔɪntli] gemeinsam

performance [pə'fɔ:məns] Leistung; Ergebnis

over time [ˌəʊvə 'taɪm] mit der Zeit

to enable [ɪ'neɪbl] in die Lage versetzen; befähigen

to underline [ˌʌndə'laɪn] unterstreichen; hervorheben

to benefit ['benɪfɪt] profitieren

unemployment [ˌʌnɪm'plɔɪmənt] Arbeitslosigkeit

to match ['mætʃ] gleichkommen; entsprechen

competitive [kəm'petɪtɪv] hart umkämpft; wettbewerbsfähig

to keep sb. on their toes [ˌki:p sʌmbədi ɒn ðeə 'təʊz] jmdn. auf Trapp halten

buoyant ['bɔɪənt] lebhaft; florierend

target group ['tɑ:gɪt gru:p] Zielgruppe

cutting-edge [ˌkʌtɪŋ'edʒ] auf dem neuesten Stand

B | Delivering a presentation

to establish eye contact [ɪˌstæblɪʃ 'aɪ ˌkɒntækt] Blickkontakt herstellen

slide [slaɪd] Folie

reminder [rɪ'maɪndə] Erinnerungsschreiben

to ensure [ɪn'ʃɔ:] sicherstellen; gewährleisten

gestures ['dʒestʃəz] Gesten; Gestik

to operate ['ɒpreɪt] bedienen

to rehearse [rɪ'hɜ:s] proben; einüben

to come across [ˌkʌm ə'krɒs] wirken; rüberkommen

prerequisite [ˌpriːˈrekwɪzɪt] Voraussetzung; Bedingung

likely [ˈlaɪkli] wahrscheinlich

to assess [əˈses] bewerten; einschätzen; abschätzen

according to [əˈkɔːdɪŋ tə] gemäß; entsprechend

evaluation scheme [ɪˌvæljuˈeɪʃn ˌskiːm] Bewertungs-schema

to award points [əˌwɔːd ˈpɔɪnts] Punkte vergeben (z. B. Wettbewerb)

heading [ˈhedɪŋ] Überschrift

well-substantiated [ˌwelsəbˈstænʃieɪtɪd] gut begründet

delivery [dɪˈlɪvri] Vortragsweise; Lieferung

confident [ˈkɒnfɪdnt] selbstbewusst; sicher sein

overall impression [ˌəʊvrɔːlˈɪmˈpreʃn] Gesamteindruck

lively [ˈlaɪvli] lebendig; spritzig

line graph [ˈlaɪn ˌɡrɑːf] Liniendiagramm

pie chart [ˈpaɪ ˌtʃɑːt] Tortendiagramm

C | Line graphs

gathering [ˈɡæðrɪŋ] Versammlung; Treffen

decline [dɪˈklaɪn] Rückgang

steady [ˈstedi] stetig

peak [piːk] Gipfel; Höchststand

drop [drɒp] Rückgang

sharp [ʃɑːp] stark; deutlich

gradually [ˈɡrædʒuəli] allmählich

turnover [ˈtɜːnˌəʊvə] Umsatz

D | Bar charts

bar chart [ˈbɑː ˌtʃɑːt] Balkendiagramm

F | Meetings

for approval [fər əˈpruːvl] zur Genehmigung

amendment [əˈmendmənt] Änderung; Korrektur

to appoint [əˈpɔɪnt] ernennen; bestellen

to keep the minutes [ˌkiːp ðə ˈmɪnɪts] Protokoll führen

absentee [ˌæbsnˈtiː] Abwesende/r

apology [əˈpɒlədʒi] Entschuldigung

vote [vəʊt] Abstimmung

to call on [ˈkɔlˌɒn] sich wenden an

to monopolise [məˈnɒpəlaɪz] an sich reißen

item [ˈaɪtəm] Tagesordnungspunkt; Artikel

to conclude [kənˈkluːd] abschließen; beenden

draft [drɑːft] Entwurf

progress [ˈprəʊɡres] Fortschritt

feasibility [ˌfiːzəˈbɪləti] Machbarkeit

to reflect [rɪˈflekt] widerspiegeln

fashionista [ˌfæʃnˈɪstə] Modefan

affordable [əˈfɔːdəbl] bezahlbar; erschwinglich

to supervise [ˈsuːpəvaɪz] beaufsichtigen

adequate [ˈædɪkwət] angemessen; ausreichend

in working order [ɪn ˌwɜːkɪŋˈɔːdə] funktionstüchtig

those involved [ˌðəʊzˌɪnˈvɒlvd] die Beteiligten

evidence in law [ˌevɪdnsˌɪn ˈlɔː] Beweis vor Gericht

proceedings [prəˈsiːdɪŋz] Verlauf; Geschehnisse

to record [rɪˈkɔːd] aufzeichnen; protokollieren

account [əˈkaʊnt] Bericht

to see eye to eye [siːˌaɪ tə ˈaɪ] einer Meinung sein

poor [pʊə] schlecht

workmanship [ˈwɜːkmənʃɪp] Verarbeitung

garments [ˈɡɑːmənts] Kleidung

to have the edge over the competition [ˌhæv ðiˌedʒ ˌəʊvə ðə ˌkɒmpəˈtɪʃn] der Konkurrenz überlegen sein

to have a point [ˌhævˌə ˈpɔɪnt] nicht ganz Unrecht haben

win-win situation [ˌwɪnˈwɪn sɪtjuˌeɪʃn] Situation, in der beide Seiten gewinnen; Win-Win-Situation

short-lived [ʃɔːtˈlɪvd] kurzlebig

to juggle [ˈdʒʌɡl] jonglieren; hin und herschieben

over and over again [ˌəʊvərˌənˌəʊvərˌəˈɡen] immer wieder

to exploit [ɪkˈsplɔɪt] ausbeuten

cheap labour [ˌtʃiːp ˈleɪbə] billige Arbeitskräfte

to feel strongly about [ˌfiːl ˈstrɒŋliˌəˌbaʊt] eine entschiedene Meinung haben

overall [ˌəʊvrˈɔːl] insgesamt; übergreifend

trade-off [ˈtreɪdɒf] Kompromiss; Abwägung

to be at stake [biˌət ˈsteɪk] auf dem Spiel stehen

re [riː] bezüglich

to call it a day [ˌkɔːlˌɪtˌə ˈdeɪ] Feierabend machen

honesty [ˈɒnɪsti] Ehrlichkeit; Aufrichtigkeit

sincerity [sɪnˈserəti] Aufrichtigkeit

privacy [ˈpraɪvəsi] Privatsphäre

to tone down [ˌtəʊn ˈdaʊn] abschwächen

Office expert

G | The structure and design of presentations

to customise [ˈkʌstəmaɪz] anpassen

to line up [ˌlaɪnˌˈʌp] organisieren

to overwhelm [ˌəʊvəˈwelm] überfordern

pace [peɪs] Geschwindigkeit

KMK Exam Training

billboard [ˈbɪlbɔːd] Plakatwand

08 | Forms of written communication

confidentiality [ˌkɒnfɪdenʃiˈæləti] Vertraulichkeit

PA [ˌpiːˈei] Assistent/in; Sekretär/in

on familiar terms [ɒn fəˌmɪliə ˈtɜːmz] auf vertrautem Fuß

brevity [ˈbrevəti] Kürze

tempting [ˈtemptɪŋ] verlockend

considered [kənˈsɪdəd] überlegt

to skip [skɪp] überspringen; auslassen

to get down to business [get ˌdaʊn tə ˈbɪznɪs] zur Sache/zum Geschäftlichen kommen

notoriously [nəˈtɔːriəsli] bekanntermaßen

recipient [rɪˈsɪpiənt] Empfänger/in

◎ **to stick to** [ˈstɪk tə] an etw. festhalten

A | E-Mails

findings [ˈfaɪndɪŋz] Ergebnisse

to capitalize [ˈkæpɪtlaɪz] in Großbuchstaben schreiben

sparing [ˈspeərɪŋ] sparsam; mäßig

chain letter [ˈtʃeɪn ˌletə] Kettenbrief

tuition [tjuˈɪʃn] Unterricht; Unterweisung

HR (Human Resources) [ˌeɪtʃ ˈɑː ˌhjuːmən ˈriːsɔːsɪz] Personalabteilung

signature footer [ˈsɪgnətʃə ˌfʊtə] Unterschriftsfußzeilen

to leave blank [ˌliːv ˈblæŋk] freilassen

◎ **to delete** [dɪˈliːt] löschen

spam folder [ˈspæm ˌfəʊldə] Spam-Ordner

colon [ˈkəʊlɒn] Doppelpunkt

punctuation [ˌpʌŋktʃuˈeɪʃn] Interpunktion; Zeichensetzung

B | Business letters

immersion course [ɪˈmɜːʃn ˌkɔːs] Intensivkurs

signatory [ˈsɪgnətri] Unterzeichner/in

marital status [ˌmærɪtl ˈsteɪtəs] Familienstand

to precede [priˈsiːd] vor(an)gehen; -stehen

bold type [ˌbəʊld ˈtaɪp] Fettdruck

C | Structure and style of business correspondence

template [ˈtempleɪt] (Dokument)vorlage

jacuzzi [dʒəˈkuːzi] Whirlpool

discount [ˈdɪskaʊnt] Rabatt

festive season [ˌfestɪv ˈsiːzn] Weihnachtszeit; Festtage

to approach [əˈprəʊtʃ] sich nähern

stocking-filler [ˈstɒkɪŋ ˌfɪlə] kleines Weihnachtsgeschenk

Office expert

D | Word processing

to paste [peɪst] einfügen

hard copy [ˌhɑːd ˈkɒpi] Computerausdruck

hyphenation [ˌhaɪfnˈeɪʃn] Worttrennung

to insert [ɪnˈsɜːt] einfügen; einlegen

justification [ˌdʒʌstɪfɪˈkeɪʃn] Bündigkeit

margin [ˈmɑːdʒɪn] Rand

word wrap [ˈwɜːd ˌræp] automatischer Zeilenumbruch

typo [ˈtaɪpəʊ] Tippfehler

to back up [ˌbæk ˈʌp] rückwärts bewegen

KMK Exam Training

score [skɔː] Auswertung; Punktestand

to slip through [ˌslɪp ˈθruː] durchschlüpfen

threshold [ˈθreʃhəʊld] Schwellenwert

quota [ˈkwəʊtə] Quote; Kontingent

default [dɪˈfɔːlt] Voreinstellung; Standardeinstellung

09 | Enquiries

to involve [ɪnˈvɒlv] mit sich bringen; einschließen

particulars (pl) [pəˈtɪkjələz] Einzelheiten

trade association [ˌtreɪd əˌsəʊʃiˈeɪʃn] Handelsverband; Wirtschaftsverband

A | Enquiries in writing

vintage [ˈvɪntɪdʒ] Oldtimer-; klassisch

00-scale [ˌəʊˈəʊ ˌskeɪl] Spur HO

demanding [dɪˈmɑːndɪŋ] anspruchsvoll

B | Enquiries by phone

◎ **I take it that** [aɪ ˈteɪk ɪt ðət] Ich nehme an, dass

my pleasure [maɪ ˈpleʒə] gern geschehen; ist mir ein Vergnügen

gift box [ˈgɪft ˌbɒks] Geschenkkarton

means [miːnz] Mittel; Methode

to retain [rɪˈteɪn] behalten; halten

to facilitate [fəˈsɪlɪteɪt] ermöglichen; erleichtern

volume order [ˌvɒljuːm ˈɔːdə] Großauftrag

to launch [lɔːnʃ] einführen; starten; in die Wege leiten receipt [rɪ'siːt] Erhalt, Eingang

incentive [ɪn'sentɪv] Anreiz

to see a point [ˌsiː ə 'pɔɪnt] einen Standpunkt verstehen

R&D (Research and Development) [ˌɑːrn'diː] Entwicklung(sabteilung)

to arrive at a solution [əˌraɪv ət ə sə'luːʃn] eine Lösung finden

clout [klaʊt] Schlagkraft

feasible ['fiːzəbl] machbar

stunning ['stʌnɪŋ] atemberaubend; überwältigend

stiff competition [ˌstɪf kɒmpə'tɪʃn] harter Wettbewerb

to commit oneself [kə'mɪt wʌnˌself] sich festlegen; verpflichten

knitting wool ['nɪtɪŋ ˌwʊl] Strickwolle

to negotiate [nɪ'gəʊʃieɪt] aushandeln; verhandeln

sole trader [ˌsəʊl 'treɪdə] Einzelkaufmann/frau

decanter [dɪ'kæntə] Karaffe

to deal with ['diːl wɪð] sich befassen mit

Office expert

C | Negotiating in trade

going rate [ˌgəʊɪŋ 'reɪt] geltender Preis

KMK Exam Training

janitorial [ˌdʒænɪ'tɔːriəl] hausmeisterlich

two-winged [ˌtuː'wɪŋd] zweiflüglig

three-story [ˌθriː'stɔːri] dreistöckig

courtyard ['kɔːtjɑːd] Hof

recess [rɪ'ses] Pause

playground ['pleɪgraʊnd] Spielplatz

tool shed ['tuːl ʃed] Geräteschuppen

staircase ['steəkeɪs] Treppe; Treppenhaus

maintenance ['meɪntnəns] Wartung

grounds keeping ['graʊndzˌkiːpɪŋ] Reinigung und Pflege von Außenanlagen

as to ['æz tə] bezüglich

flat fee [ˌflæt 'fiː] Pauschalpreis

caretaking ['keəˌteɪkɪŋ] Hausmeisterdienste

snow shoveling ['snəʊ ʃʌvlɪŋ] Schneeschippen

waste management [ˌweɪst 'mænɪdʒmənt] Abfallwirtschaft

minor repairs [ˌmaɪnə rɪ'peəz] kleinere Reparaturen

affiliated [ə'fɪlieɪtɪd] angehörig

10 | Offers

solicited offer [səˌlɪsɪtɪdˌ'ɒfə] verlangtes Angebot

unsolicited [ˌʌnsə'lɪsɪtɪd] unverlangt

quotation [kwə'təɪʃn] Angebot; Kostenvoranschlag

to designate ['dezɪgneɪt] bezeichnen; benennen

cost estimate ['kɒstˌestɪmət] Kostenvoranschlag

to be subject to [bi 'sʌbdʒɪktˌtə] unterliegen; abhängen von; unterworfen sein

to stipulate ['stɪpjəleɪt] vertraglich vereinbaren; vorschreiben

lettering ['letrɪŋ] Beschriftung

armchair ['ɑːmtʃeə] Sessel

decisive [dɪ'saɪsɪv] entscheidend

to process ['prəʊsəs] bearbeiten

to refrain [rɪ'freɪn] auf etw. verzichten; etw. unterlassen

to conclude [kən'kluːd] abschließen; beenden

A | Offers in writing

cast iron [ˌkɑːst 'aɪən] gusseisern

flooring ['flɔːrɪŋ] Bodenbelag

loop-pile [ˌluːp'paɪl] Schlingen-

woven fabric [ˌwəʊvn 'fæbrɪk] Textilgewebe

to apply [ə'plaɪ] hier: gelten; bewerben

B | Offers by phone

to run out of sth. [ˌrʌnˌaʊtˌəv ˌsʌmθɪŋ] ausgehen; zur Neige gehen

subtotal [ˌsʌb'təʊtl] Zwischensumme

C | Comparing options

to tailor to ['teɪlə tə] zuschneiden auf

resort [rɪ'zɔːt] Urlaubs-; Badeort

tuition fees [tjuː'ɪʃn ˌfiːz] Kursgebühren

participant [pɑː'tɪsɪpnt] Teilnehmer/in

full board [ˌfʊl 'bɔːd] Vollpension

host family ['həʊst ˌfæmli] Gastfamilie

reasonable ['riːznəbl] akzeptabel; angemessen

balance ['bæləns] Restbetrag; Saldo

commencement [kə'mensmənt] Anfang; Beginn

D | INCOTERMS (Terms of delivery)

to draw up [ˌdrɔː 'ʌp] verfassen; aufsetzen

designation [ˌdezɪg'neɪʃn] Bezeichnung

at the disposal [ət ðə dɪ'spəʊzl] zur Verfügung

carriage ['kærɪdʒ] Transport(kosten); Fracht(kosten)

vessel ['vesl] Schiff

to expire [ɪk'spaɪə] ablaufen; verfallen

to bother to do sth. [ˌbɒðə tə 'duː ˌsʌmθɪŋ] sich die Mühe machen etw. zu tun

Office expert

KMK Exam Training

shiny ['ʃaɪni] glänzend
welded ['weldɪd] geschweißt
fixed base [ˌfɪkst 'beɪs] starres Fußteil
fabric covered [ˌfæbrɪk'kʌvəd] stoffbespannt
heavy-duty [ˌhevi'dju:ti] strapazierfähig; robust
reclining [rɪ'klaɪnɪŋ] mit Liegefunktion
hydraulic controlled [haɪˌdrɔ:lɪk kən'trəʊld] hydraulisch gesteuert
piston ['pɪstn] Kolben
adjustable [ə'dʒʌstəbl] verstellbar
customized ['kʌstəmaɪzd] maßgeschneidert
sturdy ['stɜ:di] fest; stabil
wheeled steel base [ˌwi:ld ˌsti:l 'beɪs] Stahlfuß mit Rollen

11 | Orders

administrative assistant [əd'mɪnɪstrətɪv əˌsɪstnt] Kaufmann/-frau für Büromanagement
resale [ˌri:'seɪl] Wiederverkauf
the latter [ðə 'lætə] letztere(r/s)
procurement [prə'kjʊəmənt] Beschaffung; Bezug
to establish [ɪ'stæblɪʃ] einführen
to grant [grɑ:nt] gewähren
terms *(pl)* [tɜ:mz] Bedingungen; Konditionen
trial order [ˌtraɪəl 'ɔ:də] Probeauftrag
initial [ɪ'nɪʃl] anfänglich; Erst-
secure [sɪ'kjʊə] sicher

A | Orders in writing

offer ['ɒfə] Angebot
consumer safety group [kənˌsju:mə 'seɪfti ˌgru:p] in Deutschland z. B. Verbraucherzentrale
favourable ['feɪvrəbl] positiv; günstig
impressed [ɪm'prest] beeindruckt
as per ['æzpə] gemäß; wie ersichtlich
to indicate ['ɪndɪkeɪt] angeben; nennen; hinweisen
sum [sʌm] Summe
to transfer [træns'fɜ:] transferieren; überweisen
to settle an account [ˌsetl ən ə'kaʊnt] Konto ausgleichen; Rechnung begleichen
consignment [kən'saɪnmənt] Lieferung (bestellter Ware)
reference ['refrns] Referenz; Bezug
relevant ['reləvənt] entsprechend; sachdienlich

complimentary close [ˌkɒmplɪmentri 'kləʊz] Grußformel am Schluss (Brief/Fax/E-Mail)
enclosure [ɪn'kləʊʒə] Anlage (Brief)
applicable [ə'plɪkəbl] zutreffend
quantity ['kwɒntəti] Menge
purchasing department ['pɜ:tʃəsɪŋ dɪˌpɑ:tmənt] Einkauf(sabteilung)
stationery ['steɪʃənri] Schreibwaren; Büromaterial
leaflet ['li:flət] Prospekt
multilingual [ˌmʌltɪ'lɪŋgwəl] vielsprachig; mehrsprachig
architectural [ˌɑ:kɪ'tektʃrl] architektonisch; Architektur-
calendar ['kælɪndə] Kalender
superb [su:'pɜ:b] hervorragend
magnificent [mæg'nɪfɪsnt] großartig; prächtig
spectacular [spek'tækjələ] spektakulär; eindrucksvoll
Silk Road ['sɪlk ˌrəʊd] Seidenstraße
Bee Farmers' Association ['bi: ˌfɑ:məz əsəʊʃiˌeɪʃn] Imkerverband

B | Orders by phone

to supply [sə'plaɪ] liefern; bereitstellen

annual ['ænjuəl] jährlich
luncheon ['lʌnʃən] förmliches Mittagessen
buffet ['bʊfeɪ] Büfett
to charge [tʃɑ:dʒ] berechnen
sufficient [sə'fɪʃnt] genügend; ausreichend
complicated ['kɒmplɪkeɪtɪd] kompliziert
be out of pocket [bi ˌaʊt əv 'pɒkɪt] draufzahlen; zusätzlich zahlen
to square sth. with sb. ['skweə ˌsʌmθɪŋ wɪð ˌsʌmbədi] etw. mit jmdm. absprechen / vereinbaren
strip [strɪp] Streifen
chopped [tʃɒpt] kleingeschnitten
gherkin ['gɜ:kɪn] Gewürzgurke
bowl [bəʊl] Schale
to detect [dɪ'tekt] entdecken; *hier:* heraushören
scepticism ['skeptɪsɪzm] Skepsis
asparagus spears [ə'spærəgəs spɪəz] Spargelstangen
platter ['plætə] Servierplatte; (Holz-)Teller
rye [raɪ] Roggen
vegetarian [ˌvedʒə'teəriən] Vegetarier/in
the odd [ðɪ 'ɒd] der eine oder andere
frankfurter ['fræŋkfɜ:tə] Bockwurst
meat ball ['mi:t ˌbɔ:l] Fleischklops; Frikadelle
fishy ['fɪʃi] fischig
smoked salmon [ˌsməʊkt 'sæmən] Räucherlachs
horseradish ['hɔ:sˌrædɪʃ] Meerrettich; Kren
custard ['kʌstəd] Vanillesoße

raspberry ['rɑːzbri] Himbeere
sour [saʊə] sauer
to appeal to [ə'piːl tə] ansprechen; gefallen
Rhine ['raɪn] Rhein
Moselle [məˈzel] Mosel
to break the bank [ˌbreɪk ðə 'bæŋk] Unsummen kosten
perishable ['perɪʃəbl] verderblich
airfreight ['eəfreɪt] Luftfracht
to pick up [ˌpɪk 'ʌp] abholen
advice of dispatch [ədˌvaɪs ˌəv dɪ'spætʃ] Versandanzeige

vacuum cleaner ['vækjuːm ˌkliːnə] Staubsauger
to take a call [ˌteɪk ə 'kɔːl] Anruf entgegennehmen
to refer to [rɪ'fɜː tə] sich beziehen auf
to regret [rɪ'gret] bedauern
to dispatch [dɪ'spætʃ] versenden; verschicken
particular [pə'tɪkjələ] besonders; speziell
substitute ['sʌbstɪtjuːt] Ersatz
forwarder ['fɔːwədə] Spediteur
Treaties of Rome [ˌtriːiz ˌəv 'rəʊm] Römische Verträge
in favour of [ɪn 'feɪvər ˌəv] dafür sein; zugunsten
application [ˌæplɪ'keɪʃn] Antrag; Bewerbung
membership ['membəʃɪp] Mitgliedschaft
to initiate [ɪ'nɪʃieɪt] einleiten
to bring into being [ˌbrɪŋ ˌɪntə 'biːɪŋ] ins Leben rufen

Office expert

C | Ordering over the phone

despite [dɪ'spaɪt] trotz
widespread ['waɪdspred] weit verbreitet
device [dɪ'vaɪs] Gerät
to remain [rɪ'meɪn] bleiben
vital ['vaɪtl] unerlässlich
advancement [əd'vɑːnsmənt] Fortschritt
tent [tent] Zelt
foldable ['fəʊldəbl] faltbar
item ['aɪtəm] Artikel
total ['təʊtl] Gesamtsumme

KMK Exam Training

to bow [baʊ] sich verbeugen
to stuff into [ˌstʌf 'ɪntə] reinstecken in
rank [ræŋk] Rang; Rangordnung
prominently ['prɒmɪnəntli] auffällig

Phrases

previous ['priːviəs] früher; vorhergehend

12 | Transport and logistics

fundamental [ˌfʌndə'mentl] grundlegend; fundamental
importance [ɪm'pɔːtns] Wichtigkeit; Bedeutung
freight logistics ['freɪt ləˌdʒɪstɪks] Frachtlogistik; Güterspedition
to be considered [bi kən'sɪdəd] erachtet werden
significant [sɪg'nɪfɪkənt] deutlich; wesentlich
manufacturing [ˌmænjə'fæktʃrɪŋ] Fertigung; Fabrikation
operations (pl) [ˌɒprˈeɪʃnz] Geschäftstätigkeit
provider [prə'vaɪdə] Versorger; Anbieter; Lieferant
multiple ['mʌltɪpl] mehrere; mehrfach
under one umbrella [ˌʌndə 'wʌn ʌmˌbrelə] unter einem Dach
warehousing ['weəhaʊzɪŋ] Lagerhaltung / -wesen
formality [fɔː'mæləti] Formalität
documentation [ˌdɒkjəmen'teɪʃn] Dokumentation
percentage [pə'sentɪdʒ] Anteil; Prozentsatz
waterway ['wɔːtəweɪ] Wasserstraße
France [frɑːns] Frankreich
Austria ['ɒstriə] Österreich

A | Modes of transport

mode of transport [ˌməʊd ˌəv 'trænspɔːt] Beförderungsart
journal ['dʒɜːnl] Zeitschrift
recent ['riːsnt] nicht lange zurückliegend; *hier:* neueste(r/n)
twice [twaɪs] zweimal
grid [grɪd] Gitter; hier: Tabelle; Raster
separate ['seprət] eigen; separat
sheet [ʃiːt] Blatt
cargo ['kɑːgəʊ] (See-)Fracht; Ladung

⊚ **regarded as** [rɪ'gɑːdɪd ˌəz] gesehen als
field [fiːld] Gebiet
grateful ['greɪtfl] dankbar
factor ['fæktə] Faktor; Umstand
specific [spə'sɪfɪk] bestimmt; spezifisch
destination [ˌdestɪ'neɪʃn] Bestimmungsort
in relation to [ɪn rɪ'leɪʃn tə] in Bezug auf
value ['væljuː] Wert
mainland ['meɪnlənd] Festland; Kontinent
bulky ['bʌlki] sperrig; unhandlich
comparatively [kəm'pærətɪvli] vergleichsweise
pollution [pə'luːʃn] (Umwelt-)Verschmutzung
downside ['daʊnsaɪd] Kehrseite; Nachteil
lorry ['lɒri] Lkw
investment [ɪn'vestmənt] Investition
inadequate [ɪ'nædɪkwət] unzureichend; unzulänglich

machine tool [məˈʃiːn ˈtuːl] Werkzeugmaschine
railway siding [ˈreɪlweɪ ˌsaɪdɪŋ] Gleisanschluss
track [træk] (Bahn-)Gleis
to join up [ˌdʒɔɪnˈʌp] Verbindung haben mit
public [ˈpʌblɪk] öffentlich
huge [hjuːdʒ] riesig
obvious [ˈɒbviəs] offensichtlich
flexibility [ˌfleksɪˈbɪləti] Flexibilität
dependent [dɪˈpendənt] abhängig
timetable [ˈtaɪmˌteɪbl] Fahrplan
issue [ˈɪʃuː] Frage; Problem
fog [fɒg] Nebel
icy [ˈaɪsi] glatt; eisig; vereist
border [ˈbɔːdə] Grenze
risk [rɪsk] Risiko
theft [θeft] Diebstahl
to handle [ˈhændl] in die Hand nehmen; bearbeiten
spare part [speə ˈpɑːt] Ersatzteil
exotic [ɪgˈzɒtɪk] exotisch
foodstuffs *(pl)* [ˈfuːdstʌfs] Lebensmittel
inexpensive [ˌɪnɪkˈspensɪv] preisgünstig
bulk [bʌlk] Masse
inland waterway [ˌɪnlænd ˈwɜːtəweɪ] Binnengewässer
barge [bɑːdʒ] Lastkahn; Binnenschiff
coal [kəʊl] Kohle
containerisation [kənˌteɪnraɪˈzeɪʃn] Einsatz von Containern
to offload [ɒfˈləʊd] ab-/ausladen
standardised [ˈstændədaɪzd] genormt; standardisiert
conscious [ˈkɒnʃəs] bewusst
Channel [ˈtʃænl] Ärmelkanal
North Sea [ˌnɔːθ ˈsiː] Nordsee
shuttle train [ˈʃʌtl ˌtreɪn] Pendelzug
ferry [ˈferi] Fähre

seaworthy packing [ˌsiːwɜːði ˈpækɪŋ] seetaugliche Verpackung
urgent [ˈɜːdʒnt] dringend; eilig
required [rɪˈkwaɪəd] benötigt
bubble [ˈbʌbl] Blase
medical supplies [ˌmedɪkl səˈplaɪz] Sanitätsartikel
bottled [ˈbɒtld] in Flaschen abgefüllt
olive oil [ˈɒlɪvˌɔɪl] Olivenöl
Italy [ˈɪtli] Italien
generator [ˈdʒenreɪtə] Generator
orchid [ˈɔːkɪd] Orchidee
Brazil [brəˈzɪl] Brasilien
gravel [ˈgrævl] Kies
Belgium [ˈbeldʒəm] Belgien
Switzerland [ˈswɪtsələnd] die Schweiz

steel [stiːl] Stahl
girder [ˈgɜːdə] Träger
Morocco [məˈrɒkəʊ] Marokko
Argentina [ˌɑːdʒnˈtiːnə] Argentinien

C | Dispatch advice

dispatch advice [dɪˈspætʃ ədˌvaɪs] Versandanzeige
carrier [ˈkæriə] Frachtführer
contract [ˈkɒntrækt] Vertrag
to bear in mind [ˌbeər ɪn ˈmaɪnd] daran denken; im Auge behalten
polite [pəˈlaɪt] höflich
outboard engine [ˌaʊtbɔːd ˈendʒɪn] Außenbordmotor
Irish [ˈaɪrɪʃ] irisch
Republic of Ireland [rɪˌpʌblɪk əv ˈaɪələnd] Republik Irland
haulier [ˈhɔːliə] Spediteur
warehouse [ˈweəhaʊs] Lager(haus)
assurance [əˈʃɔːrns] Zusicherung
crate [kreɪt] Kiste
pallet [ˈpælɪt] Palette
consignment note [kənˈsaɪnmənt ˌnəʊt] Frachtbrief
packing list [ˈpækɪŋ ˌlɪst] Packliste
commercial invoice [kəˌmɜːʃl ˈɪnvɔɪs] Handelsrechnung
prompt [prɒmt] Vorgabe; Stichwort
arrival [əˈraɪvl] Ankunft

D | Order confirmation and inquiry by phone concerning transport

inquiry [ɪnˈkwaɪəri] Anfrage
to confirm [kənˈfɜːm] bestätigen

in stock [ɪn stɒk] auf Lager
bathroom scale [ˌbɑːθruːm ˈskeɪl] Personenwaage
stainless [ˈsteɪnləs] rostfrei
analyser [ˈænlaɪzə] Analyseprogramm
slim [slɪm] schlank
casing [ˈkeɪsɪŋ] Gehäuse
transparent [trænˈspærnt] transparent; durchsichtig
to debit an account [ˌdebɪt ən əˈkaʊnt] ein Konto belasten
settled [ˈsetld] erledigt

to place an order [ˌpleɪs ən ˈɔːdə] einen Auftrag erteilen
loyalty [ˈlɔɪəlti] Loyalität; Treue
to honour [ˈɒnə] honorieren; einlösen
at the latest [ət ðə ˈleɪtɪst] spätestens
hold the line [ˌhəʊld ðə ˈlaɪn] am Apparat bleiben
delay [dɪˈleɪ] Verzögerung
to be held up [bi ˌheldˈʌp] aufgehalten werden

security issue [sɪˈkjʊərəti ˌɪʃuː] Sicherheitsproblem

to cancel [ˈkænsl] annullieren

inconvenience [ˌɪnkənˈviːniəns] Unannehmlichkeit

Office expert

F | Just in time

to tie up [ˌtaɪ ˈʌp] binden

resources [rɪˈzɔːsɪz] Ressourcen; Mittel

to overestimate [ˌəʊvrˈestɪmeɪt] überschätzen

to pile up [ˌpaɪl ˈʌp] anhäufen

to underestimate [ˌʌndrˈestɪmeɪt] unterschätzen

shelf (pl.) shelves [ʃelf] Regal

to call for [ˈkɔːl fə] erfordern; verlangen

signboard [ˈsaɪnbɔːd] Reklameschild

billboard [ˈbɪlbɔːd] Plakatwand

added [ˈædɪd] zusätzlich

to tailor [ˈteɪlə] maßschneidern

drawback [ˈdrɔːbæk] Haken; Nachteil

volume [ˈvɒljuːm] Volumen; Ausmaß

smooth [smuːð] glatt; reibungslos

to oscillate [ˈɒsɪleɪt] pendeln

KMK Exam Training

to boost [buːst] ankurbeln; fördern

distraction [dɪˈstrækʃn] Ablenkung

overwhelmed [ˌəʊvəˈwelmd] überwältigt

bombarded [bɒmˈbɑːdɪd] bombardiert

to relate to [rɪˈleɪt tə] in Kontakt kommen mit

burgeoning [ˈbɜːdʒnɪŋ] sprießend; aufkeimend; wachsend

to collaborate [kəˈlæbreɪt] zusammenarbeiten

blip [blɪp] Bildmarke; kurzer Leuchtimpuls

to keep up [ˌkiːp ˈʌp] mithalten; Schritt halten

more often than not [mɔːr ˌɒfn ðən ˈnɒt] meistens

to juggle [ˈdʒʌgl] jonglieren; gleichzeitig erledigen

data deluge [ˈdeɪtə ˌdeljuːdʒ] Datenflut

to map out [ˌmæp ˈaʊt] entwerfen; planen; ausarbeiten

to spot [spɒt] erkennen; ausmachen

obstacle [ˈɒbstəkl] Hindernis

to clog up [ˌklɒg ˈʌp] verstopfen

inbox [ˈɪnˌbɒks] Posteingang

to tag [tæg] auszeichnen; markieren

to message [ˈmesɪdʒ] eine Nachricht senden

instantly [ˈɪnstəntli] sofort

to implement [ˈɪmplɪment] umsetzen

13 | Payment and reminders

vital [ˈvaɪtl] entscheidend; wesentlich

to monitor [ˈmɒnɪtə] beobachten; überprüfen

prompt [prɒmt] schnell; umgehend

invoice [ˈɪnvɔɪs] Rechnung

overdue [ˌəʊvəˈdjuː] überfällig

trade [treɪd] Handel treiben; handeln

frequently [ˈfriːkwəntli] häufig

foreign currency transfer [ˌfɒrən ˈkʌrnsi ˌtrænsfɜː] Auslandsüberweisung

currency [ˈkʌrnsi] Währung

Chinese [tʃaɪˈniːz] chinesisch

A | The invoice

to provide [prəˈvaɪd] angeben; zur Verfügung stellen; bieten

transaction [trænˈzækʃn] Transaktion; Vorgang

to make out [ˌmeɪk ˈaʊt] ausstellen

subsequent [ˈsʌbsɪkwənt] anschließend; nachträglich

licence [ˈlaɪsns] Lizenz

abbreviation [əˌbriːviˈeɪʃn] Abkürzung

gauge [geɪdʒ] Spurweite

scale [skeɪl] maßstabsgetreu

modelling [ˈmɒdlɪŋ] Modellbau

attachment [əˈtætʃmənt] Anhang

to appreciate [əˈpriːʃieɪt] (wert)schätzen

to instruct [ɪnˈstrʌkt] anweisen

at your earliest convenience [ət jɔːr ˌɜːliəst kənˈviːniəns] so bald wie möglich

to remit [rɪˈmɪt] überweisen

to attach [əˈtætʃ] anhängen (Datei); anbringen

craftsmanship [ˈkrɑːftsmənʃɪp] Kunstfertigkeit; handwerkliches Können

query [ˈkwɪəri] Frage

tax-exempt intra-EU delivery [ˌtæksɪgˈzemt ˌɪntrəiːˈjuː dɪˈlɪvri] steuerfreie Innergemeinschaftslieferung (innerhalb der EU)

imagination [ɪˌmædʒɪˈneɪʃn] Phantasie; Vorstellungskraft

B | Means of payment in trade

to issue [ˈɪʃuː] ausstellen; ausgeben

means of payment [ˈmiːnz əv ˈpeɪmənt] Zahlungsmittel

to advance [ədˈvɑːns] vorschießen; auslegen

cardholder [ˈkɑːdˌhəʊldə] Karteninhaber/in

to withdraw [wɪðˈdrɔː] Geld abheben; zurückziehen

ATM (automatic teller machine) [ˌeɪtiːˈem, ˌɔːtəmætɪk ˈtelə məʃiːn] Geldautomat

cheque [tʃek] Scheck

to specify [ˈspesɪfaɪ] genau bezeichnen
equivalent [ɪˈkwɪvlənt] Entsprechung

C | Payment by plastic cards

to account for [əˈkaʊnt fə] ausmachen; entfallen auf
outlet [ˈaʊtlet] Verkaufsstellen; Vertriebsmöglichkeiten
as a matter of course [əz ə ˌmætər əv ˈkɔːs] ganz
selbstverständlich
cashback [ˈkæʃbæk] Zurückerstattung von einem Teil
vom Kaufpreis als Kaufanreiz
double-digit [ˌdʌblˈdɪdʒɪt] zweistellig
presumably [prɪˈzjuːməbli] voraussichtlich
boost [buːst] Auftrieb
to oust [aʊst] verdrängen
to revolutionise [ˌrevlˈuːʃnaɪz] revolutionieren
profession [prəˈfeʃn] Beruf
plumber [ˈplʌmə] Klempner/in
electrician [ˌclɪkˈtrɪʃn] Elektriker/in
decorator [ˈdekreɪtə] Innenausstatter/in; Tapezierer/in
on the spot [ɒn ðə ˈspɒt] sofort; auf der Stelle
periodically [ˈpɪəriˈɒdɪkli] regelmäßig
to resurface [ˌriːˈsɜːfɪs] wieder auftauchen
over-indebted [ˌəʊvərɪnˈdetɪd] überschuldet
to argue [ˈɑːɡjuː] behaupten
to vet [vet] überprüfen
to phase out [ˌfeɪzˈaʊt] allmählich abschaffen
to exclude [ɪkˈskluːd] ausschließen
creditworthy [ˈkredɪtˌwɜːði] kreditwürdig
widespread [ˈwaɪdspred] weit verbreitet
availability [əˌveɪləˈbɪləti] Verfügbarkeit
statistic [stəˈtɪstɪk] Statistik

D | Terms of payment in foreign trade

creditworthiness [ˈkredɪtˌwɜːðinəs] Kreditwürdigkeit
political [pəˈlɪtɪkl] politisch
security [sɪˈkjʊərəti] Sicherheit
to manufacture [ˌmænjəˈfæktʃə] herstellen; anfertigen
specification [ˌspesɪfɪˈkeɪʃn] Spezifikation; Vorgabe
staggered [ˈstæɡəd] gestaffelt
proof [pruːf] Beweis; Nachweis
to effect payment [ɪˌfekt ˈpeɪmənt] Zahlung leisten
to be entitled to [bi ɪnˈtaɪtld tə] Anspruch haben auf
to deduct [dɪˈdʌkt] abziehen
cash discount [ˌkæʃ ˈdɪskaʊnt] Barzahlungsrabatt;
Skonto
trusted [ˈtrʌstɪd] vertrauenswürdig
customary [ˈkʌstəmri] üblich
to revoke [rɪˈvəʊk] widerrufen; stornieren
consent [kənˈsent] Zustimmung; Einwilligung

all parties concerned [ɔl ˌpɑːtiz kənˈsɜːnd] alle beteiligten Parteien
to rely on [rɪˈlaɪ ɒn] sich verlassen auf
promise [ˈprɒmɪs] Versprechen
opening bank [ˌəʊpnɪŋ ˈbæŋk] ausstellende Bank
irrevocable [ˌɪrɪˈvəʊkəbl] unwiderruflich
valid [ˈvælɪd] gültig
enquiry [ɪnˈkwaɪəri] Anfrage
Canadian [kəˈneɪdiən] kanadisch
marine [məˈriːn] See-
pump [pʌmp] Pumpe
to insist on [ɪnˈsɪst ɒn] bestehen auf
catering [ˈkeɪtrɪŋ] Catering; Verpflegung
long-standing [ˌlɒŋˈstændɪŋ] langjährig
relationship [rɪˈleɪʃnʃɪp] Beziehung
sweater [ˈswetə] Pullover

E | Mobile online banking

millennials [mɪˈleniəlz] um die Jahrtausendwende
geborene Personen
to innovate [ˈɪnəveɪt] Neuerungen einführen
Spain [speɪn] Spanien
to interact [ˌɪntəˈækt] miteinander umgehen;
interagieren
to correspond to [ˌkɒrɪˈspɒnd tə] entsprechen
need [niːd] Bedürfnis
branch [brɑːnʃ] Filiale
in response [ˌɪn rɪˈspɒns] als Antwort; als Reaktion
array [əˈreɪ] Feld
intense [ɪnˈtens] intensiv; stark
additive [ˈædɪtɪv] zusätzlich
current [ˈkʌrnt] aktuell; gegenwärtig
transfer [ˈtrænsfɜː] Überweisung
commission charge [kəˈmɪʃn ˌtʃɑːdʒ] Vermittlungsgebühr
preapproved [ˌpriːəˈpruːvd] im Voraus genehmigt
fee [fiː] Gebühr
mortgage [ˈmɔːɡɪdʒ] Hypothek
chunk [tʃʌŋk] Brocken
to switch [swɪtʃ] wechseln
rival [ˈraɪvl] Konkurrenz-
to insure against [ɪnˈʃɔːr əˌɡenst] versichern gegen
fraud [frɔːd] Betrug
fingerprint [ˈfɪŋɡəprɪnt] Fingerabdruck
recognition [ˌrekəɡˈnɪʃn] Wiedererkennung; Anerkennung

F | Reminders

insistent [ɪnˈsɪstnt] nachdrücklich
to mislay [mɪˈsleɪ] verlegen
to fail [feɪl] scheitern

desired [dɪˈzaɪəd] gewünscht

response [rɪˈspɒns] Reaktion

to threaten [ˈθretn] drohen

interest [ˈɪntrəst] Zinsen; Interesse

outstanding [ˈaʊtˌstændɪŋ] ausstehend; offen

legal [ˈliːgl] juristisch; rechtlich

to doublecheck [ˌdʌblˈtʃek] nochmals prüfen

file [faɪl] Akte; Datei

to be affected [bi əˈfektɪd] betroffen sein

hurricane [ˈhʌrɪkən] Wirbelsturm

faulty [ˈfɔːlti] fehlerhaft

smooth [smuːð] glatt; reibungslos

to occur [əˈkɜː] vorkommen

apologetic [əˌpɒləˈdʒetɪk] Bedauern ausdrücken; entschuldigend

concerning [kənˈsɜːnɪŋ] bezüglich

to apologise [əˈpɒlədʒaɪz] sich entschuldigen

to regret [rɪˈgret] Bedauern

respite [ˈrespaɪt] Atempause; Zahlungsaufschub

severe [səˈvɪə] ernst; schwer

spell [spel] Episode; Phase

power cut [ˈpaʊə ˌkʌt] Stromausfall

to affect [əˈfekt] betreffen

stock [stɒk] Vorräte

insurance [ɪnˈʃɔːrns] Versicherung

to compensate [ˈkɒmpənseɪt] entschädigen

in the meantime [ɪn ðə ˈmiːntaɪm] zwischenzeitlich; inzwischen

considerable [kənˈsɪdrəbl] beträchtlich

replacement [rɪˈpleɪsmənt] Ersatz

extension [ɪkˈstenʃn] Zahlungsaufschub; Verlängerung

G | Reminders and replies to reminders by telephone

Accounts [əˈkaʊnts] Buchhaltung

⊙ **punctual** [ˈpʌŋktʃuəl] pünktlich

Office expert

H | An ATM

to deposit money [dɪˌpɒzɪt ˈmʌni] Geld einzahlen; einlegen

to process [ˈprəʊsəs] bearbeiten

to withdraw (money) [wɪðˈdrɔː] (Geld) abheben; zurückziehen

amount [əˈmaʊnt] Betrag; Summe

alert [əˈlɜːt] wachsam

ahead of time [əˌhed əv ˈtaɪm] im Voraus

KMK Exam Training

village banking [ˈvɪlɪdʒ ˌbæŋkɪŋ] Vergabe von Mikrokrediten durch lokale Banken

loan [ləʊn] Darlehen

collateral [kəˈlætrl] Sicherheit; Pfand

expenditure [ɪkˈspendɪtʃə] Ausgaben; Auslagen

to levy fines [ˌlevi ˈfaɪnz] Geldbußen auferlegen

penalty payment [ˈpenlti ˌpeɪmənt] Strafzahlung

to exert [ɪgˈzɜːt] ausüben

14 | Complaints and adjustments

to take into account [ˌteɪk ˌɪntu əˈkaʊnt] berücksichtigen

complaint [kəmˈpleɪnt] Beschwerde; Mängelrüge

adjustment [əˈdʒʌstmənt] Ausgleich; Regulierung

unsatisfactory [ʌnˌsætɪsˈfæktri] unbefriedigend; unzureichend

to express [ɪkˈspres] ausdrücken

anger [ˈæŋgə] Wut; Ärger

firm [fɜːm] fest; bestimmt

culture [ˈkʌltʃə] Kultur

A | Making complaints

wine [waɪn] Wein

surface [ˈsɜːfɪs] Oberfläche

badly [ˈbædli] schwer; schlecht; stark

scratched [skrætʃt] verkratzt

to stress [stres] betonen

to render [ˈrendə] leisten; erbringen

surplus [ˈsɜːpləs] überschüssig

credit note [ˈkredɪt ˌnəʊt] Gutschrift

oral [ˈɔːrl] mündlich

wasp [wɒsp] Wespe

refund [ˈriːfʌnd] Erstattung

stitching [ˈstɪtʃɪŋ] Naht

defective [dɪˈfektɪv] fehlerhaft; beschädigt

botched [bɒtʃt] verpfuscht

B | Complaints in writing

to inspect [ɪnˈspekt] prüfen ; inspizieren

merchandise [ˈmɜːtʃndaɪs] Ware

inspection [ɪnˈspekʃn] Prüfung; Inspektion

adhesive [ədˈhiːsɪv] Klebstoff

insufficient [ˌɪnsəˈfɪʃnt] unzureichend

time-consuming [ˈtaɪmkənˌsjuːmɪŋ] zeitraubend

to commission [kəˈmɪʃn] beauftragen

to reglue [ˌriːˈgluː] neu verkleben

to bear [beə] tragen

fault [fɔːlt] Fehler

error ['erə] Irrtum; Fehler
aviation [ˌeɪvi'eɪʃn] Luftfahrt
principal ['prɪnsɪpl] Schulleiter/in
noisy ['nɔɪzi] laut
insulation [ˌɪnsjə'leɪʃn] Wärmedämmung; Isolierung
procedure [prə'si:dʒə] Ablauf; Verfahren
to merge [mɜ:dʒ] zusammenlegen
largely ['lɑ:dʒli] weitgehend

C | Complaints by telephone

bulb [bʌlb] Blumenzwiebel; Knolle
tuber ['tju:bə] Pflanzenknolle
numerous ['nju:mrəs] zahlreich
mix-up ['mɪksʌp] Verwechslung
paperweight ['peɪpəweɪt] Briefbeschwerer
staff [stɑ:f] Belegschaft; Personal
chip [tʃɪp] Abplatzung; Splitter
shape [ʃeɪp] Form
uniform ['ju:nɪfɔ:m] einheitlich; gleich
handcrafted ['hænkrɑ:ftɪd] handgemacht

⊙ **fair** [feə] Messe
generous ['dʒenrəs] großzügig
plenty ['plenti] reichlich; viel
at our expense [ət ˌaʊər ɪk'spens] auf unsere Kosten
consolation [ˌkɒnsə'leɪʃn] Trost
revised [rɪ'vaɪzd] geändert

Italian [ɪ'tæliən] italienisch
discrepancy [dɪ'skrepnsi] Abweichung; Diskrepanz
to differ ['dɪfə] sich unterscheiden
complainee [kəm'pleɪni:] Beschwerdeempfänger
to state [steɪt] darlegen; nennen
blunt [blʌnt] unverblümt; geradeheraus
dissatisfaction [dɪsˌsætɪs'fækʃn] Unzufriedenheit
norm [nɔ:m] Regel; Norm
to take offence [ˌteɪk ə'fens] Anstoß nehmen
no-nonsense [ˌnəʊ'nɒnsns] unverblümt; direkt
conciliatory [kən'sɪliətri] versöhnlich; konziliant
to be subjected to [bi səb'dʒektɪd tə] etwas unterworfen sein; zu etw. gezwungen werden
antagonised [æn'tægənaɪzd] vor den Kopf gestoßen
uncooperative [ˌʌnkəʊ'ɒprətɪv] unkooperativ
intercultural [ˌɪntə'kʌltʃrl] interkulturell; zwischen den Kulturen

D | Adjusting complaints

to adjust [ə'dʒʌst] anpassen
satisfactory [ˌsætɪs'fæktri] zufriedenstellend
to fob sb. off [ˌfɒb ˌsʌmbədi 'ɒf] jmdn. abspeisen

courtesy ['kɜ:təsi] Höflichkeit
patience ['peɪʃns] Geduld
to arise [ə'raɪz] entstehen
compromise ['kɒmprəmaɪz] Kompromiss
justified ['dʒʌstɪfaɪd] gerechtfertigt
sweetener ['swi:tnə] Zuckerchen
voucher ['vaʊtʃə] Gutschein
coaster ['kəʊstə] Untersetzer
to investigate [ɪn'vestɪgeɪt] nachgehen; untersuchen
completion [kəm'pli:ʃn] Fertigstellung
disruptive [dɪs'rʌptɪv] störend
ceiling ['si:lɪŋ] Zimmerdecke
glue feeder ['glu: ˌfi:də] Klebstoffdosierer
defect ['di:fekt] Fehler; Mangel
improvement [ɪm'pru:vmənt] Verbesserung
to incur [ɪn'kɜ:] anfallen
goodwill [gʊd'wɪl] Wohlwollen
to complain [kəm'pleɪn] beschweren
construction works [kən'strʌkʃn ˌwɜ:ks] Bauarbeiten
to install [ɪn'stɔ:l] installieren
heating ['hi:tɪŋ] Heizung
merger ['mɜ:dʒə] Fusion; Zusammenlegung
administrative [əd'mɪnɪstrətɪv] Verwaltungs-
to refund [ˌri:'fʌnd] erstatten
provided [prə'vaɪdɪd] vorausgesetzt
courtyard ['kɔ:tjɑ:d] Hof
to hesitate ['hezɪteɪt] zögern
to cope with ['kəʊp wɪð] schaffen; zurechtkommen mit

Office expert

E | The five R's of complaints

to redress [rɪ'dres] entschädigen
to refund [ˌri:'fʌnd] erstatten
to reimburse [ˌri:ɪm'bɜ:s] erstatten; rückvergüten
to make up for sth. [ˌmeɪk ˌʌp fə ˌsʌmθɪŋ] etwas wiedergutmachen; für etwas entschädigen
substitute ['sʌbstɪtju:t] Ersatz
to right [raɪt] richtigstellen

F | Key account management

proposal [prə'pəʊzl] Vorschlag
negotiation [nɪˌgəʊʃi'eɪʃn] Verhandlung
outgoing [ˌaʊt'gəʊɪŋ] aufgeschlossen; kontaktfreudig

H | Licence agreements

extract [ɪk'strækt] Auszug
permission [pə'mɪʃn] Erlaubnis
to violate ['vaɪəleɪt] verstoßen gegen

KMK Exam Training

legitimate [lɪˈdʒɪtɪmət] rechtmäßig; legitim
to praise [preɪz] loben
to go about sth. [ˌgəʊ əˈbaʊt ˌsʌmθɪŋ] mit etwas umgehen
temptation [tempˈteɪʃn] Versuchung
annoyed [əˈnɔɪd] verärgert
litany [ˈlɪtni] Litanei
tardiness [ˈtɑːdɪnəs] Verspätung; Unpünktlichkeit; Langsamkeit
to be rushed [bi ˈrʌʃt] unter Zeitnot sein
to gripe [graɪp] meckern; nörgeln
to pinch [pɪntʃ] stehlen
adverse [ˈædvɜːs] nachteilig; negativ
if word gets back to so. [ɪf ˌwɜːd gets ˈbæk tə ˌsʌmwʌn] wenn jemand etwas erfährt; wenn es herauskommt
to call in sick [ˌkɔːlˌɪn ˈsɪk] sich krankmelden

15 | Marketing products and services

service [ˈsɜːvɪs] Dienstleistung
concept [ˈkɒnsept] Konzept; Begriff; Auffassung
to transform [trænsˈfɔːm] verwandeln; umwandeln
stage [steɪdʒ] Bühne; *hier* Stadium
to conduct [kənˈdʌkt] durchführen
market research [ˌmɑːkɪt ˈriːsɜːtʃ] Marktforschung
potential [pəˈtenʃl] potenziell
proposed [prəˈpəʊzd] beabsichtigt
costly [ˈkɒstli] teuer
in addition [ɪn əˈdɪʃn] zusätzlich; außerdem
co-ordination [kəʊ ˌɔːdɪˈneɪʃn] Koordinierung; Abstimmung
so-called [ˌsəʊˈkɔːld] sogenannte/r/s
channel [ˈtʃænl] Kanal; *hier:* Vertriebsweg
promotional [prəˈməʊʃnl] Werbe-

A | Life cycle of a product

cycle [ˈsaɪkl] Zyklus
to consist of [kənˈsɪstˌəv] bestehen aus
phase [feɪz] Phase
growth [grəʊθ] Wachstum
to expand [ɪkˈspænd] (sich) erweitern
maturity [məˈtjʊərəti] Reife
plateau [ˈplætəʊ] Plateau
to drop off [ˌdrɒpˈɒf] abfallen
to extend [ɪkˈstend] verlängern; erweitern
to devise [dɪˈvaɪz] entwerfen

to update [ʌpˈdeɪt] aktualisieren
packaging [ˈpækɪdʒɪŋ] Verpackung
feature [ˈfiːtʃə] Eigenschaft
to peak [piːk] einen Höhepunkt erreichen

B | Branding and USP

to create [kriˈeɪt] (er)schaffen; erzeugen
brand [brænd] Markenname
distinct [dɪˈstɪŋkt] unverwechselbar; deutlich
to mark sth. off [ˌmɑːk ˌsʌmθɪŋˈɒf] etw. abgrenzen
branding [ˈbrændɪŋ] Markenentwicklung
competitive advantage [kəmˌpetətɪvˌədˈvɑːntɪdʒ] Wettbewerbsvorteil
to encourage [ɪnˈkʌrɪdʒ] ermutigen; *hier:* fördern
in comparison [ɪn kəmˈpærɪsn] im Vergleich
competition [ˌkɒmpəˈtɪʃn] Konkurrenz; Wettbewerb

C | Market research

profitable [ˈprɒfɪtəbl] gewinnbringend; rentabel
primary [ˈpraɪmri] primär; grundlegend
to gather [ˈgæðə] sammeln; zusammentragen
survey [ˈsɜːveɪ] Umfrage; Befragung
secondary [ˈsekndri] zusätzlich
to publish [ˈpʌblɪʃ] veröffentlichen
wealth [welθ] Fülle; Reichtum
resource [rɪˈzɔːs] Mittel; Ressourcen
to carry out [ˌkæriˈaʊt] ausführen
habit [ˈhæbɪt] Gewohnheit
mixture [ˈmɪkstʃə] Mischung
questionnaire [ˌkwestʃəˈneə] Fragebogen

groceries [ˈgrəʊsriz] Lebensmittel
household [ˈhaʊshəʊld] Haushalt
adolescent [ˌædəˈlesnt] halbwüchsig
commute [kəˈmjuːt] Pendelzeit
to lug [lʌg] schleppen
to vary [ˈveəri] sich ändern
at present [ət ˈpreznt] gegenwärtig; zurzeit
annoyed [əˈnɔɪd] verärgert
to criticise [ˈkrɪtɪsaɪz] kritisieren
slot [slɒt] Zeitfenster
conference [ˈkɒnfrns] Konferenz
function [ˈfʌŋkʃn] Festveranstaltung; Funktion
order [ˈɔːdə] Auftrag; Bestellung; Reihenfolge
slightly [ˈslaɪtli] etwas; leicht

interviewee [ˌɪntəvjuˈiː] Befragte/r
criticism [ˈkrɪtɪsɪzm] Kritik; Kritikpunkte

D | Distribution channels

link [lɪŋk] Verbindung; Bindeglied

depending on [dɪ'pendɪŋ ˌɒn] je nach; abhängig von

to bypass ['baɪpɑːs] umgehen

radical ['rædɪkl] radikal; drastisch

to shake up [ˌʃeɪk ˈʌp] durchschütteln; wachrütteln

proportion [prə'pɔːʃn] Anteil

segment ['segmənt] Marktsegment

brick [brɪk] Ziegelstein

mortar ['mɔːtə] Mörtel

physical ['fɪzɪkl] körperlich; materiell

presence ['prezns] Präsenz; Anwesenheit

High Street ['haɪ ˌstriːt] Haupteinkaufsstraße

variety [və'raɪəti] Vielfalt; Auswahl

pharmacy ['fɑːməsi] Apotheke

optician [ɒp'tɪʃn] Optiker/in

feedback ['fiːdbæk] Rückmeldungen; Feedback

satisfaction [ˌsætɪs'fækʃn] Zufriedenheit

to repack [ˌriː'pæk] neu verpacken; umpacken

thus [ðʌs] folglich; somit

to perform [pə'fɔːm] ausführen; ausführen

advisory [əd'vaɪzri] Beratungs-

to stock [stɒk] auf Lager haben; vorrätig halten

to eliminate [ɪ'lɪmɪneɪt] beseitigen; ausschließen

to cover ['kʌvə] abdecken

peculiarity [pɪˌkjuːli'ærəti] Eigentümlichkeit; typisches Merkmal

commission [kə'mɪʃn] Provision; Kommission

trade fair ['treɪd ˌfeə] (Fach-)Messe

to undermine [ˌʌndə'maɪn] untergraben

general public [ˌdʒenrl 'pʌblɪk] Allgemeinheit; breite Öffentlichkeit

frame [freɪm] Rahmen

conservatory [kən'sɜːvətri] Wintergarten

PVC [ˌpiːviː'siː] PVC (Polyvinylchlorid)

cosmetics [kɒz'metɪks] Kosmetik

overheads ['əʊvəhedz] (fixe) Kosten

accessories [ək'sesriz] Accessoires; Zubehör

head office [ˌhed ˈɒfɪs] Hauptniederlassung

standardisation [ˌstændədaɪ'zeɪʃn] Standardisierung

localisation [ˌləʊklaɪ'zeɪʃn] Lokalisierung; Anpassung an örtliche Gegebenheiten

to debate [dɪ'beɪt] diskutieren

globalised ['gləʊblaɪzd] globalisiert

multinationals [ˌmʌlti'næʃnlz] multinationale Konzerne

consistent [kən'sɪstnt] einheitlich

flop [flɒp] Misserfolg; Flop

to attempt [ə'tempt] versuchen

naive [naɪ'iːv] naiv; blauäugig

to reproduce [ˌriːprə'djuːs] nachbilden; kopieren

character ['kærɪktə] Buchstabe; Zeichen

wax [wæks] Wachs

tadpole ['tædpəʊl] Kaulquappe

diaper ['daɪpə] Windel

stork [stɔːk] Storch

myth [mɪθ] Mythos; Sage

mystified ['mɪstɪfaɪd] ratlos

pack [pæk] Packung

likewise ['laɪkwaɪz] ebenfalls; gleichermaßen

to attribute to [ə'trɪbjuːt tə] zuschreiben; zuordnen

to associate with [ə'səʊʃieɪt wɪð] in Verbindung bringen mit

mourning ['mɔːnɪŋ] Trauer

lack of ['læk ˌəv] Mangel an

awareness [ə'weənəs] Bewusstsein

to imply [ɪm'plaɪ] bedeuten

slang [slæŋ] Slang; Jargon

inventor [ɪn'ventə] Erfinder/in

to suck [sʌk] saugen

tragic ['trædʒɪk] tragisch

unaware [ˌʌnə'weə] in Unkenntnis; unwissend

pitfall ['pɪtfɔːl] Falle; Fallstrick

sensitivity [ˌsensɪ'tɪvəti] Empfindlichkeit; Zartgefühl

unforeseen [ˌʌnfɔː'siːn] unvorhergesehen

association [əˌsəʊʃi'eɪʃn] Assoziation

harmless ['hɑːmləs] harmlos

to impact [ɪm'pækt] beeinflussen

linguistic [lɪŋ'gwɪstɪk] sprachlich

E | Advertising

print [prɪnt] Druck

screen [skriːn] Bildschirm

surge [sɜːdʒ] starker Anstieg

to fuel ['fjuːəl] anheizen; verstärken

popularity [ˌpɒpjə'lærəti] Beliebtheit

portable ['pɔːtəbl] tragbar

to bounce off [ˌbaʊns 'ɒf] abprallen

to track [træk] nachvollziehen; verfolgen

effectiveness [ɪ'fektɪvnəs] Effektivität

distinction [dɪ'stɪŋkʃn] Unterscheidung

mail shots ['meɪl ˌʃɒts] Postwurfsendungen

better-off [ˌbetər 'ɒf] besser dran sein; *hier:* wohlhabend

personalised ['pɜːsnlaɪzd] personalisiert

brochure ['brəʊʃə] Prospekt; Broschüre

educational [ˌedʒʊ'keɪʃnl] Bildungs-

to target ['tɑːgɪt] ansprechen; anpeilen

male [meɪl] Mann

keen [kiːn] eifrig

gardener ['gɑːdnə] Gärtner/in

yachting ['jɒtɪŋ] Segelsport

enthusiast [ɪn'θjuːziæst] Schwärmer/in; Liebhaber/in

hoarding *(BE)* ['hɔːdɪŋ] Plakatwand

commercial [kə'mɜːʃl] Werbespot

appeal [ə'piːl] Anziehung(skraft)

lifestyle ['laɪfstaɪl] Lebensweise

visual ['vɪʒuəl] bildlich; visuell

visibility [ˌvɪzə'bɪləti] Sichtbarkeit

keyword ['kiːwɜːd] Schlüsselwort; Keyword

site [saɪt] Website

to rank [ræŋk] Rang einnehmen; einordnen

search engine ['sɜːtʃˌendʒɪn] Suchmaschine

to auction ['ɔːkʃn] versteigern

generic [dʒə'nerɪk] allgemein; generisch

affiliate [ə'fɪliət] Partner-

flow [fləʊ] Strom; Fluss

leather ['leðə] Leder

to incentivise [ɪn'sentɪvaɪz] jmdm. einen Anreiz schaffen

host [həʊst] Gastgeber; *hier:* Betreiber

prominent ['prɒmɪnənt] auffallend; hervortretend

to insert [ɪn'sɜːt] einfügen

series *(pl)* ['sɪəriːz] Serie; Reihe

recently ['riːsntli] kürzlich

consultancy [kən'sʌltnsi] Beratung

○ buzz word ['bʌz ˌwɜːd] Schlagwort

tribal ['traɪbl] Stammes-; auf eigene Gruppe bezogen

community [kə'mjuːnəti] Gemeinschaft

tribe [traɪb] Stamm

to mobilise ['məʊbɪlaɪz] mobilisieren

in-depth [ˌɪn'depθ] in die Tiefe gehend

to fine-tune [ˌfaɪn'tjuːn] feinabstimmen

to project [prə'dʒekt] herausragen; *hier:* abgeben

audience ['ɔːdiəns] Publikum

to engage with [ɪn'geɪdʒ wɪð] sich einlassen auf

creativity [ˌkriːeɪ'tɪvəti] Kreativität

to join together [ˌdʒɔɪn tə'geðə] zusammenfügen

to address [ə'dres] ansprechen

to ignore [ɪg'nɔː] ignorieren

dialogue ['daɪəlɒg] Dialog

in general [ɪn 'dʒenrl] im Allgemeinen

gratification [ˌgrætɪfɪ'keɪʃn] Befriedigung; Belohnung

impulse ['ɪmpʌls] Impuls

to get on sb.'s nerves [ˌget ɒn ˌsʌmbədiz 'nɜːvz] jmdm. auf die Nerven gehen

constantly ['kɒnstəntli] andauernd

annoying [ə'nɔɪɪŋ] ärgerlich

credits *(pl)* ['kredɪts] Abspann; *hier:* Quellenangabe

virtual ['vɜːtʃuəl] virtuell

eager ['iːgə] begierig

F | Public Relations (PR)

credentials *(pl)* [krɪ'denʃlz] Zeugnis; Zeugnis

donation [də'neɪʃn] Spende

charity ['tʃærɪti] wohltätige / gemeinnützige Organisation

to interpret [ɪn'tɜːprɪt] interpretieren; deuten

spin [spɪn] Drehung; Drall

disrespectful [ˌdɪsrɪ'spektfl] respektlos; geringschätzig

to foresee [fɔː'siː] vorhersehen; absehen

press release ['pres rɪˌliːs] Pressemitteilung

news coverage ['njuːz ˌkʌvrɪdʒ] Berichterstattung in den Medien

G | Advertising industrial goods – B2B advertising

innovation [ˌɪnə'veɪʃn] Neuerung; Innovation

competitor [kəm'petɪtə] Wettbewerber/in

medium ['miːdiəm] Mittel; *hier:* Werkzeug

H | Language and techniques of advertising

technique [tek'niːk] Technik

category ['kætəgri] Kategorie; Klasse

persuasive [pə'sweɪsɪv] überzeugend

to persuade [pə'sweɪd] überreden; überzeugen

to awaken [ə'weɪkn] erwecken

subjective [səb'dʒektɪv] subjektiv

recognisable ['rekəgnaɪzəbl] wiedererkennbar

to imprint [ɪm'prɪnt] einprägen

memory ['memri] Erinnerung; Gedächtnis

memorable ['memrəbl] unvergesslich

angle ['æŋgl] Winkel

symbolism ['sɪmblɪzm] Symbolik

to calibrate ['kælɪbreɪt] graduieren; abstimmen

jingle ['dʒɪŋgl] Jingle; kurze Tonfolge

diamond ['daɪəmənd] Diamant

pun [pʌn] Wortspiel

fanciful ['fænsɪfl] fantasievoll

alliteration [əˌlɪtə'reɪʃn] Alliteration; Stabreim

exaggeration [ɪgˌzædʒə'reɪʃn] Übertreibung

to wow [waʊ] zum Staunen bringen

dramatisation [ˌdræmətaɪ'zeɪʃn] Dramatisierung

to indulge in [ɪn'dʌldʒ ɪn] sich gönnen

luggage ['lʌgɪdʒ] Gepäck; Reisegepäck

charged [tʃɑːdʒd] (auf)geladen

jewellery ['dʒuːəlri] Schmuck

artist ['ɑːtɪst] Künstler/in

font [fɒnt] Schriftart

to envisage [ɪn'vɪzɪdʒ] vorhersehen

Office expert

I | Incentives and customer satisfaction

inclination [ˌɪnklɪ'neɪʃn] Neigung
height adjustable [ˌhaɪtə'dʒʌstəbl] höhenverstellbar
palm rest ['pɑːm ˌrest] Handballenauflage
tilt function ['tɪlt ˌfʌŋkʃn] Kippfunktion
resolution [ˌrezə'luːʃn] Bildschirmauflösung
staff retention [ˌstɑːf rɪ'tenʃn] Personalerhaltung;
Mitarbeiterbindung

16 | Job applications in Germany and the EU

principle ['prɪnsɪpl] Prinzip
qualification [ˌkwɒlɪfɪ'keɪʃn] Ausbildung; Qualifikation
career [kə'rɪə] Karriere
majority [mə'dʒɒrəti] Mehrheit
adaptable [ə'dæptəbl] anpassungsfähig
inquisitive [ɪn'kwɪzətɪv] neugierig
open-minded [ˌəʊpn'maɪndɪd] aufgeschlossen; unvoreingenommen
globalisation [ˌgləʊblaɪ'zeɪʃn] Globalisierung
pressing ['presɪŋ] dringend
internationalisation [ˌɪntəˌnæʃnlaɪ'zeɪʃn] Internationalisierung
to fulfill [fʊl'fɪl] erfüllen
requirement [rɪ'kwaɪəmənt] Bedingung; Voraussetzung
level ['levl] Ebene
directory [dɪ'rektri] Verzeichnis

A | Job advertisements

bilingual [baɪ'lɪŋgwəl] zweisprachig
secretary ['sekrətri] Sekretär/in
to recruit [rɪ'kruːt] anwerben; einstellen
minimum ['mɪnɪməm] Minimum; Mindest-
cosmopolitan [ˌkɒsmə'pɒlɪtn] kosmopolitisch
opportunity [ˌɒpə'tjuːnəti] Gelegenheit
fast-paced [ˌfɑːst'peɪst] tempogeladen; hektisch
varied ['veərid] abwechslungsreich
to comprise [kəm'praɪz] umfassen
to coordinate [kəʊ'ɔːdɪneɪt] koordinieren; abstimmen
minute taking ['mɪnɪt ˌteɪkɪŋ] Protokollführung
managerial [ˌmænə'dʒɪəriəl] leitend
diary ['daɪəri] Terminkalender; Tagebuch
database ['deɪtəbeɪs] Datenbank
statistical [stə'tɪstɪkl] statistisch
CV (curriculum vitae) [ˌsiː'viː, kəˌrɪkjələm 'viːtaɪ] Lebenslauf

covering letter ['kʌvərɪŋ ˌletə] Begleitschreiben
to consider [kən'sɪdə] berücksichtigen; in Betracht ziehen
similar ['sɪmɪlə] ähnlich
position [pə'zɪʃn] Stellung; Position
freight forwarder ['freɪt ˌfɔːwədə] Spediteur
per annum [pər'ænəm] pro Jahr; jährlich
fluent ['fluːənt] fließend
to require [rɪ'kwaɪə] verlangen; benötigen
ability [ə'bɪləti] Fähigkeit
to liaise [li'eɪz] zusammenarbeiten
assistance [ə'sɪstns] Hilfe
to equip [ɪ'kwɪp] befähigen; ausstatten; ausrüsten
objective [əb'dʒektɪv] Ziel
title ['taɪtl] Titel; Bezeichnung

B | Letter of application (covering letter)

to grab [græb] greifen; fassen; packen
care [keə] Sorgfalt; Pflege
to depend on [dɪ'pend ˌɒn] abhängen von; sich verlassen auf
instruction [ɪn'strʌkʃn] Anweisung
Swedish ['swiːdɪʃ] schwedisch
innovative ['ɪnəvətɪv] innovativ
face-to-face [ˌfeɪstə'feɪs] persönlich

C | CV (Curriculum Vitae)

subject ['sʌbdʒɪkt] betreffende Person
approximate [ə'prɒksɪmət] ungefähr
examination [ɪgˌzæmɪ'neɪʃn] Prüfung
probably ['prɒbəbli] wahrscheinlich
familiar [fə'mɪliə] vertraut
vocational [və'keɪʃnl] beruflich; Berufs-
continental Europe [ˌkɒntɪnentl 'jʊərəp] europäisches Festland
careerwise [kə'rɪəwaɪz] die Karriere betreffend
testimonial [ˌtestɪ'məʊniəl] Zeugnis; Empfehlungsschreiben
referee [ˌrefr'iː] Referenz; Schiedsrichter/in
independent [ˌɪndɪ'pendənt] unabhängig
advert ['ædvɜːt] Anzeige
beyond [bi'ɒnd] jenseits; außerhalb
to reverse [rɪ'vɜːs] umkehren
chronological [ˌkrɒnə'lɒdʒɪkl] chronologisch; zeitlich
secondary education [ˌsekndri ˌedʒʊ'keɪʃn] Sekundarschulbildung
to disclose [dɪ'skləʊz] offenlegen; preisgeben
final examination [ˌfaɪnl ɪgˌzæmɪ'neɪʃn] Abschlussprüfung

D | Interviews

flexible ['fleksɪbl] flexibel; anpassungsfähig
deadline ['dedlaɪn] Abgabetermin
minutes (pl) ['mɪnɪts] Protokoll
robotics [rə'bɒtɪks] Robotertechnik
developing country [dɪˌveləpɪŋ 'kʌntri] Entwicklungs-
    land
gap [gæp] Lücke
whereabouts ['weərəbaʊts] wo (in etwa)
pleasure ['pleʒə] Vergnügen

to put at ease [ˌpʊt ət 'iːz] jmdm. die Nervosität nehmen
located [ləʊ'keɪtɪd] gelegen
to demonstrate ['demənstreɪt] zeigen
to mention ['menʃn] erwähnen
press [pres] Medien
to refresh [rɪ'freʃ] auffrischen
embarrassing [ɪm'bærəsɪŋ] peinlich
smart [smɑːt] ordentlich; gepflegt; schick
informal [ɪn'fɔːml] informell; locker
enthusiasm [ɪn'θjuːziæzm] Begeisterung; Enthusiasmus
confidence ['kɒnfɪdns] Selbstvertrauen; Sicherheit
nervousness ['nɜːvəsnəs] Nervosität
failure ['feɪljə] Misserfolg; hier: Unterlassung
underlying [ˌʌndə'laɪɪŋ] unterschwellig
attitude ['ætɪtjuːd] Ansicht; Einstellung
preparation [ˌprepr'eɪʃn] Vorbereitung
emphasis ['emfəsɪs] Betonung; Nachdruck
inability [ˌɪnə'bɪləti] Unfähigkeit; Unvermögen
to nod [nɒd] nicken
entitlement [ɪn'taɪtlmənt] Anspruch
satisfying ['sætɪsfaɪɪŋ] befriedigend; zufriedenstellend
strength [streŋθ] Stärke
rapport [ræ'pɔː] Verhältnis
scope [skəʊp] Umfang; Reichweite; Spielraum
to gain [geɪn] sammeln; gewinnen; erwerben
rate [reɪt] Tarif; Satz
motivated ['məʊtɪveɪtɪd] motiviert
to faze [feɪz] aus der Fassung bringen
humour ['hjuːmə] Humor
ethnic ['eθnɪk] ethnisch
diversity [daɪ'vɜːsəti] Unterschiedlichkeit; Vielfalt
profile ['prəʊfaɪl] Profil; Beschreibung
competence ['kɒmpɪtns] Kompetenz; Können
to toy with ['tɔɪ wɪð] mit etw. spielen
to set up [ˌset 'ʌp] gründen; eröffnen
guideline ['gaɪdlaɪn] Richtlinie

hectic ['hektɪk] hektisch
atmosphere ['ætməsˌfɪə] Atmosphäre
loner ['ləʊnə] Einzelgänger/in
concentration [ˌkɒnsn'treɪʃn] Anhäufung; Dichte
proactive [ˌprəʊ'æktɪv] proaktiv
track record ['træk ˌrekɔːd] Erfolgsbilanz
respect [rɪ'spekt] Hinsicht

E | The European Union

creation [kri'eɪʃn] Schaffung; Entstehen
to unify ['juːnɪfaɪ] vereinigen
capital ['kæpɪtl] Kapital
advanced [əd'vɑːnst] fortgeschritten; fortschrittlich
imperfection [ˌɪmpə'fekʃn] Unvollkommenheit;
    Mangelhaftigkeit
immense [ɪ'mens] gewaltig; riesig
to take up residence [teɪk ʌp 'rezɪdns] wohnhaft
    werden; sich niederlassen
to estimate ['estɪmeɪt] schätzen
regulation [ˌregjə'leɪʃn] Vorschrift; Verordnung
to originate [ə'rɪdʒneɪt] entstehen; Ursprung haben
institution [ˌɪnstɪ'tjuːʃn] Institution; Organ
to nominate ['nɒmɪneɪt] ernennen; nominieren
commissioner [kə'mɪʃnə] Kommissar/in
portfolio [pɔːt'fəʊliəʊ] Aufgabenbereich
to endorse [ɪn'dɔːs] im Amt bestätigen
treaty ['triːti] Vertrag (zwischen Staaten)
to violate ['vaɪəleɪt] verstoßen gegen
to impose [ɪm'pəʊz] verhängen; auferlegen
directive [dɪ'rektɪv] Direktive; Anordnung
proposal [prə'pəʊzl] Vorschlag
legislation [ˌledʒɪ'sleɪʃn] Gesetze; Gesetzgebung
budget ['bʌdʒɪt] Haushalt; Etat
Council of Ministers [ˌkaʊnsl əv 'mɪnɪstəz] Ministerrat
financial [faɪ'nænʃl] finanziell; Finanzen-
fiscal ['fɪskl] Steuer-
indirect [ˌɪndɪ'rekt] indirekt
democratic [ˌdemə'krætɪk] demokratisch
legitimacy [lɪ'dʒɪtɪməsi] Legitimität; Rechtmäßigkeit
origin ['ɒrɪdʒɪn] Ursprung
prime minister [ˌpraɪm 'mɪnɪstə] Premierminister/in
to resolve [rɪ'zɒlv] lösen; klären
prestige [pres'tiːʒ] Prestige; Ansehen
to suffer from ['sʌfə frəm] leiden an/unter
participation [pɑːˌtɪsɪ'peɪʃn] Teilnahme
to reject [rɪ'dʒekt] zurückweisen
renewable [rɪ'njuːəbl] erneuerbar
embassy ['embəsi] Botschaft(sgebäude)

responsibility [rɪˌspɒnsəˈbɪləti] Verantwortung;
  Zuständigkeit

policy [ˈpɒləsi] Politik

citizen [ˈsɪtɪzn] Bürger/in

Bulgaria [bʌlˈgeəriə] Bulgarien

Croatia [krəʊˈeɪʃə] Kroatien

Cyprus [ˈsaɪprəs] Zypern

Czech Republic [ˌtʃek rɪˈpʌblɪk] Tschechische Republik

Denmark [ˈdenmɑːk] Dänemark

Estonia [esˈtəʊniə] Estland

Finland [ˈfɪnlənd] Finnland

Greece [griːs] Griechenland

Hungary [ˈhʌŋgəri] Ungarn

Latvia [ˈlætviə] Lettland

Lithuania [ˌlɪθjuˈeɪniə] Litauen

Luxemburg [ˈlʌksmbɜːg] Luxemburg

Malta [ˈmɔːltə] Malta

the Netherlands [ðə ˈneðələndz] die Niederlande

Poland [ˈpəʊlənd] Polen

Portugal [ˈpɔːtʃəgl] Portugal

Romania [rʊˈmeɪniə] Rumänien

Slovakia [sləˈvækiə] die Slowakei

Slovenia [sləˈviːniə] Slowenien

Sweden [ˈswiːdn] Schweden

total [ˈtəʊtl] Gesamt-

area [ˈeəriə] Bereich; Gebiet

population [ˌpɒpjəˈleɪʃn] Bevölkerung; Einwohnerzahl

GDP (gross domestic product) [ˌdʒiːdiːˈpiː ˌgrəʊs
  dəˌmestɪk ˈprɒdʌkt] BIP (Bruttoinlandsprodukt)

Office expert

F | Office jobs

internship [ˈɪntɜːnʃɪp] Praktikum

hands-on [ˌhændzˈɒn] praktisch; praxisnah

intern [ˈɪntɜːn] Praktikant(in)

to advance [ədˈvɑːns] weiterentwickeln

setting [ˈsetɪŋ] Rahmen; Umfeld; Umgebung

domestic [dəˈmestɪk] inländisch; heimisch

corporate [ˈkɔːprət] Firmen-

to meet the criteria [ˌmiːt ðə kraɪˈtɪəriə] die Kriterien
  erfüllen

to submit [səbˈmɪt] einreichen; vorlegen

résumé [ˌreszjuːˈmeɪ] Lebenslauf

KMK Exam Training

promotional event [prəˌməʊʃnl ɪˈvent] Werbeveranstal-
  tung

outstanding [ˌaʊtˈstændɪŋ] hervorragend; herausragend

to achieve [əˈtʃiːv] erreichen; erzielen

admission [ədˈmɪʃn] Zulassung; Zugang; Eintritt

to enrol [ɪnˈrəʊl] sich einschreiben; anmelden;
  immatrikulieren

to implement [ˈɪmplɪment] umsetzen; durchführen

to liaise [liˈeɪz] zusammenarbeiten

recruitment [rɪˈkruːtmənt] Anwerbung; Einstellung

desirable [dɪˈzaɪərəbl] wünschenswert

audition [ɔːˈdɪʃn] Vorsprechen

Alphabetical word list

A

abbreviation Abkürzung 177

ability Fähigkeit 227

abseiling Abseilen 75

absentee Abwesende/r 108

to absorb aufnehmen 101

access Zugang 64

accessories Accessoires, Zubehör 216

to accommodate Unterkunft bieten, entgegenkommen, aufnehmen 54

accommodation Unterkunft 72

to accompany begleiten 25

according to gemäß, entsprechend 104

account Bericht 109

to account for ausmachen, entfallen auf 180

accounting Buchhaltung, Rechnungswesen 16

accounts Kunden, Buchhaltungsabteilung 55

Accounts Buchhaltung 187

accurate genau, präzise 70

to achieve erreichen, erzielen 101

to acquire sich aneignen 100

to act as *hier:* fungieren als 9

actual tatsächlich 30

adaptable anpassungsfähig 226

to adapt to (sich) anpassen an 42

added zusätzlich 173

added benefit Zusatznutzen 75

additive Zusatzstoff, Zusatz 47, zusätzlich 183

to address ansprechen 219

addressee Adressat, Empfänger/in 77

adequate angemessen, ausreichend 109

adhesive Klebstoff 195

adjacent angrenzend, daneben 88

to adjourn verschieben, vertagen 97

to adjust anpassen 201

adjustable verstellbar 152

adjustment Ausgleich, Regulierung 193

administration and finance Verwaltung und Finanzen 57

administrative Verwaltungs- 203

administrative assistant Kaufmann/-frau für Büromanagement 155

admission Zulassung, Zugang, Eintritt 242

adolescent halbwüchsig 213

to adore lieben, verrückt sein nach 31

to advance vorschießen, auslegen 179, weiterentwickeln 241

advanced fortgeschritten, fortschrittlich 239

advancement Fortschritt 163

adventurous abenteuerlich 9

adverse nachteilig, negativ 208

advert Anzeige 234

advice of dispatch Versandanzeige 160

advisory Beratungs- 215

to affect betreffen 186

affiliate Partner- 218

affiliated angehörig 136

to afford sich leisten 64

affordable bezahlbar, erschwinglich 108

a good command of English gute Englischkenntnisse 86

ahead of time im Voraus 189

airfreight Luftfracht 160

airy luftig 30

aisle Gang 89

alert wachsam 189

alliteration Alliteration, Stabreim 220

all parties concerned alle beteiligten Parteien 181

all the more important umso wichtiger 67

alongside nebeneinander 30

ambitious ehrgeizig, anspruchsvoll 34

amendment Änderung, Korrektur 108

amount Betrag, Summe 93

analyser Analyseprogramm 171

anecdotal evidence Anhaltspunkte 27

anger Wut, Ärger 193

angle Winkel 220

annoyance Unmut, Ärger 93

annoyed verärgert 207

annoying ärgerlich 219

annual jährlich 160

antagonised vor den Kopf gestoßen 200

anxious besorgt, ängstlich 26

apologetic Bedauern ausdrücken, entschuldigend 185

apologies entschuldigte Abwesenheiten 97

to apologise sich entschuldigen 186

apology Entschuldigung 108

appeal Anziehung(skraft) 217

to appeal to ansprechen, gefallen 160

appliances Geräte 65

applicable zutreffend 156

application Antrag, Bewerbung 162

to apply *hier:* gelten, bewerben 141

to apply to betreffen, zutreffen 18

to appoint ernennen, bestellen 108

to appreciate (wert)schätzen 177

apprenticeship Lehre, Ausbildung 9

approach Herangehensweise, Ansatz 42

to approach sich nähern 122

appropriate geeignet, passend, angebracht 73

to approve genehmigen, billigen 97

approximate ungefähr 230

archery Bogenschießen 75

architectural architektonisch, Architektur- 158

area Bereich, Gebiet 240

Argentina Argentinien 167

to argue behaupten 180

*to arise entstehen 201

armchair Sessel 139

array Feld 183

arrival Ankunft 170

to arrive at a solution eine Lösung finden 133

artist Künstler/in 220

as a matter of course ganz selbstverständlich 180

asap (as soon as possible) so bald wie möglich, schnellstmöglich 66

as a rule in der Regel 93

to deposit money Geld einzahlen, einlegen   189

deputy director stellvertretende/r Direktor/in   30

to designate bezeichnen, benennen   138

designation Bezeichnung   146

desirable wünschenswert   242

desired gewünscht   184

desperate *hier:* verzweifelt vor Hunger   56

despite trotz   163

dessert Nachspeise   31

destination Bestimmungsort   167

to detect entdecken, heraushören   160

detergent Waschmittel   55

developing country Entwicklungs-land   235

device Gerät   48

to devise entwerfen   212

dialogue Dialog   219

diamond Diamant   220

diaper Windel   216

diary Terminkalender, Tagebuch   227

to differ sich unterscheiden   200

digit Ziffer   66

directive Direktive, Anordnung   239

directory Verzeichnis   226

to disclose offenlegen, preisgeben   234

discount Rabatt   121

discrepancy Abweichung, Diskrepanz   199

dish Speise, Gericht, Schüssel   88

to dismantle auseinandernehmen   99

to dispatch versenden, verschicken   161

dispatch advice Versandanzeige   169

to display zeigen   93

disrespectful respektlos, gering-schätzig   219

disruptive störend   202

dissatisfaction Unzufriedenheit   200

distinct unverwechselbar, deutlich   212

distinction Unterscheidung   217

distraction Ablenkung   174

diversity Unterschiedlichkeit, Vielfalt   237

documentation Dokumentation   166

domestic inländisch, heimisch   241

donation Spende   219

to doublecheck nochmals prüfen   185

double-digit zweistellig   180

*****to do without** ohne etw. aus-kommen   31

downside Kehrseite, Nachteil   167

draft Entwurf   108

dramatisation Dramatisierung   220

*****to draw attention to** Aufmerksamkeit lenken auf   101

drawback Haken, Nachteil   173

*****to draw up** verfassen, aufsetzen   146

dreadful schrecklich   27

drizzle Nieselregen   28

drop Rückgang   105

to drop off abfallen   212

due fällig   76

due to wegen, aufgrund   27

duration Dauer   89

duties Aufgaben   8

E

eager begierig   219

to edit redigieren, bearbeiten   61

educational Bildungs-   217

effectiveness Effektivität   217

to effect payment Zahlung leisten   181

efficient effizient   45

elaborate sorgfältig ausgeführt, gut durchdacht   49

electrician Elektriker/in   180

to eliminate beseitigen, aus-schließen   215

embarrassed silence peinliche Stille   93

embarrassing peinlich   235

embassy Botschaft(sgebäude)   240

emphasis Betonung, Nachdruck   236

to emphasise betonen, hervorheben   42

to enable in die Lage versetzen, befähigen   27

to enclose beifügen   79

enclosure Anlage (Brief)   156

to encourage ermutigen   212

to endorse im Amt bestätigen   239

engaged besetzt (Telefon)   65

to engage with sich einlassen auf   219

to enjoy doing sth. etw. gern tun   9

enquiry Anfrage   182

to enrol sich einschreiben, anmelden, immatrikulieren   242

to ensure sicherstellen, gewähr-leisten   103

enterprising unternehmungslustig, geschäftstüchtig   10

to entertain sich um jmdn. kümmern, unterhalten   24

enthusiasm Begeisterung, Enthusias-mus   236

enthusiast Schwärmer/in, Liebhaber/in   217

entitlement Anspruch   236

environmentally-friendly umwelt-freundlich   43

to envisage vorhersehen   222

to equip befähigen, ausstatten, ausrüsten   228

equivalent Entsprechung   179

error Irrtum, Fehler   195

escalator Rolltreppe   57

essential wesentlich   64

essential oils ätherische Öle   43

to establish einführen   155

to establish eye contact Blickkontakt herstellen   103

to estimate schätzen   239

Estonia Estland   240

ethnic ethnisch   237

EU-funded loan EU-finanziertes Darlehen   43

evaluation scheme Bewertungs-schema   104

event consultant Veranstaltungs-berater/in   11

event management Veranstaltungs-management   9

event management assistant Veranstaltungskaufmann/frau   11

eventually letztendlich, schließlich, irgendwann   10

evidence Beweis, Nachweis   30

evidence in law Beweis vor Gericht   109

exaggeration Übertreibung   220

examination Prüfung   230

to exclude ausschließen   180

executive leitende/r Angestellte/r   88

to exert ausüben   190

exotic exotisch   167

to expand (sich) erweitern   212

expenditure Ausgaben, Auslagen   190

to experience erleben   37

to expire ablaufen, verfallen   149

expiry date Ablaufdatum, Verfallstermin   89
to exploit ausbeuten   109
to express ausdrücken   193
to extend verlängern, erweitern   212
extension Zahlungsaufschub,
Verlängerung   186
extract Auszug   206

F

fabric covered stoffbespannt   152
face-to-face persönlich   229
facial expression Gesichtsausdruck   67
to facilitate ermöglichen,
erleichtern   132
factor Faktor, Umstand   167
to fail scheitern   184
failure Misserfolg, *hier:* Unterlassung   236
fair Messe   199
familiar vertraut   230
family-owned company Familienunternehmen   57
fanciful fantasievoll   220
to fancy doing sth. Lust auf etw.
haben   8
fashion chain Kette von Modegeschäften   25
fashionista Modefan   108
fast-paced tempogeladen,
hektisch   227
fault Fehler   195
faulty fehlerhaft   185
favourable positiv, günstig   156
to faze aus der Fassung bringen   237
feasibility Machbarkeit   108
feasible machbar   133
feature Eigenschaft   212
fee Gebühr   183
feedback Rückmeldungen,
Feedback   215
*to feel strongly about eine entschiedene Meinung haben   109
ferry Fähre   167
fertiliser Dünger   43
festive season Weihnachtszeit, Festtage   122
field Gebiet   167
file Akte, Datei   185

final examination Abschlussprüfung   234
to finalise zum Abschluss bringen   73
financial finanziell, Finanzen-   239
findings Ergebnisse   116
to fine-tune feinabstimmen   219
fingerprint Fingerabdruck   183
Finland Finnland   240
firm fest, bestimmt   193
firm booking feste Buchung   88
fiscal Steuer-   239
fishy fischig   160
fitted out with ausgestattet mit   54
fixed base starres Fußteil   152
to flash blinken   80
flat fee Pauschalpreis   136
flexibility Flexibilität   167
flexible flexibel, anpassungsfähig   235
flooring Bodenbelag   141
flop Misserfolg, Flop   216
flow Strom, Fluss   218
fluent fließend   227
to fob sb. off jmdn. abspeisen   201
fog Nebel   167
foldable faltbar   163
foldable bicycle Klapprad   48
folder Ordner   61
font Schriftart   221
foodstuffs (pl) Lebensmittel   167
for approval zur Genehmigung   108
foreign currency transfer Auslandsüberweisung   176
foreign language correspondent Fremd-
sprachenkorrespondent/in   14
foreign language secretary Fremd-
sprachensekretär/in   10
*to foresee vorhersehen, absehen   219
for instance zum Beispiel   8
forklift truck Gabelstapler   58
form Formular   72
formality Formalität   166
forwarder Spediteur   161
forward-looking zukunftsorientiert   42
frame Rahmen   216
France Frankreich   166
frankfurter Bockwurst   160
fraud Betrug   183
freelance freiberuflich   30
free-range freilaufend   30
freight forwarder Spediteur   227

**freight forwarding and logistics ser-
vices clerk** Kaufmann/frau für Spedition und Logistikdienstleistung   9
freight logistics Frachtlogistik, Güterspedition   166
frequently häufig   176
fridge Kühlschrank   56
fried potatoes Bratkartoffeln   31
from the outset von Anfang an   45
front office Büro mit Publikumsverkehr   54
to fuel anheizen, verstärken   217
to fulfill erfüllen   226
full board Vollpension   144
function Festveranstaltung,
Funktion   213
fundamental grundlegend,
fundamental   166
funding finanzielle Unterstützung   49
fusion cooking Fusionsküche   30

G

to gain sammeln, gewinnen,
erwerben   237
game Wild   31
gap Lücke   235
gardener Gärtner/in   217
garments Kleidung   30
to gather sammeln, zusammentragen   213
gathering Versammlung, Treffen   105
gauge Spurweite   177
GDP gross domestic product
BIP (Bruttoinlandsprodukt)   240
general public Allgemeinheit, breite
Öffentlichkeit   216
generator Generator   167
generic allgemein, generisch   218
generous großzügig   199
gestures Gesten, Gestik   103
*to get mitbekommen, verstehen   68
*to get down to business zur Sache /
zum Geschäftlichen kommen   116
*to get off to a good start einen guten
Start erwischen, sich gut ein-
führen   10
*to get on sb.'s nerves jmdm. auf die
Nerven gehen   219

*to get on well with someone sich gut mit jemandem verstehen 14

ghastly entsetzlich 27

gherkin Gewürzgurke 160

gift box Geschenkkarton 131

girder Träger 167

globalisation Globalisierung 226

globalised globalisiert 216

glue feeder Klebstoffdosierer 202

*to go about sth. mit etwas umgehen 207

*to go ahead fortfahren 73

*to go clubbing in die Disko gehen 11

*to go for sich entscheiden für 56

going rate geltender Preis 135

goodwill Wohlwollen 202

gossip Klatsch 55

to grab greifen, fassen, packen 228

gradually allmählich 106

to grant gewähren 155

grated gerieben, geraspelt 32

grateful dankbar 167

gratification Befriedigung, Belohnung 219

gravel Kies 167

Greece Griechenland 240

grid Gitter, hier: Tabelle, Raster 167

to gripe meckern, nörgeln 208

groceries Lebensmittel 213

ground floor Parterre, Erdgeschoss 30

grounds keeping Reinigung und Pflege von Außenanlagen 136

*to grow (Pflanze:) anbauen 43

grower Bauer, Bäuerin, Pflanzer, Pflanzerin 43

growth Wachstum 212

*to grow up aufwachsen 14

guideline Richtlinie 237

H

habit Gewohnheit 213

handcrafted handgemacht 199

to handle in die Hand nehmen, bearbeiten 167

hands-on praktisch, praxisnah 241

hard copy Computerausdruck 125

harmless harmlos 216

to hatch ausbrüten 30

haulier Spediteur 169

*to have a point nicht ganz Unrecht haben 109

*to have in common gemeinsam haben 14

*to have the edge over the competition der Konkurrenz überlegen sein 109

heading Überschrift 104

head office Hauptniederlassung 216

heating Heizung 203

heavy-duty strapazierfähig, robust 152

hectic hektisch 237

height adjustable höhenverstellbar 223

hemp Hanf 43

herbicides Unkrautvernichtungsmittel 47

to hesitate zögern 204

high-end Luxus-, Nobel- 25

High Street Haupteinkaufsstraße 214

hitch Haken, Problem 26

hoarding (BE) Plakatwand 217

*to hold warten 65

hold the line am Apparat bleiben 171

honesty Ehrlichkeit, Aufrichtigkeit 110

to honour honorieren, einlösen 171

horseradish Meerrettich, Kren 160

hospitality and catering Hotel- und Gaststättengewerbe 16

hospitality package Besucherpaket, Bewirtungspaket 36

host Gastgeber, Betreiber 218

host family Gastfamilie 144

hourly rate Stundensatz 94

to house unterbringen 55

household Haushalt 213

household appliances Haushaltsgeräte 49

HR (Human Resources) Personalabteilung 117

huge riesig 167

humanely menschenwürdig 30

humour Humor 237

Hungary Ungarn 240

hurricane Wirbelsturm 185

hydraulic controlled hydraulisch gesteuert 152

hyphenation Worttrennung 125

I

icy glatt, eisig, vereist 167

I didn't quite catch that Ich habe das nicht ganz verstanden 68

if word gets back to so. wenn jemand etwas erfährt, wenn es herauskommt 208

to ignore ignorieren 219

imagination Phantasie, Vorstellungskraft 178

immense gewaltig, riesig 239

immersion course Intensivkurs 118

impact Auswirkung, Einfluss 43

to impact beeinflussen 216

imperfection Unvollkommenheit, Mangelhaftigkeit 239

to implement einführen 97

to implement umsetzen 174, durchführen 242

to imply bedeuten 216

importance Wichtigkeit, Bedeutung 166

to impose verhängen, auferlegen 239

impressed beeindruckt 156

impression Eindruck 24

to imprint einprägen 220

improvement Verbesserung 202

impulse Impuls 219

inability Unfähigkeit, Unvermögen 236

in addition zusätzlich, außerdem 211

inadequate unzureichend, unzulänglich 167

incentive Anreiz 133

to incentivise jmdm. einen Anreiz schaffen 218

in charge of verantwortlich für, betraut mit 25

inclination Neigung 223

to include einbeziehen, einschließen 8

inclusion Einbeziehung, Aufnahme 78

in comparison im Vergleich 212

inconvenience Unannehmlichkeit 171

to incur anfallen 202

independent unabhängig 234

in-depth in die Tiefe gehend 219

to indicate angeben, nennen, hinweisen 156

indicator Anzeigetafel 93

indirect indirekt 239

to indulge in sich gönnen 220

industrial business management assistant Industriekaufmann/frau 11

linen Leinen   43

to line up organisieren   10

lingua franca (Latin) internationale
   Verkehrssprache   24

linguistic sprachlich   216

link Verbindung, Bindeglied   214

litany Litanei   208

literally wortwörtlich, buchstäblich   16

Lithuania Litauen   240

lively lebendig, spritzig   104

loan Darlehen   190

localisation Lokalisierung, Anpassung
   an örtliche Gegebenheiten   216

located gelegen   235

log cabin Blockhütte   76

loner Einzelgänger/in   237

long-standing langjährig   182

to look after sich kümmern um   9

to look into sth. einer Sache nachgehen   66

loop-pile Schlingen-   141

lorry Lkw   167

low-interest loans Niedrigzinsdarlehen   45

low-maintenance wartungs-
   freundlich   49

loyalty Loyalität, Treue   171

luckily glücklicherweise   58

to lug schleppen   213

luggage Gepäck, Reisegepäck   220

luncheon förmliches Mittagessen   160

Luxemburg Luxemburg   240

M

machine tool Werkzeugmaschine   167

magnificent großartig, prächtig   158

mail merge Serienbrief   61

mail shots Postwurfsendungen   217

main course Hauptgericht, Hauptgang   32

mainland Festland, Kontinent   167

mainly hauptsächlich   9

to maintain pflegen, führen   19, *hier:*
   aufrechterhalten   64

maintenance Wartung   136

major groß, wichtig, Haupt-   25

major concerns Hauptsorgen   30

majority Mehrheit   226

*to make a complaint sich beschweren,
   reklamieren   65

*to make a fool of oneself sich
   blamieren   67

*to make a note notieren   68

*to make out ausstellen   177

*to make s.o. feel at home dafür sor-
   gen, dass sich jmnd. wohlfühlt   24

*to make up erfinden   70

*to make up for sth. etwas wieder-
   gutmachen, für etwas entschädigen   205

male Mann   217

Malta Malta   240

to man besetzen, betreuen   88

management assistant for tourism and
   leisure Kaufmann/frau für Tourismus
   und Freizeit   14

management assistant in advertising
   Werbekaufmann/frau   10

management assistant in freight
   forwarding Speditionskaufmann/
   frau   11

management assistant in retail
   business Kaufmann/frau im Einzelhandel   11

management assistant in wholesale
   and foreign trade Kaufmann/frau im
   Groß- und Außenhandel   9

managerial leitend   227

to manufacture herstellen,
   anfertigen   181

manufacturing Fertigung,
   Fabrikation   166

to map out entwerfen, planen,
   ausarbeiten   174

margin Rand   125

marine See-   182

marital status Familienstand   119

market research Marktforschung   211

to mark sth. off etw. abgrenzen   212

mashed potatoes Kartoffelpüree   31

to match gleichkommen, entsprechen   102

mature reif, alteingesessen   42

maturity Reife   212

means Mittel, Methode   132

means of payment Zahlungsmittel   179

meat ball Fleischklops, Frikadelle   160

medical supplies Sanitätsartikel   167

medium Mittel, Werkzeug   220

medium-sized company mittelständisches Unternehmen   49

*to meet the criteria die Kriterien
   erfüllen   241

membership Mitgliedschaft   162

memorable unvergesslich   220

memory Erinnerung, Gedächtnis   220

to mention erwähnen   235

menu Speisekarte   32

merchandise Ware   195

to merge zusammenlegen   196

merger Fusion, Zusammenlegung   203

to message eine Nachricht senden   174

to microwave im Mikrowellenherd
   erhitzen   56

millennial-born um die Jahrtausendwende herum geboren   55

millennials um die Jahrtausendwende
   geborene Personen   183

minimum Minimum, Mindest-   227

minor repairs kleinere Reparaturen   136

minutes (pl) Protokoll   235

minute taking Protokollführung   227

*to mislay verlegen   184

mix-up Verwechslung   198

to mobilise mobilisieren   219

modelling Modellbau   177

mode of payment Zahlungsart   75

mode of transport Beförderungsart   167

to modulate *hier:* dämpfen, abschwächen   80

to monitor beobachten, überprüfen   176

monitor Bildschirm, Monitor   29

to monopolise an sich reißen   108

more often than not meistens   174

Morocco Marokko   167

mortar Mörtel   214

mortgage Hypothek   183

Moselle Mosel   160

motion Antrag   97

motivated motiviert   237

mourning Trauer   216

to move on to weitergehen zu   9

multilingual vielsprachig, mehrsprachig   158

multinationals multinationale
   Konzerne   216

multiple mehrere, mehrfach   166

my pleasure gern geschehen, ist mir ein Vergnügen   131
mystified ratlos   216
myth Mythos, Sage   216

N

naive naiv, blauäugig   216
National Vocational Qualification staatlich anerkannte berufliche Qualifikation   16
need Bedürfnis   183
to negotiate aushandeln, verhandeln   133
negotiation Verhandlung   205
nervousness Nervosität   236
nevertheless trotzdem, dennoch   78
news coverage Berichterstattung in den Medien   220
to nod nicken   236
noisy laut   196
to nominate ernennen, nominieren   239
no-nonsense unverblümt, direkt   200
norm Regel, Norm   200
North Sea Nordsee   167
notably insbesondere   97
notoriously bekanntermaßen   116
now and again ab und zu   30
No worries Kein Problem   67
numerous zahlreich   197
nutrition-conscious ernährungsbewusst   56

O

objective Ziel   228
obstacle Hindernis   174
to obtain erhalten   74
obvious offensichtlich   167
to occur vorkommen   185
offence Anstoß, Beleidigung   27
offer Angebot   156
office administration clerk Bürokaufmann/frau   11
office management assistant Kaufmann/frau für Büromanagement, Bürokaufmann/frau   11
to offload ab-/ausladen   167
olive oil Olivenöl   167
on behalf of Namen von, im Auftrag   86

on familiar terms auf vertrautem Fuß   115
onion Zwiebel   31
on request auf Anfrage   36
on site vor Ort   76
on the job training Ausbildung am Arbeitsplatz   16
on the other line am anderen Apparat   66
on the spot sofort, auf der Stelle   180
opening bank ausstellende Bank   181
open-minded aufgeschlossen, unvoreingenommen   226
open-plan office Großraumbüro   30
to operate bedienen   103
operations (pl) Geschäftstätigkeit   166
opportunity Gelegenheit   227
opposite number Gegenüber, Kollege, Kollegin   87
optician Optiker/in   214
option Alternative, Variante   90
oral mündlich   194
orchid Orchidee   167
order Auftrag, Bestellung, Reihenfolge   213
organic biologisch, Bio-   30
organically-grown biologisch angebaut   43
organic wool Bio-Wolle   68
origin Ursprung   239
to originate entstehen, Ursprung haben   239
to oscillate pendeln   173
to oust verdrängen   180
outboard engine Außenbordmotor   169
outgoing aufgeschlossen, kontaktfreudig   205
to outlaw verbieten, für ungesetzlich erklären   80
outlets Verkaufsstellen, Vertriebsmöglichkeiten   180
to outsource auslagern   30
outstanding hervorragend, herausragend   242
outstanding ausstehend, offen   184
overall insgesamt, übergreifend   109
overall impression Gesamteindruck   104
over and over again immer wieder   109
overcast bedeckt, bezogen (Himmel)   28

overdue überfällig   176
to overestimate überschätzen   173
overheads (fixe) Kosten   216
over-indebted überschuldet   180
over the top übertrieben   78
over time mit der Zeit   102
to overwhelm überfordern   111
overwhelmed überwältigt   174

P

PA = personal assistant Assistent/in, Sekretär/in   115
pace Geschwindigkeit   111
pack Packung   216
packaging Verpackung   212
packing list Packliste   169
pallet Palette   169
palm rest Handballenauflage   223
panini italienisches Brötchen   56
paperweight Briefbeschwerer   199
to paraphrase umschreiben, paraphrasieren   16
participant Teilnehmer/in   144
participation Teilnahme   240
particular besonders, speziell   161
particulars Einzelheiten   128
to pass on weitergeben, weiterleiten   58
to paste einfügen   125
patience Geduld   201
patient geduldig   68
peak Gipfel, Höchststand   105
to peak einen Höhepunkt erreichen   212
peculiarity Eigentümlichkeit, typisches Merkmal   215
penalty payment Strafzahlung   190
per annum pro Jahr, jährlich   227
percentage Anteil, Prozentsatz   166
to perform ausführen   215
performance Leistung, Ergebnis   102
periodically regelmäßig   180
perishable verderblich   160
permissible zulässig, erlaubt   27
permission Erlaubnis   206
personalised personalisiert   217
to persuade überreden, überzeugen   220
persuasive überzeugend   220
pesticides Pestizide   47
pest-resistant schädlingsresistent   43

Q

qualification Ausbildung, Qualifikation 226

quality-conscious qualitätsbewusst 42

quantity Menge 157

query Frage 178

questionnaire Fragebogen 213

queue Warteschlange 93

quota Quote, Kontingent 126

quotation Angebot, Kostenvoranschlag 138

quote Kostenvoranschlag 75

R

radical radikal, drastisch 214

raft-building Floßbau 75

rafting Rafting 75

rag trade Bekleidungsindustrie 26

railway siding Gleisanschluss 167

raised eyebrows hochgezogene Augenbrauen 67

range Spektrum, Palette, Angebot 25

rank Rang, Rangordnung 164

to rank Rang einnehmen, einordnen 218

rapport Verhältnis 237

rarely selten, kaum 93

raspberry Himbeere 160

rate Tarif, Satz 237

raw materials Rohstoffe 58

re bezüglich 109

*****to read back** wiederholen 70

reasonable akzeptabel, angemessen 145

reasonably halbwegs 56

reasonably obvious ziemlich offensichtlich 31

recent nicht lange zurückliegend, neueste(r/n) 167

recently kürzlich 219

recess Pause 136

recipient Empfänger/in 116

reclining mit Liegefunktion 152

recognisable wiedererkennbar 220

recognition Wiedererkennung, Anerkennung 183

record Datensatz 61

to record aufzeichnen, protokollieren 109

records Unterlagen, Dokumente 94

to recruit anwerben, einstellen 227

recruitment Anwerbung, Einstellung 242

red cabbage Rotkohl 31

redcurrants rote Johannisbeeren 31

red jelly Rote Grütze 31

to redress entschädigen 205

referee Referenz, Schiedsrichter/in 234

reference Referenz, Bezug 156

to refer to sich beziehen auf 161

to reflect widerspiegeln 108

to refrain auf etw. verzichten, etw. unterlassen 139

to refresh auffrischen 235

refund Erstattung 19

to refund erstatten 203

regarded as gesehen als 167

to reglue neu verkleben 195

to regret bedauern 161, Bedauern 186

regulations Vorschrift, Verordnung 239

to rehearse proben, einüben 103

to reimburse erstatten, rückvergüten 205

to reject zurückweisen 240

to relate to in Kontakt kommen mit 174

relationship Beziehung 182

relevant entsprechend, sachdienlich 156

reliable zuverlässig 26

to rely on sich verlassen auf 181

to remain bleiben 163

remainder Rest 61

reminder Zahlungserinnerung, Mahnung 61, Erinnerungschreiben 103

to remit überweisen 177

removal services Umzugsdienste 49

to remove entfernen 99

to render leisten, erbringen 194

renewable erneuerbar 240

to repack neu verpacken, umpacken 215

replacement Ersatz 186

to replicate nachbilden, reproduzieren 20

to report to unterstehen 57

to reproduce nachbilden, kopieren 216

Republic of Ireland Republik Irland 169

request Bitte 74

to require verlangen, benötigen 227

required benötigt werden 167

requirement Bedingung, Voraussetzung 226

resale Wiederverkauf 155

to reschedule verlegen, neu terminieren 86

research (Nach)Forschung 33

resolution Bildschirmauflösung 223

to resolve lösen, klären 239

resort Urlaubs-, Badeort 144

resource Mittel, Ressourcen 213

resources Ressourcen, Mittel 173

respect Hinsicht 237

respite Atempause, Zahlungsaufschub 186

response Reaktion 184

responsibility Verantwortung, Zuständigkeit 240

résumé Lebenslauf 241

to resurface wieder auftauchen 180

retailer Einzelhändler/in 49

to retain behalten, halten 132

to retrieve abrufen 61

to reverse umkehren 234

revised geändert 199

to revoke widerrufen, stornieren 181

to revolutionise revolutionieren 180

Rhine Rhein 160

to right richtigstellen 205

ringer Telefonklingel 80

risk Risiko 167

rival Konkurrenz- 183

robotics Robotertechnik 235

rock climbing Klettern 75

Romania Rumänien 240

roughly ungefähr, in etwa 10

to round up aufrunden 93

rudimentary rudimentär, einfach 25

*****to run out of sth.** ausgehen, zur Neige gehen 142

rye Roggen 160

S

salary Gehalt 16

satisfaction Zufriedenheit 215

satisfactory zufriedenstellend 201

satisfying befriedigend, zufriedenstellend 237

scale maßstabsgetreu   177

00-scale Spur H0   129

S

scepticism Skepsis   160

schedule Terminplan, Aufstellung   96

to schedule zeitlich einplanen   87

scope Umfang, Reichweite, Spielraum   237

score Auswertung, Punktestand   126

scratched verkratzt   194

to screen überprüfen, aussondern   19

screen Bildschirm   217

scrubbed geschrubbt, gescheuert   31

search engine Suchmaschine   218

seaworthy packing seetaugliche Verpackung   167

secondary zusätzlich   213

secondary education Sekundarschulbildung   234

secretary Sekretär/in   227

sector Branche   9

secure sicher   155

security Sicherheit   181

security issue Sicherheitsproblem   171

*__to see a point__ einen Standpunkt verstehen   133

*__to see eye to eye__ einer Meinung sein   109

segment Marktsegment   214

selection Auswahl   93

self-catering Selbstversorgung   76

senior staff Führungskräfte, leitende Angestellte   30

sensitivity Empfindlichkeit, Zartgefühl   216

separate eigen, separat   167

series (pl) Serie, Reihe   218

service Dienstleistung   211

set expression feststehende Redewendung   67

set time feste Zeit   56

setting Rahmen, Umfeld, Umgebung   241

to settle an account Konto ausgleichen, Rechnung begleichen   156

settled erledigt   171

*__to set up__ gründen, eröffnen   237

severe ernst, schwer   186

to shake up durchschütteln, wachrütteln   214

shape Form   199

sharp stark, deutlich   106

sheet Blatt   167

shelf (pl.) shelves Regal   173

shiny glänzend   152

shortcut Abkürzung, Tastenkombination   20

short-lived kurzlebig   109

shuttle train Pendelzug   167

signatory Unterzeichner/in   118

signature footer Unterschriftsfußzeilen   117

signboard Reklameschild   173

significant deutlich, wesentlich   166

to sign up to sich anmelden, sich registrieren   45

Silk Road Seidenstraße   158

similar ähnlich   227

sincerity Aufrichtigkeit   110

single room Einzelzimmer   88

*__to sit an exam__ eine Prüfung machen   16

site Website   218

to skip überspringen, auslassen   116

slang Slang, Jargon   216

slice Scheibe, Anteil   31

slide Folie   103

slight leicht, gering(fügig), kaum merklich   70

slightly etwas, leicht   213

slim schlank   171

to slip through durchschlüpfen   126

slot Zeitfenster   213

Slovakia die Slovakei   240

Slovenia Slovenien   240

smart ordentlich, gepflegt, schick   235

smoked ham geräucherter Schinken   31

smoked salmon Räucherlachs   160

smooth glatt, reibungslos   173

snow shoveling Schneeschippen   136

so-called sogenannte/r/s   211

sociable gesellig, umgänglich   30

to socialise Kontakte pflegen   11

sole trader Einzelkaufmann/frau   133

solicited offer verlangtes Angebot   138

solicitor Rechtsanwalt, Rechtsanwältin   66

solidity Festigkeit, Stabilität   42

sophisticated hoch entwickelt, technisch ausgefeilt   49

sour sauer   160

to source sth. (from) etwas beziehen (von)   43

spacious geräumig   30

Spain Spanien   183

spam folder Spam-Ordner   117

spare part Ersatzteil   167

sparing sparsam, mäßig   116

sparkling mineral water Mineralwasser mit Kohlensäure   25

specific bestimmt, spezifisch   167

specification Spezifikation, Vorgabe   181

to specify genau bezeichnen   179

spectacular spektakulär, eindrucksvoll   158

spell Episode, Phase   186

spin Drehung, Drall   219

spinning mill Spinnerei   43

to spot erkennen, ausmachen   174

spouse Ehegatte, Ehegattin   36

*__to spread__ verteilen   45

spreadsheet Tabellenkalkulation   61

to square sth. with sb. etw. mit jmdm. absprechen / vereinbaren   160

staff Belegschaft, Personal   199

staff retention Personalerhaltung, Mitarbeiterbindung   223

stage Bühne, *hier:* Stadium   211

staggered gestaffelt   181

stainless rostfrei   171

staircase Treppe, Treppenhaus   29

standardisation Standardisierung   216

standardised genormt, standardisiert   167

*__to stand in for so.__ jmdn. vertreten   73

starter Vorspeise   32

to start the ball rolling den Anfang machen   9

start-up (business) Neugründung, junges Unternehmen   48

to state darlegen, nennen   200

state-of-the-art auf dem neuesten Stand (der Technik)   49

stationery Schreibwaren, Büromaterial   158

statistic Statistik   180

statistical statistisch   227

U

V

W

Y

Acronyms and abbreviations

Abbreviation: shortened form of a word
Acronym: abbreviation formed from the first letters of each word in a term

Short form **Full form** German

a.m./am **ante meridian** morgens/vormittags (24 Uhr – 12 Uhr)

approx. **approximately** ungefähr

asap **as soon as possible** so schnell wie möglich

ATM **automated teller machine** Geldautomat

Attn. **for the attention of** zu Händen (von)

B/E **bill of exchange** Wechsel

B/L **bill of lading** Konnossement, Frachtbrief

B2B **business to business** Business-to-Business

BIC **bank identifier code** internationaler Bank-Code

BOP **balance of payments** Zahlungsbilanz

BOT **balance of trade** Handelsbilanz

BRIC **Brazil, Russia, India, China** Brasilien, Russland, Indien, China

cc **carbon copy, copy circulated, cubic centimeters** (Kohlepapier-)Durchschlag, Verteiler, Kubikzentimeter

CEO **Chief Executive Officer** *(etwa:)* (Haupt-)Geschäftsführer/in, Firmenchef/in, Vorstandsvorsitzende/r

CFO **Chief Financial Officer** Finanzleiter/in

CIF **cost, insurance and freight (Incoterm)** Kosten, Versicherung und Fracht

COD **cash on delivery** Lieferung per Nachnahme

CPT **carriage paid to (Incoterm)** frachtfrei, Fracht bezahlt

CRM **customer relationship management** Kundendienst, Kundenbetreuung

CV **curriculum vitae** Lebenslauf

CWO **cash with order** Zahlung bei Auftragserteilung

D/A **documents against acceptance** Dokumente gegen Akzept

D/P **documents against payment** Kasse gegen Dokumente

DAP **delivery at place (Incoterm)** geliefert benannter Ort

DAT **delivery at terminal (Incoterm)** geliefert Terminal

DDP **delivered, duty paid (Incoterm)** frei Haus, verzollt geliefert

dept. **Department** Abteilung

e.g. **exempli gratia = for example** zum Beispiel (z.B.)

encl. **enclosed** beiliegend, in der Anlage

etc. **etcetera** und so weiter (usw.)

EU **European Union** Europäische Union (EU)

EXW **ex works (Incoterm)** ab Werk

FAO **for the attention of** zu Händen von

FAQ **frequently asked question** häufig gestellte Frage

FAS **free alongside ship (Incoterm)** frei Längsseite Schiff

FOB **free on board (Incoterm)** frei an Bord

GDP **gross domestic product** Bruttoinlandsprodukt (BIP)

GNP **gross national product** Bruttosozialprodukt (BSP)

HQ **headquarters** Hauptsitz, Zentrale

HR **human resources** Personalabteilung, -wesen

i.e. **id est (Latin) = that is** das heißt (d.h.)

IBAN **International Bank Account Number** Internationale Kontonummer

ICC **International Chamber of Commerce** Internationale Industrie- und Handelskammer (ICC)

IMF **International Monetary Fund** Internationaler Währungsfond

Inc.; inc **incorporated** *(AE)* Aktiengesellschaft

ISO **International Standards Organisation** ISO (Norm)

JIT **just-in-time** bedarfsorientierte Produktion (gerade rechtzeitig)

L / C **letter of credit** Akkreditiv

lbs **pounds** Pfunde *(Gewicht)*

Ltd. **limited** mit beschränkter Haftung

MD **managing director** Geschäftsführer/in

MNC **multinational company** multinationales Unternehmen

mph **miles per hour** Meilen pro Stunde *(Geschwindigkeit)*

NGO **non-governmental organisation** Nichtregierungsorganisation

no. **number** Nummer (Nr.)

OPEC **Organisation of the Petroleum Exporting Countries** Organisation erdölexportierender Länder (OPEC)

P&L **Profit and Loss** Gewinn und Verlust

p. a. **per annum** jährlich, pro Jahr

p. m. / pm **post meridian** nachmittags / abends (12 Uhr – 24 Uhr)

PIN **Personal Identification Number** PIN (Erkennungsnummer)

plc / PLC **public limited company** *(etwa:)* AG

pp **paginae = pages** Seiten

pp / ppa **per procurationem = on behalf of** im Auftrag von

PR **public relations** Öffentlichkeitsarbeit

R&D **research and development** Forschung und Entwicklung

Re. **regarding** bezüglich

Re. **reply (e-mail)** Antwort

Ref. **reference** Aktenzeichen

ROI **return on investment** Rentabilität, Kapitalertrag

SME **small and medium(-sized) enterprise** *(BE)*; **small to mid-sized enterprise** *(AE)*
Mittelstand; kleines und mittelständisches Unternehmen (KMU)

sq. **square** Quadrat *(Maß)*, Platz *(Ort)*

SWOT **Strengths, Weaknesses, Opportunities, Threats** Stärken, Schwächen, Möglichkeiten, Gefahren / Risiken

WTO **World Trade Organisation** Welthandelsorganisation

False friends

False friends (= falsche Freunde) sind Wörter, die in Deutsch und Englisch identisch oder ähnlich aussehen, die aber nicht dieselbe Bedeutung haben. Im besten Fall kann das zu bloß lustigen, im schlimmsten Fall aber zu peinlichen oder gefährlichen Missverständnissen führen. Die wichtigsten falschen Freunde sollte man also gut kennen.

Deutsch	Englische Bedeutung	Nicht zu verwechseln mit	Deutsch
aktuell	topical, current(ly)	actual	wirklich, tatsächlich
also	therefore, then	also	auch
bald	soon	bald	kahl, glatzköpfig
bekommen	to receive, to get	to become	werden
Billion	1,000,000,000,000.00	billion	Milliarde
blamieren	to embarrass	to blame	jemanden beschuldigen
Brief	letter	brief	kurz
Chef	boss	chef chief (adjective)	Chefkoch haupt-, Haupt-
dezent	discreet, modest	decent	anständig; nett, großzügig
Direktion	management, administration	direction	Richtung
Distanz	detachment, coolness	distance	Entfernung
Dose	can, tin	dose	Dosis
engagiert	involved	engaged	verlobt; besetzt (Telefon)
eventuell	possibly, maybe	eventually	endlich, schließlich
Fabrik	factory, works	fabric	Gewebe, Stoff
familiär	family-related	familiar	bekannt
fast	almost	fast	schnell
Fotograf	photographer	photograph	Foto
Gift	poison	gift	Geschenk
Gymnasium	secondary school, high school (AE), grammar school (BE)	gym(nasium)	Turnhalle
Handy	cellular / mobile phone	handy (adjective)	praktisch
Hochschule	college, university	high school	Gymnasium, Oberschule
irritieren	confuse, distract	irritate	ärgern, auf die Nerven gehen
Kaution	deposit	caution	Vorsicht
Klosett	toilet	closet	Verschlag, Wandschrank
Konkurrenz	competition	concurrence	Übereinstimmung
konsequent	consistent	consequently	infolgedessen
kontrollieren	check, monitor	control	steuern, regulieren
Kritik	criticism	critic	Kritiker/in
Mappe	briefcase, folder	map	Landkarte

Deutsch	Englische Bedeutung	Nicht zu verwechseln mit	Deutsch
Meinung	opinion	meaning	Bedeutung
Menü	set meal	menu	Speisekarte; Menü (Computer)
Messe	trade fair, show	mess	Unordnung
Note	mark (school)	note	Notiz
ordinär	vulgar, cheap	ordinary	üblich, normal
Pension	small hotel	pension	Rente
plump	tactless, awkward, clumsy	plump	mollig
prinzipiell	on principle	principally	hauptsächlich
Promotion	doctor's exam	promotion	Beförderung, Förderung
Prospekt	brochure, leaflet	prospect	Aussicht
Provision	commission, percentage of price	provision	Vorsorge
prüfen	check	prove	beweisen
rentabel	profitable	rentable	(ver)mietbar
Rente	pension	rent	Miete
Rezept	recipe (cooking) prescription (medical)	receipt	Quittung
Rückseite	back, rear	backside	Hinterteil
selbstbewusst	self-confident	self-conscious	schüchtern, gehemmt
sensibel	sensitive	sensible	vernünftig
seriös	reliable	serious	ernsthaft
spenden	donate	to spend	ausgeben
Sympathie	a liking, a feeling of solidarity	sympathy	Mitleid
sympathisch	likable, nice	sympathetic	mitfühlend
übersehen	overlook, miss something	oversee	überwachen
Unternehmer	businessman, businesswoman, employer	undertaker	Leichenbestatter
Warenhaus	department store	warehouse	Lagerhalle

Glossary

Communication

Written communication

agenda Tagesordnung
application Bewerbung, Antrag
attach, to anhängen
attachment Anhang *(E-Mail)*
brochure Broschüre, Prospekt
catalogue *(BE)*, catalog *(AE)* Katalog
contract Vertrag
documents Unterlagen
draft Entwurf
enclosure Anlage *(Brief)*
enquiry *(BE)*, inquiry *(AE)* Anfrage
leaflet Flugblatt, Infoblatt, Prospekt
letter Brief
message Nachricht
minutes Protokoll
notice Aushang
offer Angebot
order Auftrag, Bestellung
paperwork Verwaltungsarbeit, Schreibarbeit
post-it note Haftnotiz, Klebezettel
reminder (Zahlungs-)Erinnerung, Mahnung
report Bericht
schedule (≈ itinerary, timetable) Zeitplan, Fahrplan, Stundenplan
subject *(in a letter / e-mail)* Betreff
memo (*short for:* memorandum) interne Notiz, Vermerk
paragraph Absatz, Paragraph

Spoken communication

advise, to beraten
advice Rat, Ratschlag
announce, to ankündigen, bekannt geben, ansagen
announcement (to make an announcement) Ankündigung, Bekanntgabe, Durchsage
apologise for something, to sich für etwas entschuldigen
apology Entschuldigung
available erhältlich, erreichbar, verfügbar
chat, to plaudern, schwätzen
controversy Kontroverse, Auseinandersetzung
debriefing Nachbesprechung
demonstration (to give / do a demonstration) Vorführung, Demonstration

dispute Streit
gossip, to schwätzen, plaudern
interview (to hold / give an interview) Interview, Vorstellungsgespräch
lecture (to hold / give a lecture) Vortrag, Vorlesung
negotiate, to verhandeln
negotiation Verhandlung
phone call (= telephone conversation) Telefongespräch
presentation (to give / do a presentation) Präsentation, Vortrag, Referat
speech (to hold / give a speech) Rede
thank somebody for something sich bei jemandem für etwas bedanken

Collocations relating to communication

circulate the agenda, to die Tagesordnung verteilen
clarify a matter, to eine Angelegenheit klären
co-ordinate an event, to eine Veranstaltung koordinieren / organisieren
confirm an agreement, to eine Vereinbarung bestätigen
have an objection to something, to (= to object to something) Einwand gegen etwas erheben, etwas beanstanden
liaise with colleagues / business partners, to zusammenarbeiten mit, in Verbindung stehen mit
make a complaint about something, to (= to complain) etwas reklamieren, sich über etwas beschweren
make an appointment, to einen Termin vereinbaren
make an enquiry, to (= to enquire about something) eine Anfrage machen
make an offer, to ein Angebot machen
make arrangements, to Vorkehrungen treffen
notify somebody of something, to jemanden über etwas informieren, jemandem Bescheid geben
place an order, to (with a firm / for a product) einen Auftrag erteilen
postpone an appointment, to einen Termin verschieben
solve a problem, to ein Problem lösen
take the minutes, to das Protokoll führen
update information, to Daten / Informationen aktualisieren
write up the minutes, to das Protokoll schreiben

"I'll put you through." „Ich stelle Sie durch."
"Speaking." „Am Apparat."
"The line is busy."/"The line is engaged."
  „Die Leitung ist besetzt."
answerphone *(BE)*, **answering machine** *(BE)*,
  voice mail *(AE)* Anrufbeantworter
bad line schlechte Verbindung
dial the wrong number, to sich verwählen
dial, to wählen
extension Durchwahl
hang up, to auflegen
hold the line, to am Apparat bleiben
landline phone Festnetztelefon
leave a message, to eine Nachricht hinterlassen
mobile phone *(BE)*, **cell(ular) phone** *(AE)*
  Mobiltelefon, Handy
put through, to durchstellen, verbinden
receiver Hörer
return a call, to zurückrufen

cursor Cursor, Positionsmarke
click on something, to etwas anklicken
digital / computer projector Beamer
keyboard Tastatur
screen Bildschirm
text message SMS

Company organisation

affiliate Schwestergesellschaft, Schwesterfirma
agency Agentur, Vertretung
board of directors Geschäftsleitung, Vorstand und
  Aufsichtsrat
branch Filiale, Niederlassung, Zweigstelle
company Firma, Gesellschaft
conglomerate Firmengruppe
consultancy Beratungsfirma
cooperative Genossenschaft
core business Hauptgeschäft, Kerngeschäft
cost centre Kostenstelle
executive board Vorstand
firm Firma
franchise Franchise
go public, to an die Börse gehen
group Konzern

headquarters Hauptsitz, Firmenzentrale,
  Hauptgeschäftsstelle
Inc. (= incorporated) *Abkürzung für amerikanische*
  Kapitalgesellschaft
joint stock company *(BE)*, **stock corporation** *(AE)*
  Kapitalgesellschaft
limited liability beschränkte Haftung
limited partnership Kommanditgesellschaft
Ltd. (= limited company) *(etwa:)* GmbH
mail order business Versandhandel
multinational company (MNC) multinationales
  Unternehmen
offshoring das Auslagern ganzer Geschäftsprozesse
  ins Ausland
outsourcing Produktionsverlagerung *(z. B. ins Ausland)*
parent company Muttergesellschaft
partnership Personengesellschaft, *(etwa:)* OHG
PLC (= public limited company) *(BE)* britische
  Aktiengesellschaft
private limited company britische Gesellschaft mit
  beschränkter Haftung
retail outlet Verkaufsstelle
retailer Einzelhändler
self-employed selbständig
service provider Dienstleister
sole trader *(BE)*, **sole proprietorship** *(AE)*
  Einzelunternehmer / in
stakeholder Interessenvertreter, Mitglied einer
  Interessengruppe
subcontractor Sub-Unternehmer
subsidiary Tochtergesellschaft, Tochterfirma
supervisory board Aufsichtsrat
supplier Lieferant, Zulieferer
wholesaler Großhändler

accounts, accountancy Finanzbuchhaltung,
  Finanzabteilung
advertising Werbung
after-sales service Kundendienst
board of directors Direktion, Geschäftsleitung
customer service Kundendienst, Kundenbetreuung
department (dept.) Abteilung
distribution Vertrieb
executive board Vorstand
finance Finanz-
human resources (HR) / personnel Personal
legal department Rechtsabteilung
logistics Logistik
maintenance Wartung

marketing Marketing

organisation chart Organigramm

payroll Lohn- und Gehaltsabrechnung

PR (= public relations) Öffentlichkeitsarbeit

production Produktion

purchasing (≈ procurement) Einkauf, Beschaffung

quality assurance Qualitätssicherung

recruitment Personalbeschaffung

research and development (R&D) Forschung und Entwicklung

sales Verkauf

security Sicherheit

supervisory board Aufsichtsrat

Jobs and responsibilities

accountant Bilanzbuchhalter / in

administration Verwaltung

agent Vertreter / in *(auf Provisionsbasis)*

apprentice Lehrling, Auszubildende / r, Praktikant / in

automated teller machine (ATM) Geldautomat

back office Büro ohne Publikumsverkehr

blue-collar worker Arbeiter / in *(in der Produktion)*

board (of directors) Geschäftsleitung, Vorstand

boss Chef / in

caretaker *(BE)*, janitor *(AE)* Hausmeister / in

Chief Executive Officer (CEO) Vorstandsvorsitzende / r, Hauptgeschäftsführer / in

Chief Financial Officer Leiter / in der Finanzabteilung

clerical staff (= clerk) Büroangestellte

co-worker *(AE)* Mitarbeiter / in

colleague Kollege / Kollegin

consultant Berater / in

department head Abteilungsleiter / in

director Mitglied des Vorstands / Aufsichtsrats

employee Arbeitnehmer / in, Mitarbeiter / in

employer Arbeitgeber / in

executive leitende / r Angestellte / r

executive board Vorstand

founder Gründer / in

freelancer Freiberufler / in, freie / r Mitarbeiter / in

head of department / department, head Abteilungsleiter / in

internee Praktikant / in

management Geschäftsleitung

management assistant in office communication Kaufmann / -frau für Bürokommunikation

management assistant (industrial business) *(etwa:)* Industriekaufmann / -frau

managing director (MD) Geschäftsführer / in

office management assistant, office administration clerk Kaufmann / -frau für Büromanagement

owner Eigentümer / in, Besitzer / in

PA (= personal assistant) *(etwa:)* Chefsektretär / in

person responsible Verantwortliche / r

predecessor Vorgänger / in

project manager Projektleiter / in, Projektmanager / in

sales representative Außendienstmitarbeiter / in, Vertriebsmitarbeiter / in

staff (= personnel) Personal

successor Nachfolger / in

supervisor Vorgesetzte / r, Betreuer / in, Aufseher / in, Kontrolleur / in

supervisory board Aufsichtsrat

team leader Teamleiter / in

technical support Technischer Dienst

temp (= temporary staff) Aushilfe, Zeitarbeiter / in

trainee Praktikant / in

trainer Ausbilder / in, Trainer / in

white-collar staff Büroangestellte

workforce Arbeiterschaft, Belegschaft

Places at work

canteen (= cafeteria) Kantine, Mensa

conference room Konferenzraum, Sitzungszimmer

conference venue Konferenzort, Tagungsort

desk Schreibtisch

environment Umwelt

factory Fabrik

infrastructure Infrastruktur

lift *(BE)*, elevator *(AE)* Aufzug

located, to be (≈ situated) sich befinden

location Ort

on the outskirts am Rande von (einer Stadt)

open-plan office Großraumbüro

plant Anlage

premises Räumlichkeiten, Firmengelände, Geschäftsräume

reception Empfang

relocation Standortwechsel, Umzug

shop floor (= production area) Produktionsbereich, Fertigungsbereich

stockroom Lager, Lagerraum

venue Veranstaltungsort

warehouse Lager, Lagerhalle

work station Arbeitsplatz, Arbeitsstation

workshop Werkstatt

Bildquellennachweis

Textquellennachweis

Office Milestones

Englisch für Kaufleute für Büromanagement

Autoren: Dr. Richard Hooton, Ulrich Boltz, Ruth Feiertag, Annely Humphreys, Jason Humphreys, Veronica Leary

Werkübersicht:

Schülerbuch, 978-3-12-800141-8
Workbook, 978-3-12-800146-3
Workbook mit Prüfungsvorbereitung KMK-Fremdsprachenzertifikat + Multimedia-CD, 978-3-12-800147-0
Lehrerhandbuch mit 3 Audio-CDs + DVD-ROM, 978-3-12-800145-6

1. Auflage

1   5   4   3   2   1 | 21   20   19   18   17

Alle Drucke dieser Auflage sind unverändert und können im Unterricht nebeneinander verwendet werden. Die letzte Zahl bezeichnet das Jahr des Druckes.

Im Lehrwerk befinden sich ausschließlich fiktive Internet- und E-Mailadressen sowie fiktive Telefon- und Faxnummern, die alle mit „…" versehen sind.

Die Mediencodes leiten ausschließlich zu optionalen Unterrichtsmaterialien, sie unterliegen nicht dem staatlichen Zulassungsverfahren.

Redaktion: Volker Wendland
Herstellung: Julia Trabel

Gestaltung: kognito gestaltung, Berlin
Umschlaggestaltung: kognito gestaltung, Berlin
Satz: Satzkiste, Stuttgart
Reproduktion: Meyle + Müller Medien-Management, Pforzheim (Inhalt);
Schwabenrepro GmbH, Stuttgart (Cover)
Druck: DBM Druckhaus Berlin-Mitte GmbH, Berlin

Printed in Germany
ISBN 978-3-12-800141-8